Shattered, Cracked, or Firmly Intact?

D1562601

Shattered, Cracked, or Firmly Intact?

Women and the Executive Glass Ceiling Worldwide

FARIDA JALALZAI

OXFORD
UNIVERSITY PRESS

Oxford University Press is a department of the University of Oxford.
It furthers the University's objective of excellence in research, scholarship,
and education by publishing worldwide.

Oxford   New York
Auckland   Cape Town   Dar es Salaam   Hong Kong   Karachi
Kuala Lumpur   Madrid   Melbourne   Mexico City   Nairobi
New Delhi   Shanghai   Taipei   Toronto

With offices in
Argentina   Austria   Brazil   Chile   Czech Republic   France   Greece
Guatemala   Hungary   Italy   Japan   Poland   Portugal   Singapore
South Korea   Switzerland   Thailand   Turkey   Ukraine   Vietnam

Oxford is a registered trademark of Oxford University Press in the UK
and certain other countries.

Published in the United States of America by
Oxford University Press
198 Madison Avenue, New York, NY 10016

© Oxford University Press 2013

First published as an Oxford University Press paperback, 2016

Library of Congress Cataloging-in-Publication Data
Jalalzai, Farida.
Shattered, cracked or firmly intact?: women and the executive glass ceiling
worldwide / Farida Jalalzai.
p. cm.
Includes bibliographical references and index.
ISBN 978-0-19-994353-1 (hardcover); 978-0-19-060209-3 (paperback)   1. Women executives.
2. Glass ceiling (Employment discrimination)   3. Sex discrimination.   I. Title.
HD6054.3.J35 2013
331.4'81658—dc23
2012034145

For my parents, husband, and son

CONTENTS

ACKNOWLEDGMENTS

I was first drawn to studying women presidents and prime ministers as an undergraduate at SUNY College at Brockport. Professor William G. Andrews of the Political Science Department became my mentor and inspiration for this body of research. We conversed on numerous occasions about how in Pakistan, from which my family originally hailed, a woman managed to break the executive glass ceiling; of course, such an event existed as only a hypothetical in the United States. Benazir Bhutto's ascension to the Pakistani prime ministership appeared counterintuitive given Pakistani women's lower status relative to men's. Women's lack of presidential success in the United States, given their relatively equitable position, provided a stunning contrast. Professor Andrews, in essence, encouraged me to pose and solve a two-part puzzle relating women's rise to power within varied contexts: First, how do women enter executive offices in countries that afford women few political, social, and economic opportunities? Second, why do other countries (such as the United States) boasting higher percentages of women in the professions, educational institutions, and various political bodies fail to promote female national leaders?

This research line grew in importance to me over the years while I embarked on numerous personal and professional visits to Pakistan. My relatives practiced purdah, a system of sex segregation common to specific Muslim cultures. As a result, women's mobility tended to be restricted. Although highly interconnected with class status, family dynamics, religious and cultural norms, and ethnic identities, women's inequality seemed palpable throughout many regions of the country. My parents immigrated to the United States in part to provide their children, particularly their daughters, with educational opportunities. Yet again, this only underlined the seeming disconnect between women's general status and the success of individual women as they aspired to executive offices.

Years after my conversations with Professor Andrews first began, Hillary Clinton's run for the 2008 Democratic Party presidential nomination fueled a related question: Is the United States ready for a woman president? While coming very close to being the first female major party nominee, Clinton ultimately failed at what many other women around the world have accomplished: becoming executive of her country. While a female president of the United States still remains only a theoretical scenario, more women around the world are occupying presidential and prime ministerial offices in diverse settings. Thus, the original question that arose in dialogues with my mentor appears just as relevant today, maybe even more so.

This book attempts to answer the two-part puzzle posed two decades ago, providing explanations as to why the executive glass ceiling has been cracked in some countries (as in Pakistan), has been shattered in others (such as Finland), and remains firmly intact almost everywhere else (including the United States). It explores how women's ascensions to executive office, or lack thereof, connect to political institutions, societal structures, historical forces, and global statures of countries. My concentration on women world leaders later extended to graduate study at SUNY Buffalo and subsequently informed my current academic career as an associate professor of political science at the University of Missouri–Saint Louis. Deliberating the democratic consequences of representation, my research agenda analyzes political minorities. Striving to fill various gaps in our knowledge regarding women national leaders, I connect their potential representational impacts to powers and paths. In the spirit of scholarly discourse, this work answers many essential questions but raises still more along the way.

This book would not have been possible without the help of scores of people, including my family, mentors, and colleagues. I thank Professor William G. Andrews and the Ronald E. McNair Program at SUNY College at Brockport for nurturing my love for research and enabling me to conduct the fieldwork in Pakistan that served as the inspiration for this book many years later.

I am also thankful to the faculty at SUNY Buffalo, Professors Claude E. Welch Jr., D. Munroe Eagles, and the late Franco Mattei, who formed the committee for my dissertation, "Women Leaders in Comparative Perspective." While this book bears little resemblance to the dissertation, the research and writing experience proved critical to future theoretical and empirical developments contained in this current work. I owe a special debt of gratitude to Karen Beckwith, Flora Stone Mather Professor of Political Science at Case Western Reserve University, who served as my external dissertation reader and continues to provide comments on other projects, including this one. I am especially appreciative to Karen for encouraging me to pursue the highest-quality university press as I sought publication.

I am grateful to the Department of Political Science at the University of Missouri–Saint Louis, for providing me support as I pursued this research.

Many centers, colleges, and programs at the University of Missouri–Saint Louis support my research. I express appreciation to the Gender Studies Program (formally the Institute for Women's and Gender Studies) for providing academic, financial, and emotional support. I also wish to thank Joel Glassman, director of International Studies and Programs, and Ron Yasbin, dean of the College of Arts of Sciences, for offering me resources over the years for projects related to women leaders.

I am indebted to all of the local organizations that invite me to share my work on women leaders, including but not limited to the American Association for University Women–Ballwin Branch, the Ethical Society of Saint Louis, the Wednesday Club, and the Saint Louis Chapter of the National Women's Political Caucus. These talks continually remind me of the larger relevance of my research and the practical application of findings. I am always impressed by the enthusiasm and expertise of these audiences. Such organizations do remarkable work to advance the status of women at all levels of society. I count myself very fortunate for this support.

Dayna Stock is an excellent example of the benefits mentorship offers for both faculty and graduate students. Now "Dr. Stock," she remains an important colleague. I also thank her for being a great friend and, along with Sudarsan Kant, for providing a tasty collection of topics to devour.

I give thanks to my graduate assistants, including Jennifer Edwards and Janet Drake, who helped collect data at earlier stages of this project and aided in the writing of many of the biographies of women leaders contained in the appendix. I offer special gratitude to Young-Im Lee, whose enthusiasm for this topic and gift for detail helped me navigate my final revisions.

Beyond my local colleagues and supporters, I am privileged to interact with a superb domestic and international network of scholars. Current or former editors of journals offering excellent feedback on various articles on women national leaders include Heidi Hartmann, Carol Hardy-Fanta, and Karen O'Connor of the *Journal of Women, Politics & and Policy* (formerly *Women & Politics*); Karen Beckwith, Kathleen Dolan, and Ailie Mari Tripp of *Politics & Gender*; and Yvonne Galligan of the *International Political Science Review*.

Many scholars encouraged me to apply lessons I derived from my global analysis of women leaders to country or regional case studies. Too often, area specialists and academics engaging in broad cross-national studies view each other with suspicion. I am obliged to colleagues who support my passion for integrating case studies with large-N analysis and combining quantitative and qualitative techniques. Multimethod approaches provide the most complete pictures of very complex phenomena. In this spirit I thank Louise Davidson-Schmich of the University of Miami, who included me within her network of gender scholars studying Germany and Chancellor Angela Merkel, resulting in the publication of a special edition of *German Politics* (2011, Volume 20:2), as well as Gretchen Bauer of the University of Delaware and Manon Tremblay of the University of Ottawa, editors of *Women in Executive Power* (Routledge 2011), who approached me to coauthor a chapter on women in North American cabinets. I also thank Michael Genovese of Loyola Marymount University, editor of *Women World Leaders*, who offered me an opportunity to write on President Ellen Johnson Sirleaf of Liberia (Routledge 2013).

I give special recognition to Angela Chnapko, the editor with whom I worked most closely at Oxford University Press. She showed great commitment to this project at the outset and provided enduring support throughout the revision and publication processes. I greatly thank the anonymous reviewers whose insights and recommendations significantly strengthened the final product.

I cannot thank my family enough. It is only through my parents' self-sacrifice that my siblings and I realized our full potentials. I am fortunate to have five caring siblings—four sisters and a brother. Among my sisters, I credit Zubeda with first instilling in me the desire to pursue academia. I also thank her for taking time out of her busy life as a mother of three and professor of English at Rhode Island College to edit drafts of this manuscript. For Sajida, I echo the sentiment she has expressed to me over the years, "You would so be my friend even if you were not my sister," and I wish her luck as she now completes her dissertation. I am continually impressed by Abida, who combines exhausting schedules of work, schooling, and parenting. I am always delighted by my "little" sister Medina, and look forward to seeing her future unfold. To my only brother, Waheed—the only "real" doctor among my siblings—I wish all the best to his beautiful family. All of my family members have expressed a great deal of interest and support through countless stages of this research, keeping me motivated throughout the process.

Lastly, I thank my husband, Chad Alan Hankinson, for all of his love and support over these many years. He is not only a wonderful husband but a colleague and coauthor. He continually helps me think through research ideas and problems. Above all, he is an amazing father to our darling son, Elam Jalalzai Hankinson. Elam proves to be the child I always desired. He is well behaved but never provides us a dull moment. More than anything, I appreciate his sense of humor and beautiful heart. And thanks to our cat Willoughby, who sat on my lap over the course of countless days as I worked through revision after revision. I would not be where I am today if not for my family; I dedicate this work to them.

Shattered, Cracked, or Firmly Intact?

Introduction

Since 1960, the numbers of women national leaders worldwide, though still minute, have increased dramatically. More than fifty years have passed since Sirimavo Bandaranaike became the first woman to break through the executive glass ceiling by assuming the Sri Lankan premiership, yet fewer than eighty women have joined her ranks since. While experiencing record high numbers as presidents and prime ministers, women still account for only 8 percent of all national leaders today.[1] Presidential offices remain particularly devoid of women. Although Isabel Perón ascended to the office of president of Argentina in 1974, women have acquired a mere 2 percent of all presidential posts.[2] Despite increased levels of education (surpassing men in many countries) and their rising presence in both the professions and legislatures, women remain seriously underrepresented as national leaders around the globe. In this volume, I ask how and why prime ministerships and presidencies remain male bastions. What are the clearly exceptional circumstances that allow women to govern in national positions? What conditions continually prevent women's incorporation as high-level political leaders? Have women really made much progress in the attainment of national executive office?

MAIN ARGUMENTS

Women's success in gaining executive posts mostly depends on executive selection processes and institutional structures, which, in turn, are intricately connected to gender. Far greater numbers of women have attained prime ministerial and presidential posts over the past two decades than in previous periods. Given that the strongest and most visible executive positions continue to constitute a male reserve, we should question women's ultimate success. Rather than focusing merely on the numbers of women leaders, we need to evaluate women's location in the power hierarchy and their actual leadership responsibilities.

Women become prime ministers more often than they become presidents. A major difference distinguishing the two posts involves routes to power. Parties select prime ministers, whereas the public votes for presidents. Appointments to premierships present more auspicious opportunities for women to gain office. Even if a country evinces a socially conservative electorate, a woman may work her way up through the party ranks, win the respect of her colleagues, and become party head and, ultimately, prime minister.

The distribution of power across the political system, the decision-making abilities of executives, and the status of the executive's term in office (fixed tenure versus possible removal at any time) play a crucial role in women's leadership opportunities. Women more often hold executive offices in systems in which the executives have dispersed powers. Presidential powers within a presidential system appear very strong. These elites often assume the role of commander in chief and make high-profile appointments. Moreover, as the lone executive, a president does not have to share office with others. Lastly, presidents enjoy predetermined tenures. Prime ministers, by comparison, come to power through appointment, lack fixed terms, and remain vulnerable to a vote of no confidence or an unfavorable party ballot. Moreover, prime ministerial governance depends heavily on parliamentary collaboration rather than on independent leadership. Perceptions of women's negotiation and collaboration skills limit them less than their supposed inability to act unilaterally, aggressively, and decisively—all necessary presidential traits—which likely explains their relative success in attaining premierships. One advantage enjoyed by prime ministers over presidents, however, is that they may command a parliamentary majority, a significant source of power in enacting a legislative program. This advantage depends on whether the prime minister belongs to a single- or multiparty government; a prime minister's policy authority may lessen during coalition governance. In spite of this, prime ministers usually cede policy powers to their cabinet members, once again emphasizing collaborative governance.

Women's progress depends on power differentials within and between executive offices. Some presidents wield very strong powers, while others act as symbolic heads of their nations. The same is true for prime ministers. A country's political system determines executive powers. Many systems combine presidential and parliamentary structures in a dual-executive arrangement featuring both a prime minister and a president. Women fare better in mixed systems, largely because the dual executive signifies a lower concentration of powers. With twice as many posts available, women's odds of assuming executive office increase. Power imbalances, still the norm in dual-executive systems, result in more women in weaker positions. As such, not all executive positions are created equal. Women are also well represented as prime ministers in unified systems. While women increasingly serve as presidents in unified systems, nearly all such leaders to date have benefited from family ties to power. Regarding the quantity and quality of positions, gender limits women's paths to success in acquiring strong executive posts.

Structural factors play a mixed but still important role in women's rule. Individual female executives hail from the most elite backgrounds, evidenced by their high levels of education and close relationships with upper-class, politically prominent families. Women's rise to power, however, does not necessarily comport with women's general status in their countries. In fact, women routinely ascend to high office in countries where women's social standing lags far behind men's. Furthermore, though largely disadvantaged in attaining executive positions worldwide, in contexts where political power stems from such factors as ethnicity and kinship, some women, like men, occasionally rise as members of preferred groups. This explains women's executive office holding where their overall condition appears low. Neither Bandaranaike nor Perón—the pioneers mentioned at the opening of this chapter—came to power in contexts where women achieved economic and educational parity with men; both bypassed the popular vote to achieve their positions. Perhaps most conspicuously, they followed their deceased husbands to office. Both served in countries struggling with democratic transition and consolidation, which circumscribed their rule and authority. Bandaranaike repeatedly lost her premiership, and a much stronger presidential post was created by the opposition specifically to limit her authority as head of government. Though she tried, she never gained the presidency. President Perón held a very powerful position but faced ouster in a coup less than a year after taking office. These stories exemplify the indirect routes to power women have taken and the numerous obstacles they have confronted in their exercise of authority.

As a result, even in the most seemingly repressive contexts, women wield complicated kinds of authority. They frequently rise through the ranks as members of privileged groups, particularly in politically unstable contexts and countries lacking political institutionalization. Some male leaders benefit from similar circumstances. The same backgrounds and situations propelling women to office, however, also constrain them, and women far less often than men become leaders in the first place. Overall, we should question women's ability to exercise real power. Men continue to dominate even though vastly more women than ever before have broken through the executive glass ceiling.

THE IMPORTANCE OF WOMEN'S EXECUTIVE REPRESENTATION

Though they constitute an essential research subject, women prime ministers and presidents, as a field, remain understudied. Women's lack of representation in scholarship on executive officeholders is analogous to their marginalization overall. If not at the helms of power, women are less represented formalistically, descriptively, substantively, or symbolically. Formalistic representation involves the rules that empower representatives to act and by which constituents hold representatives accountable, and generally includes the procedures by which representation transpires (Pitkin 1967; Schwindt-Bayer 2010). In this vein, applicable mechanisms can select, elect, or remove women. They can also entail executive authorities. Descriptive representation relates to the extent to which representatives possess the same physical or social characteristics as their con- stituents (Pitkin 1967) and share experiences with them (Mansbridge 1999). Rather than resulting from deliberate actions, women's descriptive representa- tion is simply a by-product of women executives' ascensions. In contrast, sub- stantive representation involves women leaders' responsiveness to the political interests of women. "If the mechanics of a particular electoral system exclude to a large degree members of a particular ascriptive group (women or otherwise) then more often than not that is damning evidence that the system is excluding the interests of that particular group from the structures of decision-making power" (Reynolds 1999, 549). Several comparative studies suggest that women legislators do act more on behalf of women's policy interests, even after other relevant dynamics, such as party, are controlled for (Bratton and Ray 2002; Childs 2002; Dodson 2006; Swers 2002; Taylor-Robinson and Heath 2003). Similar investigations of women executives offer less decisive claims regarding women's tendencies to act as substantive representatives (Sykes 1993). The con- tinued lack of research on women national executives, however, limits scholars' ability to form clear conclusions.

Finally, symbolic representation engages emotional responses and relates to the extent to which constituencies believe their representatives support their interests. While some literature relates numerous positive impacts of women leaders on women's political engagement and participation (Wolbrecht and Campbell 2007; Burns, Schlozman, and Verba 2001; Atkeson 2003; Lawless 2004), none deals directly with similar effects of female executives. The pres- ence of female presidents and prime ministers may increase women's politi- cal participation, interest, and engagement. Additionally, the examples set by these leaders could increase public support for women politicians and erode stereotypes that associate only men with executive office. Increased scholar- ship on women national leaders can shed light on these four main types of representation.

This book concerns primarily the connections between descriptive and for- malistic representation. The processes involved in executive selection practices generally work against women's formalistic representation. Moreover, compared with men, women rise to power in weaker positions containing more dispersed powers; rules, processes, and institutions heavily shape women's descriptive representation. Women executives have increased dramatically in number but still constitute only a small fraction of all leaders.

The research presented here also has relevance to the symbolic representation of women. Visible examples of powerful women leaders shape the general public's and party elites' beliefs regarding the suitability and openness of politics to women.[3] Finally, findings suggest important implications for substantive representation. The paths, powers, autonomy, and security of women executives play critical roles in their capacities to promote women's interests. If weak, women executives cannot offer substantive representation even if they so desire.

METHODOLOGICAL PERSPECTIVES AND FOCI

Large-*N* Comparative Analysis

I conduct a large-number (*N*) comparative analysis in this investigation of national leaders. Nearly all the existing literature on women executives involves single case studies or small regional analyses (Opfell 1993; Richter 1991). The largest collection of works on female national leaders (Genovese 1993b) is still modest in numbers of cases explored as well as in geographic scope and only briefly examines women executives comparatively. Of all women presidents and prime ministers, 75 percent took office in the past two decades. In contrast to the 1960s and 1970s, when women leaders arose only in the developing world, now women rule substantially more diverse countries, including Costa Rica, Liberia, the Philippines, Bangladesh, Croatia, Trinidad and Tobago, and Germany. Even though women leaders came to power first in the developing world, most existing scholarship virtually ignored them. This study integrates women executives from all geographic, cultural, religious, and institutional contexts, including those from democratic and nondemocratic countries. This breadth is especially critical given that research concerning gender and politics repeatedly finds that greater proportions of women do not necessarily ascend to high office in more democratic contexts (Krook 2009; McDonagh 2009; Ritter 2007). Some women govern in autonomous, highly institutionalized, peaceful, and stable democracies. Others do so in conflict-prone and politically fragile environments that only recently attained political independence. These nations experience difficulty transitioning to democracy and consolidating representative institutions. We must account for and rigorously explain this regional variation in women's leadership. Viewing women executives in a large-scale comparative framework also advances generalizable theories regarding gender and executive leadership across space (Przeworski and Teune 1970).

This large-*N* comparative analysis focuses on countries where women have served as executives and where they have not. Examining only countries where women have governed provides no variation in the phenomenon investigated. Selection of cases should allow for some deviations (King, Keohane, and Verba 1994, 129). Going beyond successes to including failures permits a more thorough comprehension of both the necessary and the sufficient conditions related to the advancement of women leaders. How can we assess the obstacles facing women in particular countries if we analyze only those places where they have surmounted any hurdles?

Qualitative and Quantitative Analysis

The number of women executives has grown substantially in recent decades. Quantitative analysis permits a systematic and rigorous investigation of the possible connections between various factors and women's ascensions to office. At the same time, qualitative analysis is still critical. Assessing the lives of women executives exposes important conditions relevant to their ultimate rise as well as their powers. This vital information assists in the formation of several of my main hypotheses and the selection of variables utilized in the statistical models.

I do not aim to construct in-depth, thick descriptions of each woman executive or her country in the qualitative analyses. Instead, I paint a complex picture of the obstacles women face in attaining strong executive posts and the role that gender plays in their paths and their authority. Analyzing the world over fifty years, I intentionally focus on breadth rather than depth. The literature on women executives consists largely of collections of narratives (Liswood 2007; Opfell 1993) as well as descriptive case studies of their behaviors once in office (Genovese 1993b). As such, the larger institutional, structural, and historical dimensions of executive power remain underexamined. Biographical and country-specific details stemming from this body of work inform my research as well, but they serve as catalysts for appreciating the broader patterns of paths and powers of women executives. Through these inquiries, I address how far women have really come over the past five decades in achieving their executive aspirations. Unfortunately, I find that women have not made as many gains as generally thought when I account for paths, positions, and powers. Focusing on a handful of cases of women leaders from a restricted number of countries cannot adequately address questions concerning women's overall progress.

Women in Politics and Gender in Politics Approaches

This book recognizes the conceptual differences between "women in politics" and "gender in politics." *Women* refers to biological, physical, and anatomical distinctions. A "women in politics" approach selects women based on their perceived biological similarities (Caraway 2010). Incorporating women, still seldom analyzed, questions the dominant norm of male leaders and other assumptions about national leadership. According to Karen Beckwith (2005):

> The need for research on women and politics persists.... We still lack a wide range of knowledge, especially comparative and longitudinal, about women's political behavior, political beliefs and attitudes, means of organizing, behavior in governmental office, experience in campaigning, response to power inequalities, and exclusion from political power—among other concerns. The subfield of women and politics research still requires this basic investigatory, cumulative research. (128–29)

In this book I utilize a "women in politics" approach to the extent that I select female leaders as my main subject, although I also engage male executives throughout.

Gender, "the culturally constructed meaning of biological sex differences" (Duerst-Lahti 2006), is "how we come to understand and often magnify the minor differences that exist between biological males and females" (Duerst-Lahti and Kelly 1996, 13). As a category, gender is a "multidimensional mapping of socially constructed, fluid, politically relevant identities, values, conventions, and practices conceived as masculine and/or feminine" (Beckwith 2005, 131). "Masculine" and "feminine" do not necessarily correspond to a person's sex or biological characteristics. As a process, gender encompasses "behaviors, conventions, practices and dynamics engaged in by people, individuals, institutions and nations" (Beckwith 2005, 132). Seeing gender as a process helps us analyze gendered constructs relating to institutions and identify several critical questions virtually ignored in the existing literature: How are executive selection processes and political systems gendered? To what extent do gendered norms, processes, and institutions aid or inhibit women's quests for and exercise of executive powers?

A "gender in politics" approach encompasses work in which gender is an independent or dependent variable (Caraway 2010). Gender analysis can focus on women or men (or both). "Gender points us to situations where all the actors are male (e.g., the military) or primary actors are female (e.g., care work) and permits us to investigate the political construction and ramification of variations of masculinity and femininity within these contexts" (Beckwith

2005, 132). Gender analysis often pushes the biological boundaries of men and women and dichotomies of masculinity and femininity. It also recognizes that we continually renegotiate gendered constructs specific to certain places and times (Lorber 1994).

I use a "gender in politics" approach throughout this book. I scrutinize the numerous gender norms and stereotypes around the world that continue to inform political practices and limit women's gains as world leaders. For example, I construct a systematic typology of executive positions, based on both constitutional design and governance in practice, and relate powers and systems to gender. I also devise various categories of political systems. This analysis highlights both the progress women have made as national leaders and the continuing obstacles they face. Ultimately, this gendered lens enables us to see that despite women's recent advances, executive office remains nearly entirely a male domain, rendering women's progress uncertain.

At the same time, this research recognizes the importance of examining women leaders *because* they are women. Most scholarship on national leaders focuses on men, and generalizations drawn from these works view the male experience as the standard (Neustadt 1990). As Richter (1991) notes, "The experience of politically prominent women offers empirical 'reality checks' on theories of leadership that have derived exclusively from the experiences of men" (527). Much of the existing literature highlights the fact that gender, though not the only important variable in the examination of national leadership, emerges as a significant force:

> Indeed, when political scientists examine the factors that affect male leaders, they frequently find it difficult to isolate the impact of a single variable or to distinguish one factor from another. In several respects, feminist analysis can enhance our understanding of political leadership: A feminist perspective paints an alternative picture of women as national leaders, but it also points to even larger lessons for the study of leadership in general. (Sykes 1993, 227)

Moreover, research on male executives, though probing men as the primary reference group, generally lacks explicit gender analysis.

Scholars of both women in politics and gender in politics must grapple with potential challenges, including essentialism—the "assumption that members of certain groups have an essential identity that all members of that group share and of which no others can partake. Insisting that women represent women or Blacks represent Blacks, for example, implies an essential quality of womanness or Blackness that all members of that group share" (Mansbridge 1999, 637). While studying mainly women executives, I do not assume that women constitute a monolithic group, possessing identical identities and values. In fact, the various hypotheses engaged in this work demonstrate considerable divergences among women leaders and address how these relate to various social constructions rather than nature. Furthermore, integrating women does not necessarily occur at the expense of gender analysis. "It is impossible to talk about gender without talking about women and about men, even as we recognize that 'gender is not a synonym for women'" (Beckwith 2005, 134). This work recognizes the need to study women executives, given the many gaps in knowledge, but stresses the importance of placing the findings in a gendered perspective.

Indeed, the various approaches used here—quantitative and qualitative methodologies, large-N comparative analysis, and women and gender in politics—emerge as mutually supportive. According to Karen Beckwith (2010a), comparative political research is open to many questions concerning women and gender and emphasizes the value of methodological pluralism. All of these features aid in answering the main question posed: How far have women really come in their attainment of executive office? I argue that men continue to dominate as presidents and prime ministers and this will undoubtedly persist for the foreseeable future. Despite women's recent strides, they are still drastically underrepresented as executives, particularly among those nations where the executives hold significant powers. Much of this continued male dominance relates to the ways that gender informs executive political institutions and processes.

CASE SELECTION

In some chapters, I limit my analysis to countries where women have served as prime ministers or presidents, extending back to 1960. Women ruled long before that as queens and regents and proved their political prowess in "masculine" endeavors, including war. Moreover, as women, they fought to wield and retain power in the face of many challenges to their rule (Fraser 1989; Jansen 2002). While these women were no doubt important actors, the current research is limited to the modern period and to positions representative of the current political landscape.[4] Aside from monarchs, I also exclude women leaders who have served in positions not conforming to presidential or prime ministerial offices, such as collective presidencies with no apparent head (as in San Marino) and executives in nonautonomous countries (such as Netherlands Antilles). I analyze acting or interim women leaders throughout, although to a lesser extent. In other chapters, I examine nearly all countries around the globe, both where women have broken through the executive glass

ceiling and where women have not. To provide consistency among the chapters,
I exclude nonautonomous countries and those lacking more traditional executive institutions.

ROAD MAP

In Chapter 2, I evaluate the growing literature on women, gender, and politics to uncover possible theoretical explanations for women's rise to power as
presidents and prime ministers. While scholars rely a great deal on research on
women executives, this literature is very small and generally outdated; I utilize the much larger body of research on women in national parliaments, since
some of the same conditions related to women's legislative representation may
be critical to their rise to executive office.

Chapter 3 analyzes trends in women's executive office holding from 1960
through 2015. It outlines the positions in which women govern and specific
gender constructs involved in executive selection, powers available to prime
ministers and presidents, respective levels of autonomy, and selection processes
for leaders through 2010. It develops a systematic typology of executive positions and categories of political systems based on both constitutional designs
and governance observed in practice.

Having established the importance of positions and systems, I focus more thoroughly in Chapter 4 on the women who represent various types of executive positions. Here I also engage data related to the party systems and labels attributed to
women. In order to assess women's ultimate progress in advancing to executive
offices, I offer more specific details of their routes to office and authority.

Chapter 5 sketches the educational and political backgrounds of nearly all
women national leaders who came to power from 1960 through 2010. For each,
I highlight age upon entering office, tenure in the position, and reasons for
leaving (if applicable). I also offer similar information on the male leaders the
women succeeded, to show whether the women's backgrounds and tenures differ or diverge from those of their male predecessors. Chapter 6 concerns two
significant factors linked to women leaders also identified in Chapter 5: family
ties and participation in activist movements.

Based on the many dynamics associated with women's successful advancement to executive office, I combine key variables derived from the qualitative
chapters in a statistical model in Chapter 7. Instead of analyzing solely the
countries women have governed, I integrate nearly all autonomous countries
across the globe into the model.

Chapter 8 presents data on female presidential candidates worldwide as well
as information on the percentages of votes that women have attained. Questions

probed include the following: Do women fail to come to office as presidents *because they do not run*? Are women candidates competitive, or do they tend to lose by substantial margins? Do any important regional patterns surface in the types of positions women compete for and the types of races in which they appear most viable? Among the women who have been successful in presidential elections, did their victories hinge on the absence of male incumbents vying for power? By inspecting actual candidacies and election results, I make clearer the presidential positions most elusive to women.

Chapter 9 thoroughly examines two women—Ségolène Royal (France) and Hillary Clinton (the United States)—who came closer than any other women in their respective countries to attaining the presidency but ultimately failed. While others have engaged these candidacies (Carroll 2009; Lawrence and Rose 2010; Murray 2010a), this chapter represents the first attempt to compare their bids systematically. Like Chapter 8, it deciphers the aspects of presidential posts that appear most resistant to women's inclusion. The presidencies of France and the United States are very strong domestically and are also highly influential on the world stage. Additionally, Chapter 9 details specific candidate strategies implemented to navigate various executive processes.

Chapter 10 highlights some of the main conclusions drawn throughout the analysis and poses crucial questions related to women's national leadership not yet explored or adequately answered. Finally, the appendix contains brief biographies of all the women who served as prime ministers and presidents from 1960 through 2010.

In this book, I hope to uncover factors related to the advancement of women executives and to evaluate the extent to which women still require political parity. In so doing, rather than issuing the final word on women executives, I want to suggest a starting point for increased scholarship, discourse, and deliberation in an effort to move the gender and executive research forward. Given that more than fifty years have passed since Sirimavo Bandaranaike became the world's first female prime minister, this seems an especially ripe time to chart such a long-neglected course.

2

Women Executives

The Literature

This chapter evaluates the growing literature on women, gender, and politics to uncover possible explanations for women's ascensions to presidencies and premierships. To begin, I assess the research on women executives. I also utilize results drawn from examinations of women officeholders in other positions, particularly legislative, in order to assert critical ways that paths and powers may differ depending on office type. Based on these works, we can identify potential variables associated with the rise of women national leaders across the globe.

Research suggests that any explanations for women's political ascensions must account for a number of institutional, structural, historical, and cultural conditions (Reynolds 1999; Inglehart and Norris 2003; McDonagh 2009). Moreover, linking these factors to gender is essential. At the same time, existing work has not yet fully explored women prime ministers and presidents. As such, we do not entirely understand the variables that are critical to women's executive advancement.

RESEARCH ON WOMEN EXECUTIVES

The existing scholarship on women executives is quite meager. A landmark work is *Women as National Leaders,* a collection edited by Michael A. Genovese (1993b). Since the collection features only seven women presidents and prime ministers, the scope is relatively modest, although the cases vary temporally and geographically. The findings suggest that women leaders rise to power in varied contexts. Preliminary assessments of gendered leadership styles differ greatly, ultimately raising more questions for future research. As Genovese (1993a) notes, "None of these women has been a 'revolutionary' leader, and overall they have tended to be spread across the ideological spectrum" (215). Some women, however, provide transformative and feminist leadership. Transformative leadership helps to bring about change in individual citizens, states, and societies (Sykes 1993, 220). It need not include a feminist agenda, but it fundamentally changes the status quo. In contrast, feminist leadership explicitly concerns the alteration of the place and perception of women in society, acknowledges that gender is socially constructed, and aims for equal status between men and women. Gro Harlem Brundtland, as prime minister of Norway, transformed environmental policies as well as cabinet posts by appointing numerous women. Margaret Thatcher ended the forty-year postwar consensus in the United Kingdom and ushered in a revolutionary era of economic transformation; most notably, she ruled by conviction—*not* compromise (King 2002). Others, such as India's Indira Gandhi (Sykes 1993), are neither transformative nor feminist but still challenge prevailing assumptions about women's rule through exhibiting highly "masculine" traits. Indeed, Gandhi claimed the "title of only man in a cabinet of old women" (Masani in Everett 1993, 112).

Genovese's 1993 collection offers many important findings utilized in several chapters of this book. Since the majority of women executives have entered office since its initial publication, however, specific conditions related to the current expansion of women leaders remain unclear. Patterns identified in the early 1990s may no longer hold. While a revised edition integrating four additional women leaders is forthcoming (Genovese and Steckenrider 2013), only two of the women have ascended since 2000.[1] Further, Genovese's volumes utilize solely qualitative analysis, but given the sharp increase in cases, we can also integrate quantitative techniques to uncover factors related to women's paths.

Other important works on women leaders include Olga Opfell's *Women Prime Ministers and Presidents* (1993) and Laura Liswood's *Women World Leaders* (1995, 2007). Opfell examines the lives of twenty-one female presidents and prime ministers. While an extremely valuable resource, this work engages only very short summaries of the women's lives prior to entering office and their times in power. In contrast, Liswood compiles excerpts of interviews with women national leaders containing anecdotes that center on the women's backgrounds, personal influences, and lessons learned in office.[2] These leaders articulate their struggles for acceptance and concerns about representing women around the world. Liswood attempts to derive some general findings, including geographic influences on women's leadership. I utilize these works to identify important personal details of women executive's lives.

More recently, Rainbow Murray (2010a) edited a collection detailing nine female executive aspirants. The authors utilize gender analysis and offer greater diversity in case selection than do the previous works noted. The book is timely in that it mainly features campaigns that only recently concluded. Above all, it hones in on the pervasive gender stereotypes limiting women's success in securing executive posts. While the conclusions offered in the collection inform the current analysis, the authors focus on a very small sample of candidates and concentrate mainly on campaign dynamics and media reporting.

Women in Executive Power, edited by Gretchen Bauer and Manon Tremblay (2011), analyzes women presidents and prime ministers and cabinets in all major world regions. Each chapter examines sociocultural, economic, and political variables shaping women's access to cabinet posts and to the positions of head of state and government over the past few decades and offers insight regarding the substantive representation of women.[3] The contributors use mainly qualitative analysis, and their findings largely suggest that women increasingly attain stereotypically "masculine" positions and their tendency to act on behalf of women's policy interests varies.

Several authors have published biographies of women national leaders. Works on Margaret Thatcher and Mary Robinson are among the most numerous (Hughs 2000; Moskin 1990; Young 1990; Siggins 1997). Outside Europe, popular subjects include Corazon Aquino (Komisar 1987), Benazir Bhutto (Akhund 2000), and Golda Meir (Burkett 2008). These works effectively establish various timelines and document women's educational and political backgrounds and family ties. However, few examine the specific details of women's lives in relation to their larger contexts. None systematically investigate the role of gender in women's rise to power and leadership styles. Moreover, they analyze individual leaders in isolation from other cases.

Several female executives have penned their own life stories. Some prominent titles include *The Downing Street Years* (Thatcher 1995), *Dreams of the Heart* (Chamorro 1996), *Madam Prime Minister: A Life in Power and Politics* (Brundtland 2002), *My Truth* (Gandhi 1980), *Daughter of Destiny* (Bhutto 1989), *Reconciliation: Islam, Democracy, and the West* (Bhutto 2008),[4] and *This Child Will Be Great: Memoir of a Remarkable Life by Africa's First Woman President* (Johnson Sirleaf 2009). While disclosing details regarding upbringings and political ambitions, autobiographies obviously fixate on strengths and successes, given that it is in a woman leader's interest to focus solely on the positive aspects of her life and political tenure. As such, we must view these sources through a critical lens.

A number of journal articles examine case studies of women premiers and presidents (Clemens 2006; Ferree 2006; King 2002; Thompson and Lennartz 2006; Wiliarty 2008). Several provide important insights into women's backgrounds and paths. Two related themes surface repeatedly: (1) women are often outsiders before their rise to executive power, and (2) they frequently gain office through chance circumstances, such as the aftermath of major electoral defeats of the ruling party and political scandals (Clemens 2006; King 2002; Thompson and Lennartz 2006). Therefore, an important explanation for women's executive advancement relates to the opening of political space. Still, these studies concentrate only on high-profile European leaders such as Margaret Thatcher and Angela Merkel. Further, this research fails to situate cases within a comparative gendered framework.[5]

Essays published in the "Critical Perspectives" section of *Politics & Gender* in 2008 position female leaders within a global gendered context (Adams 2008; Tobar 2008; Wiliarty 2008; Holli 2008). Although these offer relatively short treatments of four women leaders (Merkel, Halonen, Johnson Sirleaf, and Bachelet), each executive is placed within the larger milieu of women prime ministers and presidents.[6] Women's mobilization contributed to the victories of the women presidents analyzed (see also Bauer 2009). All have relatively interesting backgrounds compared to typical executives from the same countries. For example, each is divorced and some are single mothers, which, particularly in Latin America and Africa, may be considered somewhat controversial.[7] Thus, these women challenge multiple gender norms. Among this more diverse array of cases, the public entrusted Bachelet, Merkel, and Johnson Sirleaf with ushering in new political eras when politicians (mainly men) left them disappointed and seeking an end to corruption (see also Tripp 2008). Again, a common pattern among women world leaders concerns the availability of a political vacuum.[8]

Other regionally based research links executives in a number of countries. Richter (1991) and Hodson (1997) apply critical understandings of gender to their case studies of South and Southeast Asia.[9] These analyses allow me to engage many of their theories regarding women's activism and family ties to women's rise to power in more diverse settings.

FACTORS RELATED TO WOMEN'S ASCENSIONS TO EXECUTIVE OFFICE

Some of the factors that promote women to legislative power may also contribute to their gaining executive posts. However, we can also draw some important contrasts between respective offices. Likely explanations for women's enhanced descriptive representation encompass structural, cultural, institutional, and historical conditions.

Structural Factors and Women's Descriptive Representation

SOCIETAL STATUS AND SUPPLY AND DEMAND

Within the gender and politics research, the "supply" of eligible contenders is typically associated with women's promotion to political positions. We can discern the supply by investigating women's rates in educational institutions and professional occupations. Early studies typically confirmed a connection between the educational and employment levels of women to the proportions of women legislators (Darcy, Welch, and Clark 1994; Rule 1985). Women's education and employment participation creates a pipeline of qualified contenders for political offices. More contemporary research, however, fails to establish a positive connection between women's general status and their political representation (Matland 1998a; Moore and Shackman 1996; Yoon 2010), rendering mixed empirical findings.

The United Nations Development Programme's Gender-Related Development Index (GDI) may also measure the supply of eligible women by evaluating their poverty, education, and life expectancy rates in comparison to men's. Reynolds (1999) finds that greater parity in GDI corresponds to higher percentages of women in parliament (567). While it is important to account for GDI as a control variable, mixed results make it unlikely that GDI positively relates to women executives.

Women's presence in other political offices perhaps best captures their supply in the executive pipeline. Obtaining these positions requires prior political experience. Thus, the larger the pool of eligibles (those holding legislative or lower-level executive seats), the greater the odds that a woman will become president or prime minister. Legislative experience could yield executive aspirations. Parliamentarians may eventually become prime ministers; many countries require the premier to hold a parliamentary seat. Legislative experience also situates an individual as a credible presidential aspirant. Female legislators may gain temporary executive power when a position opens up suddenly.

Likewise, proportions of women cabinet ministers may relate to the rise of a female prime minister or president. Women prime ministers appoint slightly more women to their cabinets than do men (Davis 1997, 19). Women's cabinet representation also increases with their levels in legislatures (Escobar-Lemmon and Taylor-Robinson 2005; Davis 1997; Reynolds 1999). Since it takes time for women to climb the political ladder, their access to lower offices at earlier points may be critical to their subsequent promotions as presidents or prime ministers.

Female executives arise in many contexts where women, on average, trail behind men in educational, professional, and legislative office attainment. This study explores these very paradoxes. Male political leaders generally issue from the elite facets of society, and it seems likely that these also produce women executives. To verify this, I collect here important biographical details on leaders.

Even when the backgrounds of women correspond to those of male politicians, if not actively recruited for politics, women may still be underrepresented

(Niven 2010). Women who make up the pool of eligibles do not run for office as often as do their male counterparts. Their lack of confidence in their credentials forms part of the explanation (Lawless and Fox 2010). The disproportionately low levels of encouragement that women receive from political gatekeepers (Lawless and Fox 2010) also contribute to the dearth of women candidates. Not just the supply of women but also their lack of demand among political elites clarifies this candidate void (but see Cheng and Tavits 2011).

Family duties continue to keep politics out of reach for many women (Henderson and Jeydel 2007; Lawless and Fox 2010). The strain of combining political careers with family lives may overwhelm some women and result in fewer female aspirants. If women decide to pursue executive office, they may forgo marriage and children. If not, they delay their political careers until their children have grown up (Burrell 1994; Dolan and Ford 1995; Thomas 1994). In contrast, men rarely cite family considerations as reasons they decline or delay political careers (Lawless and Fox 2010).

GENDER STEREOTYPES

Attitudes toward women figure prominently in explanations for their political status. Scandinavian societies evince egalitarian attitudes toward women's political leadership and boast elevated proportions of female parliamentarians (Inglehart and Norris 2003). In contrast, Middle Eastern cultures display low levels of support for women's equal political participation and produce few women legislators. Still, we should note several striking outliers. Americans largely support women's political roles, but women constitute only a small fraction of the US Congress. Greater percentages of female parliamentarians exist in China, amid more negative views of women in politics (Inglehart and Norris 2003). As such, neither positive nor negative attitudes toward women's engagement adequately explain the proportions of women in political institutions.[10]

Virtually every culture is saturated with gender stereotypes, viewing women and men as competent in different issue areas and possessing varying traits. The "masculine" association of toughness favors men in executive positions, while compassion is a liability for women (Huddy and Terkildsen 1993; Fox and Oxley 2003). In cross-national studies, people tend to view leaders as possessing "masculine" traits, which they associate with men, not women (Sczesny et al. 2004). The public considers women and men to be proficient in different policy areas. They see women as more skilled in "feminine" areas, such as social welfare and health care, and men as stronger on national defense and other "masculine" issues (Huddy and Terkildsen 1993).

Media portrayals of political candidates continually reinforce gender stereotypes. Women receive less coverage and lower viability ratings than do men.

Additionally, the press associates women with "feminine" issues regardless of the policies they promote on the campaign trail (Kahn 1994). Stories on women candidates include reporting on their physical appearances and family backgrounds that trivializes women (Kahn 1994). While most gender and media research conducted to date has focused on the United States, gender stereotypes abound in the coverage of women candidates around the world (Kittilson and Fridkin 2008). Uneven reporting particularly hurts female prime ministerial and presidential candidates. Women executive aspirants are routinely subjected to more petty and negative coverage that may contribute to their downfall (see Murray 2010b). Even victorious women maneuver through stereotypical coverage; common gendered frames include the wife of (Murray 2010b), the peacemaker, the nurturer, and the unifier (Cantrell and Bachman 2008). Moreover, once in office, women executives typically receive less attention than their male counterparts (Norris 1997).[11]

While countries differ in the extent to which media coverage affects the electoral process, campaigns all over the globe, especially in postindustrial democracies, increasingly depend on media coverage (Norris 1997). Additionally, gender stereotypes play a role even in parliamentary contests where more cohesive parties influence candidate selection processes (Kittilson and Fridkin 2008). Since national executive candidates compete for the highest offices, the media likely have more influence in those races.

Most American and comparative research has failed to support claims of gender discrimination against women legislative candidates (Black and Erickson 2003; Hunter and Denton 1984; Rasmussen 1983; Seltzer, Newman, and Leighton 1997; Studlar and McAllister 1991). We still largely do not know, however, the dynamics of voter stereotypes in non-Western settings. Comparative public opinion data show that respondents continue to express negative views of women in politics, especially in Eastern Europe, Latin America, Asia, and Africa. Countries displaying a strong belief in male political superiority tend to have lower levels of women in parliament (Paxton and Hughes 2007), though, as I previously noted, there are various exceptions. Comparative research evaluating voting choices for executive office is largely nonexistent, but it is likely that sexism plays some role in voting decisions among members of the general public and possibly in the decisions of political party gatekeepers in certain contexts (Kittilson 1999). On the other hand, female party officials may promote women's candidacies (Cheng and Tavits 2011).[12] Furthermore, women's mobilization contributed to the presidential victories of at least Johnson Sirleaf of Liberia, Bachelet of Chile, and Halonen of Finland (Adams 2008; Holli 2008; Tobar 2008).[13] Thus, gender sometimes works to women's advantage, though this depends on the particular time and setting (Dolan 2004).

Family Ties and Political Openings

Family ties may explain how women break the glass ceiling in some contexts, particularly where women lag behind men in educational and professional achievement (Hodson 1997; Richter 1991; Jalalzai 2004, 2008). Women exercising executive power in Asia and, until very recently, Latin America issue from political families, whereas men's backgrounds vary (Jalalzai 2008). Dependent on males for their political significance, women often "inherit" power. More apt to lead in unstable settings, they capitalize on gendered conceptions to advance unity in postconflict societies (Saint-Germain 1993a), benefiting from the familiarity of their names and numerous related perks. While helping women overcome barriers to their empowerment, family ties reinforce "feminine" characterizations of women as political proxies, diminishing their agency.

Party gatekeepers mobilize women candidates with family links because of perceived advantages. The party's interest is to maintain or achieve power; its backing of a woman candidate may have less to do with supporting female governance than with preserving control, possibly until one of the "boys" can take over. Still, rather than acting as pawns, these women often stand firm as candidates, and some seek office despite the disapproval of party elites actively pursuing their own candidacies. Complicating things further, women may compete with other family members for the title of heir (Hodson 1997). Therefore, the skillful use of familial ties can prove critical to success.

Family links relate to political stability and institutionalization. Nations that are new to political independence often see the resurfacing of ethnic and religious factions suppressed during colonialism. Frequent regime changes, often coupled with assassinations or imprisonments of male leaders, plague the aftermath (Hodson 1997). As a result, outliers may challenge others for executive posts more often than in relatively stable climates, occasionally benefiting certain women in their pursuits (Jalalzai 2008).

Instability or a lack of institutionalization provides avenues for marginalized actors, including women, to enter the political fold. Political institutionalization suggests that "a regularized and stable process of succession of political leaders is assured" (Katzenstein 1978, 481). Frequent leadership changes make executive office more open to challenge, increasing the odds that a female leader will arise. This aspect of turnover does not benefit women exclusively but results from the greater number of openings.

When rules of succession are unclear, other factors, such as group affiliation, inform political success; patronage reigns supreme. According to Matland (1998b): "In a patronage based system, there are far less likely to be clear rules and even when they exist there is a distinct possibility that they are not carefully followed. Authority is based on either traditional or charismatic leadership, rather than legal-rational authority. Loyalty to those in the party is paramount" (70).

Conceivably, women achieve executive posts *because* gender hastens political advantages. In some cases, powerful men help certain women (especially those with kinship links to former male leaders, as mentioned) advance to executive offices; women gain power because they exhibit "feminine" traits such as dependence. Frequent coups and violent conflict, often stemming from religious and ethnic divisions, characterize many newly independent countries. Consistent with women's traditional maternal role, the public looks to women as unifiers. Though such gender stereotypes generally confine women, they also promote some to power (Tripp et al. 2009).

Even within more stable political contexts, sudden openings help advance select women to power, many of whom have stood outside male political circles. Anthony King (2002) characterizes Margaret Thatcher as an outsider in three ways:

1. Socially, she was from a more modest socioeconomic status than her male counterparts within the Conservative Party, *and* a woman.
2. Psychologically, she acknowledged her marginalization within the Tory network, explained in part by her gender.
3. Tactically, she consciously exploited her outsider status for personal gain.

Women's attainment of leadership through chance is often engaged as a trope. King (2002) identifies Thatcher as an "accidental leader," largely promoted because of the weaknesses of others rather than her own strengths:

Thatcher...was an accidental leader, only because the party wanted to be rid of Heath, and became prime minister because the British wanted the Labour government out, but became leader and prime minister because she was the only one of Heath's former cabinet who was prepared to stand against him for the leadership. (452)

King downplays Thatcher's twenty years of parliamentary experience before she gained the prime ministership. Thatcher's taking on a potentially formidable adversary suggests a high degree of political ambition. Her exploitation of favorable circumstances indicates skill. Still, King views the opening of political space as critical to women's advancement in more stable political systems.

Several recent studies document German chancellor Angela Merkel's path to power (Clemens 2006; Ferree 2006; Thompson and Lennartz 2006; Wiliarty 2008).[14] Similar to King (2002), most conclude that Merkel's rise was aided, in part, by her outsider status. As a Protestant from East Germany, she was a rarity among the Catholic and Western German–dominated Christian

Democratic Union (Clemens 2006). According to Thompson and Lennartz (2006): "Merkel's fifteen year rise to the chancellorship was improbable, accidental, and unexpected....Her earlier appointments were largely coincidental" (108). Her premature promotion in Helmut Kohl's government reflected Kohl's desire to have an East German and a woman in his cabinet (Clemens 2006). Her exclusion from the party's inner circle due to her gender actually insulated her from the financial scandals that ruined the careers of several male colleagues, including Kohl, her former mentor. Moreover, the stereotype of women's greater honesty convinced some that she could clean up corruption (Thompson and Lennartz 2006). Merkel's relative youth also worked in her favor (Wiliarty 2008). Like Thatcher, she is thus an outsider and an accidental leader; her political savvy seems to play no role. However, even though auspicious circumstances and descriptive characteristics aided her success, we should not undervalue her political prowess. She carefully rose to party leadership (and ultimately the chancellorship) through meticulous exploitation of favorable conditions. She was "uniquely able to convert these challenges into opportunities because she embodied something new, lacked compunction about breaking with tradition, proved open to new ideas, and was not too closely linked with or dependent upon any of the CDU's traditional power centers" (Clemens 2006, 70).

We can derive more general conclusions from Thatcher's and Merkel's stories. Women in more stable political settings benefit from sudden openings. Exclusion from the inner realms of male networks shelters even the most politically seasoned women from the same scandals that embroil their male counterparts (Beckwith 2010b). In the aftermath of major electoral defeats, remaining high-quality male contenders sometimes hesitate to throw their hats into the ring, seeing their chances for victory as better in the future (Beckwith 2010b).[15] In these situations, high-quality senior women stand the greatest chances of attaining party headships, and sometimes premierships (Beckwith 2010b).[16]

Religious and Cultural Traditions

Countries with large Catholic populations recruit fewer female candidates (Rule 1985). Christian countries, however, produce a higher proportion of women in legislatures and cabinet offices than do those with other religious traditions (Reynolds 1999).[17] Some studies evince a negative link between Islam and women's political status (Fish 2002), although others cast doubt on these findings (Donno and Russett 2004).[18]

Cultural constructions heavily shape religious conceptions of women's proper roles. Hinduism promotes views of women's duality; the powerful influences of women may be regarded as both decidedly negative and highly positive

(Waldley 1977). According to Hodson (1997), South Asian women enjoy many benefits stemming from religious interpretation:

> The Hindu goddess Kali both gives life and destroys it, although she is more associated with destruction. Hindus also believe that women are the sources of creative energy. Buddhism views the power of women through the same dual lens of creation and destruction. Benazir Bhutto's autobiography cites several positive images of powerful public Muslim women in Islamic history and notes that "Muslim history was full of women who had taken a public role and performed every bit as successfully as men. Nothing in Islam discouraged them, or me, from pursuing that course."[19] Western religions offer no similarly pervasive images of female power. (37)

Society also invests South Asian women with other significance. Older women from middle- and upper-class families match marital partners (Hodson 1997). Since family connections transmit political power, women's influence transcends private spaces.

WOMEN'S INVOLVEMENT IN ACTIVIST MOVEMENTS

Women's activist participation may influence their subsequent incorporation in more formalized political institutions, including executive offices. Scholars tend to identify three broad categories of movements involving women (Beckwith 2000). First, women's movements involve the systematic organizing of female actors on behalf of a common political cause. While ideologies vary, some seek to preserve women's traditional roles.[20] Second, feminist movements may include both male and female actors but aim to overcome female subordination. Finally, nationalist movements lack gender content and feature men dominating leadership positions (Beckwith 2000) but also strongly rely on female participants.

Women's movements appear common to Latin America. The Bolivian Housewives Committee organized in the 1970s to protest government displacement of miners. According to Geske and Bourque (2001):

> The pattern noted in the Bolivian case came to be repeated in a variety of contexts throughout Latin America....Women frequently justified their political involvement by reference to their maternal roles and the need to protect their homes and families. They had been driven not out of a desire for an expanded political voice but rather to protest government violation of their loved ones—the appropriate roles of mother. (254–55)

In the Madres de Plaza de Mayo movement, women acted on behalf of their children who disappeared during the Argentinean "Dirty War" (Bouvard 2002). Although their participation focused on others and reinforced maternal roles, many of the women involved subsequently became politically engaged on a broader array of issues and interests.

African women's movements have engaged a wide range of issues and actors (Tripp 2001; Tripp et al. 2009). As a result, several new organizations formed in the 1990s, opening both domestic and international networks of participation. According to Adams (2008, 481) women in Liberia played critical roles in initiating peace talks and creating the interim Council of State. These movements relied on traditional notions of women as peacemakers and their unique contributions as mothers. Women had played peace-building roles throughout Liberian history and benefited from this accumulation of leadership experience. Perhaps most strikingly, during the democratic transition, women activists united for the first time across class, ethnic, and religious divides. They opened a space, seizing new opportunities that resulted from the destruction of existing social and political institutions (Bauer 2009). While the women gained a great deal of political ground, they neither included men in their struggles nor explicitly utilized feminist ideology.

Activism is more accurately characterized as feminist in other countries. South African female activism formed across various cleavages in strategic feminist alliance. Women's gender consciousness developed simultaneously with political transition, uniting actors in challenging patriarchy (Salo 2010). Feminist activism during this critical juncture enabled women to write gender equality guarantees into the new constitution (Salo 2010).

Baldez (2003) cites three factors critical to women's mobilization during democratic transitions: (1) organizational networks and resources, (2) direct contact with international feminism, and (3) women's exclusion from the process of decision making in the democratic movements.[21] Based on these conditions, democratic transitions mobilized women along gender lines to advocate for their own empowerment in Brazil, Chile, and East Germany. This did not occur in Poland (Baldez 2003). In fact, in most Central and Eastern European transitions, women tended not to mobilize as women or to advocate feminist ideologies (Baldez 2003).

Women may first organize on behalf of larger movements and subsequently gain political positions, including presidencies and prime ministerships. Activism also may aid their ascensions when voters mobilize on behalf of women's issues, agendas, and candidacies. Liberia, again, provides a good example. Voter registration campaigns organized by female activists increased women from 30 percent to 50 percent of the voting pool, directly contributing to Johnson Sirleaf's presidential victory in 2005 (Adams 2008, 482; National Elections Commission 2005).

Political Institutions and Women's Representation

ELECTORAL SYSTEMS

Since the publication of Maurice Duverger's classic 1955 work *The Political Role of Women,* institutional designs have been considered crucial to women's political inclusion. The legislative literature shows that multimember and proportional representation systems produce more women legislators than do single-member majoritarian districts (Darcy, Welch, and Clark 1994; Lovenduski and Norris 1993; Matland 1998a; Rule 1985; Rule and Zimmerman 1994; Paxton 1997; Salmond 2006; Yoon 2010). The benefits of multimember districts for women depend on district magnitude. Districts with fewer seats less often elect women (Matland 1993; Rule 1985; Taagepera 1994). As Matland (1998b) observes, "When a party expects to win several seats, parties are much more conscious of trying to balance their tickets" (76). Furthermore, "as the number of seats per district increases, parties will go further down their lists (that is, win more seats) and more parties will have multi-member delegations. Both should increase women's representation" (80). Salmond (2006) suggests that scholars overestimate the positive effects of proportional representation when they employ linear regression models. Still, he finds a strong connection between proportional representation and women's elevated levels in parliament.[22] Closed lists may aid women candidates when the electorate has more traditional views than party elites (Matland 1998b, 82). However, when the opposite holds true, open lists could benefit women more (Rule and Zimmerman 1994).

QUOTAS

Gender quotas affect the proportion of women legislators. Quotas are of three main types: reserved seats, party quotas, and legislative quotas (see Krook 2009). Within the past fifteen years, more than one hundred countries have adopted these kinds of affirmative measures (Jalalzai and Krook 2010). Still, the ultimate impact of quotas on women's representation varies depending on their interaction within political environments and configurations of a multitude of conditions, including electoral systems (Krook 2009). Quotas work best within proportional representation systems with closed lists and high district magnitudes (Htun and Jones 2002). Left-wing party ideologies tend to support women, and the leaders of left-wing parties, compared to their more conservative counterparts, offer a greater commitment to gender equality and more seriously enforce quota regulations (Kittilson 1999; Davidson-Schmich 2006).

According to Krook (2009), quotas generally succeed when conditions provide a "harmonious" fit with political institutions and candidate selection practices.[23] Unsuccessful implementation efforts, in contrast, witness unresolved clashes and tensions and appear "disjointed." Pakistan's quota reserving National Assembly seats for women is an illustration of a harmonious case; it rapidly produced striking results.[24] Women's levels increased from 2.3 percent to 22 percent between 1997 and 2002, the year the quota took effect.[25] In other countries, including France, quota adoption led to stagnation, at least initially (Krook 2009; Tripp and Kang 2008).[26] Additionally, changes in women's proportions depend on quota specifications and the repercussions triggered by unmet mandates (Jones 1998; Schmidt and Saunders 2004). While quotas do not directly relate to countries' electing or appointing women executives, they shape the contents of the political pipeline.[27]

EXECUTIVE SYSTEMS AND STRUCTURES

Political systems and structures, shaped by gender ideologies, affect women's ascension to executive offices. A separation between the executive and the legislature generally characterizes presidential systems. The president need not answer to the legislature, nor can she or he dismiss it. While requiring some collaboration with other political actors, the president acts independently. Though presidential terms are fixed, impeachment may curtail a term. Presidents are thus relatively protected from dismissal; as the lone executive, a president is separate from the legislature in terms of political survival and enjoys greater autonomy than does a prime minister. Finally, presidents are elected through some form of popular vote.

In contrast, prime ministers, after being appointed through a variety of procedures, effectively avoid the public vote.[28] It is relatively easier to depose prime ministers if they fall out of favor; votes of no confidence or unsuccessful party elections hasten their dismissals. This vulnerability connects to ideal prime ministerial traits. The essence of parliamentary politics is collaboration. To achieve their policy agendas, prime ministers depend on parliamentary cooperation and enjoy less room to take unilateral action than do presidents. Prime ministers are afforded greater control over policy making than their presidential counterparts, but cabinet ministers manage their respective policies. It is the prime minister's responsibility to ensure the government's smooth operation. While vulnerable to ouster, a prime minister generally enjoys the benefit of being able to call early elections.

Compared with presidencies, prime ministerial appointments present more auspicious opportunities for women. Even if the country has a socially conservative electorate, a woman can work her way up through party ranks, win her colleagues' respect, and head the party and ultimately become prime minister. According to Whicker and Isaacs (1999):

> In aspiring to leadership of a political party, parliamentary members start with an equally recognized legitimacy: All have been elected from their districts or in national elections....Party members seem to operate on a rough merit system, which provides rewards of power and leadership based on political and legislative performance. Both male and female party members, once elected, have similar opportunities to excel in the tasks of creating national agenda, developing legislation, and shepherding proposals around or over legislative hurdles. In this arena, paying one's professional dues is important, recognized, and generally rewarded. (222)

Executive office is generally considered a highly masculinized realm. Exploring the United States, Georgia Duerst-Lahti (1997) argues that this characterization relates to centralized and hierarchical power arrangements:

> Executive power is characterized by unity of command, hierarchical arrangements, and—with centralized control—a capacity to act quickly and decisively when circumstances dictate. These factors create circumstances in which women are understood as "other" in contrast to a masculine norm, and they do so in a way that is predictable inside gender ideology. (18)

Preferred presidential traits likely exist in other systems featuring strong presidencies. Strength, leadership, quick decision making, and unilateral command contribute to executive power. Moreover, depending on the electorate, gaining office through popular vote potentially poses a problem for women. Presidents often serve as commanders in chief, a "masculine" duty. Women experience more difficulty in attaining presidencies because of the connection of presidencies to popular election, "masculine" leadership traits and responsibilities, and insulation from removal. On the other hand, women leaders proliferate as prime ministers. The deliberative nature of parliamentary legislatures indicates slower decision-making practices (Duerst-Lahti 1997, 18). Perceptions of women's abilities to collaborate and deliberate impede them less in attaining prime ministerial roles than perceptions of their lesser capacities to lead quickly, decisively, and independently hamper them in attaining presidencies. Gradual appointment processes to leadership and less protection in their posts also makes prime ministerial office a more likely option for women.

Research on women in cabinets makes the relationship between gender and executive office clearer. The gender dynamics of cabinet assignments correlate to prevailing stereotypes. As a result, some cabinet departments are considered "masculine" and others "feminine." "Feminine" departments generally issue from the private sphere, whereas "masculine" departments operate in the public domain (Borrelli 2002; see also Escobar-Lemmon and Taylor-Robinson 2009). For example, various explorations of women within the US executive branch have found that women rarely achieve positions wielding vast powers, though the cases of Janet Reno, Madeleine Albright, Condoleezza Rice, and Hillary Clinton challenge these findings. Still, women largely occupy posts within less potent departments, particularly ones more removed from the president and those managing "feminine" issues (Borrelli 2002; Martin 2003). Comparative research reveals similar patterns. While women worldwide have increasingly secured more high-profile and "masculine" cabinet posts, including finance, state, and even defense, they are still underrepresented in "masculine" ministries and overrepresented in all "feminine" positions (Escobar-Lemmon and Taylor-Robinson 2009). "Masculine" appointments tend to be more prestigious, while more "feminine" ones, such as those concerned with family, women's issues, health, and education, occupy the margins (Blondel 1988; Davis 1997; Dolan 2001; Escobar-Lemmon and Taylor-Robinson 2005; Paxton and Hughes 2007). Women's tendency to head less prestigious and more "feminine" ministries with weaker connections to the president or prime minister reinforces the "masculine" structure of cabinet office. Still, women appear to be gaining ground in obtaining more "masculine" cabinet posts worldwide (see Bauer and Tremblay 2011).

While women are more likely to serve as prime ministers than as presidents (Jalalzai 2008), prime ministers are not afforded identical authority from nation to nation; likewise, presidential powers vary significantly across countries. Power divergences exist both within and across executive positions. Some political systems stray away from the simplistic parliamentary/presidential dichotomy; these are typically classified as semipresidential.

Hodson (1997) argues that semipresidential systems, like parliamentary structures, benefit women because they enable women to rise to premiership through appointments. Other positive aspects of such systems for women include party financing of elections, which alleviates the potential problem of discrimination against women in fund-raising. The instability within semipresidential systems may also advantage women, since many nations with such systems only recently instituted hybrid governments (Hodson 1997).

Still, semipresidential systems are themselves extremely diverse, and the differences among them can potentially affect women's success. Not all presidencies or prime ministerships are created equal, and this inequality offers substantial gendered consequences. Rather than limit discussion here to three types of systems—presidential, prime ministerial, and the "catchall" semipresidential—I devise five political systems and five political positions, as explained in Chapter 3.

PARTIES AND PARTY SYSTEMS

Parties officially nominate executive candidates. Women's executive leadership prospects, therefore, depend greatly on the ideologies and structures of parties. In advocating for women's greater political access, parties prove critical to women's chances. Women's divergent demands and party responses shaped by rules and organizational structures in part explain women's varying levels of success. Do national or more localized parties pick candidates? Are selection processes more or less formalized (Norris and Lovenduski 2010)? Gender discrimination may affect the demand for women by parties, especially when elites possess little candidate information. Descriptive characteristics may affect perceptions regarding candidate quality. Weaker party organizations often promote fewer women, since they enjoy limited control over local parties (Lovenduski 1993). Less competitive parties tend to nominate more women candidates, given their more restricted choices (Lovenduski 1993). Competition also guides the relative power of parties and the voting public. Generally, voters exercise more sway in marginal districts and parties appear more influential over safer seats (Norris and Lovenduski 2010, 135).

Leftist parties, on balance, advocate women's parliamentary leadership; compared with more conservative parties, they ascribe to more egalitarian gender roles and list more women in prime ballot positions (Kittilson, 1999). However, some prominent women leaders, including Angela Merkel, Margaret Thatcher, and Kim Campbell (Canada), rose on conservative tickets. According to Wiliarty (2008), corporatist "catchall" parties appeal to many segments of the general electorate while recognizing important societal interests. This internal party organizational structure sometimes drives members of particular minority groups to power. Wiliarty further argues that the corporatist catchall party structure is more common among right-wing parties since they are less concerned with democratic procedures for promotion, often propelling women through the ranks. Conflicting findings surface as parties spanning the ideological spectrum promote women for different reasons (Lovenduski, 1993).

Beyond specific parties, party systems determine women's exercise of power. Multiparty parliamentary systems commonly feature coalition governments. We need to ask whether coalition governments increase women's odds of appointment to prime ministerships. Leading a coalition limits autonomy, resulting in a more tenuous tenure. Further, coalition governments require more consensus-driven leadership to bring parties together. Women may be seen as particularly apt to unite parties lest the dissolution of coalitions diminishes their personal power.[29]

Historical Factors and Women's Representation

Scholars generally expect that the longer women have access to basic political rights in a country, the greater the odds they will achieve legislative and executive posts (Reynolds 1999). As women become habituated in political roles, the more elites and the mass public consider them political contenders. This results in a larger pool of female aspirants.

A difficulty arises in how one measures historical political incorporation. Dating access from the year women gained national suffrage rights or the ability to run for office is the most common approach (Reynolds 1999). Women tend to win both these rights simultaneously, but this propensity has deviated worldwide. Western women obtained suffrage through prolonged periods of activism, and the enfranchisement of different groups proceeded incrementally. Typically at first only some men could vote (such as property owners), followed by all men, and then, only after that, women (Caraway 2004, 454). Sometimes women gained gradual incorporation. For example, although Australia extended suffrage to white women in 1902, Aboriginal women did not receive the franchise until 1967 (Henderson and Jeydel 2007). Women sometimes faced different age restrictions than men, which eased over time. When women in the United Kingdom gained suffrage in 1918, their voting age was thirty years, although the voting age for men was twenty-one.[30] More often than not, however, women were incorporated as an entire group. According to Caraway (2004), the *sequence* of suffrage expansions appears critical. Therefore, instead of assuming that women in the West enjoy advantages because of their longer histories of voting rights, women in the developing world may benefit from their simultaneous inclusion on the voting rolls with men.

Reynolds (1999) finds that earlier dates women first could stand for office correspond with greater quantities of female parliamentarians and cabinet members. Longer histories of political rights might likewise account for the ascension of women as presidents and prime ministers. Given Caraway's (2004) arguments, however, it appears that the sequencing of suffrage rights plays an important role.

Global Considerations

Do executives wield influence outside their countries? G-20 countries represent major industrial or emerging economies, while the G-8 countries are the most elite. National leaders' influence on global economic matters is enhanced when they govern countries enjoying heightened international status. For example, Chancellor Angela Merkel's power is bolstered by Germany's economic strength, which makes her the key player in crafting foreign policy agreements with Germany's neighbors. Merkel plays the leading role in mediating economic debates in other European states and those states' adoption of various reforms.

Nuclear capabilities and defense spending signify military might and provide countries with increased leverage in global discussions. Given the greater association of masculinity with foreign affairs, economics, and defense, women may face greater challenges leading countries with more global import in these realms. Thus, perhaps it is not surprising that women have gained executive office in less politically crucial countries, such as Trinidad and Tobago and Costa Rica, but *not* in the United States. Scholars repeatedly neglect global dimensions when explaining women's political incorporation. With the inclusion of this variable, this book breaks new ground in the study of gender in executive politics.

CONCLUSION

Any thorough discussion of women's ascension to executive offices must link critical institutional, structural, historical, cultural, and global factors to gender. In developing this comprehensive account, we need to investigate closely those who have successfully navigated their way to the top. We must also examine, however, candidacies that *did not* prove successful. Combining qualitative and quantitative comparative analysis appears an especially fruitful approach to exploring the many remaining questions related to women's attainment and exercise of executive powers.

Women Executives

Positions, Selections, Systems, and Powers

The previous chapter evaluated the growing literature on women, gender, and politics to uncover possible explanations for women's ascensions to presidencies and premierships. Engaging some of these works, I uncovered potential variables associated with the rise of women national leaders across the globe. Explanations for women's political ascents must account for a number of institutional, structural, historical, cultural, and global conditions (Reynolds 1999; Inglehart and Norris 2003; McDonagh 2009). Still, current scholarship has not yet fully explored women prime ministers and presidents, leaving some unclear conditions relevant to their expansion. This chapter provides more depth regarding institutional factors and processes critical to women's rise.

I outline here the quantity of women rulers and the positions occupied through 2015. Attention to both offices and selection procedures aids in answering a main question posed in this book: Have women made substantial progress in attaining executive posts? While we may learn a great deal from the numbers of women leaders, we must also address the powers at their disposal. Women leaders' relegation to weak positions, for example, necessarily limits their progress. To assess the powers of leaders, I distinguish presidential systems, parliamentary systems, and hybrid types as well as prime ministerial and presidential posts. I am particularly concerned with executive powers and autonomy and how these relate to selection procedures. I construct a typology of executive positions, based on both constitutional designs and governance in practice, to derive various categories of political systems. I follow with an analysis of the systems and positions in which women executives arise through 2010. In order to verify whether women disproportionately cluster into weaker positions, I also incorporate data on male leaders. In this way I probe the question of whether women face greater constraints than men in terms of power and independence. The limits of women executives' powers and positions, more than numbers alone, suggest that executive office continues to constitute a male domain such that women's progress in shattering the executive glass ceiling remains dubious.

TRENDS IN WOMEN'S EXECUTIVE DESCRIPTIVE REPRESENTATION

Descriptive representation is the extent to which representatives possess the same physical or social characteristics of their constituents (Pitkin 1967) and also share experiences with them (Mansbridge 1999). Women's descriptive representation is accomplished as simply a by-product of women executives' ascension rather than through specific actions taken in their offices. In this section, which analyzes women's descriptive representation in executive posts, I address the following questions: How many cases of women executives exist historically? What changes in the numbers of women executives arise by decade? What geographic regions do women executives come from?

Historically, female national leaders are rarities. The first woman to enter a position of national leadership (excluding female monarchs) was Sirimavo Bandaranaike, who became prime minister of Sri Lanka in 1960. Indira Gandhi of India and Golda Meir of Israel also held premierships beginning in that decade. Women's progress in breaking through to presidencies began later, when Isabel Perón rose to power in Argentina in 1974.[1]

From 1960 through August 2015, 108 women joined the elite ranks of national leaders (see Table 3.1) but ruled in seventy countries. More were prime ministers than presidents, sixty-two (57 percent) and forty-six (43 percent), respectively. Eighty-three (77 percent) were elected or appointed through normal procedures, whereas twenty-five (23 percent) served on an interim basis. Since these twenty-five did not undergo the same processes that more permanent leaders do, I note their numbers and do not treat them identically to the others.

When only the eighty-three nontemporary leaders are included, the gap in positions is even bigger, with fifty (60 percent) serving as prime ministers and thirty-three (40 percent) as presidents. Still, executive powers may not necessarily be gleaned through position title alone, a point discussed throughout this chapter.

Twenty-eight countries witnessed multiple women coming to power: twenty-one (Argentina, Bangladesh, Central African Republic, Croatia, Gabon, Germany, Guinea Bissau, Iceland, India, Ireland, Israel, Latvia, Malta, Moldova, New Zealand, the Philippines, Poland, São Tomé and Príncipe, Senegal, Serbia, and Sri Lanka) elected or appointed two different women leaders, and four (Finland, Lithuania, Norway, and South Korea) saw the ascensions of three distinct female leaders. Haiti and Switzerland have had four and five women leaders respectively. Countries with multiple women executives account for 40 percent of the total sample of nations with female leaders to date. Put differently, sixty-six of 108 women executives cluster within twenty-eight countries; together these leaders represent over sixty percent of all cases of women executives. Perhaps a woman holding office weakens the association of executive office with masculinity, ultimately

Table 3-1. WOMEN LEADERS AND THEIR DATES IN OFFICE BY COUNTRY,
WORLDWIDE, 1960–2010

Region/Country	Position	Name	Dates in Office (MM/DD/YYYY)
Africa			
Burundi	Prime Minister	Sylvie Kinigi	07/10/1993–02/11/1994
Central African Republic	Prime Minister	Elisabeth Domitien	01/03/1975–04/07/1976
Central African Republic	President*	Catherine Samba-Panza	01/23/2014–present
Gabon	President	Rose Francine Rogombé*	06/10/2009–10/16/2009
Guinea-Bissau	President*	Carmen Pereira	05/14/1984–05/16/1984
Guinea Bissau	Prime Minister*	Maria Adiatu Diallo Nandigna	02/10/2012–04/12/2012
Liberia	President	Ellen Johnson Sirleaf	01/16/2006–present
Madagascar	Prime Minister*	Cécile Manorohanta	12/18/2009–12/20/2009
Malawi	President	Joyce Banda	04/07/ 2012–05/31/2014
Mali	Prime Minister	Cissé Mariam Kaïdama Sidibé	04/03/2011–03/22/2012
Mauritius	President*	Catherine Samba-Panza	03/31/2012–07/21/2012 05/29/2015–06/05/2015
Mauritius	President	Ameenah Gurib-Fakim	05/06/2015–present
Mozambique	Prime Minister	Luísa Dias Diogo	02/17/2004–01/18/2010
Namibia	Prime Minister	Saara Kuugongelwa-Amadhila	03/21/2015–present
Rwanda	Prime Minister	Agathe Uwilingiyimana	07/18/1993–04/07/1994
São Tomé and Príncipe	Prime Minister	Maria das Neves Ceita Batista de Sousa	10/07/2002–07/16/2003
São Tomé and Príncipe	Prime Minister	Maria do Carmo Silveira	06/08/2005–04/21/2006
Senegal	Prime Minister	Mame Madior Boye	03/03/2001–11/04/2002
Senegal	Prime Minister	Aminata Touré	09/01/2013–07/08/2014
South Africa	President*	Ivy Matsepe-Casaburri	09/14/2005–09/18/2005 09/25/2008
Asia			
Bangladesh (South Asia)	Prime Minister	Khaleda Zia	03/20/1991–03/30/1996, 10/10/2001–10/29/2006
Bangladesh (South Asia)	Prime Minister	Sheikh Hasina	06/23/1996–07/15/2001 01/06/2009–present
India (South Asia)	Prime Minister	Indira Gandhi	01/19/1966–03/24/1977
India (South Asia)	President	Pratibha Patil	07/25/2007–07/25/2012
Indonesia (Southeast Asia)	President	Megawati Sukarnoputri	07/23/2001–10/20/2004
Kyrgyzstan (Central Asia)	President	Roza Otunbayeva	05/19/2010–12/1/2011
Mongolia (Central Asia)	Prime Minister*	Nyam Osoryn Tuyaa	07/22/1999–07/30/1999
Pakistan (South Asia)	Prime Minister	Benazir Bhutto	12/02/1988–08/06/1990 10/19/1993–11/05/1996
Philippines (Southeast Asia)	President	Corazon Aquino	02/25/1986–06/30/1992
Philippines (Southeast Asia)	President	Gloria Macapagal-Arroyo	01/20/2001–06/30/2010
South Korea (East Asia/Pacific)	Prime Minister*	Sang Chang	07/11/2002–07/31/2002

(continued)

Table 3-1. CONTINUED

Region/Country	Position	Name	Dates in Office (MM/DD/YYYY)
South Korea (East Asia/Pacific)	Prime Minister	Myeong-Sook Han	04/19/2006–03/07/2007
South Korea (East Asia/Pacific)	President	Park Geun-hye	02/25/13–present
Sri Lanka (South Asia)	Prime Minister	Sirimavo Bandaranaike	07/21/1960–03/27/1965 05/29/1970–07/23/1977 11/14/1994–08/10/2000
Sri Lanka (South Asia)	President	Chandrika Kumaratunga	11/14/1994–11/19/2005
Thailand (Southeast Asia)	Prime Minister*	Yingluck Shinawatra,	05/8/2011–07/05/2014
Caribbean			
Bahamas	Prime Minister	Cynthia A. Pratt	05/4/2005–06/06/2005
Dominica	Prime Minister	Eugenia Charles	07/21/1980–06/14/1995
Jamaica	Prime Minister	Portia Simpson-Miller	03/30/2006–09/11/2007 01/05/2012–present
Haiti	President*	Ertha Pascal-Trouillot	03/13/1990–02/07/1991
Haiti	Prime Minister	Claudette Werleigh	11/07/1995–02/27/1996
Haiti	Prime Minister	Michèle Pierre-Louis	09/05/2008–11/08/2009
Haiti	Prime Minister*	Florence Duperval Guillaume	12/20/2014–01/16/2015
Trinidad and Tobago	Prime Minister	Kamla Persad-Bissessar	05/26/2010–present
Europe			
Bulgaria	Prime Minister*	Reneta Indzhova	10/16/1994–01/25/1995
Croatia	Prime Minister	Jadranka Kosor	07/06/2009–12/23/2011
Croatia	President	Kolinda Grabar-Kitarovic	02/19/15–present
Denmark	Prime Minister	Helle Thorning-Schmidt	10/02/2011–06/28/2015
Finland	President	Tarja Halonen	03/01/2000–03/1/2012
Finland	Prime Minister	Anneli Tuulikki Jäätteenmäki	04/17/2003–06/24/2003
Finland	Prime Minister	Mari Kiviniemi	06/22/2010–06/22/2011
France	Prime Minister	Edith Cresson	05/15/1991–04/02/1992
Georgia	President*	Nino Burdzhanadze	11/23/2003–01/25/2004
Germany (East)	President*	Sabine Bergmann-Pohl	04/05/1990–10/02/1990
Germany (Unified)	Chancellor	Angela Merkel	11/22/2005–present
Iceland	President	Vigdís Finnbogadóttir	08/01/1980–08/01/1996
Iceland	Prime Minister	Jóhanna Sigurðardóttir	02/01/2009–05/23/2013
Ireland	President	Mary McAleese	11/11/1997–11/10/2011
Ireland	President	Mary Robinson	12/03/1990–09/12/1997
Kosovo	President	Atifete Jahjaga	04/07/2011–present
Latvia	President	Vaira Viķe-Freiberga	06/17/1999–07/08/2007
Latvia	Prime Minister	Laimdota Straujuma	01/22/2014–present
Lithuania	Prime Minister	Kazimira Danutė Prunskienė	03/17/1990–01/10/1991
Lithuania	President	Dalia Grybauskaitė	07/12/2009–present
Lithuania	Prime Minister*	Irena Degutienė	05/04/1999–05/18/1999
Macedonia	Prime Minister*	Radmila Šekerinska	05/12/2004–06/12/2004 11/18/2004–12/17/2004
Malta	President	Agatha Barbara	02/15/1982–02/17/1987
Malta	President	Marie-Louise Coleiro Preca	04/04/2014–present
Moldova	Prime Minister	Zinaida Greceanîi	03/31/2008–09/14/2009
Moldova	Prime Minister*	Natalia Gherman	06/22/2015–07/30/2015

Table 3-1. CONTINUED

Region/Country	Position	Name	Dates in Office (MM/DD/YYYY)
Norway	Prime Minister	Gro Harlem Brundtland	02/04/1981–10/14/1981
			05/09/1986–10/16/1989
			11/03/1990–10/25/1996
Norway	Prime Minister*	Anne Enger	08/31/1998–09/23/1998
Norway	Prime Minister	Erna Solberg	10/16/2013–present
Poland	Prime Minister	Hanna Suchocka	07/08/1992–10/26/1993
Poland	Prime Minister	Ewa Kopacz	09/22/2014–present
Portugal	Prime Minister*	Maria de Lourdes Pintasilgo	08/01/1979–01/03/1980
Serbia	President*	Nataša Mićić	12/29/2002–02/04/2004
Slovenia	Prime Minister	Alenka Bratušek	03/20/2013–09/18/2014
Slovakia	Prime Minister	Iveta Radičová	07/08/2010–04/04/2012
Switzerland	President	Ruth Dreifuss	01/01/1999–12/01/1999
Switzerland	President	Micheline Calmy-Rey	01/01/2007–12/31/2007
Switzerland	President	Doris Leuthard	01/01/2010–12/31/2011
Switzerland	President	Eveline Widmer-Schlumpf	01/01/2012–12/31/2012
Switzerland	President	Simonetta Sommaruga	01/01/2015–present
Turkey	Prime Minister	Tansu Çiller	06/25/1993–03/07/1996
Ukraine	Prime Minister	Yuliya Tymoshenko	01/04/2005–09/08/2005
			12/18/2007–03/04/2010
United Kingdom	Prime Minister	Margaret Thatcher	05/04/1979–11/28/1990
Yugoslavia	Prime Minister	Milka Planinc	05/16/1982–05/15/1986
Latin America			
Argentina	President	Isabel Perón	07/01/1974–03/24/1976
Argentina	President	Cristina Fernández	12/10/2007–present
Brazil	President	Dilma Rousseff	01/01/2011–present
Bolivia	President*	Lidia Gueiler Tejada	11/17/1979–07/18/1980
Chile	President	Michelle Bachelet	03/11/2006–03/11/2010
			03/11/2014–present
Costa Rica	President	Laura Chinchilla	05/08/2010–05/08/2014
Ecuador	President*	Rosalía Arteaga	02/09/1997–02/11/1997
Guyana	Prime Minister	Janet Jagan	03/06/1997–12/19/1997
	President		12/19/1997–08/11/1999
Nicaragua	President	Violeta Chamorro	04/25/1990–01/10/1997
Panama	President	Mireya Moscoso	09/01/1999–09/01/2004
Peru	Prime Minister	Beatriz Merino Lucero	06/28/2003–12/15/2003
Peru	Prime Minister	Rosario Fernández	03/19/2011–07/28/2011
Peru	Prime Minister	Ana Jara	07/22/2014–04/02/2015
Middle East			
Israel	Prime Minister	Golda Meir	03/17/1969–06/03/1974
Israel	President*	Dalia Itzik	01/25/2007–07/15/2007
North America			
Canada	Prime Minister	Kim Campbell	06/25/1993–11/05/1993
Oceania			
Australia	Prime Minister	Julia Gillard	06/24/2010–06/27/2013
New Zealand	Prime Minister	Jenny Shipley	12/08/1997–12/10/1999
New Zealand	Prime Minister	Helen Elizabeth Clark	12/10/1999–11/19/2008

SOURCES: Author's analysis of data from Worldwide Guide to Women in Leadership and Zárate's Political Collections.

*Interim leader.

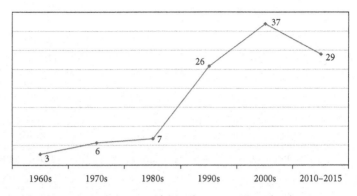

Figure 3.1 Women Prime Ministers and Presidents over Time (108)

influencing individual women to throw their hats into the ring, parties to recruit
women more actively, and the public to become more accepting of them. This
suggests that women's descriptive representation can give way to symbolic representation—the public's belief that their leaders can credibly represent their
interests (Wolbrecht and Campbell, 2007; Burns, Schlozman, and Verba 2001;
Atkeson 2003; Schwindt-Bayer and Mishler 2005; Lawless 2004).

Women made sluggish progress in earlier decades (see Figure 3.1), but dra-
matic changes have occurred from the 1990s onward. The number of new
female leaders nearly quadrupled in the 1990s, and this pattern repeated again
in the 2000s. In fact, more than three-quarters of all female presidents and
prime ministers entered office in the past twenty years. However, women still
represent only a minuscule number of all leaders worldwide. As noted, by the
early years of the twenty-first century, multiple women had ascended in many
of the same countries that welcomed other women leaders previously.

The immense expansion in the numbers of women executives in the 1990s
and 2000s is similar to the timing of women's more substantial inroads into
parliaments. Legislatures containing a "critical mass" of women (at least 30
percent) increased by nearly five times from 1998 through 2008 (Jalalzai and
Krook 2010).[2] Gains in women's legislative representation relate to the rapid
diffusion of candidate gender quota policies across the globe in the 1990s and
2000s (Jalalzai and Krook 2010), although throughout many countries this
uneven progress links to quota types and enforcement (Krook 2009). Quotas
for women national executive candidates appear extremely rare.[3] Conceivably,
however, the greater inroads made in lower offices allowed women to form
a larger eligibility pool and compete for the top political posts. Alternatively,
countries with quotas might be more open to women in other political offices,
though findings on this greatly diverge (Krook 2009). More generally, gains in
women's employment and higher educational attainment may play a role in

their subsequent political successes, although I challenge this claim throughout this book.

We can explain women's recent growth as executives typically through political transitions. Military dictatorships dominated several regions, including Asia, Africa, and Latin America, between the 1960s and the early 1990s. In Africa, according to Gretchen Bauer (2011),

> part of the explanation for this executive-power deficit lies in sub-Saharan Africa's post-colonial trajectory of single party rule and military regimes that precluded women's independent organizing and denied free and fair election to women or men candidates. (85)

Some regimes controlled politics for such long periods that competing in elections failed to present as an option for *anyone*, regardless of gender. In Asia, President Ferdinand Marcos of the Philippines stayed in power for twenty-six years; he effectively insulated the presidency from competition. As militaries appear among the most masculine institutions in the world, women do not take the military coup path to power. Political transitions involving women, however, relate to takeovers. After years of martial rule, the public may look to women as potential unifiers; such women include Corazon Aquino, who ended Marcos's tenure through a bloodless democratic revolution (Komisar 1987). The fact that many of these dictatorships were dismantled in the late 1980s and the 1990s could possibly explain women's greater success in attaining executive posts in the past two decades (Bauer 2011).

When temporary leaders are included, sixty-two of the 108 women executives held prime ministerships (57 percent) and forty-six occupied presidencies (43 percent). While women began their ascent to premierships in the 1960s, the 1990s and first decade of the 2000s witnessed important expansions in numbers (see Figure 3.2). During the 1990s, more women became prime ministers than had attained that position between 1960 and 1989. Twice the number have ascended since the year 2000 than in the first three decades of analysis combined.

Women enjoyed some limited success in gaining presidencies in the 1970s, one decade after female premiers. Though fewer, women presidents display a pattern of growth that mimics that of prime ministers; they made substantial gains in the 1990s and dramatically more into the first decade of the 2000s (see Figure 3.3). Nearly double the number of women presidents came to power in the 1990s as did in the 1970s and 1980s combined; the level tripled by 2010.

As Table 3.2 shows, women executives hail from geographically diverse locations. Europe lacked female leaders until the late 1970s (nearly two decades after Asian women ascended), but, with forty-five to date, now surpasses all

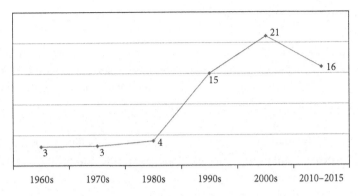

Figure 3.2 Women Prime Ministers over Time (62)

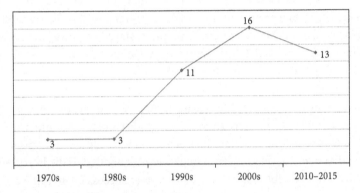

Figure 3.3 Women Presidents over Time (46)

regions in quantities. In fact, European cases account for 41 percent of the entire sample of women leaders. Similar to general trends, more substantial inroads occurred in the 1990s and 2000s. Western Europe claims the majority, though vastly increasing quantities have arisen in the East. In terms of positions, twenty-six European prime ministerships (58 percent) and nineteen presidencies (42 percent) have been held by women.

Asia follows Europe with sixteen cases. At least one female leader has governed nearly every South Asian country. Again, in this region the greatest growth of women executives occurred in the 1990s and the 2000s. Moreover, two different female leaders have ruled Sri Lanka, Bangladesh, and India. South Asia, however, recently stalled in promoting women to these high offices. We may, therefore, question whether women will see many future gains in executive offices in the region. Women have also secured power in Southeast Asia, in the Philippines (Corazon Aquino and Gloria Macapagal-Arroyo) and Indonesia (Megawati Sukarnoputri). Among the five women rising in Central Asia (Mongolia,

Table 3-2. Numbers of Women Executives by Region, 1960–2015

Region		Countries (number)	Number
Africa		Burundi, Central African Republic (2), Gabon, Guinea Bissau (2), Liberia, Madagascar, Malawi, Mali, Mauritius (2), Mozambique, Namibia, Rwanda, Sao Tome and Principe (2), Senegal (2), South Africa	20
Asia	South Asia	Bangladesh (2), India (2), Pakistan, Sri Lanka (2)	16
	Southeast Asia	Indonesia, Philippines (2), Thailand	
	Central Asia, East Asia/Pacific	Mongolia, South Korea (3), Kyrgyzstan	
Caribbean		Bahamas, Dominica, Haiti (4), Jamaica, Trinidad/Tobago	8
Europe	Western Europe	Denmark, Finland (3), France, East Germany, Germany, Iceland (2) Ireland (2), Malta (2), Norway (3), Portugal, Turkey, Switzerland (5), United Kingdom	45
	Eastern Europe	Bulgaria, Croatia (2), Georgia, Kosovo, Latvia (2), Lithuania (3), Macedonia, Moldova (2), Poland (2), Serbia (2), Slovakia, Slovenia, Ukraine, Yugoslavia	
Latin America		Argentina (2), Bolivia, Brazil, Chile, Costa Rica, Ecuador, Guyana, Nicaragua, Panamá, Perú (3)	13
Other Areas	Middle East	Israel (2)	6
	North America	Canada	
	Oceania	Australia, New Zealand (2)	
Total			108

sources: Author's analysis of data from Worldwide Guide to Women in Leadership and Zárate's Political Collections.

Kyrgyzstan) and East Asia (South Korea), most have led only temporarily and or held weak positions with the exception of President Park of South Korea.

Twenty women to date have taken power in sub-Saharan Africa. Africa registered a rapid increase in women leaders at the same time other regions, such as South Asia, slowed in pace. Many gains occurred from the 1990s onward, but a more speedy promotion of women leaders began later than in most areas, primarily in the first decade of the 2000s. More recently, however, African expansions in the numbers of women leaders appear impeded.

With thirteen cases so far, Latin America enjoyed a major growth of women leaders in the 1990s. Progress rapidly continued into the first decade of the 2000s. Perhaps most strikingly, advances appear widespread as of late, trending toward different countries electing women as opposed to women leaders clustering within particular locations.[4] Of the eight Caribbean women leaders, half hail from Haiti. Only two women have ascended in the Middle East (Israel), with one governing on an interim basis (see Table 3.2).

The numbers of women executives worldwide indicate substantial growth. Regional diversity suggests that women lead where women as a whole trail behind men, but they also surface in more egalitarian contexts.[5] An analysis of where women fail to come to power indicates limited progress. Women's relative absence from leadership positions in critical regions such as the Middle East and Central Asia is glaring. China and the United States are noticeably absent from the list of countries with female executives in Table 3.2.

In sum, women have indeed made strides to executive office over the past five decades. However, they total only 108 cases to date. Among these, several contexts have witnessed multiple women ascending, whereas others have stalled at one. The majority of countries, however, completely lack women national leaders; men continue to dominate executive posts. The glass ceiling indeed appears shattered in some contexts, such as Finland, only cracked in the United Kingdom, and firmly intact in the United States. Based on analysis of quantities and relevant regional dynamics alone, we may question women's ultimate progress.

RELATING GENDER TO PATHS, POSTS, POWERS, AND SYSTEMS

Going beyond the numbers, do women occupy powerful posts? To answer this question, I analyze political systems and authorities within executive positions, restricting my analysis to the women executives gaining power between 1960 and 2010. I also investigate paths to office and security within positions. Women more often gain appointment rather than election, serve in dual-executive systems, and, though certainly not always, exercise weak powers in their executive capacities. I argue that women's lack of progress as executives stems from the gendered nature of executive offices and selection processes. Gender stereotypes associate men more squarely with the executive arena, especially as it pertains to dominant offices.

This section links women's formalistic representation to their descriptive representation. Formalistic representation involves the rules that empower representatives to act and by which constituents hold them accountable, and encompasses the procedures by which representation transpires (Pitkin 1967; Schwindt-Bayer 2010). In this vein, women could be selected, elected, or removed through applicable mechanisms. Such representation also entails the processes through which executives exercise their authority. Selection or electoral practices connect to women's ability to attain offices, as do executive powers. While not directly concerning substantive representation (whether women executives act on behalf of women's interests; Pitkin 1967), selection procedures and powers are interrelated and critical to an executive's ability to exercise authority. Strong, independent leaders who are elected by the public and serve fixed terms may be better situated to pursue their agendas; in doing so, some might advocate women's substantive representation.

Presidential systems generally feature an executive distinct from the legislative branch, while parliamentary configurations fuse these. Müller, Bergman, and Strøm (2003) draw a second, though related, distinction between presidential and parliamentary types: "Parliamentary government refers to the institutional relationship by which the executive is accountable, through a confidence relationship, to any parliamentary majority…either through an ordinary or constructive vote of confidence" (12–13). An ordinary vote of no confidence simply requires a vote against the prime minister for dismissal; the constructive form necessitates that parliament select a new prime minister beforehand. This form, used only in a small minority of parliamentary systems, including Germany, results in greater prime ministerial insulation. Either way, the prime minister's survival depends on these processes.

Presidents leading presidential systems are neither directly accountable to their legislatures nor able to dismiss these bodies. The respective role of the cabinet constitutes another important distinction. Presidents enjoy considerably more autonomy than do prime ministers, who govern through cabinets. Cabinets in presidential systems usually wield less authority than those in parliamentary systems. They help execute policy while the president ultimately steers his or her preferred course of action. Still, favorable policy outcomes for the president rely on legislative relationships. Presidential terms are fixed, although most countries specify conditions for impeachment in cases where presidents commit serious abuses or offenses (Lijphart 1999, 17). Compared to prime ministers, presidents within presidential systems generally evade dismissal, depend less on the legislature, and assert more autonomy.

Presidents act as the chiefs of state; this role involves receiving foreign dignitaries, participating in various ceremonies, including extending high awards and honors, and promoting national traditions. Presidential functions generally entail providing symbolic leadership for the country. Ceremonial duties support "feminine" leadership because of their symbolic and apolitical nature (Jalalzai 2010b). However, presidents acting simultaneously as heads of government and chiefs of state exercise substantive powers, several of which are highly "masculine" in nature (Duerst-Lahti 2006).

The paths of prime ministers and presidents also differ. Popular vote (which may be connected to an electoral college) elects presidents in presidential

systems, whereas legislators select or appoint prime ministers in parliamentary configurations (Lijphart 1999), although these procedures diverge greatly
throughout the world (Müller, Bergman, and Strøm 2003). Different scenarios
include the appointment of the prime minister through parliamentary vote,
which in some countries first requires the candidate to win a party election
to become leader. Presidents select prime ministers in some dual-executive
systems, though they may have to choose from a limited pool of candidates
commanding a majority of parliamentary support. In other cases a presidential
appointment of a prime minister cannot officially take effect until the prime
minister and his or her cabinet receive a vote of confidence within a specified
time frame. Coalition governments complicate matters even more. When no
party attains a parliamentary majority, prime ministers emerge when governing partners reaches a consensus. In several dual-executive systems, however,
the president plays an essential role in deciding who forms the government.
While relevant procedures differ greatly, women's paths to prime ministerships
are aided by their ability to bypass a public vote.

Tenures in office also distinguish presidents and prime ministers. Unlike
most presidents, prime ministers do not face term limits. However, they generally have a limited number of years they can serve before new parliamentary
elections. Since they are subject to votes of no confidence resulting in the dissolving of parliament, they are more likely than presidents to succumb to ouster
and, in some cases, face legislative removal through an unfavorable party vote.
The legislature may also be dissolved. Prime ministers may trigger this alone or
through consultation with the head of state (if applicable), cabinet, parliament,
or some combination (see Strom and Swindle 2002).[6]

Prime ministers, therefore, possess a number of advantages in comparison
with presidents. While vulnerable to ouster, they may also enjoy the benefit of
calling early elections, especially when their chances for victory appear most
promising. Presidents in presidential systems lack this ability. However, many
consider this prime ministerial authority as the necessary counterweight to
parliamentary discharge of prime ministers. In fact, scholars suggest that the
possibilities of dismissal and dissolution foster cooperation between executive
and legislative institutions in parliamentary systems (Lupia and Strom 1995).[7]

The formal process of governance in each system relates to gender norms and
stereotypes. Prime ministers possess the advantage over presidents in crafting
policies. To achieve their policy agendas and stay in power, however, prime ministers must collaborate. Because they rely on parliament so much for survival,
they rarely take unilateral action. In cabinet systems, the ministers act as the
chief players of their respective policies while the prime minister ensures the government's smooth operation and resolves potential conflicts. This restrains the
prime minister's free exercise of power relative to presidents but again rewards

compromisers.[8] In governments where no party possesses a majority, cooperative governance, particularly with coalition partners, proves even more essential. Research suggests that women legislators are more likely than their male
counterparts to espouse leadership styles based on consensus building, whereas
men exert control and power (Kathlene 1994, 1995; Rosenthal 1998; Reingold
2000). Women legislators also more generally view their leadership roles contex-
tually (Kathlene 1995), emphasizing webs of relationships and interconnections
as highlighted in the literature on gender formation theory (Chodorow 1994).

The fusion of the prime ministership with the legislature in parliamentary
systems, as well as the prime minister's clear dependence on the parliament and
cabinet, stands in contrast to presidential rule. Constituencies more often associate presidentialism with unilateral command and the noncollegial exercise
of power (Lijphart 1999). Hierarchical, top-down governing styles commonly
coincide with masculinity (see Duerst-Lahti 1997). The greater association with
"feminine" traits, heightened vulnerability to ouster at any time, and bypassing
of the public vote make the prime ministership less resistant to women than the
presidency.[9]

Several divergences exist from the pure presidential and parliamentary
patterns of governance, leading to debates about systems that straddle the
presidential and parliamentary types (Duverger 1980; Shugart and Carey
1992; Sartori 1997). As previously noted, a minimalist definition of parlia-
mentarianism focuses on the distinguishing feature of its having an executive accountable to a parliamentary majority (Müller, Bergman, and Strøm
2003). This problematizes the role of a president in such systems, particularly
where the president's significance extends beyond symbolism. Scholars also
debate various aspects of presidential systems. For example, Elgie (1998) considers a presidential system to be a system with a unified executive featuring
a president. Lijphart (1999) classifies a system as presidential if the president
acts as head of government but shares power with a symbolic head of state.
Uniting these views, Siaroff (2003) argues that in all the various presidential
systems "there is a single individual, normally but not invariably called 'president'...popularly elected for a fixed term who plays the...central role in the
political system" (289).

Some countries, such as France, feature a popularly elected president unaccountable to parliament who appoints a prime minister who is responsible to
the parliament. The president holds a fixed term in office, while the prime minister (following parliamentary procedures) can dissolve parliament. Presidents
do not discharge prime ministers from parties different from their own, but they
can dismiss prime ministers with whom they share party affiliation (Shugart
and Carey 1992, 123–24). Thus, to assess executive autonomy accurately, we
must consider partisanship.

Given the complicated nature of political systems in the real world, where offices and processes vary widely, even the development of a semipresidential category leaves much to be desired. Several hybrid types exhibit wide divergences (Shugart and Carey 1992; Siaroff 2003). We may see, however, a basic distinction between political systems in whether they feature a unified or a dual-executive structure. Unified systems exist in both presidential and parliamentary types and have only one national executive post: *either* a prime minister *or* a president.[10] Dual-executive systems include both a president and a prime minister and may utilize predominantly presidential or parliamentary structures. While dual-executive types somewhat disperse powers, one leader typically wields more authority than the other. If women are disproportionately placed in weaker positions in dual-executive systems, this limits their ultimate influence. If they instead serve in more powerful positions, even in systems with dual-executive configuration, this may indicate that they hold substantial sway. Since constituents more often associate women with collaboration and submissiveness, women executives are more likely to govern in dual-executive systems and in the weaker, less autonomous posts in those systems.

We must also consider paths to power as well as procedures for dismissal. Women's ability to gain powerful and more secure presidential positions through the popular vote would signal a major development given the plethora of gender stereotypes that women encounter (as discussed in Chapter 2). If, however, they primarily are *selected* to positions from which they can be ousted at any time or the public elects them to secure but mainly symbolic posts, women's advancement is tenuous. We therefore need to analyze the formal procedures through which women come to office, their security, and their powers. For this purpose, I construct a typology of executive systems and positions.

Systems Typology

While several studies classify comparative systems and executive powers, Siaroff (2003) most parsimoniously details both constitutional and practical powers. Based partially on the work of Siaroff (2003) and on my own original analysis, I categorize systems as one of the following unified or dual-executive types:

1. *Unified presidential:* These configurations include presidents, elected directly by the public or an electoral college tied to popular sentiment, possessing both substantive and symbolic powers. These systems often limit total or consecutive presidential terms; presidents generally remain in office unless impeached. Examples include the United States, the Philippines, and Latin American countries.

2. *Dual-presidential dominance*: These systems feature a very powerful president, elected in some fashion, serving with a much weaker prime minister. The president often directly appoints the prime minister, although this selection sometimes requires legislative approval. The prime minister frequently faces presidential dismissal but is also usually subject to parliamentary discharge (as in Haiti). Legislative dependence through votes of confidence makes these systems—at the most basic level—parliamentary. Though rarely, sometimes the prime minister is unaccountable to the parliament and acts as more of a presidential aide, similar to a presidential system as in Guyana, Sri Lanka, and South Korea. Even if presidential powers prove substantial, however, I hesitate to classify these countries as simply presidential given their dual nature.

3. *Unified parliamentary*: These systems incorporate a prime minister sharing powers with a cabinet in a typical parliamentary form of government. Though subsequent terms are unlimited, the prime minister's tenure is dependent on his or her staying in favor with the legislature and or sometimes party. The United Kingdom and New Zealand are unified parliamentary systems.

4. *Dual-powerful president*: These systems feature a president who, though not dominant, exerts considerable powers (possibly to dissolve the legislature), while the prime minister, still vulnerable to parliamentary ouster, exercises more influence. The executives in such systems generally appear the most evenly matched in power. Among dual-executive systems, this is also the rarest configuration. Representative countries include Turkey and Pakistan (at various points in time) and Croatia currently.

5. *Dual-weak or figurehead president*: These systems typically function with a president who possesses no substantive powers or very limited authority serving with a prime minister who, though unquestionably dominant, remains subject to a vote of confidence. Such a system operates very similarly to a traditional parliamentary structure. The president may be elected directly by the public or by the legislature. Unless impeached, the president enjoys security. Term limits may exist, but these vary in length. The president cannot unilaterally dismiss parliament. Examples of countries with this type of system include India and Ireland.

Executive Powers

Though related to systems, executive power still needs further clarification. I use a multimethod approach to determine executive powers, including analysis of country constitutions, media articles, scholarly works, country reports, and Web sites, as well as biographies of leaders. Legal and constitutional designs provide an important first glimpse into offices and processes. While the powers specified on paper do inform, reality sometimes diverges from prescribed procedures, particularly over time. For example, the Irish and Icelandic presidents are much stronger constitutionally than in practice. Thus, integrating other sources provides a more comprehensive picture of power. It is also important to take into consideration the situations existing when women first come to their posts; major changes in political structures occur temporally, particularly in unstable systems. Institutions and processes may even change during a leader's reign or when he or she begins a new term after a brief absence.

I examine many of the same presidential powers as Siaroff (2003). Additionally, I focus on whether the executive plays a defense role, generally considered one of the most "masculine" available (Duerst-Lahti 2006). I am particularly concerned with whether presidents serve as commanders in chief. Unlike Siaroff, I also assess prime ministerial powers.

Based on ranges of points, I classify each executive as one of five types; later, I engage relevant examples among women occupying these offices more deeply (see Chapter 4). I assign the executives one point for each of the powers listed below that they possess.[11] In some dual-executive systems, both the president and the prime minister exert sway in the same domain. In such cases, they each receive a point.[12] If, however, one is clearly charged with the larger share of the responsibility, I credit him or her alone one point. In other cases, legislatures solely assume powers (such as declaring emergencies); here I award neither executive a point.

1. *Making appointments:* This category of powers involves authorizing pivotal appointments of various governmental officials, including cabinet ministers, judges, and, in some dual-executive structures, the prime minister. While the exercise of these powers may require legislative approval, the executive plays an important rather than a nominal role in nominations. This excludes executives who formally approve officials but do not engage in real decision making. Appointment powers allow an executive to have a substantive effect on the composition of government and policy.

2. *Chairing cabinet meetings:* Presiding over cabinet meetings signifies some control over deliberation. This goes beyond serving as chair solely for the first cabinet session of the administration, which is customary in some countries.

3. *Vetoing legislation:* Veto power suggests an important policy-making role. In cases where the legislature cannot override an executive veto, it is especially likely that this individual exercises substantial powers. Although prime ministers often work to resolve disputes over policy between their cabinet ministers, they do not have veto power as some presidents do, thus this power pertains only to presidents.

4. *Authorizing emergency decrees:* This includes the power to circumvent the legislature to declare emergencies and unlimited authority to extend emergencies beyond the dates set by the legislature.

5. *Setting foreign policy:* Foreign policy powers include the ability to appoint officials who craft foreign policy, the authority to act as the representative of the country at political summits, and the standing to influence foreign policy. As discussed in Chapter 2, the public generally considers this a "masculine" domain, and it has thus remained relatively impermeable to women.

6. *Playing a defense role:* Involvement in national defense includes being commander in chief of the armed forces, another role seemingly requiring stereotypically "masculine" attributes. This role must extend beyond symbolic authority. For example, if a president acts as commander in chief but exercises this policy under the direction of the prime minister, the point for this power is awarded to the prime minister instead.

7. *Playing a major role in governmental formation:* This power is indicated by the executive's ability to appoint or retain members of the cabinet or possibly even the prime minister in some contexts. While this at first blush appears similar to the power to make appointments, some presidents within dual-executive systems make some important individual appointments, but the prime minister plays the leading role in governmental formation.

8. *Dissolving the legislature:* Prime ministers typically possess this power. For presidents in dual-executive systems, dissolving the legislature requires the government's receiving a vote of no confidence or prime ministerial approval.

Election by popular vote underscores legitimacy, providing some presidents an additional power. Further, a partisan identity generally suggests a more substantive role.[13] It also makes sense to deduct a point from prime ministers facing presidential dismissal. Therefore, presidential powers range from 0 to 10 points; those for prime ministers range from –1 to 7.

1. Dominant president (6 to 10 points)
2. Dominant prime minister (4 to 7 points)
3. Powerful president but weaker than the prime minister (4 to 5 points)
4. Weak president (0 to 3 points)
5. Weak prime minister (–1 to 3 points)

Obviously, greater power variations exist among presidents than among prime ministers; prime ministers generally act in clearly dominant or submissive roles. Assessing prime ministerial powers presents more difficulty, since constitutional documents less often directly reference those powers. Such documents routinely focus on presidents as independent actors in terms of requirements for their positions, paths, and authorities, while they reference prime ministers indirectly as members of the "cabinet" or "government."

Based on the stereotypes relating gender and executive power outlined in Chapter 2, one would generally expect women to govern in dual systems and in weaker positions. While women prime ministers within unified parliamentary systems may also be common, seldom will women become presidents within unified systems or hold the stronger post in a dual-executive model. These divergences relate to the greater association of women with collaboration rather than with independent, authoritative action. Based on numerous gender expectations, the public generally hesitates to vote women into strong positions, particularly those requiring more stereotypically masculine strength and expertise. Likewise, party elites could be less inclined to recruit and support female candidates.

Patterns of Women National Leaders: System, Powers, and Paths

In analyzing the paths and powers of the sixty-three nontemporary women leaders to date, important patterns emerge. Table 3.3 displays the positions, systems, and paths of women executives and the regions where they surface. Among the sixty-three noninterim leaders, forty-one function in dual-executive as opposed to unified systems, representing 65 percent of the sample. Thus, as expected, the vast majority of women leaders share powers with others. With twice the numbers of positions at stake, women are more likely to come up through the ranks in these contexts. They also ascend to positions with a lower degree of autonomy. However, a greater quantity of women hold dominant power within their systems. Specifically, thirty-six are either dominant presidents or prime ministers (57 percent), while twenty-seven are weaker executives (43 percent). Still, nearly all dominant female prime ministers occupy their posts with other executives, face ouster at any time, and must exercise power with the government as a whole. While this does not prove women's disproportionately greater tendency than their male counterparts to govern in these capacities, I provide confirmation of this claim in the next section.

EXPLORING GENDER DIFFERENCES IN POSITIONS AND POWERS
Women executives, though increasing in presence, still exist only rarely. The data analysis thus far, however, does not evaluate whether women leaders are more likely to hold weaker positions than men. Only by integrating information on male executives can we address this important issue. In doing so, I utilize data available on the World Political Leaders page of the Zárate's Political

Table 3-3. Numbers of Female National Leaders by Systems, Powers, and Paths

Category	REGION					
	Europe*	Asia	Africa	Latin America	Other	Total
Unified Systems	7	3	1	6	5	**22**
Presidential	3	3	1	6	0	**13**
Parliamentary	4	0	0	0	5	**9**
Dual Systems	19	9	7	2	4	**41**
President Dominance	4	4	7	2	2	**20**
Powerful President	7	1	0	0	1	**9**
Symbolic President	7	4	0	0	1	**12**
Total	**25**	**12**	**8**	**8**	**9**	**63**
Powers						
Dominant President	0	5	1	7	0	**13**
Weak President	8	1	0	0	0	**9**
Powerful but Weaker President	2	0	0	0	0	**2**
Dominant Prime Minister	11	4	0	0	8	**23**
Weak Prime Minister	4	2	7	1	2	**16**
Total	**25**	**12**	**8**	**8**	**10**	**63**
Paths						
Popular Vote	5	2	1	6	0	**14**
Legislative Appointment	15	3	1	0	7	**26**
Presidential Appointment	5	5	6	1	3	**20**
Constitutional Succession	0	2	0	1	0	**3**
Total	**25**	**12**	**8**	**8**	**10**	**63****
Other Temporary Appointments	7	2	3	2	2	16

sources: 'Constitution Finder', 'Worldfactbook' (https://www.cia.gov/library/publications/the-world-factbook/index.html), International Foundation *for Electoral Systems Election* Guide (http://www.idea.int/), Siaroff, A. (2003) 'Comparative Presidencies: The Inadequacy of the Presidential, Semi-Presidential and Parliamentary Distinction', *European Journal of Political Research*, 42 (3), 287–312.

*Europe tally includes presidents of the Swiss confederation.

**The total of 63 does not include temporary appointments.

Kazimiera Prunskiene (Lithuania) is not reflected in the position classification since the specifics of the office are unclear; as such, the European total drops from 19 to 18 and the total for all dual system categories decreases from 41 to 40.

Collections Web site, which collects information on all prime ministers and presidents in power since 1945.[14] I analyze the data for 162 countries, using the percentages of male and female leaders in office in 2009.[15]

This section departs from the previous analysis by concentrating on one particular period. Ideally, similar to the approach used with women leaders, I would interrogate all cases of men in power throughout history. It is impossible, however, to offer a direct comparison of the entire universe of male leaders to female leaders. Not only are men's numbers enormous compared to women's, they also extend much farther back in time. Furthermore, countries have radically altered their institutions during various periods, making meaningful comparisons over such a long duration even more difficult.

Of the 162 countries, 90 (56 percent) utilize dual-executive structures, and 72 (44 percent) have unified structures. Women's tendency to serve in dual-executive systems may issue from the greater usage of these forms of government. As a proportion, however, women are much more prone than men to govern in dual-executive systems (75 percent versus 55 percent, significant at the .0001 level).

Overall, 134 presidencies and 118 prime ministerships exist, resulting in a total of 252 executive posts. In 2009, 236 of these posts were occupied by men, while only 16 of them, or 6 percent, were held by women (see Figure 3.4).

To push this point further, I also incorporate data for presidents worldwide from 1960 (the first year a woman came to power) through 2009. I examine presidencies only because individual presidents are much easier to identify, while separating cases of prime ministerships appears exceedingly cumbersome, as several of the same actors hold these posts at many different points in time.

Women constitute only 20 of the 802 presidents holding power since 1960. Over the past nearly fifty years, women have held only 2 percent of all presidential offices, while men have held nearly 98 percent. Prior to fifty years ago, no women executives ascended.[16] If we were to extend this time frame back

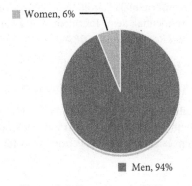

Figure 3.4 Executives in 2009

just to the beginning of the post–World War II era, men would represent virtually 100 percent of cases; executive office, particularly the presidency, remains a masculine domain.

Most presidential posts worldwide are dominant rather than weak. In contrast, roughly equal numbers of dominant and weak prime ministerships exist, although a greater percentage of prime ministerships wield dominant authority. It is critical to understand women's and men's power placements.

Among the 10 women presidents in office in 2009, 5 are dominant, 2 are weak, and 3 are powerful (see Figure 3.5). In contrast, among the 124 male presidents, 90 are dominant, 18 are weak, and 16 are powerful (see Figure 3.6). Only 6 women are prime ministers—2 dominant prime ministers and 4 weak (see Figure 3.5). A total of 112 men occupy prime ministerships: 65 dominant and 47 weak (see Figure 3.6). Regardless of powers, men occupy the preponderance of presidencies and prime ministerships.

We can look at these numbers another way by simply comparing proportions of men and women within positions. Nearly one-third of women leaders fall within the dominant president classification. The majority of women, however, still occupy weaker posts. Across all executive types, the vast preponderance

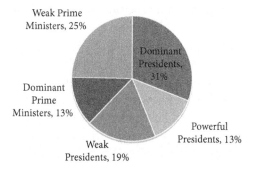

Figure 3.5 Female Executives and Positions in 2009

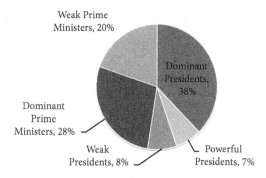

Figure 3.6 Male Executives and Positions in 2009

of men hold dominant as opposed to weak positions. In fact, barely over one-quarter of men hold feeble presidencies and prime ministerships.

GENDER DIFFERENCES IN POSITIONS AND TENURES

A remaining issue concerns whether women serve shorter terms in office than their male counterparts. Do women's durations compromise their ultimate influence even if they hold comparatively strong posts? Longer tenures likely better situate executives to navigate political waters, establish critical alliances, and craft policy expertise. Thus, career length may relate to potential substantive representation. I compare women's durations to those of their immediate predecessors. Making these more limited contrasts allows for meaningful assessments, as many (though certainly not all) country conditions can be held constant. If we accumulate data over a large span of years, we cannot assume that differences correspond to gender rather than to various transformations within that country.[17] I also evaluate regional dynamics and position types in relation to tenure.

Table 3.4 organizes tenure data geographically.[18] I first analyze the numbers of years women leaders and their predecessors held power. I then calculate the average lengths of tenure within and across regions, noting any statistically significant findings.[19] Equivalent numbers of men and women (twenty-two each) held power longer than their comparators. Further, six pairs exhibit identical tenures.[20] The greatest gaps in lengths of service manifest in Africa and Latin America; women serve much shorter terms than their male predecessors in these regions (see Table 3.4). Larger disparities exist in Asia, although they benefit women. No major gender differences emerge in Europe. Little evidence suggests women's disadvantage in years served within regions, though this appears true in Africa and Latin America. Even in these areas, however, gaps do not achieve statistical significance.

Instead, do greater gender divergences manifest within positions? Tenures of women presidents average nearly five years, while men serve about six months longer, indicating a slight advantage for men. Still, no noticeable gaps surface between prime ministers. Further, none of the tenure variances reach statistical significance. Finally, to get a sense of whether premiers, regardless of gender, govern for fewer years than presidents, I compare the average tenures between both main executive types. As predicted, presidents stay in power longer than prime ministers, resulting in two additional years of service. These gaps encompass the first statistically significant tenure differences.

In analyzing tenures, I find women do not generally experience limited career lengths. At the same time, since they tend to hold prime ministerships, their durations appear more constricted. While time in office does not directly

Table 3-4. GENDER DIFFERENCES IN AVERAGE YEARS SERVED

Region	Women	Men	Number of Cases
Africa	1.71	3.86	14
Asia	6.4	4.3	24
Caribbean	4.5	4.5	8
Europe	3.74	3.16	38
Latin America	3.5	6.3	10
Middle East	5.2	5.8	2
North America	.4	8.9	2
Oceania	2	7.1	2
Total Cases	4.06	4.18	100
Position	Women	Men	Both
All Prime Ministers	3.69	3.6	3.35
All Presidents	4.93	5.53	**5.23

NOTE: Totals do not include the following:

Pairs where the successor was still in office as these calculations were made: Johnson Sirleaf and Blah (Liberia), Otunbayeva and Bakiyev (Kyrgyzstan), Persad-Bissessar and Manning (Trinidad and Tobago), Kiviniemi and Vanhanen (Finland), Merkel and Schröder (Germany), Grybauskaitė and Adamkus (Lithuania), Radičová and Fico (Slovakia), Gillard and Rudd (Australia).

Pairs where a woman succeeded another woman: Hasina and Zia (Bangladesh), Bandaranaike and Kumaratunga (Sri Lanka), McAleese and Robinson (female predecessor).

Cases where there was no predecessor: Prunskienė (Lithuania).

Totals include women serving nonconsecutive terms multiple times: Bhutto (Pakistan), Bandaranaike (Sri Lanka), Brundtland (Norway), Tymoshenko (Ukraine).

See also Table A.1 in the appendix, "Tenures of Women Leaders and Their Predecessors," for specific information on pairs and years served.

**Significant at < .05 level.

relate to gender, women surface within the very posts offering fewer advantages in career duration. We need to understand the dynamics related to longer tenures, especially because holding power for more extended periods of time may allow executives to act as women's substantive representatives. I speculate here and call overall for more research.

GLOBAL BACKDROPS WHERE WOMEN LEAD

If we broaden the scope of power to include a country's standing on the world stage, what would this tell us about women's ultimate executive powers? Two indications of a country's global importance involve economic strength and military prowess. Leading a G-20 country illustrates an executive's status in a major industrial or emerging economy. Argentina, France, Germany, India, the United Kingdom, Canada, South Korea, and Turkey are all currently part of this collective and, at some point, were governed by women. We should, however, keep in mind that this grouping has existed formally only since 1999 and does not necessarily reflect economic conditions during women's times in power. G-20 countries currently led by women include Argentina, Germany, Australia, and India.[21] India's female president, however, possesses nominal power. The G-8 represents the world's most elite economic players, including Canada, Germany, France, and the United Kingdom. Kim Campbell of Canada and Edith Cresson of France held power for very brief periods, and a dominant president rivaled the latter's authority. Further, the economic influence of other women leaders should not be overstated in that they all represent forms of parliamentary systems where their respective finance ministers exert sway.

A country's nuclear capabilities are a measure of military might. Among nuclear powers, women leaders have surfaced in the United Kingdom, France, India, Pakistan, and Israel.[22] Among these, however, only Margaret Thatcher headed a nuclear power. The others did not occupy posts exercising influence in this realm or predated their countries' development of nuclear capabilities. Findings demonstrate that women executives rarely lead highly influential countries (with exceptions duly noted).[23] It might be quite unlikely, therefore, for a woman to gain the American presidency.

CONCLUSIONS

The numbers of women national leaders have vastly increased over the past two decades. Their geographic expansion, however, appears somewhat limited. More commonly, when one woman makes it through the executive glass ceiling, another follows her. Research findings demonstrate that women still serve only rarely as executives, and when they govern, they occupy weaker posts than men in systems with less concentrated executive authority. Since the numbers of women executives are currently at the highest levels in history, we may assume women's relegation to even fewer and less powerful positions in years past. This puts into question women's ultimate progress in attaining executive posts.

Women prime ministers and presidents still remain scarce, particularly those wielding high degrees of power. Gender stereotypes contribute to the limitations experienced by women in leadership roles. Rarely identified as strong actors taking unilateral control, women are more often connected to softer and collaborative leadership styles. Because of these stereotypes, women experience greater difficulty in being popularly elected and rely more on appointment. Party elites occasionally recruit them, and they also rise through sudden openings left by men. Most women executives occupy prime ministerships rather than presidencies, in part because prime ministerial terms are not fixed and can end at any moment. Beyond domestic constraints, women rarely rule in more visible and globally critical countries. In this way, women premiers pose a less meaningful threat to the gender order. While no major tenure differences among executives are directly attributable to gender, women more often hold prime ministerships. Given that prime ministers generally enjoy shorter tenures than presidents, women's ability to wield influence more generally and to act as women's substantive representatives seems compromised.

A More In-Depth Analysis of Executive Positions and Paths

As discussed in the preceding chapter, women seldom rise to power, and when they do, in comparison with men they occupy weaker posts with less concentrated authority. We must, therefore, question women's success in shattering the executive glass ceiling. Indeed, the numbers of women national leaders have increased substantially, but women executives, especially those wielding strong powers, are still uncommon. The public still associates women with collaborative forms of governance, reinforcing ties between masculinity and dominant executive office types.

This chapter focuses more on the powers and paths of women within the various typologies of positions derived thus far. The first section concerns women presidents as categorized into the three main presidential types. This is followed by an analysis of women serving in the two main prime ministerial posts. I also provide data on the party systems and labels with which women are affiliated. I offer more specific details of women's routes to office and their authorities to evaluate women's ultimate progress. In so doing, I engage the stories of women leaders who are illustrative of various typologies. Overall, more variation exists in powers and paths than might have been expected. Still, the findings tend to support the main argument of this book: that women executives wield limited and dependent authority. Their trajectories are fairly similar to men's, but with some differences. These disparities likely connect to gendered notions related to executive governance.

WOMEN PRESIDENTS

Table 4.1 displays the powers that the twenty-four women presidents held in their posts as well as their initial paths to office. Eight female presidents have shared power with a stronger prime minister, several serving mainly as

Table 4-1. WOMEN PRESIDENTS: PATHS AND POWERS

Region/Name (Country)	PV	Party	AP	CM	VT	EP	FP	DF	GF	DL	Total Powers	Position
Africa												
Johnson Sirleaf (Liberia)	1^	1	1	1	1	0	1	1	1	0	8	Dominant
Asia												
Patil (India)	0	0	1	0	1	0	0	1	0	0	3	Weak
Aquino* (Philippines)	1	1	1	1	1	0	1	1	1	0	8	Dominant
Kumaratunga* (Sri Lanka)	1	1	1	1	1	1	1	1	1	1	10	Dominant
Macapagal-Arroyo* (Philippines)	0>	1	1	1	1	0	1	1	1	0	7	Dominant
Sukarnoputri* (Indonesia)	0>	1	1	1	0	0	1	1	1	0	6	Dominant
Europe												
Barbara (Malta)	0	0	0	0	0	0	0	0	0	1	1	Weak
Calmy-Rey (Switzerland)	0	1	0	1	0	0	0	0	0	0	2	Weak
Dreifuss (Switzerland)	0	1	0	1	0	0	0	0	0	0	2	Weak
Finnbogadóttir (Iceland)	1	0	0	0	1	0	0	0	0	0	2	Weak
McAleese (Ireland)	1	0	1	0	1	0	0	0	0	0	3	Weak
Robinson (Ireland)	1	0	1	0	1	0	0	0	0	0	3	Weak
Vīķe-Freiberga (Latvia)	0	0	0	0	1	0	0	1	0	0	2	Weak
Grybauskaitė (Lithuania)	1	0	1	0	1	0	1	1	0	0	5	Powerful
Halonen (Finland)	1	0	1	0	1	0	1	1	0	0	5	Powerful
Leuthard (Switzerland)	0	1	0	1	0	0	0	0	0	0	1	Weak
Otunbayeva (Kyrgyzstan)	0	1	1	1	1	0	1	1	1	1	8	Dominant
Latin America												
Bachelet* (Chile)	1^	1	1	1	1	1	1	1	1	0	9	Dominant
Chamorro* (Nicaragua)	1	1	1	1	1	0	1	1	1	0	8	Dominant

(continued)

Table 4-1. CONTINUED

Region/Name (Country)	PV	Party	AP	CM	VT	EP	FP	DF	GF	DL	Total Powers	Position
Chinchilla (Costa Rica)	1	1	1	1	1	0	1	0	1	0	7	Dominant
Jagan* (Guyana)	1	1	1	1	1	0	1	1	1	1	9	Dominant
Fernández* (Argentina)^	1	1	1	1	1	1	1	1	1	0	9	Dominant
Perón* (Argentina)	0 >	1	1	1	1	1	1	1	1	0	8	Dominant
Moscoso* (Panama)	1	1	1	1	1	0	1	0	1	0	7	Dominant

SOURCES: Author's analysis of data from Constitution Finder, CIA World Factbook, International Institute for Democracy and Electoral Assistance, and Siaroff (2003).

ABBREVIATIONS: PV = popular vote, AP = discretionary appointment powers, CM = chair cabinet meetings, VT = veto, EP = emergency long-term or decree powers, FP = central role in foreign policy, DF = central role in defense (such as commander in chief), GF = central Role in governmental formation, DL = ability to dissolve the legislature.

*Possession of familial ties to power; ^runoff election; >presidential succession.

SCORING: 0–3 = weak or minimal power; 4–5 = powerful but not dominant, 6–8 = dominant power.

NOTE: Macapagal-Arroyo (Philippines) did not enter through popular election her first term, but did the second term. Her subsequent terms she would move up to a 7. Chinchilla and Moscoso lack control over standing military forces; as such they are not traditional commanders in chief. Panama's president, however, can engage militarily against external forces.

figureheads in countries such as Iceland, Ireland, and India. Only two, Tarja Halonen (Finland) and Dalia Grybauskaitė (Lithuania), have held substantial influence, though still not as great as that of their prime ministers. Three presidents of Switzerland (Ruth Dreifuss, Micheline Calmy-Rey, and Doris Leuthard) technically served as presidents in a unified system, but they are classified as weak leaders because the Federal Council exercises most executive authority. In a unified system, even the president may be invested with weak powers, although this appears applicable here only to Switzerland.[1] Overall, thirteen of the women presidents are considered dominant, two powerful, and nine weak. I begin by analyzing the dominant non-interim leaders.

Table 4.2 distributes dominant women presidents who may have governed either in unified systems or with weaker prime ministers in dual-executive structures. Thirteen women occupy dominant presidencies, representing 21 percent of non-interim leaders and just slightly more than half of all women presidents. Seven dominant presidents come from Latin America. Considering that unified systems are nearly ubiquitous in this region, Latin American women, not surprisingly, govern as dominant presidents. Five Asian women are also dominant presidents. Finally, one dominant president hails from Africa. Therefore,

Table 4-2. DOMINANT WOMEN PRESIDENTS

Leader	Country	System	Popular Vote
Aquino	Philippines	Unified Presidential	Yes
Bachelet	Chile	Unified Presidential	Yes
Chamorro	Nicaragua	Unified Presidential	Yes
Chinchilla	Costa Rica	Unified Presidential	Yes
Fernández	Argentina	Unified Presidential	Yes
Jagan	Guyana	Dual–Presidential Dominance	Yes
Johnson Sirleaf	Liberia	Unified Presidential	Yes
Kumaratunga	Sri Lanka	Dual–Presidential Dominance	Yes
Macapagal-Arroyo	Philippines	Unified Presidential	No
Otunbayeva	Kyrgyzstan	Dual–Presidential Dominance	No
Perón	Argentina	Unified Presidential	No
Moscoso	Panama	Unified Presidential	Yes
Sukarnoputri	Indonesia	Unified Presidential	No

$N = 13$

SOURCES: Author's analysis of data from Constitution Finder, CIA World Factbook, International Institute for Democracy and Electoral Assistance, and Siaroff (2003).

though still a minority, dominant presidents actually constitute a substantial portion of all female leaders.

Almost all dominant presidents possess veto power. Typically, however, the legislature can reconsider the legislation vetoed by the president; legislative support, therefore, informs veto applications.[2] Dominant presidents make key appointments, chair cabinet meetings, play important roles in government formation, and perform foreign affairs and defense functions.[3] Though still critical to making security appointments, Chinchilla and Moscoso have questionable roles as commanders in chief.

Often appointments made by the president, especially in Latin America, do not require parliamentary approval to take effect. Through these selections, presidents may play decisive roles in governmental formation. This is particularly true in the two cases of dominant presidents in Guyana and Sri Lanka, Jagan and Kumaratunga, respectively. Both served as heads of state and heads of government, although they appointed prime ministers. Here prime ministers generally act as presidential aides rather than as independent political players.[4]

For the most part, dominant presidents cannot unilaterally and indefinitely extend states of emergency. Some Latin American presidents, including Bachelet, Fernández, and Jagan, have enjoyed greater emergency powers. Kumaratunga's case illustrates the particular pressures on presidents to curb political violence in some contexts. The Sri Lankan government's enduring conflict with the Tamil Tigers continually led her to declare states of emergency, ultimately weakening the opposition as she rationalized her sacking of cabinet officials and dissolution of parliament (BBC News 2005a). Some presidents can dissolve the legislature, a critical power. Therefore, even though their authorities appear more dispersed, dominant presidents such as Jagan and Kumaratunga exercise a great deal of influence, sometimes more than executives within unified presidential systems.

Some form of popular vote determines the paths for dominant presidents. Still, the public elected only nine of the thirteen dominant presidents when they first entered office. Three vice presidents succeeded their presidents when openings occurred (Sukarnoputri, Macapagal-Arroyo, and Perón).[5] It is important to note that all dominant women presidents represent party labels. Both popular election and partisanship indicate more substantive roles for women executives.

While many dominant female presidents have bypassed direct public election, most have still risen initially through a popular vote. I have suggested that it is difficult for women presidential candidates to appeal to a majority of the public, especially in more culturally conservative contexts. Any candidate, however, may not gain a majority of the vote initially in multiparty systems. This situation triggers runoff elections, pitting the two highest vote getters against each other. If a woman places in the top two, this may signal her ability to garner public support and set her on a path to ultimate victory.

Many women occupying dominant presidencies avoid the public vote altogether in their ascensions. Beyond individual powers, a president's ability to exercise authority depends on myriad factors. Even dominant presidents may be constrained in Latin America and Asia because of political instability and military intervention, evident in Perón's ousting by the military after she had been in office barely one year. Corazon Aquino survived several coup attempts during her term, and advisers kept her out of many important governmental negotiations, denied her access to information, and usurped presidential powers (Roces 2000). Gloria Macapagal-Arroyo faced several aborted military coups and survived impeachment proceedings. When she largely adhered to their demands, military officials protected her from opposition parties and the public's call for her resignation (Associated Press 2008b). Many also question Violeta Chamorro's authority. To stay in office, Chamorro continually appeased the Nicaraguan military (Opfell 1993, 178). We must consider the larger context in which executives operate before we attempt to draw firm conclusions about their ultimate influence.

Nine women presidents have held very few powers. Overall, six of the nine weak women presidents are European (see Table 4.3). In most Western European dual-executive systems, the president acts as chief of state. Monarchs (in Norway and the United Kingdom, for example) or governors-general (as in Australia and Canada) serve these functions in the unified ones.

Table 4-3. WEAK WOMEN PRESIDENTS

Leader	Country	System	Popular Vote
Barbara	Malta	Dual–Parliamentary/Weak President	No
Calmy-Rey	Switzerland	Unified Presidential	No
Dreifuss	Switzerland	Unified Presidential	No
Leuthard	Switzerland	Unified Presidential	No
Finnbogadóttir	Iceland	Dual–Parliamentary/Weak President	Yes
McAleese	Ireland	Dual–Parliamentary/Weak President	Yes
Robinson	Ireland	Dual–Parliamentary/Weak President	Yes
Patil	India	Dual–Parliamentary/Weak President	No
Vīķe-Freiberga	Latvia	Dual–Parliamentary/Weak President	No

$N = 9$

SOURCES: Author's analysis of data from Constitution Finder, CIA World Factbook, International Institute for Democracy and Electoral Assistance, and Siaroff (2003).

One of the weakest presidents was Vigdís Finnbogadóttir of Iceland. She possessed a power not included in this analysis: deciding which party forms the government when a majority fails to surface following elections. Since Iceland utilizes a multiparty system, she may have regularly exercised this authority. Presidents officially sign bills into law and can veto by refusing to do so. If this transpires, the matter may come to the public for a referendum (Blondal 1996). Like all of her predecessors, Finnbogadóttir never declined a bill. She once delayed approval, however, to make a political point regarding workers' rights (Liswood 1995).[6] Iceland has had no standing army since 1869, reinforcing Finnbogadóttir's lack of a defense role.

Though more powerful than Finnbogadóttir, both former female presidents of Ireland, Mary Robinson and Mary McAleese, occupied weak presidencies. Their potential powers included making appointments and exercising vetoes. However, presidential authorities appear greater in the Irish constitution than in practice. The Oireachtas (parliament) plays a dominant role in military and defense matters, as do specific cabinet members. Some constitutional provisions clearly curb presidential autonomy. Irish presidents require permission from the government to travel abroad, and they are strictly prohibited from making partisan declarations. Still, growing evidence suggests that both Robinson and McAleese increased their influence compared to previous presidents (Sykes 1993; Hardy 2008). Irish presidents are permitted to run as partisans and to keep their partisan status upon their ascensions. However, several have governed as independents for at least parts of their tenures.[7]

The president of Malta, Agatha Barbara, also played only a very limited political role. The Maltese constitution permits the president to dissolve parliament, but he or she must do so on the advice of the prime minister and cabinet. Media reports and governmental Web sites describing the nature of the Maltese presidency, however, indicate that presidents do not exercise these powers. Further, the president is unaffiliated with a party and not popularly elected. The three Swiss women presidents—Ruth Dreifuss, Micheline Calmy-Rey, and Doris Leuthard—only chaired cabinet meetings, although they affiliated with political parties.

Weak presidents outside Western Europe include Vaira Vīķe-Freiberga of Latvia. The Latvian presidency's powers encompass a veto and a defense role. Although the president can propose dissolving parliament, a majority of the popular vote in favor is required for dissolution to take effect. In fact, the defeat of the referendum triggers presidential removal. This explains why Latvian presidents do not use this power. While Vīķe-Freiberga served as more than just a symbol, her powers proved unsubstantial. She also lacked a party affiliation.

Only one case of a weak woman president exists outside Europe: President Pratibha Patil of India. As president, she officially renounced her affiliation with the Congress Party. While the president commands the armed forces and can dissolve parliament, the Indian constitution's forty-second amendment places clear restrictions on this: "There shall be a Council of Ministers with the Prime Minister at the head to aid and advise the President who shall, in the exercise of his functions, act in accordance with such advice."[8] Choosing the party forming the government when no party holds a majority affords greater significance to presidents. Although some Indian presidents, such as Rajendra Prasad and Neelam Sanjiva Reddy, have played more substantive roles, India's prime ministers have exercised the preponderance of executive power. The extreme ethnic/religious/caste divisions in India increase the importance of the symbolic nature of presidents. In fact, political minorities, including Muslims (President A. P. J. Abdul Kalam) and Dalits (President Kocheril Raman Narayanan), have served as presidents. Their selections suggest an acceptance of historically oppressed groups within political positions. Given the lack of presidential authority, however, this claim seems questionable. Currently no evidence suggests that Pratibha Patil pushed the boundaries of her power.

While the popular vote elects most weak women presidents, exceptions include the Swiss, Latvian, and Indian cases. While not a specific power, election by popular vote underscores legitimacy. Interestingly, the first female president elected by the popular vote, Finnbogadóttir, wielded very little power. In contrast, a host of political actors elected Patil to the presidency; she possessed the highest number of powers among weak women presidents.

Weak women presidents face many power limitations. Other executives or political institutions constrain them. Though the public may vote them in, this is more typically the case for the weakest presidents. Their ability to win national popular elections likely relates to their less substantive powers. Finally, several lack partisan affiliations, indicating apolitical roles. Weak women presidents ultimately do not challenge the gendered nature of executive office or signal much progress for women. At the same time, more symbolic presidents push various boundaries to exert greater influence. Furthermore, a woman occupying even a weak presidency conveys women's inclusion in the public sphere. She provides a model of female leadership to girls and women, potentially enhancing women's symbolic representation.

Between the two extremes of dominant and weak presidents lie those possessing midrange powers. Only two women in this sample fit this category: Tarja Halonen of Finland and Dalia Grybauskaitė of Lithuania (see Table 4.4). Since 1994, two-round majoritarian elections determine the Finnish president. Previously, the public voted for an electoral college, which in turn chose the president (Holli 2008). Perhaps not so coincidentally, a popularly elected woman ascended when presidential powers became limited.[9] Constitutional changes transferred certain authorities to the parliament, the cabinet, and, most notably, the prime minister. The president and the prime minister now share

Table 4-4. POWERFUL WOMEN PRESIDENTS

Leader	Country	System	Popular Vote
Halonen	Finland	Dual–Powerful President	Yes
Grybauskaitė	Lithuania	Dual–Powerful President	Yes
N = 2			2 (100%)

SOURCES: Author's analysis of data from Constitution Finder, CIA World Factbook, International Institute for Democracy and Electoral Assistance, and Siaroff (2003).

responsibility over foreign affairs, although the latter leads European policy. The legislative assembly nominates and dismisses the government and prime minister (Holli 2008). The president does not carry out day-to-day domestic policy. Some of the president's powers, nonetheless, prove important, including appointing and discharging military officials and defense and foreign ministers as well as selecting key financial officers and some judges. Still, appointments and removals require prime ministerial consultation. Halonen, who left office in March 2012, was visible as a leader as she conducted foreign policy meetings and summits worldwide.

As president, Halonen was able to invoke emergency powers in exceptional circumstances; parliament had to approve any such decree, however, within three months. In addition, she possessed a veto.[10] She appointed the prime minister in response to parliamentary elections. In Finland, dismissal of the prime minister can result only from a vote of no confidence, which is also the one condition under which the president may dissolve parliament. Halonen needed to renounce her party affiliation upon taking office. Overall, the Finnish prime minister appears at least marginally more powerful than the president, although President Halonen possessed significance beyond the symbolic.

The popular vote elects the Lithuanian president, who may serve up to two consecutive terms. Dalia Grybauskaitė possesses more power than most female Eastern European leaders. As president, she appoints state officials and some judges, as well as the commander of the armed forces and head of security services. The Seimas (parliament) must approve some of her appointees. While she appoints ministers, the prime minister officially selects them. The prime minister must countersign all executive decrees, and the Seimas can override presidential vetoes. President Grybauskaitė can declare martial law or emergency, but parliament must subsequently approve such actions. The president may not dissolve parliament at will. She heads the State Defense Council, which consists of the prime minister, defense minister, speaker of parliament, and commander of the armed forces. She conducts foreign policy in coordination with the government. Powerful women presidents hold substantial influence within their systems, but they are very rare. Moreover, in these contexts, the prime minister dominates.

Women Presidents: Party Dynamics

Virtually all women presidents issue from multiparty systems (twenty-three of twenty-four, or 96 percent).[11] As anticipated, several have headed coalitions, including Ellen Johnson Sirleaf, Aquino, and Chamorro. Multiparty parliamentary systems commonly feature coalition governments. Research examining the particular ideological thrust of the parties women have represented in office shows that leftist parties promote women to office more often than do rightist parties (Kittilson 2006). Nearly all female presidents stand in the center, at center left, or in the left wing. McAleese leaned more to the right during her first term, with no party affiliation during her second. Still, female presidents have tended to be grounded more in leftist parties.

Women Presidents: Conclusions

Overall, the powers and paths of women presidents vary significantly. A slightly greater portion of women presidents actually exercise dominant power (thirteen of twenty-three, or 54 percent). However, a nearly equal segment of them are fairly weak (46 percent). More of them enter office initially through a popular vote (fourteen of twenty-three, or 61 percent) than through other means. Nearly all hail from multiparty systems. Several weak presidents lack party affiliations. Dominant and powerful women presidents tend to represent centrist or left-leaning parties. At this point in the analysis, women's progress in achieving presidential positions appears somewhat mixed, though perhaps better than anticipated.

WOMEN PRIME MINISTERS

Among the thirty-nine female prime ministers, power scores range from –1 to 6 (see Table 4.5). No woman prime minister holds the maximum possible score of 7. Women prime ministers routinely possess fewer authorities than presidents. This substantiates claims that women's greater tendency to occupy premierships translates into weaker power potential. Sixteen (41 percent) female prime ministers appear weak, all occupying office with a dominant president. Many of these cases arise in Africa and Europe. Still, twenty (59 percent), a substantial quantity, serve in dominant prime ministerships, yet even they possess relatively limited autonomy and policy authority.

Regarding paths, presidents appointed twenty of the women prime ministers (57 percent); in ten of these cases (50 percent) the presidents selected the

Table 4-5. Women Prime Ministers: Paths and Powers

Region/Name (country)	Appointment	PR	AP	CM	EP	FP	DF	GF	DL	Total	Position
Africa											
Kinigi (Burundi)	Legislative	-1	1	0	0	0	0	1	0	1	Weak
Domitien (Central African Republic)	Presidential	-1	0	0	0	0	0	0	0	-1	Weak
Diogo (Mozambique)	Presidential	-1	1	1	0	0	0	1	0	2	Weak
Uwilingiyimana (Rwanda)	Presidential	-1	1	0	0	0	0	1	0	1	Weak
Das Neves (São Tomé and Príncipe)	Presidential	-1	1	1	0	0	0	1	0	2	Weak
Silveira (São Tomã and Príncipe)	Presidential	-1	1	1	0	0	0	1	0	2	Weak
Boye (Senegal)	Presidential	-1	1	1	0	0	0	1	0	2	Weak
Asia											
Hasina (Bangladesh)	Presidential (limited)	0	1	1	0	1	1	1	1	6	Dominant
Zia (Bangladesh)	Presidential (limited)	0	1	1	0	1	1	1	1	6	Dominant
Gandhi (India)	Presidential (limited)	0	1	1	0	1	1	1	1	6	Dominant
Bhutto (Pakistan)	Legislative	-1	1	1	0	1	0	1	1	4	Dominant
Han (South Korea)	Presidential (legislature approval)	-1	1	0	0	0	0	1	0	1	Weak
Bandaranaike (Sri Lanka)	Presidential	-1	0	0	0	0	0	0	0	-1	Weak
Caribbean											
Charles (Dominica)	Presidential (limited)	-1	1	1	0	1	0	1	1	4	Dominant
Werleigh (Haiti)	Presidential (legislature approval)	-1	1	0	0	0	1	1	0	2	Weak
Pierre-Louis (Haiti)	Presidential (legislature approval)	-1	1	0	0	0	1	1	0	2	Weak
Simpson-Miller (Jamaica)	Legislative	0	1	1	0	1	0	1	1	5	Dominant
Persad-Bissessar (Trinidad and Tobago)	Legislative	0	1	1	0	1	0	1	1	5	Dominant

Europe

		PR	AP	CM	EP	FP	DF	GF	DL		
Brundtland (Norway)	Legislative	0	1	1	0	1	1	1	0	5	Dominant
Çiller (Turkey)	Presidential	0	1	1	1	0	1	1	1	5	Dominant
Cresson (France)	Presidential	-1	1	1	0	0	1	1	1	2	Weak
Greceanîi (Moldova)	Presidential (legislature approval)	-1	1	1	0	0	0	0	1	1	Weak
Jäätteenmäki (Finland)	Legislative	0	1	1	0	1	1	1	1	5	Dominant
Kiviniemi (Finland)	Legislative	0	1	1	0	1	1	1	1	5	Dominant
Kosor (Croatia)	Presidential (legislature approval)	0	1	1	0	1	1	1	1	6	Dominant
Merkel (Germany)	Legislative	0	1	1	0	1	1	1	1	6	Dominant
Planinc (Yugoslavia)	Legislative	0	1	1	0	1	1	1	0	5	Dominant
Prunskienė (Lithuania)	Legislative	0	1	1	0	1	1	1	0	4	Dominant
Radičová (Slovakia)	Legislative	0	0	1	0	1	1	1	1	4	Dominant
Sigurðardóttir (Iceland)	Legislative	0	1	1	0	1	1	1	1	6	Dominant
Suchocka (Poland)	Legislative	0	1	1	0	0	0	1	0	3	Weak
Thatcher (United Kingdom)	Legislative	0	1	1	0	1	1	1	1	6	Dominant
Tymoshenko (Ukraine)	Presidential (legislature approval)	-1	1	1	0	0	0	0	0	2	Weak

Others

		PR	AP	CM	EP	FP	DF	GF	DL		
Gillard (Australia)	Legislative	0	1	1	0	1	1	1	1	5	Dominant
Meir (Israel)	Legislative	0	1	1	0	1	1	1	1	6	Dominant
Campbell (Canada)	Legislative	0	1	1	0	1	1	1	1	6	Dominant
Shipley (New Zealand)	Legislative	0	1	1	0	1	1	1	1	6	Dominant
Clark (New Zealand)	Legislative	0	1	1	0	1	1	1	1	6	Dominant
Merino (Peru)	Presidential	-1	1	1	0	0	0	0	1	3	Weak

SOURCES: Author's analysis of data from Constitution Finder, CIA World Factbook, and International Institute for Democracy and Electoral Assistance.

ABBREVIATIONS: PR = presidential removal, AP = discretionary appointment powers, CM = chair cabinet meetings, EP = emergency long-term or decree powers, FP = central role in foreign policy, DF = central role in defense (such as commander in chief), GF = central role in government formation, DL = ability to dissolve the legislature.

prime ministers independently, in four cases (20 percent) they were limited in their choices by the partisan composition of the legislature, and in six cases (30 percent) their nominations had to be confirmed by the legislature before the appointments could take effect. The remaining nineteen prime ministers (49 percent) did not gain office through presidential selection. Instead, they arose through party appointment and or legislative elections, although the exact procedures vary.

As stated, most female prime ministers fall into the dominant category. This group of twenty-three women represents all major world regions except Latin America, where nearly all countries utilize unified presidential systems. Power scores range from a high of 6 to a low of 4 within this category (see Table 4.6). Indeed, an impressive eleven prime ministers wield at least six powers, including chairing cabinet meetings, making important cabinet appointments, and playing pivotal roles in government formation. They shape foreign and defense policies,[12] and they assert important policy impacts, in part through cabinet appointments and retention powers. These prime ministers chart their preferred course, but respective ministers steer policy. The prime ministers can, however, intervene in cases where the cabinet disagrees, although this varies with specific circumstances. Because of the relatively large numbers of women prime ministers within each category, I engage a few case studies to illustrate various points regarding paths and powers. In doing so, it is useful to differentiate between dominant prime ministers leading in dual-executive systems in contrast to those leading in unified ones.

Dominant Women Prime Ministers in Dual-Executive Systems

I draw mainly here from the cases of Angela Merkel of Germany and Benazir Bhutto of Pakistan. Merkel's example shows both the power and the vulnerabilities of dominant prime ministerships within dual-executive systems. Chancellor Merkel asserts more influence than the federal president and is the single most important policy actor in Germany.[13] Her cabinet appointees, however, wield authority over their respective policy domains while she resolves conflicts between the ministries. Since Germany is a multiparty system, party coalitions generally arise. Instead of solely appointing their fellow partisans to their cabinets, chancellors (who, in essence, appear identical to prime ministers) must also select coalition partners. Upon her first term, Merkel appointed a greater share of ministers from the Social Democratic Party (SPD) than from her own party, the Christian Democratic Union (CDU).

Like many of her female counterparts, Merkel ascended through an indirect election, not a popular vote.[14] Though the president formally proposes the

Table 4-6. DOMINANT WOMEN PRIME MINISTERS

Leader	Country	System	Appointment
Bhutto	Pakistan	Dual–Powerful President	Legislative
Brundtland	Norway	Unified Parliamentary	Legislative
Campbell	Canada	Unified Parliamentary	Legislative
Charles	Dominica	Dual–Powerful President	Presidential (limited)
Çiller	Turkey	Dual–Powerful President	Presidential
Clark	New Zealand	Unified Parliamentary	Legislative
Gandhi	India	Dual–Parliamentary/Weak President	Presidential (limited)
Gillard	Australia	Dual–Parliamentary/Powerful President	Legislative
Jäätteenmäki	Finland	Dual–Parliamentary/Powerful President	Legislative
Kiviniemi	Finland	Dual–Parliamentary/Powerful President	Legislative
Kosor	Croatia	Dual–Powerful President	Presidential (legislature approval)
Meir	Israel	Dual–Parliamentary/Weak President	Legislative
Merkel	Germany	Dual–Parliamentary/Weak President	Legislative
Persad-Bissessar	Trinidad and Tobago	Dual–Parliamentary/Weak President	Legislative
Planinc	Yugoslavia	Unified Parliamentary	Legislative
Prunskienė	Lithuania	Unified Parliamentary	Legislative
Radičová	Slovakia	Dual–Parliamentary/Powerful President	Legislative
Sigurðardóttir	Iceland	Dual–Parliamentary/Weak President	Legislative
Shipley	New Zealand	Unified Parliamentary	Legislative
Simpson-Miller	Jamaica	Unified Parliamentary	Legislative
Thatcher	United Kingdom	Unified Parliamentary	Legislative
Hasina	Bangladesh	Dual–Parliamentary/Weak President	Presidential (limited)
Zia	Bangladesh	Dual–Parliamentary/Weak President	Presidential (limited)

$N = 23$

SOURCES: Author's analysis of data from Constitution Finder, CIA World Factbook, and International Institute for Democracy and Electoral Assistance.

chancellor, parties choose candidates, who must also receive a majority vote in the Bundestag. If a candidate does not secure a majority, the Bundestag may select another candidate, who must also receive a majority. If this does not occur, the president may either appoint the candidate or dissolve the Bundestag. Merkel thus required a majority vote in the Bundestag before she could officially become chancellor. When she stood as the chancellor candidate, she obtained support from 66 percent of the Bundestag (Helms 2006), and, as procedures dictated, the federal president officially pronounced her Germany's first female chancellor. Her victory appeared auspicious, given that chancellors Konrad Adenauer, Helmut Schmidt, Helmut Kohl, and Gerhard Schröder barely received majorities (Deutsche Welle 2005). Still, some speculated that a sizable number of SPD members voted against her (Helms 2006).

Merkel enjoys greater security than most female executives, particularly prime ministers. A chancellor's full term lasts four years. The German system offers two types of confidence votes that could shorten a chancellor's tenure— one initiated by the chancellor and the other by the Bundestag. If a chancellor wants to call early elections, he or she must convince his or her own party members to vote against him or her, secure presidential approval, and obtain court oversight (Helms 2006). This procedure offers the chancellor greater odds of finishing a term but diminishes his or her chances for scheduling elections at auspicious times. In most parliamentary systems, prime ministers may call early elections when victory seems likely. Still, on balance, the German chancellor benefits from a constructive vote of confidence; dismissal requires a majority of the Bundestag to elect a new chancellor (subject to the majority vote procedure already outlined).[15] The difficulty in finding a consensus replacement is likely why the constructive vote of confidence has been attempted only twice, succeeding in 1982 when Kohl ascended (Parkes 1997). This contributes to the Germany's continuity in leadership; only eight chancellors have governed since 1949.[16] Thus, in comparison with many female executives, Merkel occupies a generally safe position.

In contrast, Benazir Bhutto's tenure highlights more constraints for dominant women prime ministers. It also illustrates that power dynamics shift between prime minister and president within a country over time. In some periods, the dominant player is the prime minister, and in others the president is dominant. Most startling is the fact that Bhutto's gender determined the executive post for which she was deemed "eligible."

Though Bhutto was a prime ministerial candidate, General Muhammad Zia-ul-Haq's death in 1988 presented her an opportunity to gain the presidency. Muslim clerics, however, issued a fatwa stating that a woman could *not* be president under Islamic law. They affirmed the main difference between the positions: the prime minister led a political party, while the president stood as head of state. Though a woman could direct a party, she could not lead an entire country (Anderson 1993, 55). Ghulam Ishaq Khan—the leader of the Senate and Zia supporter—became president instead (Anderson 1993, 60). A woman could not serve in the presidency *because* of its broader power base.

Bhutto took on important duties during both her terms. Like other dominant prime ministers, she appointed cabinet ministers, formed the government, and chaired meetings. Her influence was marginal in her first term but not in her second, and much of the difference relates to the presidents with whom she shared power. During her first stint (1988–1990) she could not pass legislation because of clashes with President Khan (from the opposition), military supporters, and former Zia loyalists. She gained visibility, however, in foreign policy, likely more so than any other prime minister in Pakistan history. President Khan removed her, ending her first term abruptly. She forged a better relationship with the military and shared party affiliation with President Farooq Leghari when she regained the prime ministership in 1993. These circumstances, however, did not prevent the president from discharging her three years later (*Telegraph* 2007).[17]

The president of Pakistan serves important functions, including commander in chief of the armed forces, and appoints several military officials, although generally in consultation with the prime minister.[18] Scholars consider the military Pakistan's most developed political institution (Shah 2002). We see this influence within the executive branch. Several generals, including Zia and Pervez Musharraf, have gained the presidency through military coups, reshaping institutions and processes to reflect presidential might.

Upon his government takeover in 1998, President Musharraf altered Pakistan's constitution to give the president broader emergency powers and set a two-term maximum for prime ministers.[19] Around the world, term limits for executives generally apply only to presidents, but Musharraf took this action because he anticipated Bhutto's reappearance. During one of Musharraf's emergency periods in 2007, Bhutto returned to Pakistan from exile as debates for political reform gained traction. While staging her comeback in hopes of gaining a third prime ministerial term, Bhutto was assassinated that December (*New York Times* 2010a).[20]

Bhutto's case suggests at least four lessons. First, executive power arrangements are dynamic, especially relationships between presidents and prime ministers. Second, we need to account for the contexts in which executives operate to understand their ultimate influence. Third, presidential dismissal power places the prime minister in a tenuous position even when he or she holds the more dominant post. Fourth, women have been barred from seeking powerful executive positions *because* they are women.

Dominant Women Prime Ministers in Unified Executive Systems

Other dominant women prime ministers govern in unified executive systems. They tend to exercise powers comparable to those exercised by prime ministers who share authority with weaker presidents, although variation exists. Several make appointments, chair meetings, form governments, play foreign policy and defense roles, and may dissolve the legislature. They still suffer limitations, including sudden ouster, and exercise power in a more collaborative framework of governance. This may propel women to these positions, given the perception of women as consensus-seeking rather than autonomous actors.

Where prime ministers operate within unified systems, why do they not exercise maximum powers? Lithuania's dual-executive structure, officially established in 1992, predated Kazimira Prunskienė's ascension (Krupavicius 2008). However, some accounts recognize Vytautas Landsbergis, the president of the Supreme Council Reconstituent Seimas, as the chief of state, probably limiting Prunskienė's powers (Krupavicius 2008). Unlike most European prime ministers, especially those in unified systems, Brundtland (Norway) could not call for the early dissolution of parliament (Strom and Swindle 2002), nor could Planinc (Yugoslavia). Finally, Simpson-Miller (Jamaica) lacked a clear defense role.

Even among dominant prime ministers, none holds unlimited power to declare emergencies, an important departure from some dominant presidents. Overall, prime ministers exercise substantial powers, though the strongest presidents enjoy greater autonomy and authorities. They also lack the ability to dismiss the president; this stands in stark contrast to dominant presidents, who may often cast out weaker prime ministers unilaterally.

The remaining sixteen women prime ministers, who constitute less than half of all prime ministerial cases (41 percent), appear weak (see Table 4.7).

Weak Prime Ministers: Powers

The power scores of the weak women prime ministers range from −1 to 3. Common to most of these prime ministers are appointment powers and the power to form the government. Not all chair cabinet meetings, indicating the president's role as chief policy player. Additionally, presidents perform defense and foreign policy duties. Presidents also commonly handpick their prime ministers, and their choices are rarely subject to legislative approval. All the weak prime ministers face the major vulnerability of dismissal by both parliament and the president. Furthermore, presidents generally dismiss at their discretion. Only one weak prime minister in this sample could call a vote of confidence.

Table 4-7. WEAK WOMEN PRIME MINISTERS

Leader	Country	System	Appointment
Bandaranaike	Sri Lanka	Dual–Presidential Dominance	Presidential
Boye	Senegal	Dual–Presidential Dominance	Presidential
Cresson	France	Dual–Presidential Dominance	Presidential
Diogo	Mozambique	Dual–Presidential Dominance	Presidential
Domitien	Central African Republic	Dual–Presidential Dominance	Presidential
Greceanîi	Moldova	Dual–Presidential Dominance	Presidential (legislature approval)
Kinigi	Burundi	Dual–Presidential Dominance	Legislative
Merino	Peru	Dual–Presidential Dominance	Presidential
Han	South Korea	Dual–Presidential Dominance	Presidential (legislature approval)
Pierre-Louis	Haiti	Dual–Presidential Dominance	Presidential (legislature approval)
Silveira	São Tomé and Príncipe	Dual–Presidential Dominance	Presidential
Das Neves	São Tomé and Príncipe	Dual–Presidential Dominance	Presidential
Suchocka	Poland	Dual–Presidential Dominance	Legislative
Tymoshenko	Ukraine	Dual–Presidential Dominance	Presidential (legislature approval)
Uwilingiyimana	Rwanda	Dual–Presidential Dominance	Presidential
Werleigh	Haiti	Dual–Presidential Dominance	Presidential (legislature approval)

$N = 16$

SOURCES: Author's analysis of data from Constitution Finder, CIA World Factbook, and International Institute for Democracy and Electoral Assistance.

Below, I use the cases of prime ministers Elisabeth Domitien (Central African Republic), Yuliya Tymoshenko (Ukraine), Myeong-Sook Han (South Korea), and Beatriz Merino Lucero(Peru) to illustrate regional power patterns, although I also draw upon the experiences of several other women leaders. African prime ministers commonly fall in the weak category because they serve with presidents who unquestionably hold the most power. Several of the African nations that have had women prime ministers were formerly French colonies that instituted governments similar to the Fifth Republic (Elgie and Moestrup 2008, 1). Domitien represents the weakest prime minister in this sample. She gained power through her long-standing friendship with General Jean-Bédel Bokassa, who staged a military coup in 1965, and helped him claim the title president for life in 1972 (Opfell 1993, 64). He subsequently appointed her prime minister, though she lacked real power. Bokassa continued to make all political decisions and soon dismissed her (Opfell 1993, 66). Since Domitien did not appear to exercise substantive powers and faced presidential dismissal, her power score is the lowest possible: −1.

Following Domitien, African prime ministers gained more authority, but not nearly as much as their presidential colleagues. Many remained only briefly in their posts, several sacked by the presidents who appointed them, including Boye (Senegal), and das Neves (São Tomé and Príncipe). In countries such as Mozambique, presidents head both government and the state.[21] Still, even weak prime ministers usually appoint cabinet ministers and assist in government formation. Presidents regularly call and chair cabinet meetings.

Semipresidentialism is the most common regime type since the collapse of the Soviet Union (Elgie and Moestrup 2008, 2). Still, the powers of Central and Eastern European prime ministers vary more than do those of their counterparts in Africa. Some systems feature symbolic presidents sharing power with stronger prime ministers, while presidents exercise dominance in others. Weak female prime ministers from this region include Zinaida Greceanîi (Moldova), Hanna Suchocka (Poland), and Yuliya Tymoshenko (Ukraine).

Upon independence, Ukraine repeatedly demonstrated the dual-executive structure's fluid power divisions, resulting from the actions of specific political leaders rather than institutional rules and processes. According to Birch (2008), "If democracy is a political arrangement where politics is governed by rules, post-Soviet Ukraine has been a context in which rules are governed by politics" (236). Since independence, presidents have exercised the bulk of powers, gaining strength as the result of a lack of parliamentary oversight (Birch 2008, 225). Ukraine's 1996 constitution reinforced presidential dominance. Provisions included a higher threshold for overturning presidential vetoes as well as broad presidential powers to appoint the cabinet and the prime minister. Unilateral presidential dismissal of the prime minister resulted in high turnover rates.

For example, President Leonid Kuchma (1994–2005) appointed eight prime ministers. Discharges commonly occurred when a president wanted the prime minister to take the fall for poor executive performance or when the prime minister became more popular than the president (Protsyk and Wilson 2003).[22]

Tymoshenko first entered executive office as acting prime minister under President Yushchenko in January 2005. Her appointment required parliamentary approval, which occurred one month later. She could appoint cabinet officials, form the government, and chair cabinet meetings. The president, however, shared these powers. The president's ability to appoint foreign and defense ministers compromised her influence over these matters. The president was also firmly positioned as commander in chief and head of the National Security and Defense Council and could oust her at will.[23] Approximately seven months after Tymoshenko's appointment, Yushchenko dismissed her government, blaming it for the economic slowdown Ukraine was experiencing. He subsequently appointed Yuriy Yekhanurov, one of his allies, to this post (Cutler 2010).

Before Tymoshenko's reemergence to the prime ministership, Yushchenko faced numerous challenges. Constitutional reforms that took effect in 2006 placed more restrictions on presidential appointment of the prime minister and eliminated presidential dismissal of the prime minister. The president's role in governmental formation was also reduced, though the president could still appoint the defense and foreign ministers.

When Tymoshenko returned to the prime ministership in 2007 after election results favored her coalition, her relationship with President Yushchenko seemed even more strained. While insulated from presidential dismissal in her second term, she confronted votes of no confidence in 2007 and again in 2008 (Cutler 2010). She survived, which likely would have been impossible under previous arrangements, suggesting that rules finally shape Ukrainian politics (Birch 2008). However, though Tymoshenko benefited from greater autonomy, the president still stood dominant. It is the presidency, not the prime ministership, to which Ukrainian politicians, including Tymoshenko, aspire.

In January 2010, Tymoshenko ran for the presidency against Yushchenko and Viktor Yanukovych. Yushchenko placed a distant third, and the results triggered a runoff election between Yanukovych and Tymoshenko. Yanukovych came in first with 38 percent of the vote, and Tymoshenko placed second with 25 percent (Levy 2010). She subsequently lost in another round of voting (Associated Press 2010). This outcome reinforces research findings indicating that women have difficulty in gaining strong presidencies, particularly through the popular vote. It also highlights that runoffs are no panacea for women candidates. Though Tymoshenko survived two previous votes of confidence, she failed to do so in March 2010 (*Telegraph* 2010).

Asia also produces weak prime ministers, as is evident in Han's ascension in South Korea. According to Chapter IV of that nation's constitution, the president serves as head of the executive branch. The president and prime minister constitute the State Council, but the president presides over cabinet meetings. Though advised by the prime minister, the president officially appoints the heads of executive ministries. Han therefore possessed appointment powers and assisted in governmental formation. In contrast to strong prime ministers, she did not lead policy; the president assumed this role. Similar to strong presidents, the South Korean president serves as commander in chief of security forces and heads the National Security Council. The president also appoints national security officials.

The president selects the prime minister, but parliament, which routinely strikes down the president's nominees, must approve the choice.[24] Article 86 characterizes the prime minister as the president's assistant. This arrangement, which also exists in Guyana and Sri Lanka, makes the prime minister akin to a vice president (see Siaroff 2003, 295). In South Korea, the prime minister succeeds to the presidency when an untimely opening occurs. The prime minister's not being beholden to the parliament for survival represents a major divergence from parliamentary processes. Parliament can only *recommend* removal of the government.[25] The president cannot dissolve parliament but may dismiss the prime minister and reshuffle the cabinet. It must be noted that South Korea's constitution does not explicitly provide for presidential dismissal of the prime minister, even if it is exercised in practice.[26] Han's preference for this position evinces the greater strength of the South Korean presidency. She resigned the prime ministership after only ten months in office to wage an ultimately unsuccessful presidential bid in 2007.[27]

Beatriz Merino of Peru enjoyed more power than other weak prime ministers analyzed, particularly those in Africa. Still, the president had significantly greater authority. Article 122 of Peru's constitution specifies that the president appoints and dismisses the prime minister. The prime minister usually chairs cabinet meetings, but not when the president is in attendance or has called the meeting (which the president may do at his or her discretion). The president also directs general policy. As the governmental spokesperson, the prime minister comes second, after the president. Unlike the South Korean case, the Peruvian prime minister is not akin to a vice president. In fact, two Peruvian vice presidents act as presidential aides. Though the prime minister appears to have greater powers than many other weak executives, the constitution explicitly distributes institutional power hierarchically; in descending order of power, first comes the president, then Congress, and then the Council of Ministers, including the prime minister.[28] Merino served for only five months before the president asked her to step down.[29] Unlike the South Korean case, the Peruvian prime minister depends upon parliament for survival but can call early elections through proposing the dissolving of the parliament and a no confidence vote. These vulnerabilities and advantages balance one another in many instances. The prime minister is also susceptible to presidential dismissal, however. Prime ministerial tenure, therefore, appears volatile. Furthermore, Merino's experience demonstrates that if a prime minister enjoys high levels of popularity when the president does not, she may fall prey to his unilateral dismissal authority.[30]

Other weak prime ministers include Bandaranaike of Sri Lanka. Her vulnerabilities are amply illustrated by the full detailing of presidential powers above.[31] Haiti also utilizes weak prime ministers; in fact, two women have served in this capacity, Claudette Werleigh and Michèle Pierre-Louis. Their power scores do not differ dramatically from other cases discussed. While their appointments required legislative approval, the president and parliament could oust them. Werleigh's term ended abruptly after only three months when a new president ascended; Pierre-Louis stayed in office for one year but left following parliamentary dismissal.

Finally, Edith Cresson briefly held the French premiership in the early 1990s. France is often considered the prototype of the semipresidential system. Based on both constitutional design and powers in practice, the presidency appears dominant. François Mitterrand appointed Cresson, an ally, in 1991 after he forced the resignation of Michel Rocard. Her selection may have been an attempt by Mitterrand to gain the support of women voters (Jensen 2008, 49). While her personal relationship with Mitterrand aided her advancement, because they were both members of the Socialist Party, he enjoyed wide latitude in nominating her and retaining her, diminishing her influence. She exercised little independent power in appointing her cabinet; instead she selected Mitterrand's friends (Liswood 1995, 122). Still, rather than toeing the party line, Cresson was very outspoken, repeatedly creating tensions within the executive branch. When the Socialist Party failed dismally in local elections in 1992, Mitterrand demanded her resignation (Jensen 2008, 50).

Though not as common as their dominant counterparts, weak prime ministers represent just over 40 percent of all female premiers—a substantial portion. Their potential ouster represents a major vulnerability. They enjoy limited independence and few powers.

Women Prime Ministers and Party

Nearly all female prime ministers come to power in multiparty systems (thirty-one of thirty-nine, or 79 percent). While this may at first glance be attributed to the preponderance of multiparty systems worldwide, 69 percent of countries feature multiple competitive parties. As such, women still disproportionately cluster within multiparty contexts. In contrast to women presidents, almost all prime ministers represent party affiliations. The one exception is Pierre-Louis of Haiti.[32] Partisan linkages among prime ministers vary greatly. Perhaps tied to their activist roots, several represent nationalist parties (see the biographies in the appendix). Ethnically based parties commonly exist in Africa and Asia. Still, at least eighteen women appear situated on the left end of the ideological spectrum. Two represent the Communist Party (Planinc in Yugoslavia and Greceanîi in Moldova). Several women representing right-leaning parties have also ascended, including Thatcher, Campbell (Canada), Merkel, Çiller (Turkey), Tymoshenko, and Shipley (New Zealand). While certainly conservative women are less numerous than others, it must be noted that Thatcher, Campbell, and Merkel represent globally important countries and relatively strong positions. Campbell's premiership, however, lasted only very briefly, and Merkel led a conservative-liberal coalition during her first term.

CONCLUSIONS

A slightly greater proportion of women presidents actually exercise dominant power, though a substantial number do not. A larger percentage enters office initially through a popular vote. Powers seemingly relate to party leanings and systems. Nearly all women presidents hail from multiparty systems. The dominant and powerful presidents tend to represent centrist or left-leaning parties, while weak presidents routinely lack official partisan connections. At this point in the analysis, women's progress in achieving presidential positions appears somewhat mixed, though perhaps better than anticipated.

Women's greater tendency to serve as prime ministers suggests major consequences, since they routinely possess fewer powers than presidents. While a larger segment of women prime ministers play dominant roles within their systems, they still suffer from important vulnerabilities, including ouster, and exercise power in more collaborative systems of governance. Moreover, several weak prime ministers face dismissal by both parliament and the president. Women's greater tendency to hold prime ministerships likely relates to their depiction as consensus-driven players rather than autonomous actors. Once again, women's ultimate progress in attaining executive offices appears rather questionable, although perhaps the outlook is more hopeful than expected.

General Backgrounds of
Women Leaders

The preceding chapter's deeper look at executive powers presented encouraging findings suggesting that women sometimes acquire presidential positions that go beyond symbolic authority and require a popular vote. Nonetheless, the still substantial segment of weaker and appointed women executives suggests mixed progress overall. The fact that most women executives serve as prime ministers reaffirms this point. Prime ministers generally exercise fewer powers than do dominant presidents, govern within more collaborative frameworks, and remain vulnerable to early dismissal. The perception of women as consensus-driven players rather than autonomous actors explains in part their greater tendency to hold prime ministerships. We should question, therefore, women's overall advancement.

This chapter primarily concerns the backgrounds of women leaders, including their educational statuses, levels of political experience, and ages upon entering office. By comparing women leaders to their predecessors (almost exclusively male), we can scrutinize fears that women boast fewer qualifications. If underqualified, women may seldom gain promotion to strong positions. This chapter, however, explores the distinct possibility that women possess even *greater* political credentials than their male counterparts. If women fail to achieve powerful positions despite their amassing more impressive qualifications than the men with whom they compete, this potentially indicates gender discrimination. Analysis of women executives' backgrounds may also identify alternate routes that women take to executive positions. If no divergences surface between male and female executives, this means that the influx of women has failed to produce a shift in the backgrounds seemingly required for office (Schwindt-Bayer 2011).

I compare women executives to their male predecessors. This strategy may appear to set male backgrounds as the normative standard to evaluate women,

but it must be noted that I first operationalize categories of education and political experience. Only after doing so do I assess if and how women's backgrounds
and career trajectories differ from men's *without* establishing men's experience
as the default.

GENDER AND AGE DIFFERENCES

I analyze age upon first entrance to the prime ministership or presidency, limiting analysis to nontemporary leaders.[1] Age suggests women's ability to rise
through the political ranks quickly enough that they can forge long careers in
the highest offices. Women's gaining office at older ages might indicate hesi-
tance in promoting women. Alternatively, as a consequence of traditionally
"feminine" obligations such as taking care of family, women may delay their
careers. American and comparative research reveals that women legislators
generally get a later start in politics than do their male counterparts (Thomas
1994; Dolan and Ford 1995; Burrell 1994; Chaney 1979; Saint-Germain 1993b;
Schwindt-Bayer 2010). Does this also hold true for women executives?

The average ages of female and male executives do not diverge (see Table 5.1).[2]
An individual typically starts serving as president or prime minister in his or
her early fifties. An examination of ages by regions reveals that age gaps exist
only in Asia, where women usually lead at younger ages than men, and the
Caribbean, where women are older. These differences are slight, however; both
across and within regions, few differences are seen between men and women
in their ages upon first coming to power. Further, none of the differences that
do exist are statistically significant. Analysis of the paired cases within the same

Table 5-1. MALE AND FEMALE EXECUTIVES AND AGE (YEARS)

Region	Women	Men	Cases
Africa	49.9 (10.3)	49.5 (7.7)	16
Asia	54 (10.2)	56.3 (10.5)	22
Caribbean	57.2 (5.21)	51.4 (8.85)	10
Europe	53.2 (5.6)	54 (9.7)	46
Latin America	53.9 (10.7)	54.6 (14)	16
Total	53.2 (8.6)	53.7 (10)	59

SOURCES: BBC News profiles, Council of Women World Leaders, Worldwide Guide to
Women in Leadership, *New York Times* profiles, and Zárate's Political Collections.

NOTE: The total cases also include leaders from other areas—North America, Oceania,
and the Middle East—who are not analyzed separately by region. Three pairs are
excluded because women followed women into office and there was no predecessor to
one leader. This reduces the total cases from 63 to 59.

positions and countries shows that twenty-nine women were younger than their male predecessors, twenty-eight were older, and two the same age (4 percent).[3] Once again, no major age differentials arise.

GENDER AND EDUCATIONAL DIFFERENCES

In order to advance to executive positions, candidates must typically possess specific educational and political credentials. In contrast to age, governments rarely mandate educational qualifications for executives, but, of course, informal ones exist.[4] Do women ascend only if they boast higher levels of education than men? If so, do these higher standards for eligibility keep executive offices out of the reach of most women?

Table 5.2 provides information on the educational levels that women executives and their male predecessors completed prior to occupying their executive posts (grammar school, high school, college, and graduate or professional school).[5] The table presents these data both geographically and for the entire sample. The p values were derived from chi-square tests to assess statistical significance. As the table shows, 60 percent of the women leaders attained professional or graduate degrees, as did 62 percent of the men. Of the women, 25 percent completed university studies, while 23 percent of their male counterparts did so.[6] Finally, equal proportions completed high school or elementary educations. Nearly all women who have achieved executive office since 2000 have held doctorates or other professional degrees. Those rising to power in the 1960s and 1970s often only finished high school but nonetheless gained higher levels of education than most women of their time in their nations. As with age, very few gender differences are apparent in the educational attainment of executives. The vast majority of both men and women earn at least a master's degree before entering executive office. Women more often have pursued doctoral degrees, suggesting their slightly greater educational credentials.

Regardless of gender, executives often gain degrees in more "masculine" fields, such as science, finance, and economics.[7] The men in this sample typically completed engineering and technology degrees; no women completed degrees in these fields. Perhaps it is no surprise that the most common training for both male and female leaders is in law.

Regionally, nearly all European female national leaders achieved college degrees and more typically the equivalent of master's or doctorate degrees; their fields of study varied. Asian women's educational backgrounds appear even more diverse than those of their European counterparts, and Latin American women generally earned professional degrees. African women leaders, while

Table 5-2. MALE AND FEMALE EXECUTIVES AND EDUCATION BY REGION

Education	Sex	REGION/PERCENTAGE								Total	p
		Africa	Carib	Euro	LA	Asia	Ocea	ME	NA		
Grammar School	Women	0	0	4(1)	13(1)	0	0	0	0	3 (2)	.62
	Men	0	0	0	0	0	50(1)	0	0	1 (1)	
High School	Women	13(1)	0	0	13(1)	33(4)	0	100 (1)	0	11 (7)	.78
	Men	50(2)	0	5(1)	25(2)	9(7)	0	100 (1)	0	13 (7)	
College	Women	25(2)	40(2)	20(5)	25(2)	33(4)	33(1)	0	0	25(16)	.83
	Men	0	25(1)	14(3)	0	9 (1)	50(1)	0	0	23(12)	
Graduate or Professional School	Women	63(5)	60(3)	76 (19)	50(4)	33(4)	67(2)	0	100 (1)	60(38)	.85
	Men	50(2)	75(3)	81 (17)	75(6)	27(6)	0	0	100 (1)	62(33)	

SOURCES: BBC News profiles, Council of Women World Leaders, *New York Times* profiles, and numerous biographies listed in the references as well as information from embassies cited in text endnotes.

NOTES: Total of women = 63; total of men = 53. Three women were preceded by other women, one was preceded by no one, and there was no information available for six men. Parentheses note the number of leaders in the category.

ABBREVIATIONS: Carib = Caribbean, Euro = Europe, LA = Latin America, Ocea = Oceania, ME = Middle East, NA = North America.

highly educated, did not attain doctorate-level degrees. Several, however, completed graduate degrees in economics or finance.

Earlier in their educations, many female leaders attended Catholic schools, irrespective of their own religious upbringings. Catholic private schools provided them with high-quality education where public funding for schooling proved inadequate.[8] The sex segregation of these schools also quelled familial concerns over culturally inappropriate mixing of boys and girls. In contrast, Catholic education is not a prevalent factor in the backgrounds of male executives.

Regardless of region or gender, several executives traveled outside their home countries for university studies, often in the most respected institutions of higher learning in the United States and Europe.[9] South Asian female leaders frequently interrupted their university or graduate-level educations, while their male counterparts did not. Political instability often facilitated women's sudden return to their home countries. Another gendered educational difference is that at least three male leaders trained in military high schools or colleges.[10] This coincides with the fact that military careers constitute a route to power for male executives but not for women—a point discussed below.

By and large, the data indicate that, regardless of region, extensive education precedes the political careers of both women and men, implying their equal preparation to rule.[11] In fact, given women's greater proportion of doctorates, their educational credentials are slightly higher than those of men. While women increasingly fit the traditional mold of political elites, their entrance to executive posts does not signal a shift from the qualifications deemed necessary for the job. Thus, the largely male-defined pattern prevails.

GENDER DIFFERENCES IN POLITICAL EXPERIENCE

Political experience prior to holding presidential or prime ministerial office sheds light on the springboards to power, which likely differ from country to country. Executive office remains a male bastion. Must women attain greater political credentials than their male counterparts to gain entrance to this elite club?

Measuring political experience is a particularly daunting task, and the results are necessarily ultimately imperfect. Michael Genovese (1993a, 212–13) classified the political experience of each of several women leaders in one of three ways: none, limited, or extensive. However, Genovese did not develop a scientific measure.[12] His category of limited experience signified little or no national government experience and limited state/regional experience, and his extensive experience category signified holding a position in a national government or a shadow cabinet/party leadership position. I attempt to improve upon Genovese's categories (see also Jalalzai 2004). Several possible types of political experience emerge: membership or activism in a political party; appointment or election to various political offices at a multitude of levels, including national, local, and regional; and appointment to cabinet ministerships. Ideally, numbers of years and levels of politics should figure into any classifications. I assigned different weights to different levels of office. For example, serving in parliament for two years absent appointments to ministerial posts does not count the same as accumulating twenty years in parliament while holding several ministerial posts.[13]

Unfortunately, not much literature guides this venture (Bond, Covington, and Fleisher 1985). Coding should account for different levels of office but also address years of experience. Even when one considers both level and years in office, however, further problems arise. What if an individual gains experience at multiple levels of government, including local and national? Furthermore, how do we measure political clout? Lastly, should we completely discount experience in party organizations and political movements? Ultimately, such assessments appear imperfect.

In this book and a previous article (Jalalzai 2004), I measure political experience in the following ways. First, it entails involvement in any of these activities: holding political office, engaging in party work, and participating in a political movement, including revolutionary or independence struggles. As much of the literature on gender in politics demonstrates, the tendency to analyze only formal office holding substantially underestimates women's political participation (see Banaszak 2008). Political experience ranges from none to high and accounts for the type, level, and number of years engaged in the activity. Political clout is determined by the ministerial positions and party leadership posts held. Coding results in the four levels of political experience that I apply to women leaders and their immediate predecessors:

1. *None:* No prior political experience.
2. *Low:* One to four years of experience in one of the following activities: local office holding (such as serving as mayor), party activism, or participation in a revolutionary movement. It also includes occupying national legislative or executive office for one year or less.
3. *Medium:* Five to eight years of local office holding, party activism, or participation in a revolutionary movement, or two to three years of occupying national-level office.
4. *High:* Nine years or more of local office holding, party activism, or activism in a revolutionary movement, or four years or more occupying national-level office.

While the vast majority of the female leaders (79 percent) amassed high levels of political experience, this was true for a greater proportion of their male predecessors (89 percent). Of the women, 12 percent achieved low and medium levels (6 percent each). Roughly equal proportions of men achieved low levels. Among the women, 8 percent lacked political experience; these included political widows and weak presidents.[14] Among the men, only Kristján Eldjárn, former president of Iceland (a weak position), completely lacked political credentials. Still, all other weak male presidents accumulated political experience prior to their ascensions (a statistically significant difference). These findings demonstrate that for women, a high level of experience prior to governance is the rule, *not* the exception (see Table 5.3).

How do women's political résumés compare with those of their male predecessors? Must women attain more political experience to ascend within the same contexts? While the vast majority of women leaders have gained extensive experience, a larger proportion of men with similar backgrounds rise to executive office. Women leaders, consequently, possess somewhat fewer political credentials upon taking office. This suggests that women lacking prior political experience challenge typical executive political backgrounds.

Few regional differences surface; in both Asia and Latin America, women executives have tended to have less political experience than their male predecessors. Nearly three-quarters of the women executives have obtained high levels of political experience; in contrast, nearly all the male executives from these regions do. Such a gap, though smaller, exists also in Europe, indicating men's greater political credentials. Still, women typically acquire impressive political portfolios before rising to power.[15]

Table 5.4 breaks political experience down by whether the individuals held legislative or cabinet posts or both. Of the women, 21 percent served in the national legislature, while 8 percent held cabinet or cabinet-rank positions. However, the largest proportion of women combined cabinet and legislative backgrounds (41 percent). In comparison, a higher percentage of male predecessors occupied national legislative posts (29 percent). Men more often served as cabinet ministers (25 percent compared to 13 percent). On the other hand, a smaller proportion of men held both cabinet and legislative offices (35 percent versus 41 percent). Then again, more women occupied *neither* national legislative nor cabinet posts (25 percent and 11 percent, respectively, a statistically significant gap).

Regional patterns suggest that African leaders, male and female, regularly use cabinet appointments as routes to higher executive offices. Legislatures are not as pivotal to yielding potential executives in Africa as in other contexts, or at least for the subset of African countries where women have ascended. In contrast, to obtain the highest executive posts in Europe, men and women typically need parliamentary or ministerial histories or both. Since most European countries utilize parliamentary systems, the pool of possible prime ministers generally consists of legislative office holders. As before, gender differences

Table 5-3. MALE AND FEMALE EXECUTIVES AND POLITICAL EXPERIENCE

Political Experience	Sex	REGION/PERCENTAGE								Total	p
		Africa	Carib	Euro	LA	Asia	Ocea	ME	NA		
High	Women	5 (63)	4 (80)	21 (84)	6 (75)	9 (75)	3 (100)	1 (100)	1 (100)	50 (79)	.21
	Men	4 (80)	4 (80)	20 (91)	8 (100)	10 (100)	2 (100)	1 (100)	0	49 (89)	
Medium	Women	2 (25)	0	1 (4)	0	1 (8)	0	0	0	4 (6)	.12
	Men	0	0	0	0	1 (10)	0	0	0	0	
Low	Women	1 (13)	0	1 (4)	2 (25)	2 (25)	0	0	0	4 (6)	1
	Men	1 (20)	1 (20)	1 (5)	0	0	0	0	1 (100)	4 (7)	
None	Women	0	1 (20)	2 (8)	0	2 (17)	0	0	0	5 (98)	.03
	Men	0	0	1 (5)	0	0	0	0	0	1 (2)	

SOURCES: BBC News profiles, Council of Women World Leaders, *New York Times* profiles, and numerous biographies listed in the references as well as information from embassies cited in text endnotes.

NOTES: Total of women = 63; total of men = 55. Three women were preceded by other women, one was preceded by no one, and there was no information available for four men. Bold entries are statistically significant at the $p < .05$ level. Parentheses note the number of leaders in the category.

ABBREVIATIONS: Carib = Caribbean, Euro = Europe, LA = Latin America, Ocea = Oceania, ME = Middle East, NA = North America.

Table 5-4. MALE AND FEMALE EXECUTIVES AND PRIOR POLITICAL OFFICES

		REGION/PERCENTAGE									
Political Experience	Sex	Africa	Carib	Euro	LA	Asia	Ocea	ME	NA	Total	p
Legislative	Women	0	2 (40)	6 (24)	1 (13)	3 (25)	0	1 (100)	0	13 (21)	.67
	Men	0	1 (20)	9 (41)	1 (13)	3 (27)	1 (50)	0	1 (100)	16 (29)	
Cabinet	Women	4 (50)	0	1 (4)	2 (25)	1 (8)	0	0	0	8 (13)	**.09**
	Men	3 (60)	3 (60)	1 (5)	4 (50)	3 (27)	0	0	0	14 (25)	
Both	Women	0	2 (40)	16 (64)	1 (13)	3 (25)	3 (100)	0	1 (100)	26 (41)	.58
	Men	0	1 (20)	10 (45)	2 (25)	4 (36)	1 (50)	1 (100)	0	19 (35)	
Neither	Women	4 (50)	1 (20)	2 (8)	4 (50)	5 (42)	0	0	0	16 (25)	.05
	Men	2 (40)	0	2 (9)	1 (13)	1 (9)	0	0	0	6 (11)	

SOURCES: BBC News profiles, Council of Women World Leaders, *New York Times* profiles, and numerous biographies listed in the bibliography as well as information from embassies cited in text endnotes.

NOTES: Total of women = 63; total of men = 55. Three women were preceded by other women, one was preceded by no one, and there was no information available for four men. Bold entries are statistically significant at the $p < .05$ level. Parentheses note the number of leaders in the category.

ABBREVIATIONS: Carib = Caribbean, Euro = Europe, LA = Latin America, Ocea = Oceania, ME = Middle East, NA = North America.

persist in Latin America and Asia: 50 percent of Latin American and 42 percent of Asian female leaders obtained neither cabinet nor legislative experience, whereas nearly all of their male counterparts served in at least one of these positions previously.[16]

GENDER AND SPECIFIC CABINET PORTFOLIOS

Since many executives have had prior cabinet experience, we need to explore the types of portfolios they accumulate. Here gender relates also to the types of ministries that individuals head. Can women ascend to presidencies or prime ministerships after having been secretaries of "feminine" departments, or must they typically prove their competence in "masculine" domains first? If they are initially secretaries of "feminine" departments, do women become national executives only after they have switched to "masculine" ministries? How do their experiences compare to those of their male predecessors?

The findings thus far indicate that obtaining cabinet positions shapes women's chances of gaining presidencies and prime ministerships. But not all cabinet posts figure equally. Women ministers who hold more "feminine" or possibly gender-neutral posts seem less likely to gain presidential or prime ministerial offices, or, if they do, they occupy weaker presidencies or premierships. Women appointed to more "masculine" ministries may prove their strength through handling foreign affairs or defense. It would not be expected that male prime ministers and presidents would have experience in "feminine" ministries. Like women, they gain their expertise by serving in "masculine" ones.

To verify this, I utilize the work of Escobar-Lemmon and Taylor-Robinson (2005, 2009) examining gender and cabinet assignments in Latin America. Political institutions are gendered, replete with stereotypes regarding the traits and competencies necessary to carry out relevant duties. Considering the stereotype literature discussed in Chapter 2, some ministries are classified as "masculine" and others "feminine" (Escobar-Lemmon and Taylor-Robinson 2009). Specifically, "feminine" areas deal with the private domain, particularly anything related to nurturing or to advancing women's interests.[17] Though the label is tricky to apply, this generally includes children's and family policies, health care, social welfare, education, culture, and women's rights (Escobar-Lemmon and Taylor-Robinson 2009). "Masculine" ministries deal with the public domain and issues related to strength and power, encompassing diverse areas including agriculture, construction, defense and security, economy and finance, foreign affairs, government and interior, industry and commerce, labor, science, transportation, and communication (Escobar-Lemmon and Taylor-Robinson 2009). A few ministries, which may be classified as gender-neutral, are not stereotyped as either "masculine" or "feminine"; these include justice, sports, tourism, planning and development, and the environment.[18]

Clearly "masculine" posts abound; any overconcentration of women in "feminine" ministries may demonstrate a propensity to appoint women to stereotypically appropriate realms, usually ones affording less prestige (Escobar-Lemmon and Taylor-Robinson 2009). Further, men tend to switch from one "masculine" ministry to another while women appear more prone to change between gender-neutral and "feminine" ministries; few women shift from "feminine" to "masculine" portfolios (Escobar-Lemmon and Taylor-Robinson 2009). I ask whether these patterns evidence in Latin America cabinet appointments hold for women who eventually become presidents or prime ministers worldwide. Or, in contrast, do women executives establish competence in "masculine" departments, compensating for potential vulnerabilities stereotypically associated with "feminine" issues and traits?

Among the sixty-three nontemporary women leaders, thirty-four held cabinet posts prior to ascending to prime ministerships or presidencies (54 percent). Twenty-two (65 percent) remained in one department, while twelve (43 percent) changed assignments.[19] For those leading only one, half headed "masculine" ministries, nearly all in finance or economics, though some also held foreign affairs portfolios (see Table 5.5). No women executives first entered cabinet posts as defense ministers, though some did subsequent to their first appointments.[20] Six women (27 percent) led "feminine" departments, most commonly as minister of social affairs. Five remained within gender-neutral departments.[21] In contrast, thirty-three male predecessors (60 percent) served in cabinets.[22] Seventeen (52 percent) remained in one department, and sixteen (48 percent) switched departments.

Analysis of the leaders who stayed in one position reveals that half of the women, as opposed to three-quarters of the men, led "masculine" ones. Only one man stayed in a "feminine" ministry, and the remainder continued to occupy gender-neutral posts. However, none of these differences stands as statistically significant.

Table 5-5. Male and Female Executives and Cabinet Posts

Cabinet	Sex	One Department (%)	Total	P	One/ Combined (%)	Total	p
Feminine	Women	6 (27)	22	0.11	10 (44)	34	.39
	Men	1 (6)	17		6 (18)	33	
Masculine	Women	11 (50)	22	0.11	15 (44)	34	.18
	Men	13 (76)	17		22 (67)	33	
Neutral	Women	5 (23)	22	1	9 (26)	34	.37
	Men	3 (18)	17		5 (15)	33	

Among those who changed their portfolios, twelve women switched cabinet assignments. No obvious gendered patterns emerge in these department shifts.[23] Women, however, never entered the position of defense minister until they had proved their worth in other positions.[24] Among the sixteen male shufflers, 38 percent stayed within "masculine" ministries during their entire cabinet careers. About one-third switched from "feminine" departments to "masculine" ones. The rest alternated from "masculine" to gender-neutral positions except for one who moved from a "feminine" post to a gender-neutral one. No man transferred from a "masculine" or gender-neutral portfolio to a "feminine" one prior to his ascension as president or prime minister.

Analysis of the entire sample of women executives with cabinet experience shows that 44 percent headed "masculine" departments, 29 percent headed "feminine" departments, and 26 percent headed gender-neutral departments (see Table 5.5).[25] Among all sixty-three noninterim women presidents and prime ministers in this study, nearly one-quarter directed "masculine" ministries; it appears that women may move up the executive ladder by first establishing their more "masculine" credentials.[26]

The overall breakdown of male predecessors occupying cabinet portfolios is as follows: 67 percent led "masculine" ministries, 18 percent led "feminine" ones, and 15 percent led gender-neutral ones. Again, the percentage of men heading "masculine" ministries soars above the percentage of women executives who managed such ministries, while men had less experience in "feminine" ministries. Still, statistically significant differences fail to surface. Surprisingly, only one male leader held the defense portfolio. Men's ability to gain military positions, however, may explain this.

These findings affirm that women executives largely have backgrounds similar to those of their male counterparts, fitting the traditional "masculine" norm. Women generally obtain legislative or ministerial experience or a combination prior to gaining prime ministerships or presidencies. Some, however, do not serve in these posts. How can we explain these notable exceptions?

GENDER AND POLITICAL MOVEMENTS

While the vast majority of women executives held formal positions prior to becoming prime ministers or presidents, some came to power absent these backgrounds, raising questions about the particular contours of these women's lives prior to their assumption of national executive office.

Several women accumulated long histories working as activists in political parties or movements. Conflict and strife hampered others in their abilities to serve in official capacities. South Asian leaders in particular faced exile or house

Table 5-6. GENDER, POLITICAL MOVEMENTS, MILITARY, AND FAMILIAL TIES

	Sex	Number (%)	*p*
Movements	Women	23 (37)	**.0001**
	Men	4 (7)	
Military	Women	0	**.02**
	Men	5 (12)	
Familial Ties	Women	15 (25)	**.0002**
	Men	2 (4)	

NOTE: Bold entries are statistically significant at the *p* < .05 level.

arrest. Therefore, based on specific circumstances, women could not always acquire traditional political experience. These same conditions, however, permitted women's presidential or prime ministerial ascensions in the first place. In contrast, only one male predecessor possessed an activist background as his *sole* political credential.

More than one-third of the sixty-three nontemporary women leaders engaged in independence or democratization movements prior to their ascensions to executive positions (see Table 5.6). This route is particularly important in Africa, Asia, and Latin America, where between half and three-quarters of all women executives share these backgrounds. Only about one-quarter of European women leaders, mostly those from Eastern Europe, took this path. A regional dimension therefore surfaces, related to anticolonial movements and third-wave democratization processes. When women leading on a temporary basis are incorporated, the percentages of women activists increase further (see the biographies in the appendix for more details). In contrast, once again, few of the women's male predecessors had experience as activists (see Table 5.6).[27] These differences register high levels of statistical significance and are the first indication that women can broaden some of the traditional characteristics related to executive leadership. At the same time, since even women activists also had more customary political backgrounds, the prevailing patterns remain largely intact.

GENDER AND THE MILITARY ROUTE TO POWER

Men often use the military as a route to power, serving as army generals or colonels; in contrast, no women leaders have thus far done so (see Table 5.6). While men commonly accrue other types of political experience in addition to their military service, experience in the military appears relevant particularly in Latin America, Asia, and Africa.[28] This may explain why male leaders' résumés do not feature defense posts whereas women assert such experience;

men demonstrate their military prowess more overtly than do women. As a result, women have enjoyed less access to power when military regimes, coups, and dictatorships have flourished (Bauer 2011). While these dynamics initially constrained women in their paths to executive power in Latin America, Asia, and Africa, some women advanced when these same contexts consequently underwent political transition.

GENDER AND THE "FAMILY PATH"

Delving even further into women leaders' backgrounds, I find that one of the greatest commonalities between Latin American and Asian women executives lies in their issuing from elite ruling families. As defined in this study, familial ties are connections through blood or marriage to former prime ministers, presidents, or opposition leaders.[29]

Out of the sixty-three nontemporary women leaders, fifteen capitalized on such ties (see Table 5.6). This background thus features prominently for nearly one-quarter of women leaders, though this phenomenon is limited to South and Southeast Asia and Latin America. In fact, except for President Pratibha Patil of India, the remaining nine South and Southeast Asian women leaders boasted familial ties.[30] Of course, Patil held a fairly nominal post. Six out of eight (75 percent) Latin American executives possessed familial linkages. Only Beatriz Merino, former prime minister of Peru, and President Laura Chinchilla of Costa Rica lacked such connections.[31] In contrast, two male predecessors possessed familial ties.[32] Along with political activist backgrounds, family connections register the highest levels of statistically significant gender differences thus far in this analysis.[33]

CONCLUSIONS

The discussion presented in this chapter demonstrates that women executives amass impressive political and educational credentials before ascending to presidencies and prime ministerships, though this varies geographically. Among the most recent cases of women leaders, almost all have achieved graduate degrees. Both men and women who enter executive posts generally accumulate high levels of political experience before doing so. Whereas a greater proportion of men have acquired either legislative or ministerial experience, women more often have served in both legislative and cabinet posts. Women move up the executive ladder by obtaining appointments to more "masculine" positions. Yet, in comparison to their male counterparts, women appear to lack experience in either "feminine" or "masculine" institutions. We should consider the political pipeline of women in attempting to explain women's rise to presidencies and prime ministerships.

Given these findings, it appears that women's educational and political creden-tials do not hold them back from occupying powerful executive offices. Rather, the gendered nature of executive office still typically promotes men instead of women. Despite their impressive educational backgrounds, professional experi-ence, and associations with politically active families, women remain underrep-resented at the highest levels of power *everywhere*. Men continue to dominate prime ministerships and presidencies and gain stronger positions; we cannot explain this discrepancy by citing women's lack of preparation.[34]

Specific Pathways to Power

Political Families and Activism

While women leaders generally amass impressive political and educational credentials, as discussed in Chapter 5, two other factors are strongly related to women's ascensions to executive posts: activist histories and familial ties. In this chapter, I investigate why women leaders benefit from these backgrounds and how this connects with volatile contexts and gendered norms. In doing so, I examine all cases of women executives with familial ties and activist backgrounds, making some comparisons to their male counterparts when relevant.

Women may attain more dominant and autonomous executive posts when they successfully exploit familial ties, political vacuums, or activist backgrounds, or some combination of these. They benefit from gender stereotypes of women as healers, reformers, or dependents often during critical political trajectories. As such, women's progress is decidedly mixed. Though some women gain office where they might not otherwise, members of political families are the *only* women ascending to executive offices in some parts of the world. Men rarely depend on these same connections to secure power in such locations. Moreover, men continue to dominate executive offices globally. Though the numbers of women leaders have vastly increased, we must continue to question the overall advancement of women to political office.

A CLOSER LOOK AT FAMILY TIES

Family links to executive power frequently surface in unstable and less institutionalized contexts. Moreover, female leaders with political activist backgrounds ascend after fighting for independence and democracy. Upon achieving political autonomy or democratic transition, however, the countries in which they serve often experience a resurfacing of formerly suppressed cleavages. Frequent regime changes transpire, creating critical executive openings that benefit certain women's electoral pursuits (Hodson 1997; Jalalzai 2008).

Though recurrent turnover does not exclusively advantage women, some women successfully exploit traditional gender stereotypes during critical junctures. Women are typically viewed as dependents and therefore appropriate inheritors of power (McDonagh 2009). As stereotypical nurturers, women play mothers of their nations, healing and unifying people in postconflict societies (Saint-Germain 1993a). Women from political families capitalize on their names and numerous related advantages unavailable to the mass public. Party gatekeepers also mobilize the candidacies of such women because of these same advantages (Col 1993). Familial ties must be employed skillfully; some women seek candidacies despite the disapproval of party elites desiring the same executive positions and may battle family members for the title of heir (Hodson 1997). Still, women who have attained dominant executive positions in Latin America and Asia have almost always had kinship ties to power, while the backgrounds of their male counterparts in these same contexts vary.

Fifteen of sixty-three women leaders (24 percent) possess familial ties to power. In fact, Ellen Johnson Sirleaf of Liberia and Laura Chinchilla of Costa Rica are the only popularly elected presidents exercising dominant power absent kinship ties as defined.[1] I begin by presenting short narratives of the ascensions of women with family ties in Latin America and Asia as a means of developing a larger though still nuanced understanding of the kinship phenomenon in relation to gender and executive office holding.

Family Ties in Latin America

Six of the seven noninterim female presidents in Latin America possess family ties to power, generally being the wives of executives or opposition leaders. I briefly analyze each below in the order of ascension to the presidency.

ISABEL PERÓN, ARGENTINA (JULY 1974–MARCH 1976)

Isabel Perón of Argentina was the world's first female president. She was married to President Juan Domingo Perón, an army colonel who rose to power through a military coup.[2] Her husband appointed her to the vice presidency one year prior to his death as part of a deliberate succession plan (Weir 1993). Opponents questioned her legitimacy when she took over the presidency, arguing that governmental procedures did not provide for the vice president to succeed the president. She was ousted in a military coup less than two years later. Instability, therefore, factors into both Perón's ascension and her downfall; unstable contexts offer a mixed bag for women.

Violeta Chamorro, Nicaragua (April 1990–January 1997)

Other widows include Violeta Chamorro of Nicaragua. Her husband, activist Pedro Chamorro (the descendant of several former Nicaraguan presidents), opposed the Somoza military regime. Violeta Chamorro ascended to the presidency in 1988, a decade after her husband's assassination. She had limited political experience, having served only briefly in a junta. The United National Opposition (UNO), made up of factions sympathetic to and financially supported by the United States (Saint-Germain 1993a, 83), recruited her to run in the 1990 presidential election. Her supporters hoped that the widow of a popular political leader would unify competing blocs. Though initially hesitant, she entered the race and defeated incumbent president Daniel Ortega. Chamorro, therefore, unlike Perón, gained popular election. Chamorro's case illustrates that political elites sometimes mobilize women to enter the political game *because* of their family linkages.

Janet Jagan, Guyana (December 1997–August 1999)

Janet Jagan's independent political ambition and experience distinguishes her from early Latin American female presidents. She cofounded the People's Progressive Party (PPP) with her husband, Cheddi Jagan, and served as its general secretary from 1950 until 1970. A member of the House Assembly and a senator, she gained nearly forty years of experience prior to her presidency. Cheddi Jagan was elected president in 1992 and died of natural causes five years later. After seven months as interim prime minister, Janet Jagan gained the presidency in December 1997.[3] She resigned two years later for health reasons (Wilkinson 1999). Though Guyana provided a more stable environment than others discussed here, Jagan first entered the political scene through activism, gaining formal office subsequently.

Mireya Moscoso, Panama (September 1999–September 2004)

Panama's former president Arnulfo Arias died of natural causes in 1988 while in exile following a third ouster (Associated Press 1988).[4] His widow, Mireya Moscoso, led Partido Arnulfista for ten years, narrowly losing the 1995 presidential election. She proved successful, however, in her 1999 bid (Ortiz 1999). Male presidents in Panama have also benefited from family ties; Arnulfo Arias's brother, Harmodio, preceded him. Like Argentina and Nicaragua, Panama has had an unstable political history. Unlike Jagan, Moscoso acquired limited political experience prior to her husband's death, making her more akin to Perón and Chamorro.

Cristina Fernández, Argentina (December 2007–present)

More recently, Latin America has boasted very politically experienced female presidents possessing both family ties and independent political ambitions.

As such, they resemble Jagan more than Perón, Chamorro, or Moscoso. In 2007, Cristina Fernández became the second female president of Argentina.[5] She followed her husband, Néstor Kirchner, who declined a second term. Political observers asserted that the couple strategized alternating presidential terms (Rohter 2007a).[6] Kirchner reportedly played a leading role in economic policy and held the Perónist coalition together (Barrioneuvo 2010).This depiction, however, trivializes Fernández's experience as a Perónist party activist and regional and national politician (Piscopo 2010; Rohter 2007b). Many wondered how Kirchner's sudden death from a heart attack in October 2010 would affect his wife's reelection plans (Schweimler 2011), but she easily sailed to victory, attaining some of the highest vote totals in the country's history (Garlow 2011). Not only does Fernández's case reaffirm that family ties can coincide with independent political experience and ambition, but also she entered the presidency while her male relative lived, distinguishing her from all other cases of women executives with family ties.[7]

Michelle Bachelet, Chile (March 2006–March 2010)
Michelle Bachelet also gained extensive political experience prior to her election to Chile's presidency. Her father, air force general and Pinochet opponent Alberto Bachelet Martínez, died of heart failure during political imprisonment. Bachelet and her mother were also jailed for protesting the Pinochet regime, and they continued their prodemocratic activism upon their release. Bachelet entered institutionalized politics once Pinochet was toppled, serving as minister of health and then minister of defense before successfully running for the presidency (Franceschet and Thomas 2010). Academics and journalists rightly characterize her as a self-made politician (see Paxton and Hughes 2007; Thomas and Adams 2010). While we should not completely ignore her father's political significance, an important shift obviously took place in Latin America in 2006; women's previous dependence on family connections to achieve executive office eroded.

Explaining Women and Family Ties in Latin America
Why do familial ties present some women in Latin America with political opportunities? In addressing this question, it is helpful to link women's political empowerment to gendered cultural conceptions, particularly marianismo, the feminine counterpart of machismo. "Under this system, women derive their identities through their male relatives—fathers, brothers, husbands, and sons—and achieve their highest fulfillment as wives and mothers" (Saint-Germain 1993a, 77). Women otherwise unable to attain office thus may gain political promotion to further their husbands' political agendas. Since women derive their identities from men, they can use their ties to men to gain political advantage.

Marianismo derives from Catholicism, a religion traditionally confining to women. Several women executives, particularly in Latin America, have originated from majority-Catholic populations. Many of these leaders have actively engaged Catholic symbols, including the Virgin Mary, while campaigning for office. Violeta Chamorro is one example: "During the campaign, Violeta's image was modeled after that of the Virgin Mary. She was dressed in white with a simple gold crucifix to symbolize her almost mystical Catholicism.... Chamorro was introduced at political rallies as Nicaragua's 'Maria'" (Saint-Germain 1993a, 85). In Chamorro's (1996) own words:

> Why did I run? Because I was driven to fulfill my late husband Pedro's dreams that Nicaragua become a truly democratic republic. My metamorphosis—from mother and wife to widow of a slain opposition leader and finally ... to democratically elected president of a country—was the ultimate result of a series of unyielding acts of defiance against a military dictatorship. This defiance led to Pedro's assassination and propelled me as the custodian of Pedro's dream into the center of Nicaragua's political arena. (9)

Chamorro's rise to power fits squarely within marianismo ideology.

Marianismo simultaneously empowers and confines women. Although women may be afforded political roles, they do not play those roles for their own benefit. Similarly, the focus on the "moral superiority" of women, who act on behalf of the greater good, originates from traditional stereotypes of proper "masculine" and "feminine" roles. Related to marianismo, womanhood equates to motherhood. Idyllic women fuse spiritual strength and submissiveness (Craske 1999, 12). Though traditional gender divisions remain, political space opens to women. These same dynamics surface in women's engagement in social movements (Basu 2010). Bolivia's Housewives Committee formed in the 1970s to protest government plans to remove miners from their homes (Geske and Bourque 2001; Friedman 2010). Argentina's "Dirty War" similarly inspired women's activism in movements such as that of the Mothers of the Plaza de Mayo. Although the women in these movements participated on behalf of loved ones, many ultimately advocated their own interests as well.

FAMILY TIES: EDUCATION AND POLITICAL EXPERIENCE IN LATIN AMERICA

In drawing out some implications of family connections to power, it is worth mentioning that women political leaders with family ties repeatedly face scrutiny by the media and the public regarding their ambitions and credentials (Murray 2010b). In order to gauge the legitimacy of arguments about qualifications,

I compare the educational backgrounds and political experience of this subgroup of women executives to those of their immediate male predecessors.

Only two of six women executives (33 percent) with family ties accumulated low levels of education, the same quantity as male predecessors. Another two (33 percent) attained college degrees. A greater percentage of men (67 percent) than women (33 percent) come to power having earned the highest levels of education.[8]

Four women (67 percent) entered executive office with high degrees of political experience. As such, they were politically active in their own right, independent of their male relatives. Perón and Chamorro, in contrast, possessed very limited political experience (representing 33 percent of the total). All male predecessors obtained the highest credentials. Claims of women's lower qualifications for executive posts largely lack grounding, particularly in regard to women who have entered positions more recently. Perhaps most interesting is that more women devoid of familial ties are gaining the presidency in Latin America as of late.

The Erosion of Family Ties in Latin America?

The addition of women executives absent family ties is evident in Laura Chinchilla's election to the Costa Rican presidency in 2010. Though Chinchilla lacks familial ties as defined here, her father, Rafael Ángel Chinchilla Fallas, served as the national comptroller. As vice president, she was handpicked and mentored for the presidency by outgoing President Óscar Arias (Campbell 2010). Although Costa Rica is relatively stable, Chinchilla benefited from the fallout that occurred following the investigations of three former presidents for corruption. She successfully constructed a campaign highlighting her scrupulousness, which was especially convincing given her father's reputation as honest.[9]

While she gained power after the time period examined in this book, Dilma Rousseff of Brazil further illustrates the broadening pathways for Latin American female presidents beyond kinship connections. Like many women leaders, however, Rousseff fits the political activist category. Both Chinchilla and Rousseff utilized their relationships to outgoing presidents (Arias and Luiz Inácio Lula da Silva, respectively) and thus still relied on male connections.

As more women absent family connections and within more stable political settings gain ground, we may ask the questions *why now* and *to what effect*? Perhaps women executives with family ties make the presidency appear less "masculine" and more accessible to other women. Female descriptive representatives defy the dominant characteristics commonly associated with officeholders (Mansbridge 1999). This chips away at perceptions held by the public and party elites of politics as a men-only club (Sapiro 1981), creating opportunities for women who have no family ties. I speculate here and call for more research explaining the increasing variation in backgrounds of women leaders in Latin America.

Family Ties in Asia

Familial ties also surface in the backgrounds of South and Southeast Asian women leaders and remain salient as of late. To gain nonsymbolic offices, women still require family connections. More recent cases, however, suggest that kinship coincides with strong political credentials. Nine of ten (90 percent) female leaders from South Asia and Southeast Asia possess family links (see Table 6.1).[10] I briefly analyze them below in chronological order.

Sirimavo Bandaranaike, Sri Lanka (July 1960–March 1965; May 1970–July 1977; November 1994–August 2000)

Sri Lanka's Sirimavo Bandaranaike was married to Prime Minister Solomon Bandaranaike (Opfell 1993, 4). After his assassination in 1959, members of his party, the Sri Lankan Freedom Party (SLFP), approached her to run in the 1960 elections. She did not readily agree to participate but campaigned on the party's behalf, ultimately becoming SLFP's head. She lacked a formal political seat, but the governor-general appointed her to parliament so she could lawfully compete in upcoming elections, which SLFP eventually won (Opfell 1993, 7). Along with family ties, an unstable environment and elite recruitment facilitated her rise as premier.

After she lost a confidence vote in 1965, Sirimavo Bandaranaike led the opposition. However, she regained the prime ministership in 1970. She also served as the minister of planning and economic affairs and as the minister of defense and foreign affairs. In 1978, Sri Lanka established a presidential dominance system to alleviate ethnic tensions between the government and Sinhalese Tamils; opponents saw Bandaranaike as incapable of bringing about cross-ethnic unity. Charged with abuse of power for delaying the 1975–1977 elections, she lost her parliamentary seat in 1980 and was prohibited from running for president in 1983. Three years later, she ran for the presidency but lost. She eventually regained her parliamentary seat in 1989, and her daughter (President Chandrika Kumaratunga) appointed her prime minister in 1994 (Liswood 1995, 8). Bandaranaike resigned in August 2000 and died the following October (BBC News 2000).

Indira Gandhi, India (January 1966–March 1977; January 1980–October 1984)

Indira Gandhi arose to become India's prime minister shortly after Bandaranaike's first term ended. Her father, Jawaharlal Nehru, served as prime minister of India following partition with Pakistan. During India's struggle for self-government from Great Britain, Indira Gandhi and her family participated in the All India Congress Committee and faced detention at various points in

Table 6-1. WOMEN EXECUTIVES AND FAMILY TIES

Country	Woman Executive	Position	Relationship	Male Leader	Position
Bangladesh	K. Zia	Prime Minister	Husband	Z. Rahman	President
	H. Hasina	Prime Minister	Father	M. Rahman	Prime Minister
India	I. Gandhi	Prime Minister	Father	J. Nehru	Prime Minister
Indonesia	M. Sukarnoputri	President	Father	K. Sukarno	President
Pakistan	B. Bhutto	Prime Minister	Father	A. Bhutto	President and Prime Minister
Philippines	C. Aquino	President	Husband	B. Aquino	Opposition Leader
	G. Macapagal-Arroyo	President	Father	D. Macapagal	President
Sri Lanka	S. Bandaranaike	Prime Minister	Husband	S. Bandaranaike	Prime Minister
			Daughter	C. Kumaratunga	President
	C. Kumaratunga	President	Father	S. Bandaranaike	Prime Minister
			Mother	S. Bandaranaike	Prime Minister
Argentina	I. Perón	President	Husband	J. Perón	President
	C. Fernández	President	Husband	N. Kirchner	President
Chile	M. Bachelet	President	Father	A. Martínez	Opposition Leader
Guyana	J. Jagan	President	Husband	C. Jagan	President
Nicaragua	V. Chamorro	President	Husband	P. Chamorro	Opposition Leader
Panama	M. Moscoso	President	Husband	A. Arias	President

SOURCES: BBC News profiles, Council of Women World Leaders, *New York Times* profiles, World Political Leaders, and numerous biographies listed in the references as well as information from embassies cited in text endnotes.

time. After India gained independence, she forged a career in party politics and gained the Congress Party presidency, though only briefly, in 1959 (Gandhi 1980, 74).[11]

Nehru, in very poor health, ceded some political responsibilities to his daughter (Opfell 1993, 24) but did not plan for her to succeed him. Rather, her recruitment as prime minister stemmed from the political calculations of Congress Party elites. According to Everett (1993), "Congress President Kamaraj orchestrated Mrs. Gandhi's selection as prime minister because he perceived her to be weak enough that he and other regional party bosses could control her, yet strong enough to beat Desai in party elections because of the high regard for her father" (110).

Gandhi was often criticized for her heavy-handed governance. In 1975, India's High Court ruled that Gandhi's reelection in 1971 stemmed from electoral fraud. Rather than step down, Gandhi declared a state of emergency during which she initiated economic development programs and reduced inflation. However, many of her policies were oppressive (Kohli 1990). After free elections, Gandhi lost her parliamentary seat, although she returned to power in 1980 and governed until her assassination in 1984 by Sikh extremists.

The Nehru family legacy facilitated Indira Gandhi's rise, but she exhibited more political ambition and experience than many of her counterparts in this study. While her male relative did not orchestrate her succession, party elites utilized her family connections as a means of preserving power and unifying factions.

Corazon Aquino, Philippines (February 1986–June 1992)

Corazon Aquino was the first woman to gain executive office in Southeast Asia. President Ferdinand Marcos imprisoned Corazon Aquino's husband, Benigno Aquino, a political activist and de facto opposition leader, on subversion charges from 1972 through 1980. During his imprisonment, Benigno Aquino continued to oppose Marcos (Col 1993, 23). His family went into exile in the United States after his release (Komisar 1987), and upon their return in 1983 in anticipation of parliamentary elections, Benigno Aquino was assassinated (Opfell 1993, 134).[12]

Corazon Aquino, like Sirimavo Bandaranaike, immediately began working on behalf of opposition party candidates. Having won parliamentary seats, many of these figures asked her to run for president. "Corazon set two conditions for accepting the challenge: Marcos ... must call quick presidential elections, and she must see 1 million signatures endorsing her candidacy" (Opfell 1993, 134). She subsequently defeated Marcos in 1986. Marcos still declared himself president, however, triggering massive strikes and a "bloodless" coup (Col 1993, 25). Numerous Marcos loyalists remained in the military following his exile, and their opposition plagued Aquino's entire presidency. Like Violeta Chamorro and Sirimavo Bandaranaike, Corazon Aquino had never aspired to power or attained political office before her husband's death.

Benazir Bhutto, Pakistan (December 1988–August 1990; October 1993–November 1996)

Benazir Bhutto was the daughter of former president and prime minister of Pakistan Zulfikar Ali Bhutto. Benazir Bhutto, the eldest of four, returned from her oversees postgraduate studies just prior to her father's execution by General Zia-ul-Haq's military regime (Anderson 1993, 47).[13] She became her father's spokesperson and aide during his imprisonment. "Nusrat Bhutto [her mother] had become nominal head of the PPP [Pakistan People's Party] but it was always understood that Benazir would take over" (Opfell 1993, 146). Benazir Bhutto and her mother were imprisoned several times for their antigovernment protests. Even though Zulfikar Ali Bhutto had two adult sons, as her father's closest adviser, Benazir Bhutto became the heir apparent (Bhutto 1989).[14]

She worked as the newly appointed head of the PPP from England because Zia prohibited opposition parties. When this ban was lifted in 1986, she returned to Pakistan and campaigned for the PPP (Liswood 1995, 10). Zia died in a plane crash shortly before the 1988 elections. In those elections, the PPP won the most seats, although not a majority, resulting in Benazir Bhutto's prime ministership. President Ishaq Khan, however, dismissed her in 1990 on corruption charges (Liswood 1995, 10). When new elections were soon held, the PPP won only forty-five seats (Anderson 1993, 66). Bhutto remained in the National Assembly as the opposition leader and began a second prime ministerial term in 1993. President Farooq Ahmad Khan Leghari, however, discharged her in 1996, again on corruption charges (Burns 2007).[15]

After living in exile for more than ten years, Bhutto secured reentry to Pakistan in 2007 in the hope of achieving a power-sharing arrangement with President Pervez Musharraf. Most speculated that her party would handily win a majority of seats, positioning her as prime minister for a third term. After Bhutto was assassinated following a campaign rally in December 2007, her husband, Asif Zardari, assumed command of the PPP. Upon President Musharraf's resignation in August 2008, Zardari successfully ran for the presidency the following September.[16]

Sheikh Hasina, Bangladesh (June 1996–July 2001; January 2009–present)

Although Sheikh Hasina came to power after the installation of the first female prime minister of Bangladesh, Khaleda Zia, I discuss her now because her father, Mujibur Rahman, served as premier immediately after Bangladesh achieved independence from Pakistan. The narratives of both Hasina and Zia might be better understood in this order. After being installed as prime minister, Rahman pronounced himself president with absolute powers and banned all opposition parties (Opfell 1993, 194).While Hasina and her sister were in West Germany, their father, mother, three brothers, uncle, and cousin were assassinated. Hasina remained outside the country until she was elected leader of her father's party, the Awami League. Before these tragic events unfolded, her political rise seemed unexpected.

Upon her return to Bangladesh in 1981, Hasina assumed the role of opposition leader, and she was jailed a number of times while advocating for democratic processes. She refused to compete in the 1991 elections that brought Khaleda Zia and the Bangladesh National Party (BNP) to power. Hasina's first prime ministerial term commenced in 1996, when the Awami League gained a majority (BBC News 2011). She served until 2001, at which time Khaleda Zia regained power (CNN 2001). Hasina survived an assassination attempt in 2004 that claimed the lives of twenty Awami League members (Herman 2008). As clashes between the Awami League and the BNP escalated, the military enacted emergency rule, arresting leaders of both parties for corruption. Imprisoned during an emergency period in 2008, Hasina gained release after eleven months and subsequently ended the political stalemate between her and the caretaker government (Herman 2008).[17] Hasina reclaimed the prime ministership in 2009 (Adams 2011). Tensions between the BNP and the Awami League remain, however (Alam 2012).

KHALEDA ZIA, BANGLADESH (MARCH 1991–MARCH 1996; OCTOBER 2001–OCTOBER 29, 2006)

Khaleda Zia's husband, Ziaur Rahman, was a military general who took over the presidency after Mujibur Rahman's assassination in 1977.[18] After initially ruling under emergency powers, he gained election in 1978 (Opfell 1993, 192). Two years after the BNP won the parliamentary elections of 1979, he was slain (Library of Congress 1988). Evidence does not suggest that he groomed his wife to succeed him (Opfell 1993).[19]

In 1984, during military rule, the BNP elected Khaleda Zia as party chair (Liswood 1995, 41). Like Hasina, she was arrested for protesting military rule. The BNP emerged victorious in 1991, although this is largely because opposition parties, including the Awami League, refused to compete. Khaleda Zia thus became the first female prime minister of Bangladesh.[20] She led the opposition following her electoral defeat by the Awami League in 1996 but regained the premiership in 2001. The Awami League refused to recognize the election results, although international observers largely deemed the election fair. Throughout her second term, the Awami League protested Zia's government through regular strikes. Upon the conclusion of her second term, emergency rule resumed in Bangladesh for two years. Khaleda Zia was arrested on corruption charges in 2007, but, like Hasina, she gained release in 2008 (US Department of State 2010). Most recently, BNP activists have been protesting the disappearance of party members since Hasina's return to the premiership (Alam 2012).[21]

Although neither Hasina nor Khaleda Zia held formal offices until the deaths of their relatives, they both gained high levels of political experience before becoming prime ministers. Furthermore, despite their political differences, both pressed for democratic transition (Opfell 1993, 197). Political parties recruited them *because* of their family connections. Finally, they arose in politically unstable environments.

Chandrika Kumaratunga, Sri Lanka (November 1994– November 2005)

The presidency of Chandrika Kumaratunga, the daughter of Sirimavo and Solomon Bandaranaike, likewise occurred through family connections. At the same time, however, Kumaratunga evinced independent ambition. She and her husband, Vijaya Kumaratunga, were political activists and party leaders (BBC World Service). She attained high levels of political experience in executive positions, including director of the Land Reforms Commission. Kumaratunga left Sri Lanka briefly after her husband's assassination in 1988. Upon her return in 1991, she successfully organized a new coalition, ascending first to the prime ministership and then to the presidency three months later. She appointed her mother, Sirimavo Bandaranaike, to her last prime ministerial term (BBC News 2005a). Chandrika Kumaratunga gained reelection in 1999; she retired in 2005 due to term limits (BBC News 2005a).

Gloria Macapagal-Arroyo, Philippines (January 2001–June 2010)

Gloria Macapagal-Arroyo's father, Diosdado Macapagal, served as president of the Philippines from 1961 to 1965.[22] Although certainly advantaged by her father's name, she completed two Senate terms and held executive appointments under President Corazon Aquino. She won the vice presidency in 1998, boasting the largest mandate in Filipino history. Frequently clashing with President Joseph Estrada, she formed a shadow cabinet.[23] Upon Estrada's impeachment for corruption in 2001, Macapagal-Arroyo ascended to the presidency.

As president, she continued to battle with Estrada sympathizers, many of whom demanded her resignation. Ethnic and religious conflicts proved pervasive, and incidents of terrorism increased. After gaining election in a very contentious race in 2004, she survived several military coups and three impeachment proceedings (Conde 2010). The military protected her from opposition parties once she adhered to their demands. The general public, however, pressed for her resignation (Associated Press 2008b). She held on until she completed her second term and currently serves in the Philippine Congress.

MEGAWATI SUKARNOPUTRI, INDONESIA (JULY 2001–OCTOBER 2004)

Megawati Sukarnoputri's father, Sukarno (born Kusno Sosrodihardjo), success-fully led the Indonesian independence struggle against the Dutch. Sukarno tried to unite the country under a constituent assembly, but regional and factional differences plagued the newly autonomous country. He assumed full power as a dictator in 1963, declaring himself president for life. General Suharto removed him two years later in a military coup. Placed under house arrest in 1968, Sukarno died of natural causes in 1970 (McIntyre 1997, 7).

Unlike the pattern seen in many other cases presented here, in this case polit-ical parties failed to approach the Sukarno family to ask any of the members to run for office until years after Kusno Sukarno's death. In 1986, the Indonesian Democratic Party (Partai Demokrasi Indonesia, or PDI), linked to Sukarno's Indonesian National Party, opened talks with the Sukarnos, hoping "that such family involvement would affirm the PDI's pro-Sukarno orientation.... Sukarno existed as an idealized figure and increasingly a symbol of opposi-tion to President Suharto" (McIntyre 1997, 8). Enough time had passed to ele-vate Sukarno's status, especially among the nation's youth. Sukarnoputri (whose children were already grown) entered as a PDI candidate along with her hus-band. Her siblings, an older brother and two younger sisters, however, did not throw their hats into the ring. In fact, many would have preferred for her brother, Guntur, to run (McIntyre 1997, 9). Nonetheless, forces rallied behind her. Like Benazir Bhutto, Megawati Sukarnoputri was her father's closest adviser, and thus a fitting political heir (McIntyre 1997, 7).

Sukarnoputri gained a great deal of parliamentary experience, becoming head of the PDI in 1993. Feeling threatened, Suharto removed her from this position in 1996, sparking public outrage and leading her to form the PDI-P.[24] In 1998, Suharto finally resigned, providing an opening for parties to compete in free, though indirect, elections.[25] In 1999, the PDI-P won a plurality and Sukarnoputri ran for president. She reportedly gained the most votes (Sirry 2006, 477), but the parliament instead appointed Abdurrahman Wahid, a Muslim cleric, to the presidency. Wahid successfully mobilized Muslim parties against a female presidential candidacy, though they were willing to elect her vice president (Sirry 2006, 477). She succeeded Wahid after his impeachment in 2001. The first direct president election was held in July 2004. Because the winner lacked a majority vote, Sukarnoputri, who ranked second, participated in a runoff election in September 2004. She subsequently lost, and her third run in 2009 likewise proved unsuccessful (*Economist* 2009).

Explaining Women and Family Ties in Asia

How can we explain the ways in which Asian women leaders rise? Similar to their Latin American counterparts, Asian women who ascend to executive positions symbolize their fathers or husbands and essentially serve as "leaseholders of patriarchal power" (McIntyre 1997, 1). Parties tap women for leadership positions when their male relatives are assassinated or imprisoned. As Thompson (2002–2003) observes, "Female relations of martyred male politicians were best able to unite political factions because their leadership was seen as largely symbolic" (545). The public and party elites may sometimes prefer female to male candidates because they perceive women as more malleable. They presume that women who benefit from a political legacy will yield authority to male actors. In contrast, they view men as independently politically ambitious. In reality, few women with familial ties cede power to men. Indira Gandhi presided over a male "syndicate" that capitalized on her family relations while stifling her (Everett 1993, 110). In turn, Gandhi refused to surrender power. Still, we cannot ignore the expectation that she serve as placeholder, since it hastened her rise.

As in Latin America, Asian women leaders within Catholic countries can utilize confining religious gendered ideologies to gain political empowerment. Aquino of the Philippines convincingly characterized herself "as almost a Madonna, a saint in contrast to the wily, corrupt Marcos" (Richter, cited in Col 1993, 24). Outside Catholic contexts, Bartholomeusz (1999) argues that although in Asian countries women are traditionally perceived as subordinate to men, Buddhism venerates women as mothers. She notes: "Kumaratunga's motherhood was so conspicuous a part of her political campaign. Public portrayals of her stressed her motherly traits, including her abilities to mother all and to see the connections between the ethnic groups of the island" (211). Islam also glorifies the role of women as mothers (Ahmed 1992). Benazir Bhutto argued for women's empowerment by mentioning that the Prophet Muhammad was born to a woman (Thompson 2002–2003). We can still identify, however, limits to women's empowerment. Islamic parties attacked both Benazir Bhutto and Megawati Sukarnoputri for their perceived transgressions against gendered codes of behavior. In response to accusations that it would be improper for a single woman to be on the campaign trail with men, Benazir Bhutto accepted an arranged marriage (Anderson 1993). Perhaps most glaringly, Islamic interpretations deeming women ineligible for the presidency restricted Bhutto's and Sukarnoputri's access to this position (see Chapter 4). Thus, the effects of religion on women's political rise appear both contradictory and complex.

Family Ties: Education and Political Experience in Asia

Like their Latin American counterparts, Asian women from political families are often cast in a negative light. Common accusations are that these women are merely symbols or political lightweights, yet they are still venerated by the Western press (Sardar 1998). Referring to Megawati Sukarnoputri, Mohamad (1996) states: "Suppose she was not the daughter of Bung Karno, she wouldn't be any one at all: only a housewife with simple thoughts" (2).

To test the validity of these claims, I compare eight of the nine Asian female leaders to their male predecessors.[26] Four women attained a low level of education and another four achieved a medium level (44 percent each, or 88 percent). Only one amassed a high degree of education.[27] Of their male predecessors, one had a low level of education (13 percent), four had a medium level (50 percent), and three had a high level (38 percent). These women's male predecessors, therefore, appear to possess stronger educational credentials. While the education gap favors men, many women executives, particularly those holding office more recently, boast strong educational backgrounds.

More directly related to the criticisms posed, the vast majority of Asian women with family ties accumulated extensive political experience. Having gained experience in formal and informal capacities, six (67 percent) were categorized as attaining a high level of experience and one (11 percent) as achieving a medium level of experience. As mentioned throughout the short narratives above, political contexts sometimes hindered women's abilities to hold political office. While some failed to mobilize politically until the deaths of their influential relatives, they generally acquired experience before entering executive posts. Only two women (22 percent) lacked prior political involvement. Rather than the rule, Aquino and Bandaranaike are the exceptions. All male predecessors obtained high levels of political experience before gaining presidencies and prime ministerships, almost always as members of parliament or the cabinet. Yet criticisms regarding women's backgrounds appear largely unfounded; they may stem more from general beliefs about women's lack of capacity than from reality. Women executives with family links still exhibit impressive qualifications; the ascension to executive posts of women who lack educational and political credentials is a relic of the past.

THE CONTINUATION OF FAMILY TIES IN SOUTH AND SOUTHEAST ASIA

While women executives with family ties in South and Southeast Asia increasingly appear politically proficient, kinship connections remain an unofficial qualification for gaining more powerful executive offices. In contrast, female presidents in Latin America boast independent credentials, and presidential office no longer appears limited to relatives of former leaders. The latest woman to ascend in Southeast Asia, Yingluck Shinawatra, prime minister of Thailand, hails from a political family. Her brother, Thaksin Shinawatra, held the post before her but was ousted in a military coup four years before her rise. Harkening back to previous patterns, Yingluck Shinawatra lacked political experience

(Sidner 2011).[28] Why is the glass ceiling firmly intact when it comes to women who are devoid of family connections? Again, I call for more research.

COMPARING MEN'S AND WOMEN'S RELIANCE ON FAMILY TIES

Chapter 5 identified a significant number of women presidents who held dominant power within their systems. Among these thirteen cases, ten possessed familial ties. Exceptions include the popularly elected Ellen Johnson Sirleaf (Liberia) and Laura Chinchilla (Costa Rica) and the appointed Roza Otunbayeva (Kyrgyzstan).[29] Put differently, 78 percent of all female dominant presidents have family ties. Women's reliance on kinship connections decreases in correspondence with their powers. For example, none of the eight weak women presidents have family linkages. Four of the twenty-three dominant women prime ministers (23 percent) possess family connections. Finally, only one weak woman prime minister of sixteen has family linkages. Therefore, even with the broadening paths in Latin America, women who attain dominant presidential positions still generally possess kinship ties. Still, do women executives, in comparison with their male counterparts, rely disproportionately on family connections to executive power?

Compared with their immediate male predecessors, a greater percentage of women who gain executive power come from political families (see Chapter 5). Of course, these samples may not always afford comparability. I therefore enlarge the scope to include male leaders more broadly, rather than only the small number who have preceded female leaders.[30]

Being a relative of a former prime minister or president qualifies one as having a family tie.[31] Relatives include parents/children, spouses, siblings, cousins, uncles, aunts, nephews, and nieces. At least forty-five countries have witnessed men with familial ties coming to power as presidents or prime ministers.[32] In contrast to the female sample, the geographic areas in which male relatives arise appear more varied and include the Caribbean, Europe, Africa, Asia, the Middle East, North America, and Latin America (see Table A.2 in the appendix).

Women have served in executive posts in eleven of these forty-five countries, but only five of them possessed family ties.[33] Therefore, men and women may benefit from kinship connections in the same countries, but not necessarily. Although at least seventy-three different familial relationships exist within the forty-five countries, only three men succeeded female relatives.[34] Even in these three cases, their female kin were first the political heirs of men. Therefore, though family links sometimes pass from women to men, they still originate from male leaders.

The number of male leaders possessing family ties to power is greater than the quantity of female beneficiaries: seventy-three and fifteen, respectively. One-quarter of the total cases of women leaders, however, enjoy family connections. Of course, it is impossible to provide an exact count of all male leaders throughout history. Still, it is possible to approximate the proportion of men dependent on kinship connections based on the following facts:

1. In June 2011, of the 262 executive officeholders, 21 (8 percent) were women.[35]
2. More women leaders were in office in 2011 than in any previous year.
3. The first woman executive ascended in 1960.

If even only one hundred different male executives ruled annually between 1960 and 2011, the proportion of male beneficiaries of kinship connections amounts to a mere 1 percent.[36] Of course, this rough approximation *overestimates* men's kinship connections; only men occupied presidencies and prime ministerships prior to 1960. Therefore, though familial ties benefit men, women disproportionately rely on this route to power.

A CLOSER LOOK AT POLITICAL ACTIVISTS

The other pattern that surfaced in the previous chapter centered on the salience of activist backgrounds for women executives. More than one-third of women leaders gained experience as political activists (see Table 5.6). In fact, both activism and family links have frequently formed women executives' backstories. Women's relations have regularly mobilized them. Some scholars assert that activism draws women into politics during independence movements from colonial powers (Richter 1991; Katzenstein 1978). Their inclusion is not always for their own advancement but out of practical necessity. For example, women might assist male activists by cooking, sewing, and performing other grunt work. Still, the opening of real political space to women, especially ones from political families, occasionally results.

Through socialization in nationalist movements, girls within more confining cultures are sometimes afforded a degree of personal control, eventually culminating in their rise to power as women (Hodson 1997, 37). Indira Gandhi (1980) wrote of her experiences as a young child participating in the Indian homespun movement, which sought to eliminate dependence on foreign products by encouraging the production of goods at home.[37] As part of the Monkey Brigade, a children's organization, she aided the independence cause by sewing and hanging national flags, cooking for marchers, writing letters for prisoners, and providing first aid to activists injured by police. Her family connections to independence leaders no doubt encouraged her activity. Since colonial authorities frequently imprisoned family members, Gandhi's childhood often lacked traditional structure; taken together, gendered expectations did not impede her as they might have otherwise.

Similar mobilization dynamics manifest when segments of the population challenge an oppressive government within an independent state. While women have participated in democratic movements (see Alvarez 1990), they have rarely moved into leadership posts during and after transition (Waylen 1996). Constraints on women's power appear most evident following "pacted transitions" negotiated by the opposition and regime elites (Thompson 2002–2003, 535). Yet Asian women have repeatedly stood at the forefront of democratic revolutions toppling dictators and then have gone on to hold formal political offices (Thompson 2002–2003, 536). Of course, these women were not just anyone; they were daughters and wives of former leaders, as previously discussed. Female political activists, however, do not always possess family linkages to power, and they may arrive on the scene more generally within political transitions.

Political Transitions

In a more general sense, large quantities of women leaders arise amid political transitions and within unstable contexts. Utilizing the Polity IV database, country reports, and leader biographies, I examine whether particular countries underwent political transitions at the time of women's rise. I also assess whether the countries were politically unstable (defined as undergoing a major transition between 1945 and the year a woman came to power) and whether military coups or takeovers ever occurred there. As stated throughout this book, such circumstances allow for frequent political vacuums, sometimes facilitating women's promotion as unifiers in times of strife. Since women do not occupy powerful military posts from which they plot coups, military takeovers do not directly benefit them. Military seizures, however, sometimes advantage women during the subsequent transitions to civilian rule.

At least twelve of the sixty-three women in this sample (19 percent) entered during political transitions, several during shifts to democratic governance in places as diverse as Bangladesh, the Philippines, and Lithuania. Again, this number includes only nontemporary leaders; when interim executives are added, the number increases to twenty-one (27 percent)[38] At least twenty-five women (40 percent) entered contexts with histories of political instability, twenty-one where military takeovers had occurred (33 percent). Women leaders, again, do not seize power directly through coups. Stereotyped as consensual actors, women rise through peaceful democratic transitions.

Among these, European women ascending in the aftermath of communism are gaining ground as of late. This sample includes Vīķe-Freiberga (Latvia), Prunskienė and Grybauskaitė (Lithuania), Suchocka (Poland), Tymoshenko (Ukraine), and Greceanîi (Moldova). Scores of additional Eastern European women have also overseen political transitions. For example, Burdzhanadze led Georgia transitionally following that country's rigged 2004 elections.[39]

Many African women leaders, such as Kinigi of Burundi and Uwilingiyimana of Rwanda, arose within extremely volatile and violent contexts (Hill 1996a, 1996b). Johnson Sirleaf of Liberia, unlike her female predecessors, gained popular election to a presidential post. While familial ties cannot explain her rise, instability does. Decades earlier she narrowly escaped death when all but four of President William Tolbert's cabinet ministers were executed following Samuel Doe's coup (Kosciejew 2012).[40] Johnson Sirleaf protested Doe's presidency and went into exile from 1985 to 1987. In 1989, Charles Taylor led a military coup against Doe and subsequently executed him; civil war ensued. From 1989 to 1996, Liberia experienced complete state failure, characterized by extreme violence (Moran 2008). The Council of State, a six-person collective presidency led by Ruth Perry, governed during a temporary peace agreement (Jackson-Laufer 1999). Johnson Sirleaf, again in exile, returned to Liberia to compete in the 1997 presidential election, which she lost to Taylor; violence resumed shortly thereafter.

Women's groups proved to be a very strong force in Charles Taylor's removal and the subsequent peace reconciliation. These organizations maintained high levels of activity at the same time others significantly diminished their involvement (Bauer 2009). Johnson Sirleaf's victory also coincided with the most open electoral environment in decades (Harris 2006). Of course, we must not overlook Johnson Sirleaf's credentials and campaign strategies. Her experience in both the private and public sectors validated her expertise on "masculine" issues (Adams 2010, 161). She also took on stereotypically "masculine" traits to challenge the men responsible for war and corruption (Adams 2010), yet she repeatedly noted that her "feminine" traits, such as honesty and compassion, also qualified her for the presidency. In this way, she embodied the mother of a suffering nation, much as her Latin American and Asian counterparts have done (Thompson 2002–2003).

Of course, women operating within largely stable and peaceful contexts take advantage of critical openings that occur suddenly when male elites become embroiled in scandals or suffer major election upsets. Margaret Thatcher, Angela Merkel, and Gro Harlem Brundtland all benefited from unexpected power vacuums. The same male-dominated networks that had excluded women insulated these seasoned female politicians from such indignities (Beckwith 2010b). Election shocks also sometimes allow for political openings from which women may benefit, since the few unblemished high-quality male contenders may not contest in hopes of ensuring a better chance of victory at a future point (Beckwith 2010b). While family ties, activism, and political instability all play distinct roles, they tend to connect the stories of many women who successfully gain executive office.

CONCLUSIONS

This chapter illustrates the importance of the opening of political opportunities to women's leadership, often in times of crises and instability. Family ties permit some women to overcome traditional gender barriers to executive office. Stereotypically associated with the traits of nurturing, consensus seeking, and dependence, women selectively exploit traditional gender roles to promote both unity (Saint-Germain 1993a) and their own political gain. Women with politically important family names can capitalize simultaneously on their connections and on a number of positive gender stereotypes. Although, as I have outlined, several constraints work against women's ascension to executive office, women can overcome some of these hurdles, particularly within politically unstable contexts, frequently ones where kinship ties play decisive roles in power succession. In such contexts, where executive office voids are most likely to occur, some women—almost exclusively those with influential family ties— rise to the presidency or premiership.

Of course, we cannot ignore the tenuousness of this path. While some women have toppled dictatorships, their own political downfalls have occurred soon after. Many have encountered sexist attitudes and beliefs that they were unqualified and controllable. While transitions to democracy may form the backdrops of women's rise, consolidation has often proved difficult. Some women executives have been subject to criticism that rather than being genuinely concerned with ushering in a democratic era, they have pursued their own dynastic interests (Thompson 2002–2003, 540).

In other countries, while political families may not play important roles, struggles for independence or democracy routinely involve women's contributions, ultimately leading to their integration into formal political positions. Furthermore, executive posts investing a large degree of authority appear attainable only for women who exploit these factors, thus overcoming traditional opposition to their inclusion.

In light of the narratives highlighted in this chapter, how far have women really come in their struggles to obtain executive positions? Findings suggest mixed progress. In a positive vein, women can gain national leadership posts. However, in South and Southeast Asia, and to a lesser extent Latin America, women with family ties are generally the *only* women ascending to executive office; men continue to dominate presidencies and premierships.

Men in these areas as well as other regions occasionally benefit from these ties as well. More often than not, however, men do not depend solely on these same connections or unstable environments for success. As seen in Chapter 5, women experience the added burden of amassing experience within traditional political institutions after their entry through nonconventional routes. The dominant pathways to power are still set by male-defined models. Individual women's exploitation of gender constructions to gain empowerment illustrates the advantages of certain female stereotypes at the same time it reifies the meanings of womanhood. Overall, though some women successfully utilize alternative routes to power, men overwhelmingly dominate executive offices. Therefore, in spite of the rising numbers of women executives, we should question women's ultimate progress in achieving powerful positions.

A Statistical Analysis of Women's Rule

Thus far, I have identified a number of institutional, structural, cultural, histori-cal, and global factors connected to women's breaking through the executive glass ceiling. This chapter develops and tests a comprehensive model of these condi-tions that offers two important benefits: first, the model expands the scope of the discussion to include countries where the glass ceiling appears firmly intact; and second, it rigorously evaluates the relationships among many variables first dis-cerned from largely qualitative analyses previously described in this book.[1]

I now focus on nearly all autonomous countries in the world, rather than just those where women have successfully come to power. Including these countries reduces the critical problem of selection bias, a lack of variation on the depend-ent variable (King, Keohane, and Verba 1994), and permits a more thorough comprehension of conditions linked to women's advancement or lack thereof.

The second contribution of this chapter, the statistical analysis, links to its time frame—2000 through 2010. Because so few countries at any single moment feature women leaders, this range of years provides more cases than any other decade. While analyzing an eleven-year stretch may be ambitious, focusing on only one year greatly undercuts the diversity of countries where women come to power and may not be representative of larger patterns of women's rule (Hughes and Paxton 2007). Substantial quantities of data on non-Western countries have become available only recently. Also, investigating a period when larger numbers of women governed makes quantitative analysis possible and interpretations more meaningful. I do not extend the analysis even farther back than 2000, however, because countries may have altered their political institutions and processes over time and data are more limited.

Having identified several conditions as relevant to women's promotion to executive office in previous chapters, I incorporate variables into a logistical regression model to verify their statistical associations with women executives while controlling for other factors. These include the institutional, structural, cultural, and historical variables identified as important to women's attainment of executive office in other portions of the analysis.

This data set integrates 147 countries. I exclude nonautonomous states, hereditary monarchies, military dictatorships or juntas, and one-party communist states because executive office cannot be contested in these contexts. I exclude others, frequently very small countries, owing to issues of data availability.[2] Since the model extends back through 2000, countries may be omitted because they were ineligible for any of the four reasons noted above during this time frame. For example, East Timor lacked autonomy until 2002, resulting in its exclusion. State demise during this time frame also warrants elimination. For instance, Serbia and Montenegro, previously part of Yugoslavia, existed from 2003 to 2006 before its separation into two republics. Bahrain's premiership has been open to challenge only since 2006.

Though exceptions exist, the statistical findings generally reinforce the main arguments made throughout this book. Though women have made tremendous strides in attaining executive office, these positions are still occupied almost exclusively by men. While the period of 2000 through 2010 showed the greatest gains in history for women executives, women led only thirty-two countries, or 22 percent of the contexts analyzed. Moreover, many of these female leaders held fairly nominal powers.

VARIABLE CODING AND HYPOTHESES

The dependent variable, Executive Sex, assesses whether a country had a woman president or prime minister in power between 2000 and 2010 (1 = yes, 0 = otherwise). She may have entered her post prior to this time frame, though would have likely done so in the late 1990s. To remain consistent with other portions of the analysis, I exclude acting or interim leaders because they tend to serve for very short periods of time and, more important, do not come to power through traditional channels.

Institutional Variables

Independent variables include a number of institutional factors.

Dual Executive assesses whether the country has both a prime minister and a president (1 = dual, 0 = unified). In dual-executive systems, women's odds of promotion increase, since twice as many positions are in play. In such systems, the more diffused nature of executive institutions affords women a weaker base of power than in unified structures.

Hypothesis 1: Women executives will be positively associated with countries utilizing dual-executive systems.

Government Type, coded as a series of dummy variables, corresponds with the five systems developed in Chapter 3:

1. *Presidential*: unified presidential system (1 = yes, 0 = otherwise)
2. *Dominant President*: dual-executive system with a dominant president and weak prime minister (1 = yes, 0 = otherwise)
3. *Parliamentary*: unified parliamentary system (1 = yes, 0 = otherwise)
4. *Powerful President*: dual-executive system with a powerful but not dominant president and a stronger prime minister (1 = yes, 0 = otherwise)
5. *Weak President*: dual-executive system featuring a weak president and a dominant prime minister (1 = yes, 0 = otherwise)

System types 2 through 5 feature more dispersed power arrangements and appointed executives exercising fewer powers. These factors hasten women's greater inclusion. In contrast, women's prospects are limited in unified presidential systems, where powers and authority are stronger and unrivaled.

Hypothesis 2: Women executives will be positively associated with system types 2 through 5 and negatively associated with system type 1.

This model also explores party structures. The variable Multiparty accounts for whether the system features more than two competitive parties (1 = multiparty, 0 = otherwise). In presidential systems, countries utilizing multiple competitive parties frequently rely on presidential runoff elections, which allows female candidates to place in the top two without attaining a majority popular vote. This signals their credibility to the public and political elites, increasing their likelihood of victory in the next election round. Multiparty parliamentary systems also rarely result in a single party commanding a majority. Based on gender stereotypes, as outlined earlier, the resulting coalition governments may especially benefit a female consensus candidate sharing more dispersed powers.[3]

Hypothesis 3: Women executives will be associated with multiparty systems.

To assess the political pipeline, I integrate data on women in lower offices. The variables Women Legislators and Women Ministers measure women's proportions in these offices in 2000.[4] I incorporate data from the earliest point of the time period since the political pipeline should have a lagged rather than immediate effect on women's representation. Chapter 5 demonstrated that women typically work their way through national political institutions for several years before ascending to prime ministerships and presidencies. The levels as of 2000 will likely capture a key number of the women in such positions, some rising as national executives during this decade. Furthermore, using this data point lessens the chance that a positive relationship between women ministers and executives results from female leaders appointing higher percentages of women to these posts.[5]

Hypothesis 4: Countries with larger percentages of women in their legislatures are more prone to have a woman president or prime minister.

Hypothesis 5: Countries with higher levels of women in their cabinets have a greater likelihood of being governed by a woman president or prime minister.

Structural Variables

Structural variables examined include Fragility, evaluating political institutionalization and stability of a country. The Polity IV project collects state authority data, systematically appraising regime type, political conflict, and state capacity. I utilize the Polity IV State Fragility Index, which bases a country's effectiveness and legitimacy on the following four areas: security, politics, economics, and social capacity.[6]

The State Fragility Index sums eight scores, with totals ranging from 0, indicating no fragility, to 25, signifying extreme fragility (Marshall, Goldstone, and Cole 2009). I average values from 1995, 2001, and 2007. Given findings thus far, I expect women executives to arise in countries with higher levels of fragility. These years cover a period corresponding with women's likely entrance to power. As opposed to the pipeline variables (Women Legislators and Women Ministers), fragility hastens a more immediate promotion of women. I expect women leaders to surface in comparatively fragile contexts given the more frequent shifts of power in those contexts. Furthermore, the general public and party elites may see women (particularly those from particular ethnic groups and families) as potential unifiers in postconflict societies.

Hypothesis 6: Countries scoring higher on the State Fragility Index will be more apt to be governed by a woman.

Global Factors

To obtain a sense of the international stature of a country and the resulting global influence of the leader, I incorporate the variable G-20, which indicates if a country ranks among the world's largest economies (1 = G-20 country, 0 = otherwise). The public routinely views women as weaker than men on economic issues (Huddy and Terkildsen 1993). Based on this stereotype, elites and the public within more economically powerful countries could hesitate to promote women leaders. Preferences for masculine traits also abound within the military (Duerst-Lahti 2006). One measure of military might relates to nuclear capability. The variable Nuclear assesses the country's military influence and strength worldwide (1 = nuclear power, 0 = otherwise).

Hypothesis 7: Women leaders seldom ascend within nuclear states.

Hypothesis 8: Women leaders surface less often within G-20 countries.

Historical Factors

Among historical factors, women's suffrage (Suffrage) verifies whether longer histories of enfranchisement foster women executives (Studlar and McAllister 2002). The general public or party elites could provide women with enhanced future support given women's greater historical grounding in the political sphere.[7]

Hypothesis 9: Countries where women obtained suffrage at earlier points in time will be more prone to advance women executives.

The variable Prior Women Rule gauges whether women ruled in executive office before the year 2000 (1 = yes, 0 = otherwise). Given the findings thus far, more than one woman leader ascended in several countries, including Ireland, Bangladesh, Finland, Haiti, and New Zealand. The earlier occurrence of a woman executive may hasten future female leadership. Women presidents and prime ministers inspire other women to compete for political office and signal women's suitability for public office to the general population and party leaders. Having more female descriptive representatives alters social meanings attached to the dominant characteristics of officeholders (Mansbridge 1999). Male and masculine associations within this domain weaken (Sapiro 1981), while perceptions of women as political actors intensify (Dahlerupe 2006), providing women with enhanced symbolic representation, subsequent descriptive representation, and possibly substantive representation.

Most of the research that has examined the influence of women on the participation and engagement of the larger society has focused on legislators. As a whole, studies have found positive repercussions related to higher percentages of women in legislative bodies or greater quantities of female candidates. When women constitute a larger portion of the legislature, women and girls increasingly engage in political discussions with friends (Wolbrecht and Campbell 2007, 928). Their levels of political participation also rise with the proportions of female legislators (Wolbrecht and Campbell 2007, 931).[8] Anticipation of future political activity improves with greater quantities of women legislators for both boys and girls, but especially for girls (Wolbrecht and Campbell 2007, 933). Additionally, competitive female senatorial and gubernatorial candidates correlate with women's amplified political engagement (Atkeson 2003). Larger percentages of women legislators also correspond with higher rates of women's external efficacy (Atkeson and Carrillo 2007, 92). The presence of a female governor links to heightened levels of efficacy for both women and men (Atkeson and Carrillo 2007, 90). Comparatively, studies similarly verify that augmented descriptive representation of women legislators enhances women's confidence in the legislative process and policy responsiveness (Schwindt-Bayer and Mishler 2005, 422).

Although they do not deal with the influence of existing female officeholders on other women's political ambition, Lawless and Fox (2010, 148) repeatedly note that a majority of women perceive sexism in politics, are less frequently recruited by political elites, underestimate their own qualifications, and doubt they could successfully run for office.[9] Female leaders may inspire others to seek political positions (Lawless 2004, 82). While this results from women leaders' visibility, some women executives could directly groom other women for political office and appoint them to positions, with the result that some eventually attain executive power. In other cases, female executives may indirectly influence parties to recruit other women candidates. When one woman candidate has already proved successful, party elites may view female candidacies in general more positively, conceivably as a means of attracting female constituents.

In sum, women's descriptive representation relates to important political orientations, fostering greater rates of participation of women and girls and altering public views of politicians (Mansbridge 1999).The potential effects of women presidents and prime ministers should, therefore, not be discounted.

Due in part to the high levels of media attention they receive, presidents and prime ministers are likely more well-known by the public than are legislators or governors (Heffernan 2006; Kernell 1997).[10] We may also question the public's awareness of the total percentage of female parliamentarians in office.

The potential impacts of female presidents and prime ministers on women's symbolic representation may in fact be greater than for other political posts, considering their sheer visibility.[11]

> *Hypothesis 10*: A woman leader is more likely to ascend if another woman previously came to power in that same country.

For the sake of consistency, I exclude previous interim female leaders, although even temporary cases provide visible examples of women rulers.

Finally, I consider the relationship between familial ties and executive power (Family), specifically, whether prior to the year 2000 members from the same family held executive office (1 = yes, 0 = otherwise). As discussed throughout this book, because they represent the vast majority of executives, more men benefit from these ties. Within the limited quantities of women executives, however, disproportionate numbers have utilized kinship connections. These connections enable women to work within existing gendered constructs of femininity rather than challenge prevailing gender roles when attaining power.

Familial ties occur when a prime minister or president possesses one of the following relationships with another prime minister or president from the same country: parent/child, husband/wife, sibling, cousin, uncle/nephew/niece, aunt/nephew/niece. Family members need not occupy the exact same position; one could be president and the other prime minister. In analyzing familial ties in this section, I use a narrower conception than that used previously. In earlier chapters I included relatives of national opposition leaders acting in various capacities (for example, in the cases of Chamorro, Bachelet, and Aquino). I advance a more constricted definition here for one main reason: in an examination of nearly every country in the world, family relationships spread among myriad official and unofficial political posts are very difficult to detect, making consistent application of the wider definition problematic.[12]

> *Hypothesis 11*: Women national leaders ascend more regularly in contexts where family ties to executive power surface.

Finally, I integrate the Gender-Related Development Index (GDI) as a control variable. This measures women's levels of poverty and education and life expectancy rates in relation to men's (coded 0 or 1, 1 indicating perfect parity). I average GDI scores from the period 2000–2008.[13] Many women advance within contexts where women in the general population lag far behind men; in other cases, women approach equality. Thus, societal equity does not necessarily correspond with parity in political leadership, although this topic clearly warrants further investigation.

GENERAL DETAILS OF COUNTRIES IN SAMPLE

Before discussing model performance, I offer more details on the data set. As stated, I examine 147 countries. Between 2000 and 2010, 32 countries featured women executives. However, thirty-seven distinct women served; two women ascended in Bangladesh, São Tomé and Príncipe, and Sri Lanka and three in Finland during this period, resulting in five more women than the number of countries in which they served.

Tables 7.1 and 7.2 provide specific information regarding some of these variables for the subset of countries with women leaders during this decade. Table 7.1 shows that 56 percent of systems in this sample feature dual executives ($n = 83$) and 44 percent consist of unified structures ($n = 64$). Among dual-executive systems, presidencies distribute as follows: 18 weak (22 percent), 17 powerful (20 percent), and 48 dominant (58 percent). The unified types contain 39 presidential (61 percent) and 25 parliamentary structures (39 percent). A total of 102 countries (69 percent) encompass multiparty systems, and 45 (31 percent) have two-party systems. Family members served as executives in 42 (29 percent), and 28 (19 percent) saw other female executives ascend to power previously (see Table 7.2). The average percentage of women legislators in these countries is 13 percent, though levels range between 0 and 43 percent. At 9 percent the average percentage of women in ministerial posts is slightly lower, falling between 0 and 44 percent. The country granting women suffrage earliest did so in 1893; the last, not until 1989. Typically, countries achieved suffrage by 1947. GDI scores vary from .289 to .948, with a mean of .691. Finally, fragility scores fall between 0 and 22, averaging 9.

Figure 7.1 displays the distribution among countries of the women leaders in office between 2000 and 2010. Among the thirty-seven women serving during parts of this decade, thirteen are in Europe, nearly evenly divided between Western and Eastern Europe. Nine are in Asia, and five apiece are in African and Latin American countries (totaling ten). Other countries with women leaders include New Zealand, Australia, and three Caribbean nations. Noticeably absent from Figure 7.1 are female executives in North American or Middle Eastern states. Still, women leaders reached record-breaking numbers during this period, making it a particularly beneficial one to analyze.

The model includes the following independent variables: Government Type, Dual Executive, Multiparty, Women Legislators, Women Ministers, Nuclear, G-20, Fragility, Suffrage, Prior Women Rule, and Family. GDI serves as a control. Finally, the dependent variable is Women Executives.

Table 7-1. COUNTRIES WITH WOMEN EXECUTIVES, SELECT VARIABLES, PART 1

Country		SYSTEM			POWER	
	Dual	Presidential	Parliamentary	Dominant	Powerful	Weak
Argentina	0	1	0	0	0	0
Australia	0	0	1	0	0	0
Bangladesh	1	0	0	0	0	1
Chile	0	1	0	0	0	0
Costa Rica	0	1	0	0	0	0
Croatia	1	0	0	0	1	0
Finland	1	0	0	0	1	0
Germany	1	0	0	0	0	1
Haiti	1	0	0	1	0	0
Iceland	1	0	0	0	0	1
India	1	0	0	0	0	1
Indonesia	0	1	0	0	0	0
Ireland	1	0	0	0	0	1
Jamaica	0	0	1	0	0	0
Kyrgyzstan	1	0	0	1	0	0
Latvia	1	0	0	0	0	1
Liberia	0	1	0	0	0	0
Lithuania	1	0	0	0	1	0
Moldova	1	0	0	1	0	0
Mozambique	1	0	0	1	0	0
New Zealand	0	0	1	0	0	0
Panama	0	1	0	0	0	0
Peru	1	0	0	1	0	0
Philippines	0	1	0	0	0	0
São Tomé and Príncipe	1	0	0	1	0	0
Senegal	1	0	0	1	0	0
South Korea	1	0	0	1	0	0
Slovakia	1	0	0	0	0	0
Sri Lanka	1	0	0	1	0	0
Switzerland	0	1	0	0	0	0
Trinidad and Tobago	0	0	1	0	0	0
Ukraine	1	0	0	1	0	0
Total	20	8	4	10	3	6

NOTE: Bangladesh, Finland, Sri Lanka, and São Tomé and Príncipe had two different women in executive posts during this time period. Switzerland is counted as both a unified presidential system and a system with a weak president for reasons expanded on in the text.

Table 7-2. COUNTRIES WITH WOMEN EXECUTIVES, SELECT VARIABLES, PART 2

Country	Multiparty	% Women Legislators	% Women Cabinet Members	Suffrage	GDI	Fragility	Family	Prior
Argentina	1	21	8	1947	.844	3.33	1	1
Australia	0	25	24	1902	.946	1.33	0	0
Bangladesh	1	11	2	1972	.492	15	1	1
Chile	1	9	14	1949	.832	2.67	1	0
Costa Rica	1	19	13	1949	.821	0.67	1	0
Croatia	1	16	12	1945	.821	5.33	0	0
Finland	1	37	29	1906	.933	0	0	1
Germany	1	8	33	1918	.925	0.67	0	0
Haiti	1	9	0	1922	.471	13.7	1	1
Iceland	1	35	8	1915	.932	1	0	1
India	1	9	8	1950	.573	13.7	1	1
Indonesia	1	8	3	1945	.686	11.7	1	1
Ireland	1	14	21	1918	.925	0	1	1
Jamaica	0	16	11	1944	.739	3.67	1	0
Kyrgyzstan	1	7	4	1918	.700	9.3	0	0
Latvia	1	17	7	1918	.815	2	1	0
Liberia	1	7	20	1946	.380	21.3	0	0
Lithuania	1	18	6	1921	.738	0.67	0	1
Moldova	1	9	0	1978	.605	10.7	0	0
Mozambique	0	30	0	1975	.264	16.33	0	0
New Zealand	1	30	8	1893	.920	1	0	1
Panama	1	10	6	1941	.790	7	1	0
Peru	1	11	11	1955	.740	11.7	1	0

Philippines	1	13	10	1937	.752	12	1	1
São Tomé and Príncipe	1	9	0	1975	.625	15	0	1
Senegal	1	14	3	1945	.625	12	0	0
Slovakia	1	14	19	1920	.840	2.3	0	0
South Korea	1	2	1	1948	.882	2	0	0
Sri Lanka	1	5	10	1931	.736	13	1	1
Switzerland	1	18	7	1971	.931	1	1	1
Trinidad and Tobago	1	19	13	1946	.800	3.67	0	0
Ukraine	1	8	4	1919	.760	5	0	0
Total	29		14	14				

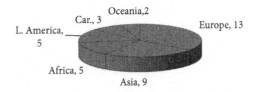

Figure 7.1 Regional Patterns: Women Executives in Office 2000–2010

RESULTS

The Nagelkerke R^2 is .338, explaining more than one-third of the variance. It correctly predicts 97 percent of cases where women do not come to power and 38 percent of those where women do. Overall, it accurately forecasts 84 percent of these circumstances.

Confirming Hypothesis 1, dual-executive systems positively and significantly relate to female-headed countries (< .05 level). Specifically, the odds ratio that countries with two executive posts will have female leaders is 9.5 (see Table 7.3). Among the thirty-two countries with women executives in power from 2000 through 2010, nineteen utilize dual-executive rather than unified structures. Therefore, dual-executive systems exist in 60 percent of countries with female leaders. The qualitative results discussed in Chapters 3 and 4 indicating the importance of dual-executive offices in improving women's chances thus receive statistical confirmation. The sheer increased quantities of positions present enhanced opportunities for women's rise. The fragmented decision-making structures in particular, however, may make women's ascensions appear less threatening to political elites and the general public. Consequently, gendered constructs operate within political institutions, sometimes supporting women.

Surprisingly, the governmental system variable fails to reach statistical significance. Countries with women executives evenly divide between unified presidential and parliamentary systems (nine countries each; see Table 7.1). Among dual-executive systems with women leaders, most employ a dominant presidency. The insignificant results may stem from the wide variation among dual-executive positions. Current coding cannot detect the particular positions women hold. Large numbers of women surfacing in presidential dominance systems may fail to occupy the more commanding position. Indeed, women occupy the presidency in only two countries utilizing presidential dominance systems (Guyana and Sri Lanka). Suspecting a high correlation between dual executives and government type, I reran the model utilizing each variable separately. However, this failed to improve model fit.

Multiparty rather than two-party systems are more prone to witness the rise of women executives (< .01 level). Only four countries that women led

Table 7-3. Logistical Regressions, Women Leaders, 2000–2010

	B	Wald	Exp(B)
Dual Executive	**2.87 (1.2)	5.1	17.7
Presidential	1.47 (1.2)	1.6	4.34
Weak President	–.454 (.823)	.305	.635
Powerful President	–.614 (.87)	.496	.541
Women Legislators	*.062 (.037)	2.738	1.06
Women Ministers	–.003 (.038)	.007	.997
Suffrage	.003 (.017)	.023	1.00
GDI	2.37 (3.2)	.523	10.66
Fragility	–.011 (.089)	.014	.989
Multiparty	***2.07 (.876)	5.58	7.93
Family	***1.43 (.561)	2.46	2.39
Prior Women Rule	*.873 (.56)	2.5	1.6
Nuclear	*–2.42 (1.3)	3.36	.089
G-20	.497 (.73)	.468	1.64
Constant	–13.153 (34)		
N	147		
Nagelkerke R^2	.338		

NOTE: Numbers in cells are regression coefficients and associated standard errors, followed by odds ratios.

*$p < .10$; **$p < .05$; ***$p < .01$.

during this time can be characterized as two-party systems, with the remaining twenty-eight being multiparty (see Table 7.2).[14] In fact, multiparty systems are more than seven times more associated with women leaders (see Table 7.3). In addition to dual-executive systems, this finding affirms the critical role institutional factors play in women's advancement, verifying Hypothesis 3. Again, statistical results confirm the qualitative findings initially derived in Chapter 3 and expanded upon in Chapter 4.

Women's levels in the legislature in 2000 significantly relate to female executives ($< .10$ level). A woman is more prone to rise to the presidency or prime ministership where women make up a greater proportion of legislators. However, since the Women Ministers variable fails to reach significance, the pipeline thesis receives only partial confirmation. Women make up less than 10 percent of the cabinet in fifteen countries where women hold presidencies or prime ministerships. Being cautious of the possibly high correlation between women legislators and cabinet ministers (Davis 1997; Reynolds 1999), I reran the model, incorporating women legislators and women cabinet ministers separately.[15] While the significance of the Women Legislators variable increased slightly (remaining variables exhibited no discernible differences), the Women

Ministers variable remained unassociated with women presidents or prime ministers. Thus, while findings validate Hypothesis 4, this is not the case for Hypothesis 5.

Contrary to Hypothesis 6, the degree of fragility in a country is not statistically related to the sex of the executive. While reinforcing previous statistical findings (Jalalzai 2008), qualitative portions of this book, including Chapter 6, repeatedly illustrate the importance of instability to women's success. Thus, this result, rather than detracting from the potential explanatory powers of these variables, should be seen as an argument for the development of better statistical indicators.[16]

The importance of executives heightens when countries command a higher status on the world stage. Women's lack of progress in attaining power might therefore hinge on countries' military and economic might. A country's nuclear capability correlates with female leaders. Specifically, as predicted by Hypothesis 7, nuclear capabilities are negatively associated with female leaders ($< .10$). While some women have led nuclear powers, many rose to executive office prior to their countries' achieving this status (Bhutto in Pakistan, Gandhi in India, and Meir in Israel). Others (Cresson in France and Patil in India) have not occupied defense-related positions. We may also question Bhutto's sway, given the Pakistani military's dominance over the executive branch in defense matters. However, contrary to the expectations of Hypothesis 8, G-20 status is irrelevant to women's ascensions. Together, these findings suggest that nuclear capability rather than economic status is detrimental to women's executive chances.

The year women received suffrage rights fails to surface as significant, contrary to the expectations of Hypothesis 9. No coherent pattern unfolds in the dates countries with women leaders granted female suffrage (see Table 7.2). For example, women in New Zealand have enjoyed suffrage rights since 1893; in Moldova, women could not vote until 1978. Women leaders, however, ascended in both countries during the time frame examined. All other contexts vary widely in their respective suffrage dates, and this holds true for those yet to be governed by a woman executive. Countries long heralded as democratic ideals routinely deprived women of suffrage rights, including Switzerland and France. The end of World War I resulted in a large wave of suffrage extensions between 1918 and 1921, primarily in the Western world, including the ratification of the Nineteenth Amendment in the United States. Even with the liberalization of voting laws, various obstacles persisted. For example, as noted in Chapter 2, Australia extended suffrage to white women in 1902, but Aboriginal women did not gain the franchise until 1967 (Henderson and Jeydel 2007). In some countries, women have sometimes needed to be older than their male counterparts to vote.[17]

Women did not win suffrage until the end of World War II in France and Japan as well as several other countries. Another major suffrage wave occurred between the late 1940s and the 1960s in the developing world, coinciding with the dismantlement of colonial governments. For example, Pakistan (1947), Algeria (1962), and Malaysia (1963) gained political autonomy and women's enfranchisement simultaneously. Advances in women's suffrage took the longest to achieve in the Middle East, a region nearly completely devoid of women national leaders.

Myriad possible problems can arise in an analysis based on the suffrage dates provided by the Inter-Parliamentary Union. As noted, many countries' suffrage dates coincide with political independence from colonial rule, including Pakistan's in 1947. Although Bangladesh and Pakistan formed the same country after India's partition, Bangladesh's women's suffrage date is 1972—the year Bangladesh gained independence from Pakistan. In contrast, the countries that made up the Soviet Union extended suffrage to women prior to the formation of the communist empire, not during the subsequent independence wave in the early 1990s. Given that women retained their voting rights under the Soviet regime, utilizing the earlier dates, as the Inter-Parliamentary Union does, appears justifiable. In both cases, however, the earlier dates seem more appropriate. Inconsistent data coding likely contributes to the failure of women's suffrage to rise to levels of statistical significance.

Another complication arises in that legal provisions allowing women the vote were not necessarily followed by the movement of women to the ballot boxes. According to Caraway (2004), the sequence of suffrage expansions proves critical: although it may seem that Western women enjoy greater advantages because of their longer histories of voting rights, women in the developing world may benefit from receiving voting rights simultaneously with men upon independence. Finally, as Salmond (2006) argues, "it is a big stretch to say that a nation's political culture today is determined by . . . a legislative decision in the 1920s or 1930s" (188). Indeed, suffrage dates correlate with women's executive ascensions in earlier periods of time (Jalalzai 2008), but not as of late.

In contrast to the negligible role of other historical factors, the statistical model provides compelling evidence for the importance of women's prior leadership to their future rise. Countries previously governed by women are twice as likely to see another woman rise to power during the next decade (< .10 level; see Table 7.3). In fact, twelve of the thirty-two countries with women leaders during the 2000–2010 period witnessed the breaking of the executive glass ceiling previous to this decade. This underscores a potential impact of women's rule, possibly a connection between women's descriptive and symbolic representation. While the first opening of executive office to a woman stems from a host of factors, this event provides an additional pull for future women. However, based on the same variables accounting for women's initial rise, the prospective benefits provided by the trailblazers vary. For example, unified executive structures and two-party systems may not be as prone to having a second or third woman in office. In contrast, countries incorporating dual-executive posts and multiparty systems are more likely to see several women leaders surfacing. This helps explains why the United Kingdom's Margaret Thatcher is yet to be succeeded by another female leader while Lithuania recently welcomed its third (Jalalzai 2010a). As such, perhaps it is most fitting to say that the glass ceiling is truly shattered in some contexts, such as Finland, only cracked in the United Kingdom, and firmly intact in the United States.

To address potential concerns regarding the correlation between variables between past and future success of women leaders, I omitted the Prior Women Rule variable, and all of the same factors remained statistically significant. The overall model fit, however, decreased. Confirming Hypothesis 10, results nicely correspond with findings presented in Chapters 3 and 4.

Another critical historical factor relates to family ties. Specifically, countries where family relations held executive office in the past more often promote women leaders (< .01 level). Family relations occupying the presidency or prime ministership prior to the year 2000 account for only forty-one countries in this sample. Fourteen of the thirty-seven women in office, however, served in such countries. Connections sometimes benefit only male family members (as in Haiti, Jamaica, Latvia, and Peru). Some of the same countries where male family relations governed, however, also afforded women from political families such opportunities. For example, both female leaders of Sri Lanka trace their initial ties to office to Prime Minister Solomon Bandaranaike (Sirimavo Bandaranaike's husband and Chandrika Kumaratunga's father). Before this family line of power developed, however, Prime Minister Don Stephen Senanayake's son Dudley gained promotion through familial connections. Other countries where male familial ties existed prior to women's ascensions but where women later benefited from their *own* kinship associations include Nicaragua, Panama, and Chile.[18] Some contexts (Argentina, Bangladesh, and the Philippines) advanced women with familial ties to executive power prior to 2000 and then again post-2000, though these women did not hail from the same families as did their male predecessors with kinship connections.

In other areas, male relatives rose to power, though women from political families (and otherwise) have yet to break through the executive glass ceiling in these same countries. Notable examples include Greece (which boasts several male family relations), Sweden, and the United States. Interestingly, while familial links to executive power exist in all areas of the world, women leaders' connections appear geographically concentrated. Specifically, as noted in Chapters 5 and 6, women from Latin America and Asia disproportionately arise through kinship networks. While male family members surface in these same locations, they also do so in Europe, North America, the Middle East, the Caribbean, and Africa. In Africa, family lines appear increasingly salient for men in countries such as Botswana and Togo.[19] Statistical findings validate Hypothesis 11 and confirm results stemming from the personal stories of women leaders presented in previous chapters.

While women's parity with men (GDI) lacks connection to women's executive leadership, this validates several findings stemming from the qualitative analysis. Women's higher social and economic status in the larger population *does not* correspond to their holding positions of national leadership. Even where women have reached near parity with men socially and economically, their executive advancement remains tentative. Women executives, however, largely arise from socioeconomically advantaged classes. This finding corroborates more contemporary research that has failed to establish positive connections between women's general status and legislative representation (Matland 1998a; Moore and Shackman 1996; Yoon 2010). Thus, women's general status fails to function as a useful pipeline variable for executive office.

Table 7.4 summarizes the hypotheses and the correspondence of the statistical to the qualitative results presented in this book, recapitulates the implications of the findings, and suggests possible avenues for future research. Most hypotheses (1, 3, 4, 7, 10, and 11) operate as expected. A few, however (2, 5, 6, 8, and 9), do not.

Statistical evidence lends greater credibility to several explanations for women's rule previously derived from more qualitative chapters. Indeed, both the qualitative and the quantitative results generally validate arguments advanced throughout this book. Women leaders rely on dual-executive structures as well multiparty systems to rise to power. They also are more prone to rise in contexts where family ties prevail. Countries where women have previously broken through the executive glass ceiling are more likely to see more women advance to executive office. This possibility, however, is highly dependent on critical factors such as the existence of dual-executive structures and multiparty systems. This chapter offers mixed findings regarding the political pipeline. Women's levels in the legislature appear more relevant to their eventual rise to presidencies and premierships than do their ministerial proportions. Women's parity among the general public neither sufficiently nor necessarily fosters their entrance to presidential and prime ministerial offices. While unstable contexts appear very critical to women's rise in the qualitative chapters, no such connection manifests statistically.[20] Furthermore, the governmental system variables fail to perform as expected.

While the statistical model offers many important benefits, one problem that cannot easily be reconciled stems from the fact that women came to power in

Table 7-4. SUMMARY OF STATISTICAL FINDINGS

Hypotheses	Findings	Implications
1. The existence of dual-executive structures will be positively associated with women leaders.	Confirmed	Reaffirms prevailing findings (Jalalzai 2008). Also confirms qualitative analysis derived in earlier chapters of this book (Chapters 3 and 4).
2. Women leaders will be less associated with unified presidential systems than with others. They will surface in dual systems featuring weak presidents as well as dominant presidents, though women will be far more likely to hold the much weaker posts of prime ministers within these contexts.	Not confirmed	Women leaders surface in dual systems featuring dominant presidents, though women are far more likely to hold the much weaker posts of prime ministers within these contexts. Partially confirms qualitative analysis derived in prior chapters of this book (Chapter 3 and 4).
3. Multiparty systems will correlate positively with women executives.	Confirmed	Had not yet been studied in scholarly work, although this appears relevant. Also confirms qualitative analysis derived in prior chapters of this book (Chapters 3 and 4).
4. Countries with greater percentages of women national legislators will be more likely to have women executives.	Confirmed	Reaffirms prevailing findings (Jalalzai 2008). Also confirms qualitative analysis derived in a prior chapter of this book (Chapter 5).
5. Countries with higher proportions of women cabinet ministers will be more prone to have women presidents and prime ministers.	Not confirmed	Reaffirms prevailing findings (Jalalzai 2008). Suggests that this factor should perhaps be abandoned as an explanation of women's rule as national leaders.
6. Countries that are more politically fragile will be more apt to have women executives.	Not confirmed	Reaffirms prevailing statistical findings (Jalalzai 2008). Does not confirm qualitative analysis derived in prior chapters of this book. Rather than abandoning this variable, researchers may need to devise better measurements.
7. Women leaders seldom ascend within nuclear states.	Confirmed	Had not yet been studied in scholarly work, although this appears relevant. Also confirms qualitative analysis derived in prior chapters of this book.

Table 7-4. CONTINUED

Hypotheses	Findings	Implications
8. Women leaders surface less often within G-20 countries.	Not confirmed	Had not yet been studied in scholarly work.
9. Countries where women obtained suffrage at earlier points in time will be positively correlated with women executives.	Not confirmed	Not consistent with prevailing findings (Jalalzai 2008). Possibly suggests that suffrage was connected to executives coming to power in early periods but not in the most recent decade analyzed (2000–2010), a finding similar to that for women legislators (Salmond 2006).
10. A country will be more likely to have a woman leader if it had another in office previously.	Confirmed	Had not yet been studied in previous scholarly work, although this appears relevant. Confirms qualitative analysis derived in prior chapters of this book.
11. Women national leaders ascend more regularly in contexts of family ties to power.	Confirmed	Though the subject of qualitative analysis in previous work (Jalalzai 2004, 2008; Jalalzai and Krook 2010), this is included in a statistical model here for the first time. Confirms qualitative analysis derived in prior chapters of this book (Chapters 5 and 6).
Control variable: Women's attainment of parity with men.	Not significant	Reaffirms prevailing finding that women's general parity is not positively related to the rise of women national leaders (Jalalzai 2008). This does not mean that professional and educational credentials have no bearing on women executives, however, since individual leaders tend to be educated and politically experienced (Chapter 5). In line with more recent legislative findings (Matland 1998a; Moore and Shackman 1996; Yoon 2010).

only thirty-two countries during the time period examined. As noted, countries repeatedly alter their institutional structures over time, and reliable data covering the earliest time frames do not exist. Seeking to maximize the numbers of countries with women in executive posts, the availability of data, and consistency in institutions, I utilized the time span of 2000–2010. Yet this clearly excludes several diverse cases of women national leaders. Therefore, we must continue to integrate quantitative analysis with more qualitative research in order to comprehend fully the dynamics related to women's rise as executives as well as their paths and powers exercised. The more descriptive chapters allowed us to gain a sense of critical themes emerging from women's backgrounds, ascensions, and the degree to which gender operates within executive offices and processes. I then confirmed some of these conditions in the quantitative analysis, which also controlled for other relevant factors and broadened the scope to the entire world.

An important topic yet be explored, however, concerns the pool of women competing for executive office. Women's best chances for success hinge on their willingness to throw their hats into the ring. While challenged by the myriad factors addressed throughout this analysis, only aspirants waging candidacies can ultimately disassociate executive office from men and masculinity. If women vying for power continually prove unsuccessful, the failure of women to advance cannot be attributed to their lack of ambition.

An Overview of Female Presidential Candidacies

I argue throughout this book that presidencies, particularly dominant ones, appear especially resistant to women. A critical dynamic needing exploration is that of the extent to which women compete for presidencies in the first place. To address this need, this chapter presents data on nearly all female presidential candidates to date worldwide. Key questions framing this analysis include the following: Do women fail to gain presidencies because *they do not run*? Do women candidates prove competitive or lose by substantial margins? What important regional patterns surface? In which kinds of contests do women more typically run and appear most viable? Which presidential positions appear most elusive to women? Among the successful women presidential candidates, did their victories hinge on the absence of male incumbents vying for power?

Findings suggest that women's candidacies have increased substantially since the 1990s. This has contributed to their greater rates of electoral success in the past two decades. Still, women rarely emerge the victors when they run for executive office, especially as candidates subject to a public vote. I have depicted the scenario of a woman attaining a majority vote as arduous, but in reality few successful women candidates ultimately require 50 percent plus one vote to gain office because of the large number of parties competing. Victorious female competitors regularly attain only 30 percent of the vote in the first round; thus, they can appeal to a much smaller segment of the population than previously thought, at least in the initial stage of competition.

A substantial portion of women's successful bids for executive office cluster within weak positions, virtually reserving all more authoritative posts for men. Female-versus-female races appear more common as of late, though most of these candidacies lack viability. Women have never run for the presidency in one-third of all countries, disproportionately ones with presidential dominance systems. The lack of female candidates guarantees the continued association of the presidency with men in some regions, particularly Africa. Overall, in spite of the greater numbers of women candidates, the maleness of the presidency appears palpable and resistant to change. We may, therefore, question women's ultimate progress in attaining presidencies.

I focus solely on presidential elections in this chapter because such elections center on individual candidates running against one another. As discussed in previous chapters, prime ministers in many dual-executive systems do not necessarily gain power through parliamentary elections; rather, they achieve office through presidential selection. Parliamentary elections, therefore, do not always similarly situate eventual winners and losers. Finally, I argue throughout this book that women rarely occupy the strongest presidential posts in both unified and dual-executive systems. By concentrating here on presidential candidates, principally those aspiring to the highest positions of power, I can more clearly discern potential hindrances facing women.

PATTERNS OF WOMEN'S PRESIDENTIAL CANDIDACIES OVER TIME

Female Presidential Bids, 1872–1980s

As noted, the world's first woman president (Isabel Perón) did not come to power until 1974. However, the earliest documented women presidential candidates ran for office in the United States in 1872 and 1884.[1] Given the harsh circumstances facing women in American politics during this time period, these candidates never expected to emerge victorious; rather, they were challenging women's unequal political status (Gutgold 2006).[2] Female candidacies were later waged in Latin America.[3] Worldwide, only five women presidential candidates surfaced prior to 1960.[4]

More women aspired to the presidencies of their countries in the 1960s than during the previous forty years combined. However, this amounted to a mere seven candidacies. During the decade in which Perón became president—the 1970s—only twelve women candidates competed.[5] They doubled their numbers by 1980, resulting in at least twenty-five distinct female bids.

Female Presidential Bids, 1990s–Present

Much of women's increased success in obtaining presidencies by the 1990s relates to their greater willingness to throw their hats into the ring. During this decade, 110 different women vied for presidential office, an astonishing increase over previous years. This progress has continued. From January 2000 through May 2010, 142 women participated in presidential contests—a record number.

NUMBERS OF WOMEN PRESIDENTIAL CANDIDATES WORLDWIDE

As of May 2010, at least three hundred different women had strived for the presidency.[6] Not all made it to election day, however, for a variety of reasons. Some voluntarily gave up their pursuits prematurely. Others, particularly in the United States, lost their party primaries. Still, I retain cases if women competed through some point of the election *and* were deemed eligible to run.[7]

While at least three hundred eligible women have attempted presidential bids, only twenty-two were ultimately victorious (see Table 8.1);[8] the remaining candidates lost, resulting in a 7 percent success rate. Still, this percentage overstates the amount of women presidents emerging from candidacies associated with the public vote. If solely the women coming through a public election are counted, the success rate falls to 5 percent. Though women have substantially increased their candidacies and attained office more often since the 1990s, women still rarely emerge as victors.

While some women have successfully secured presidencies and still more throughout many regions have waged competitive bids, most have failed to finish near the top of the ballot (see Table 8.2).[9] At least 141 of the 279 unsuccessful female presidential candidates gained 5 percent or less of the vote, routinely less than 1 percent.[10] Therefore, half of the female candidates grossly underperform, many coming in last. Only 29 attained between 5 percent and 24 percent of the vote (10 percent of the total sample of female candidates), and 17 (6 percent) received 25 percent or more support of the electorate. Another 22 (8 percent) withdrew their candidacies at some point in the competition. Others, nearly all from the United States, lost party nominating contests prior to the general election (17 candidacies, or 6 percent of the sample).

Among the remaining unsuccessful stories, 8 women ultimately fell short of the necessary votes needed to win a legislative ballot. Finally, I could not validate results for 45 women (16 percent); some sources did not always disaggregate vote totals for the poorest-performing candidates, lumping them together as "all others." Some of these candidates likely withdrew before election day.

Findings thus far generally reinforce earlier points. Women presidential candidates rarely finish among the top vote getters or garner a large percentage of the vote, suggesting the continuing obstacles women face in their executive pursuits and male domination of these positions for the foreseeable future. The resulting association of masculinity with the presidency remains a formidable impediment to women's prospects.

Table 8-1. SUCCESSFUL WOMEN PRESIDENTIAL CANDIDATES

Leader	Country	Year	Results	Position	Incumbent
Aquino	Philippines	1986	46%	Dominant	Yes
Bachelet	Chile	2005	First, 46% Second, 54%	Dominant	No
Barbara	Malta	1982	Indirect	Weak	N/A
Calmy-Rey	Switzerland	2006	Federal Council	Weak	N/A
Chamorro	Nicaragua	1990	55%	Dominant	Yes
Chinchilla	Costa Rica	2010	47%	Dominant	No
Dreifuss	Switzerland	1999	Federal Council	Weak	N/A
Fernández	Argentina	2007	45%	Dominant	No
Finnbogadóttir	Iceland	1980	34%	Weak	No
Grybauskaitė	Lithuania	2009	69%	Powerful	No
Halonen	Finland	2000	First, 40% Second, 51.6%	Powerful	No
Jagan	Guyana	1997	55%	Dominant	No
Johnson Sirleaf	Liberia	2005	First, 19.8% Second, 59.4%	Dominant	Yes
Kumaratunga	Sri Lanka	1994	64%	Dominant	No
Leuthard	Switzerland	2010	Federal Council	Weak	N/A
Macapagal-Arroyo	Philippines	2004	40%	Dominant	No
McAleese	Ireland	1997	45%	Weak	No
Moscoso	Panama	1999	45%	Dominant	No
Otunbayeva	Kyrgyzstan	2010	Referendum	Dominant	No
Patil	India	2007	66% electoral votes	Weak	N/A
Robinson	Ireland	1990	39%	Weak	No
Vīķe-Freiberga	Latvia	1999	Elected on second ballot	Weak	N/A

SOURCES: Author's analysis of data from the Worldwide Guide to Women in Leadership Web site, the African Elections Web site, the Election Guide section of the International Foundation for Electoral Systems Web site, the Political Database of the Americas, the European Election Database, and the US Department of State Web site. For the United States, analysis includes additional data from Dave Leip's Atlas of U.S. Presidential Elections Web site and the election results section of the Federal Election Commission's Web site.

NOTE: Presidents not elected by the popular vote because of institutional rules are marked N/A.

Table 8-2. ELECTION RESULTS FOR ALL UNSUCCESSFUL FEMALE
PRESIDENTIAL CANDIDATES

Vote	Number	Percentage
Less than 5%	141	49
5–10%	17	6
11–15%	8	3
16–20%	3	1
21–24%	1	0
More than 25%	17	6
Withdraw	22	8
Unclear	56	19
Lost Primary	17	6
Other*	8	3
Total	290	

SOURCES: Author's analysis of data from the Guide to the Female
Presidential Candidates section of the Worldwide Guide to Women
in Leadership Web site, the African Elections Web site, the Election
Guide section of the International Foundation for Electoral Systems
Web site, the Political Database of the Americas, the European
Election Database, and the US Department of State Web site. For
the United States, analysis includes additional data from Dave Leip's
Atlas of U.S. Presidential Elections Web site and the election results
section of the Federal Election Commission's Web site.

**These cases include women candidates facing legislative approval
who ultimately fell short of the necessary votes, some of whose
nominations were terminated after unsuccessful legislative ballots.

FEMALE CANDIDACIES BY POSITION

What powers do women presidential candidates compete for? Do women generally run for weaker positions? Given the types of presidencies discussed in
Chapters 3 and 4, I categorize candidates by the posts they aspired to fill: dominant, powerful, or weak (see Table 8.3). The vast majority of female candidates,
66 percent, contend for dominant presidencies, 16 percent for weak posts, and
15 percent for powerful positions. I cannot classify the remaining 3 percent
because the country lacked autonomy, was experiencing transition, or possessed nontraditional executive structures.[11]

Successful women presidential candidates usually vie for either dominant
(eleven, or 50 percent) or weak posts (nine, or 41 percent), while only two have
competed for midrange powers (9 percent). Therefore, successful women do
not cluster only in weak positions, although this is the case for substantial percentages. A variety of processes led to their victories. Corazon Aquino officially

Table 8-3. WOMEN PRESIDENTIAL CANDIDATES: POSITIONS

Position	Number	Percentage
Dominant	198	66
Powerful	46	15
Weak	48	16
Other	8	3
Total	300	100

SOURCES: Author's analysis of data from the Guide to the Female Presidential Candidates section of the Worldwide Guide to Women in Leadership Web site, the African Elections Web site, the Election Guide section of the International Foundation for Electoral Systems Web site, the Political Database of the Americas, the European Election Database, and the U.S. Department of State Web site. For the United States, analysis includes additional data from Dave Leip's Atlas of U.S. Presidential Elections Web site and the election results section of the Federal Election Commission's Web site.

received only 46 percent of the vote in a two-person race against President Marcos in the Filipino presidential election of 1986. Her ultimate victory rested upon the bloodless revolution that unfolded subsequent to the announcement of falsified election results.

Women presidents often win with less than majority support, since they usually run against more than one competitive candidate. Seven won with only 40 percent or 30 percent of the popular vote.[12] Still, five attained majorities.[13] Three other candidates failed to win the necessary percentage in the first electoral round but did so in subsequent runoffs.[14] Perhaps even more important, only three successful female candidates ran against incumbent presidents (see Table 8.3). Thirteen (59 percent) competed in open races, and another six (27 percent) gained election by other procedures. Results bolster claims that women gain executive office upon critical openings, specifically in the absence of entrenched incumbents. In nearly all cases, the incumbent president voluntarily stepped aside, faced impeachment, or was term limited. These scenarios, therefore, bode best for women's presidential victories.

Success stories suggest a multitude of processes and outcomes for women attaining presidencies. As noted above, while I have depicted garnering a majority vote as a difficult proposition for women, few (all powerful or dominant presidents) who have succeeded in gaining presidential office have needed to do so. Most have secured a plurality of the vote, performing well enough to compete in a second round of voting in which they ultimately commanded a majority. It is interesting that women holding weaker positions have exhibited some of the poorest electoral performances upon their first elections.[15]

Some female prime ministers have also had presidential aspirations, but failed in their pursuits. They include Bandaranaike (Sri Lanka), Greceanîi (Moldova), Prunskienė (Lithuania), and Tymoshenko (Ukraine).[16] Sukarnoputri (Indonesia) ascended through presidential succession but never gained election in her own right, despite several attempts. Even though women presidential candidates rarely make it to the top, do substantial portions prove competitive in their contests?

Women rarely place among the top finishers in presidential elections. Aside from the twenty-two eventual winners, only thirty-three women were positioned in the top two or three among candidates (see Table 8.4). These women did not all garner a large percentage of the vote, however, particularly when several others competed. I define competitive candidates as those receiving at least 25 percent of the vote, a very low threshold though necessary given the sometimes very

Table 8-4. Second- and Third-Place Female Presidential Finishers

Leader	Country	Year	Position	Results
Ferrero-Waldner	Austria	2004	Weak	5% (second)
Knoll	Austria	1998	Weak	14% (second)
Rosenkranz	Austria	2009	Weak	15% (second)
Gadijeva Hejiyeua	Azerbaijan	2009	Dominant	4% (third)
Sanin Posada	Colombia	1998	Dominant	27% (third)
Dabčević-Kučar	Croatia	1992	Powerful	5% (third)
Kosor	Croatia	2005	Powerful	First, 30% (second)
				Second, 34% (second)
Ergma*	Estonia	2006	Powerful	Less than two-thirds vote
Elisabeth Rehn	Finland	1994	Powerful	First, 30% (second)
				Second, 40% (second)
Royal	France	2007	Dominant	First, 26% (second)
				Second, 47% (second)
Renger*	Germany	1970	Weak	45% (second)
Gunera de Melger	Honduras	1997	Dominant	43% (second)
Katalin*	Hungary	2005	Weak	Second
Thorsteindóttir	Iceland	1988	Weak	5% (second)
Agnarsdóttir	Iceland	1996	Weak	26% (third)
Sehgal	India	2002	Weak	9% (second)
Banotti	Ireland	1997	Weak	30% (second)
Scallon	Ireland	1997	Weak	14% (third)
Kretuse*	Latvia	1996	Weak	25% (second)
Paegle*	Latvia	1996	Weak	< 50%
Prunskienė	Lithuania	2004	Powerful	First, 21% (second)
				Second, 47.4% (second)

(continued)

Table 8-4. CONTINUED

Leader	Country	Year	Position	Results
Greceanîi*	Moldova	2009	Dominant	1 vote short
Jinnah*	Pakistan	1963	Dominant	< 36% (second)
Khalil	Palestinian Territories	1996	Dominant	11.5% (second)
Herrera	Panama	2009	Dominant	38% (second)
Overar	Paraguay	2008	Dominant	31% (second)
Nano	Peru	2002	Dominant	24% (third)
Santiago	Philippines	1992	Weak	20% (second)
Radičová	Slovakia	2009	Weak	First, 39% (second) Second, 44% (second)
Breziger	Slovenia	2002	Weak	First, 39% (second) Second, 44% (second)
Bandaranaike	Sri Lanka	1988	Dominant	45% (second)
Dissanayake	Sri Lanka	1994	Dominant	34% (second)
Tymoshenko	Ukraine	2010	Dominant	First, 25% (second) Second, 46% (second)

SOURCES: Author's analysis of data from the Guide to the Female Presidential Candidates section of the Worldwide Guide to Women in Leadership Web site, the African Elections Web site, the Election Guide section of the International Foundation for Electoral Systems Web site, the Political Database of the Americas, the European Election Database, and the US Department of State Web site. For the United States, analysis includes additional data from Dave Leip's Atlas of U.S. Presidential Elections Web site and the election results section of the Federal Election Commission's Web site.

*Elections in these cases are not based on the popular vote but on indirect vote by the bodies of an electoral institution such as parliament.

large numbers of candidates arising in multiparty systems. Among the twenty-four female second-place finishers, sixteen received 25 percent or more of the vote, whether popular or indirect. Five women gained less than 10 percent of the vote, while the rest secured between 10 percent and 15 percent. Two of the third-place winners proved competitive greater than 25 percent, while the remaining three garnered very low percentages. In addition, three women gained presidential nominations but fell short of attaining the necessary support within the legislature. This results in a total of thirty-three cases considered "close" because the candidates were positioned a place or two behind the eventual winner; however, even they sometimes lost by wide margins. Taken together, equal numbers competed for weak and dominant presidencies (fourteen, or 42 percent, each, totaling 84 percent) and five for powerful presidencies (15 percent). Like successful presidential candidates, those coming closest to victory do so while competing for both weak and dominant presidential positions.

REGIONAL VARIATIONS

Europe

Most female presidential candidates are found in Europe. At least 118 European women have run for the presidency, representing 37 percent of all cases. While about half of all successful female presidential candidates come from this region, these victors are clearly a minority of the pool attempting bids. In fact, only 9 percent of European female presidential candidates have won their races. At the same time, European female candidates appear more competitive than their counterparts in other regions. Scores of the closest competitors are found in Europe, many in Eastern Europe in recent years.

Since the transition from communism, numerous Eastern European countries have instituted presidential dominance systems. The strength of these positions precludes women's incorporation. At the same time, recent elections placing women higher in the polls indicate their greater competitiveness. Women's future presidential aspirations may benefit "in the context of destabilization of the presidency" (Forest 2011, 75). As countries begin to disperse executive powers more evenly between presidents and prime ministers, women's prospects for attaining presidential offices may improve.

With the exceptions of Greece, Croatia, Albania, and Portugal, countries utilizing presidencies witnessed at least one female presidential aspirant. Most electoral contests, particularly from the 1990s onward, contain at least one female contender. Additionally, Eastern European legislatures indirectly selecting presidents regularly fail to provide women with the requisite votes.[17] Since women frequently throw their hats into the ring (generally at least one female candidate competes in each Eastern European presidential contest) and perform strongly, more women presidents may surface here in the future. The fact that women presidents rarely ascend in this part of the world despite the existence of several aspirants is, however, still troubling.

Latin America

At least sixty-two Latin American women have attempted to gain their countries' presidencies. Six eventually won, resulting in a 10 percent success rate. A minimum of two women per country waged candidacies. Countries fielding the most women are Colombia (eight), Argentina (seven), Ecuador (six), Venezuela (six), Peru (six), and Costa Rica (five). Among these, only Argentina and Costa Rica yielded female presidents.

Although women in Latin America routinely vie for the presidency (a dominant position), they experience mixed outcomes. While several of the more successful female candidates have possessed family ties to power, more recently women such as Blanca Ovelar (Paraguay) and Balbina Herrera (Panama) established political careers absent ties to important men. This signifies a potential shift in the necessary backgrounds of women presidential candidates in this region.

Africa

As noted in previous parts of this book, women experience difficulty in attaining presidential office in Africa, a region where the presidency appears both ubiquitous and dominant. Is this just a function of the lack of female competitors? To date, at least thirty-eight women in twenty-five African countries have sought the presidency, with only Johnson Sirleaf emerging victorious (following an unsuccessful attempt in a prior presidential election).[18] This suggests that women's failure to break the executive glass ceiling in Africa does not stem from a lack of trying. Election results indicate that no women, apart from Johnson Sirleaf, have placed anywhere near the top among presidential candidates.[19] At least ten candidates run in nearly all African presidential elections. As many as twenty or thirty people may face off in the first round. Women do not perform well in these elections, regularly receiving less than 1 percent of the vote. Not only do African women presidential candidates lose, but they do not even come close to victory. Whether their lack of viability derives from gendered obstacles is unclear. Johnson Sirleaf's victory remains anomalous.

Asia

At least twenty-six women have competed for the presidency in Asia, with four winning, representing a 7 percent success rate.[20] Of these, ten women ran in the Philippines, two of whom claimed victory. Only two other women came relatively close to winning in the region; both possessed family ties to power (Dahlburg 1994).While many women have governed as prime ministers in majority-Muslim countries, to date, no woman has reached the presidency of such a country as a result of a popular mandate. This suggests a potential obstacle to female presidential aspirants in these contexts, particularly women lacking familial ties.

North America

Mexico has fielded at least four female presidential candidates, all between 1982 and 2006.[21] None attained more than 3 percent of the vote. Many more women have attempted to gain the US presidency, dating back to Victoria Woodhull in 1872. Since that historic bid, at least thirty-seven women have run in US presidential elections. A woman has never received a major party nomination (Democrat or Republican). Those who have attempted this feat, including Hillary Clinton in 2008, have all failed. All American women candidates who have advanced to the general election did so on the tickets of minor parties or forged independent candidacies, and none has ever gained even 1 percent of the popular vote or secured a single electoral vote.[22]

Middle East

Gaining presidencies in the Middle East has proven especially daunting for women. To date, approximately one hundred women in Iran have placed their names on presidential election lists. The Supreme Guardian Council, which must officially approve all presidential candidates, has deemed them all ineligible (Siamdoust 2009). Hundreds of people attempt candidate registration in Iran, but few succeed. The Supreme Guardian Council approved only 4 men out of 404 applying for candidacy in 2009. It did not sanction any of the forty-two female candidacies that year. The council claimed that the rejections were related to the would-be candidates' lack of competence, not their gender (see Siamdoust 2009). Still, gendered norms may cause some to perceive women as incompetent.

The Iranian case demonstrates a larger point. Executive office in the Middle East appears effectively closed to both women and most men. In religious theocracies and hereditary monarchies, executive positions seem to be open only to particular men. If a contestable executive office exists, it is usually the prime ministership, also closed in practice to women. Only three official female presidential candidacies have occurred in the Middle East, two in the Palestinian Territories (1996 and 2005) and one in Israel (2007).[23] No women finished in the top. This area of the world appears particularly resistant to women's executive leadership.[24]

WHERE WOMEN NEVER COMPETE

To what extent does women's lack of presidential success stem from the absence of female aspirants? At least 45 of the 134 countries featuring presidential positions have failed to field a single female candidate to date. This amounts to one-third of the entire sample.[25] While I noted previously that women in Africa routinely seek presidential power (though almost always unsuccessfully), it is

Table 8-5. COUNTRIES LACKING FEMALE PRESIDENTIAL CANDIDATES

Country	Position	Country	Position
Albania	Weak	Lebanon	Powerful
Bangladesh	Weak	Maldives	Dominant
Botswana	Dominant	Marshall Islands	Dominant
Cape Verde	Dominant	Mauritius	Weak
Cameroon	Dominant	Mongolia	Powerful
Chad	Dominant	Montenegro	Powerful
Comoros	Dominant	Mozambique	Dominant
Cyprus	Dominant	Namibia	Dominant
Djibouti	Dominant	Nepal	Weak
Dominica	Powerful	Niger	Dominant
Egypt	Dominant	Palau	Dominant
Equatorial Guinea	Dominant	Portugal	Powerful
Eritrea	Dominant	Seychelles	Dominant
Ethiopia	Weak	Singapore	Weak
Gambia	Dominant	Somalia	Dominant
Ghana	Dominant	South Africa	Dominant
Greece	Weak	Suriname	Dominant
Honduras	Dominant	Tajikistan	Dominant
Iraq	Weak	Trinidad	Weak
Kazakhstan	Dominant	Tunisia	Dominant
Kiribati	Dominant	Turkmenistan	Dominant
Kyrgyzstan	Dominant	Uruguay	Dominant
		Zimbabwe	Dominant

SOURCE: Author's analysis of data from the Guide to the Female Presidential Candidates section of the Worldwide Guide to Women in Leadership Web site.

also true that numerous countries in this region, particularly in the north, have never seen women competitors (see Table 8.5). Several former Soviet republics in Central Asia with Muslim majorities similarly lack female candidates.

Of the forty-five countries devoid of women candidates, thirty-one (69 percent) utilize dominant presidential structures. These positions appear most daunting for women to achieve; as such, women candidates fail to compete. If women eschew vying for power altogether, the executive glass ceiling will assuredly remain intact.

PRESIDENTIAL RACES FEATURING MULTIPLE WOMEN

One fact gleaned through this analysis needs more specific attention: several presidential races have included multiple female candidates. At least thirty-seven countries have featured races with at least two different female candidates, encompassing sixty-three distinct races (see Table A.3 in the appendix). The greatest quantity of competitive women candidates appeared in the Irish presidential elections of 1997, when four of the five competitors were women. The sole male candidate—Derek Nally—came in last, with 4 percent of the vote. Mary McAleese attained 45 percent, but unlike in most races with more than one female candidate, her closest rival, Mary Banotti, was also a woman. Banotti won 30 percent of the vote. Even the third- and fourth-place finishers, Dana Scanlon and Adi Roche, received higher percentages of the vote than most women candidates do worldwide—14 percent and 7 percent, respectively.

Rarely do races featuring multiple women position the female candidates among the top two vote getters, although this has occurred—in Iceland (1988), Sri Lanka (1994), Argentina (2007), and Ireland (1997).[26] The importance of races in which women compete with women appears clear: the greater the number of female candidates, the more likely it is that a woman will win. Yet parties may strategically field female candidates to split the women's vote, ultimately hindering their chances. Of course, as noted above, few female presidential aspirants ever garner more than 1 percent of the vote, rendering their influence on the larger electoral outcome negligible.

The dynamics involved in presidential races featuring multiple female competitors constitutes a fruitful topic for future research. Possible areas of study include linking female candidate recruitment patterns to parties' electoral strategies, especially in contexts in which women have previously attained executive posts. In these scenarios, party elites may perceive the benefits of running women candidates, resulting in greater female recruitment.

CONCLUSIONS

This chapter has established several points. First, though a handful of women competed for their countries' presidencies prior to the 1970s, women did not actively pursue these posts until the 1990s. By the 2000s, their participation increased even more dramatically, explaining their greater success in attaining these positions over the past two decades. Still, one-third of all countries, disproportionately those with dominant presidencies, have never seen female presidential competitors. Strong presidential powers contribute to the dearth of women's candidacies, possibly pointing to a lack of support for female candidates by both party elites and the public. Of course, given the limited data analyzed, this claim remains speculative. Regions in which women least often compete include Africa (particularly North Africa) and the Middle East.

As discerned in the previous chapters, multiparty systems aid women's candidacies. In fact, many women have not needed to secure a majority vote to gain office or obtained one only after the first electoral round.

Although women candidates are generally less viable, they do compete for office in the remaining eighty-nine countries featuring presidencies. Several contexts have witnessed multiple female candidates, some running simultaneously. At least three hundred different women to date have vied for presidential office worldwide, but only twenty-one have emerged victorious. This reinforces the association of presidencies, particularly dominant ones, with men and masculinity. Furthermore, few women come close to victory as second- or third-place finishers. The majority of female candidates garner less than 5 percent of the vote, routinely less than 1 percent. For their presidential prospects to improve, women must not only compete in more contexts but also perform better in gaining votes. Presidents are almost always men, and this stems in part from men's greater tendencies to aspire to these positions. At the same time, however, when women do run, *they rarely win*. Therefore, women's lack of political ambition cannot adequately explain their lack of success. Women's ultimate progress appears, once again, less than remarkable.

Unless we examine the stories of women who have sought the presidency and failed, important dynamics facing women candidates will remain unknown. Closer looks at some of the most prominent near misses can further clarify the potential obstacles to women's attaining executive office. I therefore survey the cases of Hillary Clinton of the United States and Ségolène Royal of France in the next chapter.

Close but Not Close Enough

The Historic Candidacies of Hillary Clinton and Ségolène Royal

Following up on the illumination of broad patterns of female presidential candidacies in Chapter 8, I now examine the cases of Ségolène Royal of France in 2007 and Hillary Clinton of the United States in 2008. Neither can be discounted as a "long-shot" candidate; both possessed strong credentials and competed for dominant posts in visible and critical countries. How do their ultimate failures in breaking the glass ceiling relate to political institutions and processes, societal contexts, and gender?

For each of the two candidates, I first provide a general overview of the main institutional, structural, cultural, global, and historical factors at play in her country that appear relevant to women's successful attainment of executive offices. I follow with a thorough investigation of each woman's candidacy. I begin with the United States and Hillary Clinton's bid.

THE UNITED STATES AND HILLARY CLINTON

Structural Factors

The United States ranks sixteenth in the world in GDI (.937), indicating women's near parity to men in health, education, and income.[1] Despite these promising statistics, women seldom surface at the highest ranks of corporate America, particularly in *Fortune* 500 and 1000 companies. Women earn a majority of undergraduate, master's, and doctoral degrees in the United States (Appel 2010; de Vise 2010), but they trail behind their male counterparts in attaining professional degrees in numerous fields, including law.[2] In spite of their educational qualifications, American women still face a strong and persistent wage gap resulting from gendered employment patterns and discrimination (McBride and Parry 2010).

An examination of the political pipeline in the United States reveals a more troubling scenario for female presidential hopefuls. The official qualifications for the presidency include only native-born status, being at least thirty-five years of age, and having fourteen years' residency in the United States.[3] Unofficial credentials, however, comprise a number of demographic factors, including being male, Christian, and at least forty but no more than seventy years old upon assuming office (Nelson 2009, 5). Until Barack Obama's election in 2008, this list included being white. Unofficial requirements for class and professional backgrounds appear somewhat varied; only four of ten presidents in office between 1960 and 2008 were lawyers (Nelson 2009).[4] Still, modern presidents generally attain high levels of education, often from the most elite universities.

Successful candidates also amass political experience, usually as governors, members of Congress, vice presidents, or a combination. Only thirty-one women to date have held gubernatorial office in the United States, and rarely have female governors led populous and politically consequential states.[5] Women hold a mere 17 percent of congressional seats, placing them far behind the proportions of female legislators in several other countries worldwide.[6] Finally, only two women (Geraldine Ferraro in 1984 and Sarah Palin in 2008) have received the vice presidential nomination of a major party; neither won in the general election.

Women's lack of success in attaining presidential office does not stem from a lack of trying, as Chapter 8 demonstrated. Still, no female contenders have come remotely near victory in US general elections, and only Clinton has come close to garnering a major party nomination. I analyzed the backgrounds of the thirty-seven female presidential candidates who competed through 2008. The female candidates vying for a major party nomination held elected or appointed federal office.[7] As Gutgold (2006) notes, the media dubbed nearly all of them "symbolic" candidates despite their relatively high levels of political experience. They rarely stayed in the race through the nominating conventions.

Other female candidates who have competed in the general election ran on minor party tickets or waged independent bids. They did not hold federal political office but usually were activists. Of course, many women world leaders have had activist backgrounds, but they supplemented their backgrounds with formal power before they gained executive positions.

The general US population now plays a critical role in presidential nominations. Troubling gender stereotypes exist among the American public. For example, 25 percent of Americans believe that men make better political leaders than do women,[8] and 15 percent support the notion that "women should take care of running their homes and leave running the country up to men" (Lawless and Fox 2010). Women candidates confront skepticism about their presidential qualifications and traits (Kennedy 2003; Heldman 2007). In 1937, only 33 percent of American said that they would vote for a "qualified" woman president.[9] The highest level of support among Americans for the idea of a female president, 92 percent, surfaced in 1999; that number dropped to 87 percent in the aftermath of the terrorist attacks of September 11, 2001, and has recovered only slightly since that time (Jones 2007). Thus, while Hillary Clinton positioned herself as the early frontrunner for the Democratic Party nomination, Americans seemed less favorable to the idea of a woman president than in recent years (Lawless 2004; Streb et al. 2008). Rather than viewing this body of research as affirming the public's hesitancy to vote for women, however, actual female candidates may successfully challenge the negative views encountered by abstract ones (Bystrom 2010).

As political campaigns increasingly become personality-driven contests, the media play a particularly vital function in US presidential elections (Bennett 2009). This coverage also may be gendered. Some of the most overt examples of discriminatory reporting stem from recent electoral cycles. In her analysis of Geraldine Ferraro's 1984 vice presidential attempt, Heith (2003) found that "almost 30 percent of Ferraro's coverage … contained references to clothing, makeup, hair, and other distinctly 'feminine' categorizations" (126).[10] Other notable examples of gendered media coverage of Ferraro include a *Meet the Press* moderator asking her whether she would be strong enough to "push the button" if elected, NBC news anchor Tom Brokaw commenting on her being a size six, and the immense attention given to her husband's business dealings (Braden 1996).

Elizabeth Dole, exploring a 2000 bid for the Republican Party's presidential nomination, received even more gendered coverage than Ferraro (Heith 2003). Dole trailed behind only George W. Bush in public support but received less issue attention by the press. The media also spent more time reporting on her personal background than they did for Bush, John McCain, or Steve Forbes (Aday and Devitt 2001, 60–61). Dole's personality traits and appearance also garnered much more attention compared to her male counterparts (Heldman, Carroll, and Olson 2005). Further, the press less often quoted Dole directly or supported her statements with evidence (Aday and Devitt 2001, 68). Faced with this media environment and numerous other obstacles, she quickly abandoned her presidential aspirations without ever formally competing in the primary process (Gutgold 2006). Because the media filter so much of what voters see in American presidential campaigns, media presentations have a critical impact on a candidate's chances for success.

Institutional Factors in the United States

Some of the most crucial factors that must be accounted for in an evaluation of women's chances of breaking the executive glass ceiling hinge on political institutions. Rather than a dual-executive structure, which appears much more open to women leaders, the United States has a unified presidential system.

An analysis of the eight major powers discussed in Chapter 3 reveals the American presidency to be the quintessential dominant type. As both head of state and head of government, the president fuses ceremony and substance. Symbolic and apolitical duties support "feminine" leadership. The president performs several ceremonial functions for the United States, but most presidential duties involve substantive powers, spanning domestic and international issues and stereotypically "masculine" and "feminine" roles. Obviously, the issues on the political landscape differ depending on the particular context and time. Some of today's most prominent concerns seem highly masculinized, including the economy, national security, and defense. Several substantive responsibilities of the US president appear exceedingly "masculine," including the role of commander in chief (Duerst-Lahti 2007). Further, the president's foreign policy powers abound (again, a stereotypically "masculine" realm); these include forging executive agreements and negotiating treaties with other countries (Patterson 2008).

The United States is a democratic system, and the president exercises powers in a system of vast checks and balances. While this limits the powers of the president compared to those of leaders in authoritarian regimes, few could question the dominance and influence of the American president in the executive branch. Another issue is turnover. American presidents usually finish their four-year terms and are relatively assured of political stability during their tenure.[11] Finally, the traits deemed important for the presidency, which include the ability to act quickly, determinedly, and often unilaterally, appear highly "masculine" (Duerst-Lahti 1997). Together, these conditions generally present obstacles to female presidential aspirants.

American presidents select several influential players, including cabinet members, personal advisers, military staff, and federal judges (Edwards and Wayne 2005). Some appointments require congressional oversight, which means that the American president has somewhat less autonomy than do Latin American presidents. However, presidential designates generally receive confirmation. The president may also dismiss appointees at will. The president chairs cabinet meetings and plays a pivotal role in governmental formation. Congress can override presidential vetoes. The president lacks unlimited emergency decree powers absent congressional approval. Party divisions and majority status, therefore, may curtail presidential influence.[12] The president also cannot dismiss the Congress at will. Still, on balance, the American presidency is extremely powerful.

With presidential elections held once every four years, the United States has experienced few instances of political disruption. In a highly institutionalized context, clear constitutional stipulations guide the line of succession. Only forty-three presidents have ascended during the more than two hundred years since the nation's founding.[13] Although presidents face expulsion if they commit high crimes and misdemeanors, only two impeachments have occurred, neither of which resulted in presidential termination. Only one president has resigned from office.[14] Eight presidents died while serving. In all cases where a president was unable to complete his term, the vice president (a position, once again, not yet occupied by a woman) replaced the president. The lack of turnover in the American presidency hampers women's presidential chances, as does the relative security of a president once in office.

Paths to the American presidency also present a tricky scenario for women. Federalism results in varying procedures of candidate selection (Burden 2009). The public selects nominees either at caucuses or, more commonly, through primary elections. Instead of voting directly for candidates, participants vote for delegates pledged to the public choice. Each party also now possesses a number of unpledged delegates unconnected to the public vote. Depending on party rules, US states award delegates in different ways, some in a winner-take-all fashion and some by proportional representation. Voters may not necessarily be interested in promoting women to positions of power.

The financial costs associated with securing a nomination limit the numbers of candidates with realistic chances of success. At the nomination stage, parties do not fund candidates. Relatively successful candidates can rely on federal matching funds, but acceptance of such funds subjects them to spending restrictions. In recent US elections, leading party candidates, including Hillary Clinton, have declined federal funding.[15] Once an individual becomes a successful nominee, his or her financial issues may seemingly present less of an obstacle. Party nominees, however, are now likely to decline government support to avoid spending limits.[16] While women candidates pursuing lower levels of office in the United States raise as much money if not more than their similarly situated male counterparts (Farrar-Myers 2007), all modern female presidential aspirants prior to Clinton were hindered by the large sums needed to mount a credible campaign (Farrar-Myers 2003, 2007; Gutgold 2006).

The American electoral system makes the state distribution of popular votes pivotal to presidential election outcomes (Dahl 2001). Almost all successful candidates have been white men, and almost all have come from Protestant backgrounds. The complicated task of appealing to voters in certain US states, some of which are more egalitarian than others, seems particularly discouraging for women and minority candidates.[17]

Female nominees may also lack support from party activists, who still play consequential roles in nomination contests (Haussman 2003). As Cohen et al. (2008) note:

> Faced with multiple candidates beseeching them for support, party regulars—from governors to weekend activists—have a lot of choice. But party insiders cannot hope to control the outcome of the voter primaries unless they coordinate on someone broadly acceptable. So, after meeting the candidates, party members discuss and deliberate who can best represent their own concerns, unify the party, and win the general election in the fall. (8)

Regarding party systems, unlike many other presidential systems around the world, the United States operates in a fairly restrictive two-party mode. It also utilizes single-member majoritarian districts at the federal legislative level. Such electoral designs lead to lower levels of women in Congress (Reynolds 1999) and compromise women's presidential chances. A greater presence of competitive parties on the national stage increases opportunities for a woman to win a nomination contest. Since only two competitive parties exist in the United States, a female candidate may lack viability and the broad appeal needed to win a general election contest.

The Global Status of the United States

Beyond individual powers, we must assess the status a country holds on the world stage. This, too, can present a major obstacle to women candidates for executive office. The United States is part of the influential G-8. It boasts the second-largest economy in the world, based on per capita purchasing power parity (Central Intelligence Agency 2009). The nation's international and military strength appear abundant, as the United States holds the distinction of being one of the United Nations Security Council's permanent members and possesses nuclear capabilities. The American president is one of the most powerful players on the world stage. Taken together, these facts present a major hurdle for potential female contenders, especially considering the masculinization of salient issues, most notably the global economic crisis.

Hillary Clinton's Bid for the Democratic Nomination

Hillary Clinton's presidential bid simultaneously affirms several gendered hurdles previously outlined and demonstrates her transcendence over others.

Given Clinton's unique standing as the wife of a former president, we should temper our optimism with caution. Her wide appeal depended, at least in part, on her ties to an influential man. These same marital connections presented hindrances, however.

CLINTON'S EDUCATIONAL AND POLITICAL BACKGROUND

Clinton has the distinction of being the woman who has come closest to capturing a major US party's presidential nomination. Like many women world leaders, Clinton amassed impressive educational and political credentials. She obtained a law degree from Yale University. She practiced law, engaged in child advocacy, and took on many political roles as First Lady of Arkansas and the United States. Her office location in the West Wing of the White House signified her politico role.[18] As First Lady, she took action on health care issues. She successfully ran for a US Senate seat in New York in 2000 and easily gained reelection in 2006 (*New York Times* 2011b). As a senator, she served on several prestigious committees, including the Health, Education, Labor, and Pensions Committee and the Armed Services Committee.

The media speculated about Clinton's presidential hopes for several years (Duerst-Lahti 2006), and in January 2007 she formally began an exploratory bid. The sole woman in a pack of eight Democratic contenders, Clinton soon gained early frontrunner status. Much of this resulted from her name recognition and close relationship with Democratic insiders amassed during her husband's tenure as president. She gained access to donors as well as experienced campaign staff (Nelson 2009).

Being the first "serious" female contender for a presidential nomination garnered Clinton heightened attention, given her campaign's historic nature. According to Falk (2008), however, such framing may come at a cost:

> Though the "first woman" frame may help candidates in the short term by increasing the perception of their novelty and resulting in more press coverage, the effects of reinforcing the notion of women as out of place and unnatural in the political sphere may be longer lasting and have important political consequences. (37)

In spite of Clinton's political experience, the media repeatedly questioned her qualifications. As First Lady, she lacked security clearance and access to daily briefings. Her major policy initiative—health care reform—failed (Healy 2007a). Some suggested that she boasted few significant accomplishments as a senator (Healy 2007a). As such, her frontrunner status resulted from her marital connections. As Murray (2010b) argues, men benefit from the gendered rules of the game, resulting in their being able to hold the presidency before their equally qualified partners. When the female spouse follows, she is constantly subjected to the "wife of" frame, which diminishes her credentials (Murray 2010b, 15).

Senator Barack Obama's own historic bid for the presidency soon overshadowed Clinton's. Obama's distinction as the most competitive African American Democratic Party candidate in American history elicited attention and enthusiasm. Because of his relative newness to the political stage, he enjoyed fewer connections to the Democratic Party base but carried less political baggage.[19] Once John Edwards, former US senator from North Carolina, dropped out of the race in late January 2008, it essentially became a race between Clinton and Obama for the Democratic nomination. The fight for delegates remained extremely close until late spring, when Clinton acquiesced in June.

Absent incumbent presidential or vice presidential candidates, 2008 was the most wide-open US presidential contest since 1928 (Burden 2009). Important issue backdrops included the so-called war on terror and military conflicts in Iraq and Afghanistan, as well as the economic downturn, which had not yet catapulted into the crisis it became by the time of the general election. Although the Republican Party lacked an incumbent candidate, public support for the Iraq War and George W. Bush eroded significantly, providing the Democratic Party with an advantage, given the eventual Republican nominee's possible association with the Bush administration.

CLINTON'S PARTY SUPPORT

Other chapters in this book have demonstrated that party support affects the ability of women leaders to attain power worldwide, although this connection features more prominently within parliamentary systems. In the United States, significant electoral reforms implemented in 1972 made the general public central to presidential nominations. Parties still provide important networks and access to financial contributions. Though Clinton maintained ties to important Democratic operatives, the party establishment did not overwhelmingly rally behind her (Burden 2009). Whether this lack of support stemmed from sexism is unclear. Clinton did not suffer from fund-raising shortages such as those of prior female presidential aspirants, but "campaign contributors did not shower the Clinton campaign with funds" (Burden 2009, 33). Clinton had initially been perceived as the frontrunner, but her campaign had constructed that narrative, which the media at first reinforced (Burden 2009). With mixed party support, Clinton's nomination chances began to appear tenuous.

According to Burden (2009, 24), three specific changes played integral roles in the Democratic Party's nomination results: (1) the increase in the number of states turning away from caucuses to primaries and awarding delegates on a proportional basis, (2) the increased influence of superdelegates, and (3) states' changes in their primary election schedules. Clinton performed better in

primaries than did Obama. She largely ignored the caucuses, which are typically centered in smaller and more conservative states. Obama, in contrast, won
in these competitions. Since many of the large states' contests occurred early in
the schedule, Clinton assumed she could secure the nomination by February
(Burden 2009). The awarding of delegates on the basis of proportional representation worked against Clinton, since she commanded more populous states
than Obama.[20]

The frontloading of the Michigan and Florida contests presented a more difficult scenario for Clinton than for Obama. These states decided to move up
their contests to January despite national Democratic Party opposition. Since
Clinton fared better in larger states, the party's decision ultimately to count
only half the Michigan and Florida delegates compromised her nomination.[21]
Finally, early in the election process, Clinton led in superdelegate support.
Although the Democratic Party had used superdelegates since 1984, they had
never before been as numerous or as potentially influential, given the closeness
of the Clinton/Obama contest. Since Obama secured more pledged delegates,
the public outcry framed as undemocratic the possibility of superdelegates
changing the will of the people.

Clinton's Candidacy: Gender Stereotypes and Sexism

Did sexism toward Clinton surface among the general public? In their analysis
of state exit polls in primary election states, Huddy and Carey (2009) found
little evidence of gender discrimination against Clinton by voters. Nearly all
Latino and white men and women who mentioned gender as a factor in their
vote choice supported Clinton. It is conceivable, however, that respondents
are more likely to affirm a gender connection when they have voted for the
female candidate. While Clinton received just over a majority of women's votes
(Sullivan 2008), this very slight advantage largely resulted from issue semblance
rather than gender affinity (Huddy and Carey 2009).

Clinton demonstrated wide appeal, commanding larger and more diverse
constituencies in California, Massachusetts, New Jersey, New York, Ohio, and
Pennsylvania. A woman can, therefore, attain broad support in pivotal states.
Based on the rules of the game in 2008, however, victory remained elusive.
Further, achieving general allure comes at the cost of focusing specifically on
female voters. Clinton did not face an especially sexist electorate. She appeared
only slightly aided by her appeal to women.

These findings do not suggest, however, that gender did not affect the Clinton
campaign. Instead, Clinton tried to lessen the negative impact of gender by
advocating more hawkish stances on defense and foreign policy (Carroll 2009;
Lawrence and Rose 2010). She also developed a more conservative plan for the
withdrawal of combat troops in Iraq and took a harder line on Iran's nuclear

program than did Obama. While Clinton occasionally highlighted being a role model for girls and young women (Goldberg 2008), she "did not overly stress women's issues or the historic nature of her candidacy in her campaign" (Huddy and Carey 2009, 91). This potentially lost her some support among women.

By 2008, the Bush administration had left many Americans wanting change, including an end to the Iraq War. This represented a significant departure from previously positive views of Bush's handling of the war on terror and the public's desire for a strong, "masculine" leader.[22] In 2002, Clinton voted for the Senate resolution to engage combat troops in Iraq. While not yet a US senator at the time, Obama spoke against this deployment. By 2007, when support for the Iraq War had substantially eroded, Clinton opposed the troop surge. She claimed she would not have voted for the Iraq resolution based on new evidence, but she refused to apologize for her earlier vote.[23] She likely anticipated that there would be gender-based fallout if she espoused regret (Carroll 2009), as such an action could be seen as confirming "feminine" stereotypes such as weakness and indecision. According to a Clinton campaign aide, "Apologizing would have been especially difficult for a female candidate" (quoted in Simon 2008). Her support of the resolution to enter Iraq and her more conservative plans for troop withdrawal potentially alienated liberals who wanted to usher in a new era of politics, but these stances may have been necessary given prevailing "feminine" stereotypes. This is just one example of the double binds that Clinton faced.

Throughout the campaign, she adopted more stereotypically "masculine" traits while displaying more "feminine" postures (McDonagh 2009). A primarily "masculine" woman upsets the gender order. When Clinton grew misty-eyed while speaking at a campaign event in New Hampshire, she was lambasted by some, but others felt she had finally revealed her human side. In fact, Democratic women largely evaluated this event positively (Healy and Cooper 2008). In the end, she rebounded from an upsetting loss in the Iowa caucuses to claim victory in the New Hampshire primary, a decisive campaign moment.

Because of Clinton's gender-balancing strategy, polls that asked respondents specifically about her reported results far different from those found in polls that asked about abstract female candidates. A 2001 Roper poll showed that more respondents believed that a male president could handle a crisis and make tough decisions better than could a female president. In the poll, women's advantages surfaced in two areas—trustworthiness and honesty (Kennedy 2003). The two "masculine" qualities of ability to handle crises and capacity to make difficult decisions appeared more important for leadership. Six years later, polls showed that respondents viewed Clinton as a stronger leader than her opponents and as superior on "masculine" issues such as defense, foreign policy, and economics.[24] At the same time, they rated her lower than Obama on honesty and trustworthiness

(44 percent versus 63 percent), stereotypically "feminine" advantages (Jones 2008). Yet, according to a Gallup Poll report, the most-cited quality the public desired in the next president shifted to honesty and straightforwardness (33 percent); leadership strength trailed far behind (16 percent). This demonstrates that female candidates may successfully challenge negative stereotypes:

> A review of recent public opinion polls reveals that voters associate preferred presidential traits and issues primarily with male candidates, but these gender stereotypes can disappear when they are asked about actual candidates—which seems to have benefited Clinton, at least with public perceptions of her qualifications for president. (Bystrom 2010, 71)

While Clinton did not suffer from several disadvantages women traditionally face, media coverage of her campaign proved extremely problematic. Because of her name recognition, Clinton did not lack media attention (Miller, Peake, and Boulton 2010), but she also garnered more negative and trivial coverage than did her male opponents (Lawrence and Rose 2010; Miller, Peake, and Boulton 2010). Some prominent examples include a *Washington Post* article about Clinton's display of cleavage on the Senate floor (Givhan 2007a). Journalists routinely showed preoccupation with her wardrobe (Givhan 2007b; Brady 2008), and they also criticized her laugh, calling it a "cackle," a word associated with witches (Healy 2007b). Because she was a woman, her presidential aspirations necessitated suspicion, resulting in caricatures of her as a cold and calculating politician (Goldberg 2008; Matthews 2008). Leading political commentators uttered some of the most extreme sexist comments, including references to her being a bitch (Carroll 2009; Lawless 2009; Simon 2007).

To no one's surprise, former president Bill Clinton became a major factor in the presidential race. While this connection no doubt helped Clinton's name recognition and propelled her early frontrunner status, the "Billary" watch soon ensued (Rich 2008). Missteps of the former president reflected poorly on his wife (Burden 2009).[25] Bill Clinton's potential role in the White House as First Gentleman also led to gendered questions. Would he really exercise political control or sit idly by his wife (Nelson 2009)? Neither seemed tenable. While a First Lady standing by her husband appears normal, a man (particularly a former president) doing so by his wife challenges the gendered order. His playing a more active role supports "masculine" expectations, relegating his wife to a secondary or even symbolic figure. While in keeping with a "feminine" model, this operates in tension with the public's view of the president of the United States. Such complications provide further evidence of the fusion of the "double bind" and "wife of" media framing that female presidential candidates face worldwide (Murray 2010b).

While Clinton's marital relationship may at first blush appear an idiosyncratic factor (Carroll 2009), familial ties prove pivotal for women national leaders, signifying more general import.[26] The effects of her marital ties to Bill Clinton demonstrated complexity. At times, her husband proved a major distraction and liability to the campaign. Given the 2008 electoral context, name recognition did not guarantee political success. Voters wanted change; the return of Clintons to the White House signified more of the same, despite the potential of a woman cracking the presidential glass ceiling. Being African American, Obama also represented the potential of a historic first for the presidency, and as a relative newcomer, he could more successfully conduct a campaign based on a promise of change.

Barack Obama and the 2008 Political Context

Barack Obama entered the US Senate four years before he sought the presidential nomination, having previously served in the Illinois Senate for three terms. A lawyer and former professor noted for his oratory skills, he was featured prominently at the Democratic Party's 2004 national convention. Obama's lack of ties to the Democratic Party establishment surprisingly emerged as a major benefit to his campaign, which amassed an energized base of supporters especially from younger demographics. Obama wisely utilized new media to connect to these groups and initiated the most successful political fund-raising campaign in US history, relying on an enormous amount of small donations. His campaign team crafted a clear and consistent theme of change and, unlike Clinton's, remained intact and on message.

Obama successfully distanced himself from the topic of race. Instead of focusing on issues traditionally important to African American leaders, such as poverty and affirmative action, he highlighted economics, health care, and the Iraq War. Oratorically skilled, he invoked the theme of national unity (Nelson 2009). Having a white mother, he was able to highlight subtly his transcendence of the traditional white/black divide. When his ties to Pastor Jeremiah Wright surfaced as an issue, Obama eventually was forced to discuss American race relations.[27] His white opponents, however, knew they could not raise the issue of race without risking major political fallout (Nelson 2009; Lawrence and Rose 2010).[28] When Obama won in states such as Iowa, he erased doubts that an African American candidate could woo white voters. This significantly shifted African American support to him (Nelson 2009).[29] Obama rallied African American voters concentrated within southern and more conservative states. His attractiveness to African Americans specifically and to the general public did not operate as a source of tension. African Americans form the most loyal

Democratic constituency, so a Democratic African American candidate did not present African Americans with cross pressures in the general election.[30] In contrast, women's partisan loyalties are much more closely divided, resulting in only a very limited advantage to Clinton among female voters.[31]

Clinton's Election Results

Clinton eventually secured 1,896 delegates to Obama's 2,201.[32] She therefore ran a very close race, but, like her female predecessors, she still fell short of victory (Gutgold 2006). What does this signal about the role of gender in presidential elections? Clinton enjoyed name recognition, had adequate funding, and competed well, especially in more populous states. No clear evidence exists of sexism at the polls; indeed, her gender may have exerted a marginally positive impact. It appears, however, that Clinton's support among the public and within the Democratic Party was lower than generally perceived. More than anything, Clinton suffered from an inauspicious context for the party establishment, poor campaign organization, and the fact that she faced off against a talented candidate who more convincingly encapsulated the public's hope for change.

I do not suggest, however, that gender proved irrelevant to Clinton's presidential bid. Although it is impossible to know the extent to which gender affected her standing among the public and party elites, clear examples of sexist media coverage of Clinton abound. As Jennifer Lawless (2009) observes: "Clinton was forced to navigate a sexist environment and craft a strategic response. Her response may have been sufficient to mitigate or even offset the harmful media bias she encountered. But that bias did provide an additional hurdle with which Clinton, because she was a woman, had to grapple" (73). She likely based her campaign strategies on her understanding of the strengths and weaknesses of being a female candidate, although this balancing did not always yield success (Carroll 2009).

Clinton's Democratic Bid: Conclusions

Overall, Clinton's case illustrates that although the number of women in the political pipeline is small, women's lack of success does not stem from the complete absence of qualified women candidates. Important difficulties that women face in seeking the US presidency include the unified executive structure, with its very strong president. The two-party system also presents an obstacle, as do the nomination competition and the general election contests, in which the popular vote features prominently. Though some women candidates overcome

a number of difficulties through their possession of family ties worldwide, these
links provides no guarantee of success and may sometimes present a liability.
Frequent and sudden executive office openings tend to propel women, especially those with family ties, to power where they would not otherwise ascend.
In contrast, the United States boasts a highly politically stable system. Media
coverage appears to be an additional problem facing women candidates. The
association of "masculine" traits and issues with the American presidency
proves a daunting hurdle for women to surmount, even women with money,
family ties, and name recognition. The entrenchment of men as American presidents remains unabated.

FRANCE AND SÉGOLÈNE ROYAL

Structural Factors in France

France also recently witnessed a woman closely challenging male opponents
for the presidency. As in the United States, women in France benefit from high
levels of education; at least 56 percent of French university students are women
(Lambert 2001). GDI ratings show 95 percent parity of women to men. French
women, however, suffer from many of the same setbacks as their American
counterparts; less than 5 percent are senior managers in the largest companies,
and patriarchy is deeply embedded in French corporate culture (Lambert 2001;
Gresy and Dole 2011). While 82 percent of French women between the ages of
twenty-five and forty-nine work (mostly full-time), they earn 26 percent less
than their male counterparts and devote twice as much time to household tasks
(Bennhold 2010; Gresy and Dole 2011).

Women's proportion in parliament (18.9 percent) places France sixty-sixth
among nations worldwide, ahead of the United States. Recognizing the inequality in the ratio of female to male officeholders, The French National Assembly
introduced a parity law in 2000 (Krook 2009). The resulting constitutional
amendment mandates that parties present equal percentages of male and
female candidates on ballots throughout electoral districts (Krook 2009, 195).
Various weaknesses of this measure, including inadequate repercussions for
noncompliance, resulted in very limited improvements in women's descriptive
representation in the subsequent electoral cycle (Krook 2009), but by 2007 the
number of female candidacies doubled and women rose from 10 percent of
parliamentarians to 18 percent (Murray 2010d, 96).

The proportion of women in the French cabinet (30 percent) locates France
among the highest in Europe, though still lower than in Nordic countries
(Paxton and Hughes 2007, 99).[33] While France does not have a federalist

structure of government, mayors play important roles locally. Less than 10 percent of mayors are women, however, and most women mayors serve in small towns (Lambert 2001).

French presidents have tended to be individuals who have amassed impressive educational and political credentials.[34] Prior positions held include parliamentary, ministerial, and mayoral offices. Presidents Jacques Chirac, Georges Pompidou, and Charles de Gaulle also occupied the premiership. Formal requirements include being a native-born or naturalized citizen and at least twenty-three years of age. Unofficial qualifications, of course, abound. While a woman has risen to executive power in France, Edith Cresson only briefly held the relatively weak premiership.

According to the World Values Survey, 21 percent of the French population assert men's superiority as political leaders over women.[35] A poll conducted in 2006, however, showed that 94 percent of the public believed that women are qualified to be president (Sciolino 2007b).

Institutional Factors in France

The political institutions in France differ from those in the United States, although both countries feature a dominant president at the apex of power. France, however, has altered its political system and constitution on several occasions.[36] The French presidency is the longest-running presidency in Europe, but the office has shifted over time from being of more symbolic import to holding very great significance since the Fifth Republic.

Since 2002, French presidential terms last five years, with a maximum of one reelection.[37] If a candidate receives less than 50 percent of the vote, a runoff election must be conducted.[38] In fact, since the Fifth Republic commenced in 1959, all presidential elections have consisted of two different rounds; the top two candidates regularly receive less than 20 percent of the vote each. This outcome is obviously linked to France's multiparty system.

While two large catchall parties dominate France—the right-of-center Union for a Popular Movement (Union pour un Mouvement Populaire, or UMP) and the leftist Socialist Party—several smaller parties win parliamentary seats and prove consequential to presidential election outcomes. In 2002, the National Front, headed by Jean-Marie Le Pen, an extreme right-wing party, placed second in the first round of presidential election voting, only a few points behind Chirac's UMP. Nearly all female presidential candidates worldwide run in contexts where more than two competitive parties exist.

France has a dual-executive system, and scholars debate where the balance of power rests (Siaroff 2003; Shugart and Carey 1992). According to my analysis, however, the president undoubtedly holds dominant authority in this system. A critical duty of the French president is prime ministerial selection.[39] Unlike the president, the prime minister remains vulnerable to ouster at any time, although this depends on partisan factors. During periods of cohabitation—that is, when the president's party is different from that of the majority of members of parliament—the president cannot discharge the prime minister (Shugart and Carey 1992, 123–24). When the prime minister and the president share party affiliation, the prime minister becomes vulnerable to presidential dismissal, though this appears debatable (Shugart and Carey 1992, 123–24). According to Siaroff (2003, 293), relevant examples of French prime ministers dismissed by presidents include Pompidou in 1968, Jacques Chaban-Delmas in 1972, and Michel Rocard in 1991. In fact, Chaban-Delmas won a strong vote of confidence in the National Assembly just prior to his ouster (Siaroff 2003, 293). Both the prime minister and the president can dissolve parliament.[40] Since presidential elections and parliamentary contests do not occur simultaneously, the president does not lose that position with the triggering of new parliamentary contests. Presidential dismissal occurs only through impeachment. Therefore, prime ministerial survival seems more tenuous.[41] Since the establishment of the Fifth Republic, only six French presidents have ascended, in contrast to nineteen prime ministers. Seven premiers served with President Mitterrand alone.[42]

Beyond prime ministerial selection and dismissal, the president plays a key role in governmental formation. The president makes cabinet appointments, although in consultation with the prime minister.[43] Crucially, the president, not the prime minister, presides over the Council of Ministers.[44] Other presidential duties include conducting defense and foreign affairs. As commander in chief of the armed forces, the president chairs defense-related councils and committees, stereotypically "masculine" duties. The president also may veto governmental ordinances and ask parliament to reconsider legislation.[45] Another power involves submitting bills for referendum, particularly those related to public services, governmental structure, and international agreements.[46] Still, the prime minister exercises some appointment and policy powers, although this is highly dependent on partisanship as well as presidential leadership style. Whereas many of the presidential powers noted thus far rest upon constitutional analysis, in practice French executive arrangements appear somewhat ad hoc in nature. Powers also routinely prove stronger for presidents who regularly usurp domains belonging to the prime minister on paper (Sodaro 2008).

The media play a significant role in French presidential elections. Unlike in the United States, the French media broadcast political ads for free, but they also place substantial limits on such advertising. All ads must be of the same (generally quite short) length and can be run only on state television and radio stations. Thus, French presidential hopefuls appear less hampered than their

American counterparts by the need to raise funds to buy advertising time. The parties also take responsibility for financing their candidacies. Therefore, fewer obstacles face a potential female contender in France than in the United States.

The Global Status of France

Critical within French borders, the president of France also enjoys a high position on the world stage. Like the United States, France holds one of five permanent memberships on the UN Security Council and belongs to the G-8, but France has the further distinction of being the latter organization's founder. France also boasts one of the ten largest economies in the world.[47] A nuclear power, France ranks third in arsenal size and has the second-largest military in Europe (Central Intelligence Agency 2009).

A founding member of the European Union (EU), France plays a major role in European politics.[48] This adds a complicated dimension to French presidential power. The potential influence of the French president on EU policy seems great, but one could also argue that being a part of the EU undermines Frances's internal autonomy. Still, depending on presidential leadership and influence in European policy making, EU affiliation can expand a French president's ultimate executive power. President Nicolas Sarkozy held the EU presidency as well as the French presidency in 2008, giving him an even greater degree of international visibility, similar to the experience of Chancellor Angela Merkel of Germany (see Mushaben 2009).

Royal's Presidential Candidacy

As the above discussion of France's political system, presidential election procedures, and executive powers indicates, the president of France is situated in a context different from that of the American chief of state but likewise exerts strong powers and plays a vital role in the world. This may explain why a woman has attained the French prime ministership but never the presidency. Some aspects of the French context, however, may present less of a hindrance for women, particularly the multiparty system, mandates for equal media coverage and government-paid advertising, and party financing of presidential campaigns. Further, French presidents do not win a majority of votes in the first round, which opens the door for a woman to attain a high enough total to make it to the next second stage; this is what Ségolène Royal managed to do in 2007.

An overview of the extent to which women competed for the French presidency prior to Royal's rise helps situate the 2007 contest. Apart from Royal, at least seven other women throughout French history vied for the presidency, all of whom waged their candidacies relatively recently. These female candidates had generally amassed high levels of political experience, which should not have presented obstacles to their elections. For example, nearly all had held ministerships. The first French female presidential candidate, Arlette Laguiller, first ran in 1974 and has competed in every presidential election since. The leader of the Worker's Struggle Party, she won between 1 percent and 5 percent of the vote, though her worst performance was in 2007. Including Laguiller, three women ran for the presidency in 1981, all placing near the bottom. The two women who competed in 2002 shared similar results. Though she failed to win the presidency, Royal's level of success appears unparalleled. In the remainder of this chapter, I analyze Royal's inability to win a majority vote in the second round, considering whether gender proved a hindrance. In doing so, I offer various comparisons to Hillary Clinton's experiences.

As in Clinton's campaign, gender failed to manifest as a dominant factor leading to Royal's defeat, yet it formed an important backdrop of the campaign and certainly affected electoral outcomes. Also, media coverage proved one of the most obviously gendered aspects of the race. Press coverage routinely depicted Royal as incompetent, particularly in the realms of foreign policy and defense, discussed her appearance, and centered countless stories on her private life (Murray 2010c). Opposition candidates also used the media to cast doubt on Royal's competence and invoked various gender stereotypes in their treatment of her (Murray and Perry 2008). The media and Royal's opposition routinely scrutinized her relationship with longtime partner François Hollande, with whom she had four children but whom she never married. As the leader of the Socialist Party, Hollande possessed presidential ambitions, presenting Royal with an obstacle similar to Bill Clinton for Hillary Clinton; both women wrestled with the complexities of relationships with powerful men, which became fodder for foes and the media alike.

Royal's Educational and Political Background
Like many successful presidential candidates, Royal attained a prestigious education, graduating from the École Nationale d'Administration. One of President Mitterrand's political advisers, she served as minister of environment and deputy minister of education as well in the Ministry of Family and Childhood (Smith 2007). She became a member of the National Assembly in 1988 and later president of the Poitou-Charentes region, a feat that few other women have accomplished. Thus, her political credentials seem quite impressive and did not pose an obstacle to her election. Still, opponents and journalists undervalued and dismissed her qualifications (Murray 2010c).

ROYAL'S PARTY SUPPORT, GENDER STEREOTYPES, AND SEXISM

Unlike Clinton, Royal did not have to win the support of delegates tied to the preferences of the general public to secure her nomination as a Socialist Party candidate. Still, she needed to win a party vote. Given the Socialist Party's poor showing in the 2002 presidential election, Lionel Jospin stepped down from consideration as its candidate following his losses in the previous two general elections. Royal appeared to have a better chance of taking on the UMP for the presidency if she could win the nomination. However, she soon encountered resistance stemming from her gender from fellow partisans. One of her opponents for the nomination, Laurent Fabius, questioned who would watch her children as she campaigned (Wyatt 2006). Another commented that the French presidency is not a beauty contest (Traub 2006). With her longtime partner a potential presidential contender, an additional difficulty surfaced. Royal disclosed that she decided to run for the nomination when Hollande decided against making his own bid (Traub 2006). Still, Royal handily beat her two male competitors, obtaining 60 percent of the vote among the approximately 230,000 Socialist Party members (Sciolino 2006c).

Upon her selection as the Socialist Party candidate, Royal soon positioned herself as a strong competitor in the first round and rode a wave of publicity. She generally received positive coverage during this period, but things soon changed (Murray and Perry 2008; Murray 2010c). Before long, her opponents and the media began to criticize her, particularly in the realms of foreign affairs (Smith 2007) and national security (Sciolino 2007a). Many of the charges made against her stemmed from a series of gaffes she made on the campaign trail. According to Sciolino (2007a), of the three main candidates,

Ms. Royal has been the most gaffe-prone on foreign policy terrain. On a visit to China in January, she visited the Great Wall, wearing white, the color of mourning in China.... In discussing the fate of two Frenchmen held hostage by the Taliban in Afghanistan, she called for United Nations imposed penalties for rulers like the Taliban, as if unaware that the Islamic extremists had been ousted in 2001.

While these events did indeed occur, evidence suggests that, in comparison with her opponents' mistakes, Royal's missteps were more heavily documented and commented upon by the media (Kuhn 2007; Murray 2010c). The media also condemned her as having a lack of economic prowess, accusing her of not knowing the financial costs of her own proposals. Sarkozy also appeared unaware of the budget necessary to carry out some of his programs, but the media tended to ignore this (Murray 2010c). The media also disproportionately associated Royal with women's issues. Although she stressed policies concerning women, a point discussed below, she also concentrated on other realms not focused on in the media (Murray and Perry 2008). Further, reporters questioned her competence to serve as president, whereas they did not ask similar questions about her male rivals (Murray and Perry 2008).

Royal's competitors did not contend with the same superficial coverage she received, such as being called the "socialist in stilettos" by a London *Daily Mail* reporter (Randall 2007). One of the most controversial stories involved photographs published by the magazine *Closer* featuring Royal (on a beach vacation) wearing a turquoise bikini. Interestingly, many mainstream journalists in the United States and Europe argued that the pictures placed her in a stronger position for the Socialist Party nomination, because they illustrated her youthfulness and style compared to the nearly seventy-year-old Jospin. The French public strongly desired leadership change, and the photos symbolized Royal's potential to usher in this transformation (see Bremner 2006; Sciolino 2006a). Yet the media focus on Royal's physical appeal detracted attention from more substantive concerns and wove its way into narratives of her being unfit for the presidency. A typical story I analyzed from the *New York Times* read as follows: "Historically, French presidents have been old, bald guys…. In terms of sexiness, imagine an endless line of Dick Cheneys. This time, though, both front runners have all their hair and, in one case, lipstick. Quite a novelty" (Clarke 2007).[49] While the journalist also objectifies Sarkozy, such media frames could be especially damaging to Royal, since the public still typically views female candidates as outsiders, especially within the realm of presidential politics.

Royal's relationship with Hollande became fodder for tabloid-style coverage (Clift 2007). One of the many stories on this subject included another published in the *New York Times* that asked, "Can their love survive the French election campaign?" (Bennhold 2007). It focused on the strains of Royal's campaign on the couple's relationship, which became apparent within the internal campaign organization. When Royal and Hollande championed conflicting policy positions, news stories highlighted discord in their romantic relationship. In one such case, Royal's spokesman Arnaud Montebourg told a journalist that Royal's only flaw was her partner, leading her to suspend Montebourg from the campaign temporarily (Clift 2007).

The controversies surrounding Hollande obviously insert a family-connection element into this race that is similar to the one in Clinton's presidential bid. Bill Clinton, of course, had already held the presidency before Hillary Clinton aspired to the position herself; she did not forge a political career until her husband's neared its end. Hollande's election to the National Assembly occurred the same year as Royal's entry. Thus, challenges to the authenticity of Royal's independent political credentials appeared less convincing. Still, reporting like that seen during Clinton's campaign manifested, much of which discussed whether

Hollande and Royal's relationship was a politically expedient rather than truly romantic union (Clift 2007). Although the media also subjected Sarkozy's personal escapades to tabloid-style reporting, they exposed Royal to more (Murray and Perry 2008; Murray 2010c).

As mentioned, entire articles published during the campaign centered on Royal's mistakes. However, even when the media lauded her for a good performance, they characterized her as advocating for only "pet proposals" (Smith 2007). The questioning of Royal's seriousness as a candidate continually referred to her appearance. For example: "France's Socialist presidential candidate … presented her long-awaited presidential program in a two-hour speech on Sunday, hoping to dispel criticism that she is a pretty face without fundamental policies" (Smith 2007).

In terms of quantity of coverage, a constant supply of articles focused on Royal in both election rounds. The quality of the coverage diminished after she won the Socialist Party nomination (Murray and Perry 2008; Murray 2010c). By law, French media must give equal time to each candidate, which possibly minimized differences in the quantity of coverage received by Royal and her opponents. Still, the media positioned Royal, Sarkozy, and François Bayrou of the center-of-the-road Union for French Democracy as the most visible candidates. The fact that Royal was the only woman in French history to gain a place in the second round of voting made her particularly newsworthy.

Gender surfaced in the election due in part to Royal's own campaign strategies. She tried to increase public support by framing her candidacy as a first for women. She also argued that the government needed to make up for the many injustices that had been committed against women (Sciolino 2007b). She repeatedly highlighted herself as the mother of the nation, someone who would care for the French people. At other times she invoked images of Joan of Arc (Sciolino 2006b). Utilizing female stereotypes, she conducted a three-month listening tour and focused on ushering in a new era of heightened participation among the general public (Clift 2007). Although Royal brought up her role as a mother of four throughout the campaign and linked this to serving as the mother of the nation, this strategy garnered further criticism. A reporter from *Le Telegramme* wrote that France "perhaps has more need for a father who forces us to face up to reality than a mother who whispers comforting words in our ears" (quoted in Murray and Perry 2008, 8).

Royal tried to appeal to women voters by advocating free birth control for young women (Smith 2007) and retirement benefits for stay-at-home mothers (Sciolino 2007d). She wooed women voters by stating, "I want to address myself to the women.… I need the women's vote" (Sciolino 2007b). Journalists, however, frequently questioned her concern for women and feminist issues. She announced her three top priorities for helping women at a women's forum:

ending violence against women, providing more aid for preschool programs, and moving the remains of eighteenth-century feminist Olympe de Gouges to the Panthéon (Sciolino 2007a). The last of these goals was seen as trivializing women's issues.

Royal repeatedly took the media and her opponents to task for gender discrimination, although journalists often dismissed these claims as baseless (Sciolino 2007a). Indeed, various evidence suggests she encountered direct sexism, and subtle instances were pervasive, especially those that played on negative stereotypes of women's lack of competence for presidential leadership (Murray 2010c). In a debate, Sarkozy repeatedly told Royal to calm down and said, "To be president of the republic, you have to be calm" (Sciolino 2007d). Perhaps more interesting is the much greater scrutiny Royal received in the aftermath of the debate. As the *New York Times* reported: "Even though she has a reputation of being condescending during meetings, she accused him of being condescending. Even though he has the reputation of losing his temper, she was the one who lost her temper during the debate" (Sciolino 2007d). Similar to Clinton, Royal was subjected to gendered treatment by opponents, and the media rarely noticed (Murray 2010c).

Smaller parties play critical roles in French presidential elections, and the election of 2007 was no exception. Bayrou, the candidate of the Union for French Democracy, placed third in the first round of voting with 18 percent of vote. Given that he made such a strong showing, Sarkozy and especially Royal needed to compete for his centrist supporters. While Bayrou endorsed neither candidate, he and Royal debated each other eight days before the second round. She never gained his backing, and the media criticized her for not paying enough attention to her real competitor at the most pivotal point in the race (Sciolino 2007c).

Nicolas Sarkozy and the Political Context

The French election of 2007 lacked a dominant theme, and the candidates did not focus much on a particular topic. The election occurred, however, against the backdrop of a worsening economy. At the time, France had incurred the fastest-growing debt in Europe and was struggling with very high unemployment levels. France also faced mounting immigration concerns, including issues surrounding the assimilation of Arab and African immigrants. Many of these tribulations linked to the economy. Given Sarkozy's conservatism, Royal tried to tie him to the vastly unpopular George W. Bush based on his own statements and appearances with the American president. Sarkozy, however, successfully portrayed himself as an outsider to French politics and a friend to immigrants by repeatedly highlighting his Hungarian roots. Unlike Royal and most French political elites, Sarkozy never attended an elite university. He participated in party politics for years and secured an appointment to Chirac's cabinet. Like Obama, he ran on a change message, but he knew he needed to curb this call. The clearest difference he brought to French politics related to generation. Frequently depicted as the frontrunner, Sarkozy, though criticized for various faults, was considered by the media and the public generally to be more qualified than Royal for the position of president.

Like Sarkozy, Royal represented a new generation of French leaders. Unlike her opponent, she repeatedly advocated a more compassionate government as well as a furthering of participatory democracy. She linked this to her generation by campaigning through interactive Web sites (Murray and Perry 2008). She also called for change, but in doing so, she located herself outside the mainstream of the Socialist Party. Her subsequent alienation stemmed in part from her own desire to break away from the senior party elite, whom she sometimes deliberately taunted (Clift 2007). Not only did she confront the old guard of the Socialist Party, but she also challenged the strong powers of the government and the presidency. Many of the French people did not support such a radical change. The public still did not prefer the Socialist Party, which had suffered notable presidential defeats in recent years (Murray 2010c). By distancing herself from the party elite, Royal created disunity without gaining the positive repercussions she sought.

Royal also lacked clear focus, sending contrary messages and shifting campaign strategies throughout the contest. Some portrayed her as devoid of substance (Clift 2007). These accusations appeared fair. However, she also received greater scrutiny for her gaffes than did Sarkozy (Murray 2010c). The media repeatedly questioned her competence and reported on her more negatively. It is unlikely that she would have won the presidency in any case, but this unfavorable treatment no doubt affected the outcome. At the very least, it illustrates the gendered backdrop of the campaign.

Royal's Election Results

Voter turnout in France reached 84 percent in 2007, an increase over 2002 that provides evidence of greater political engagement. This is at least in part a result of the historic nature of the race. Still, Sarkozy won with 53 percent of the vote to Royal's 47 percent (Sciolino 2007e), hardly a landslide but still a decisive victory. As noted, Royal lobbied for the women's vote, but Sarkozy received a majority of women's support: 54 percent versus 46 percent (Connelly 2007). Royal appealed more to younger voters, while Sarkozy performed better with older segments of the population. Crucially, he received two-thirds of the votes of former Bayrou supporters.

Similar to Clinton's case, no evidence exists that the electorate failed to support Royal because of her gender. Yet negative gendered portrayals of Royal by opposing candidates, Socialist Party elites, and the media possibly affected the election outcome. The "masculine" nature of the French presidency likely played a mitigating role.

François Hollande stepped down as Socialist Party leader in 2008, and he and Royal parted ways. The resulting vacuum hastened myriad internal disputes as Royal tried to gain leadership in the ensuing party election (Erlanger and Bennhold 2008). Royal won the most votes but did not have enough support to avoid a runoff, narrowly losing to Martine Aubry.[50] Royal then competed for the Socialist Party presidential nomination, but Hollande defeated her. His victory against Sarkozy in 2012 ended the Socialist Party's drought.[51]

Royal's Bid: Conclusions

Given the many obstacles outlined, it is no surprise that the presidential glass ceiling in France remained intact in 2012. This does not stem from a lack of qualified women running for executive office, nor does the French government's multiparty nature or dual-executive structure present hurdles. The biggest obstacles to women presidential candidates in France include the strong presidency elected by popular vote. Some women presidents around the world have overcome such difficulties through family ties and activist backgrounds, especially in unstable settings, but these avenues fail to open to women in France. Trivializing and hostile media coverage presents further difficulties for female presidential candidates.

CONCLUSIONS

This chapter has provided in-depth analysis of two candidacies that had not previously been directly compared—Hillary Clinton's 2008 bid for the Democratic Party's US presidential nomination and Ségolène Royal's attempt to gain the French presidency in 2007. While Chapter 8 painted in broad strokes the characteristics of female presidential aspirants, the Clinton and Royal case studies allow us to see more specific factors relating political institutions and processes to gender. Unlike most of the women analyzed in Chapter 8, Clinton and Royal cannot be discounted as "long-shot" candidates; they both possessed strong credentials. Furthermore, they competed for dominant posts in visible and politically critical countries on the world stage.

Findings suggest that the American and French presidencies likely will remain male reserves. This reinforces a major argument of this book: women fail to attain dominant presidencies through the popular vote particularly within countries that play important roles on the world stage. This is the case even when qualified, highly politically experienced women (with family ties) compete for power.

Clinton capitalized on America's tendency to promote members of political dynasties to the presidency. Her ultimate failure illustrates that family ties cannot guarantee victory. Both Clinton and Royal navigated tricky relationships with powerful men and suffered from appearance and "wife of" framing by the media (Murray 2010b). While the results from this chapter affirm many of the findings presented thus far, these cases point to an additional impediment to women presidential candidates that has been largely ignored: media coverage. While the media do not operate uniformly in every context, media coverage that amplifies negative gender stereotypes presents a further challenge to women's executive aspirations.

Overall, while Royal and Clinton presented the most successful challenges to the male presidencies in their respective countries to date, they failed to accomplish what a handful of women worldwide have managed to do—become presidents of their countries. Only by examining such "nonsuccess" stories can we accurately assess women's difficulties in reaching the highest positions of power in some of the world's most visible and influential countries. Results suggest that we must question women's ultimate progress in attaining executive office. Dominant presidencies in particular remain male bastions.

Conclusions on Women Executives and Directions for Future Research

In a special twentieth-anniversary issue, *Glamour* magazine selected the women leaders holding prime ministerial and presidential office in 2010 as "Women of the Year." In making the case for why the magazine awarded women national leaders this distinction, contributing editor Lynn Harris (2010) quoted former US secretary of state Condoleezza Rice reflecting on the benefits of women world leaders:

> They have remained focused on the issues of women's empowerment. Thanks to them, girls now have powerful models at the very top. With these women leaders inspiring the next generation, perhaps the concerns of today—girls' under-education, maternal mortality, rape as a weapon of war—will, by the fortieth Glamour Women of the Year Awards, have been resolved.

The issue presented interviews with four female leaders—presidents Ellen Johnson Sirleaf (Liberia) and Dalia Grybauskaitė (Lithuania) and prime ministers Iveta Radičová (Slovakia) and Kamla Persad-Bissessar (Trinidad and Tobago)—that emphasized the ways in which gender influences leadership styles. Some of the interviewees suggested that, as women, they are more compassionate than their male counterparts, advocate for peaceful solutions to pressing problems, and give special attention to issues affecting women and children (Harris 2010). Beyond this, many said that they feel they further the acceptance of women leaders in the public sphere and inspire other women and girls to enter the political fray.

According to President Grybauskaitė:

Concrete examples of successful women and their stories of achievement are the best inspiration and [means of] empowerment for other women to seek the heights in their professional career and take a leading role in society. The examples of female success stories are even more important on the global scale, as they help to disseminate the idea of gender equality and to spread the roots for the actual implementation of equal rights for women and men and democratic values among different cultures, societies and traditions. (quoted in Harris 2010)

President Johnson Sirleaf remarked: "I have led the way for moving women from traditional roles to strategic positions and inspired girls and women throughout Africa to seek leadership positions" (quoted in Harris 2010). Prime Minister Persad-Bissessar asserted: "I think my style defines my leadership in that it's a gentler, more compassionate approach. Rather than tell people what's good for them, I consult, I listen and I compromise where it's in the best interest of the citizens" (quoted in Harris 2010). Only Radičová hesitated in linking gender to her leadership style and policy priorities, though she recognized the long-standing resistance to women's incorporation as political leaders:

I understand that for millennia this been the traditional domain of men—and a vigorous entry of women into politics has caused a tsunami. If we take into account that women have had the right to vote only for some 100 years—in some countries even less—and that we have already won seats in governments or presidential offices, I understand that men look at this rise with some anxiety. (quoted in Harris 2010)

These excerpts from *Glamour* demonstrate many things. First, the global expansion of women presidents and prime ministers captured the imagination of the popular press (in this case, a women's style magazine), yet, as many parts of this book argue, scholarly attention to women world leaders remains lacking. Consequences of this dearth highlight the impending significance of increased scholarship in this area. The *Glamour* article suggests that women presidents and prime ministers act as women's descriptive, symbolic, and substantive representatives, but it ignores another important facet of women's representation—the formalistic (Pitkin 1967; Schwindt-Bayer and Mishler 2005). As I have argued repeatedly in this book, executive processes and structures have significant impacts on women's representation. Formalistic representation should ideally be incorporated with these other types (see Schwindt-Bayer 2010).

The title of the *Glamour* article, "Female Heads of State: The Chosen Ones," oversimplifies women leaders. Not all hold the position of head of state. A critical number actually lead governments, signifying substantially different roles. Further, executives vary in how they are "chosen"; the public directly elects some, while political elites select others. A few also move up through the line of succession when a sudden opening manifests. The article fails to discuss the extent to which women in 2010 occupy powerful executive posts, leaving readers to infer that the women featured hold the strongest leadership positions within their countries. While that is true for some, it is certainly not the case for others (see Table 10.1).[1] Finally, the article makes no mention of whether these women lead internationally influential countries.

By accounting for executive selection processes as well as presidential and prime ministerial powers, we can more fully evaluate the likelihood of women

Table 10-1. FEMALE PRESIDENTS AND PRIME MINISTERS IN OFFICE, 2010

Country	Name	Election	Office
Argentina	Cristina Fernández	2007	President
Australia	Julia Gillard	2010	Prime Minister
Bangladesh*	Sheikh Hasina	2009	Prime Minister
Chile	Michelle Bachelet	2006	President
Costa Rica	Laura Chinchilla	2010	President
Croatia	Jadranka Kosor	2009	Prime Minister
Finland	Tarja Halonen	2000	President
Finland	Mari Kiviniemi	2010	Prime Minister
Germany	Angela Merkel	2005	Chancellor
Iceland	Jóhanna Sigurðardóttir	2009	Prime Minister
India	Pratibha Patil	2007	President
Ireland	Mary McAleese	1997	President
Kyrgyzstan	Roza Otunbayeva	2010	President
Liberia	Ellen Johnson Sirleaf	2006	President
Lithuania	Dalia Grybauskaitė	2009	President
Philippines	Gloria Macapagal-Arroyo	2001	President
Slovakia	Iveta Radičová	2010	Prime Minister
Switzerland	Doris Leuthard	2010	President
Trinidad and Tobago	Kamla Persad-Bissessar	2010	Prime Minister
Ukraine	Yuliya Tymoshenko	2007	Prime Minister

SOURCE: Worldwide Guide to Women in Leadership Web site.

NOTE: Macapagal-Arroyo, Tymoshenko, and Bachelet all left office during various points in 2010.

*This is the second time Hasina has served in this office. She last served from 1996 to 2001.

occupying these positions. The connections between formalistic and descriptive representation can further or constrain abilities to represent women substantively, if that is indeed one's goal. If women executives lack real power and autonomy and depend on others for survival, their capacities to act on behalf of women's policy interests appear limited. Instead, providing that women exercise critical levels of authority and occupy secure and independent posts, they can perhaps better accomplish women's substantive representation. Formalistic, descriptive, and substantive representation may interact with symbolic representation. Women's political engagement could increase where women prime ministers and presidents ascend. Visible examples of powerful women may erode stereotypes associating men and masculinity with executive posts and heighten support for women political leaders. While this book has engaged more linkages between formalistic and descriptive representation, findings speak also to women's substantive and symbolic representation.

IMPORTANT FINDINGS RECAPPED

In this book I have focused on the degree to which women have made inroads to national executive offices and relevant links to paths and powers. Unlike most previous scholarship on women national leaders, my research has utilized large-scale comparative analysis, concentrating on nearly every country that has successfully incorporated women executives. By also integrating settings that have failed to promote women to these positions, this analysis has enabled a greater array of obstacles to women executives to surface.

Employing a women and gender in politics approach, I have incorporated the understudied group of women executives but also evaluated the degree to which women's paths and powers have proved unique or similar to men's. This obviously necessitated data collection on male leaders. At the same time, the focal point has been the degree to which gendered ideologies and stereotypes are linked to powers and paths.

Throughout, I have used quantitative and qualitative techniques to explore women's progress in attaining executive offices. This has entailed qualitative analysis of personal factors related to women's success as well as a more nuanced consideration of the systems in which women govern. The qualitative chapters have revealed a number of critical variables related to women's ascensions, enabling hypothesis formation. Quantitative models have offered the benefits of extending analysis to the rest of the world (where women do not yet govern) and confirming whether numerous factors seemingly related to women's rise, first identified in the more qualitative portions, persist after other conditions are controlled for.

Among the key findings is that women's achievement of executive posts is highly dependent upon selection processes and institutional structures, which, in turn, are intricately connected to gender. Women have attained far more prime ministerial and presidential posts over the past two decades than in the past. Rather than focusing merely on the numbers of women leaders over the past several decades, I have addressed how women's location in the power hierarchy and leadership responsibilities shape their abilities to serve as women's substantive representatives. Women's success is questionable, since the strongest and most visible executive positions continue to constitute a male reserve.

I have probed several factors related to women's advancement to executive offices, including institutional (electoral systems, governmental structures, parties and party systems), structural (women's educational and professional statuses in the general population, the percentage of female legislators and cabinet ministers in the political pipeline), cultural (gender stereotypes, family demands, views of women's roles), and historical (the timing of women's suffrage, earlier women leaders) conditions.

The quantity of women prime ministers and presidents has grown substantially since the 1990s and especially since the first decade of the 2000s. Some of the countries that women have led are highly institutionalized, peaceful, stable, and long-standing consolidated democracies. Others have only recently attained political independence, have been plagued by conflict and instability, and have experienced difficulties in democratic governance. Over the past fifty years, women have entered executive offices within many different countries. As of late, however, multiple female leaders have ascended within many of the same countries, possibly confirming the symbolic effect of women executives. At the same time, some countries have experienced women's rule once, but not since. Still more countries have *never* elected or appointed women national leaders. As such, the glass ceiling has been shattered in some contexts, such as Finland, has only cracked in the United Kingdom, and remains firmly intact in the United States.

By developing a typology of executive positions and political systems and placing leaders within these categories, I have been able to demonstrate that women govern in systems where authority is less concentrated. While more presidencies exist worldwide than premierships, most women executives serve as prime ministers. Women's progress in achieving presidential positions appears somewhat mixed but somewhat better than expected. Among presidents, a slightly greater portion of women are dominant players; still, very substantial numbers are weak. Also positive for women, a greater percentage of women presidents enter office initially through the popular vote. Nearly all women presidents are found in multiparty systems. Several weak presidents have no party affiliation, while the dominant and powerful presidents most often represent centrist or left-leaning parties.

Women's greater tendency to be prime ministers has major consequences, since prime ministers routinely possess fewer powers than presidents. While a larger segment of women prime ministers hold dominant authority in their systems, they still suffer from important vulnerabilities common to all premiers. They can be ousted from office at any point and exercise power more collaboratively than do presidents. Moreover, several female prime ministers hold weak positions. A major liability facing nearly all the weak prime ministers is that they can be dismissed by both parliament and the president. Women's greater tendency to hold prime ministerships likely relates to the depiction of women as consensus-driven players rather than autonomous actors. These limitations may be linked to stereotypes of women as softer and more collaborative leaders.

Regardless of executive type, women rarely lead the most internationally powerful countries (as measured by economic and military strength and nuclear capabilities). Even if a woman holds the bulk of political power within a country, her significance can be further enhanced by the country's being a major global player.

Assessment of more of the personal factors related to executive officeholders and potential gender divergences revealed no major age differences between men and women executives upon their elections or appointments. Women's lack of securing powerful posts appears unrelated to their lower educational and professional qualifications and, as such, may be related to gender. Women's greater tendency to be prime ministers results in their shorter durations in office.

Women disproportionately enter executive office in unstable contexts. Two related factors appear especially critical to women's ascensions to office: family ties and prior participation in independence or activist movements. Frequent regime changes sometimes propel certain women to power, especially ones with family ties. More generally, even within more stable contexts, women are apt to ascend when sudden openings occur. These findings help to explain women's limitations in attaining dominant presidencies. Nearly all dominant women presidents have enjoyed family ties to power or, as in the case of Ellen Johnson Sirleaf, relied on the route of political instability (regularly, the backstories of women leaders indicate a combination of both factors in Latin America and Asia and the importance of instability in Africa). In effect, this has greatly limited the paths women have taken to dominant presidencies.

While many of the findings summarized above are drawn from careful qualitative analysis, I incorporated several of these factors in a statistical analysis of most countries worldwide. Findings confirmed the importance of dual-executive structures and multiparty systems to the rise of women executives. Further, countries with histories of promoting leaders with family ties to power are more likely to witness women national leaders. Countries where another woman entered executive office prior to 2000 were more apt to see another woman follow her between 2000 and 2009. Many of the quantitative findings generally reinforce the findings presented throughout the more qualitative portions of this book. Though women have made tremendous strides in attaining executive office, men still hold almost all of these positions. Although 2000–2010 represents the period of the greatest gains for female national leaders, during this decade women rose to power in only twenty-seven countries, or 18 percent of contexts examined.

Given the finding that women less often gain presidencies, I investigated the extent to which this results from women's failure to compete for these posts or their inability to garner the necessary votes to win. Findings indicate that both factors are at work. Women did not vigorously pursue presidencies until the 1990s and have aspired even more to this position since 2000. Their greater willingness to throw their hats into the ring undoubtedly connects to their greater attainment of these positions over the past two decades. When women do vie for presidential offices, they rarely secure more than 5 percent of the vote. Most victorious women presidential candidates have not garnered electoral majorities but have been elected through pluralities or second-round runoffs. In nearly all cases, triumphant women did not have to spar against incumbents (almost universally male). Still, women presidential candidates rarely win.

To illustrate further the difficulties women encounter in attaining the strongest presidencies worldwide, I analyzed Ségolène Royal's historic and high-profile bid for the French presidency in 2007 and Hillary Clinton's attempt to gain the US Democratic Party's presidential nomination in 2008. Findings clearly revealed that even these strong female contenders were negatively affected by gender. While gender was not the dominant reason for the failure of either, it formed a central part of the backdrop of both women's campaigns. Together, the results of this analysis clearly reinforce arguments that dominant presidencies, especially those located within very powerful countries, appear most elusive to women. Thus, the executive glass ceilings in both the United States and France appear firmly intact, with no sign of cracking, let alone shattering, anytime soon.

Together, the findings from this assessment of women's headway in gaining prime ministerships and presidencies worldwide show mixed progress for women. Women have indeed vastly increased their numbers as prime ministers and presidents. At the same time, women executives' positions, paths, and powers are still somewhat limited. Fifty years after Sirimavo Bandaranaike became the world's first female prime minister, women hold only 7 percent of all presidencies and prime ministerships worldwide. Executive positions remain almost exclusively the domain of men. Ultimately, women's real progress is questionable.

TOPICS FOR FUTURE RESEARCH

While this book presents many important findings, I make no claim that it utters the final word on women national executives. Instead, my aim is to present a starting point for increased scholarship and discourse as a means of advancing the research agenda concerning gender and executive office. Several relevant topics remain to be explored.

Various Impacts of Women's Executive Representation

More research is needed regarding whether women's descriptive representation as national leaders hastens women's symbolic representation. Presidents and prime ministers are particularly visible actors, likely known to nearly all members of the public in their respective countries. The potential impacts of descriptive representation for enhancing women's symbolic representation seem profound. Among many possible effects is the greater acceptance of women leaders and women's increased political engagement and participation. As Ellen Johnson Sirleaf said in her *Glamour* interview, female executives may inspire other women to enter politics. However, firm proof that this inspiration takes place remains elusive, and obtaining such proof will likely require research involving interviews with a variety of women national women leaders and female candidates for executive offices as well as surveys of party elites. More research linking all potential forms of representation—descriptive, substantive, formalistic, and symbolic—to women executives is necessary (Pitkin 1967; Schwindt-Bayer 2010).

Scholars hesitate to test theories of representation in less democratic countries (Wolbrecht and Campbell 2007; Schwindt-Bayer 2010). However, integrating more diverse contexts sheds light on the limitations on women's access to political power in democracies (Baldez 2010; Ritter 2007). Political disruptions often facilitate women's advancement; democracy may be quite limited in many of these countries. Rather than ignoring these contexts, scholars should pay increased attention to divergent settings, as these may yield important insights into the complexities of democracy and representation.

Family Ties

Until very recently, all noninterim women presidents in Latin America possessed family ties to power, generally as the wives of former presidents or
opposition leaders; these ascensions usually also occurred within politically
unstable contexts. More contemporary women leaders with family connections—Michelle Bachelet of Chile and Cristina Fernández of Argentina—have
demonstrated high levels of ambition and political experience. Bachelet's independent credentials are so vast that scholars routinely fail to mention her family connections (Paxton and Hughes 2007; Thomas and Adams 2010; Cantrell
and Bachman 2008). In 2010, two women lacking familial ties as parts of their
personal stories, Laura Chinchilla of Costa Rica and Dilma Rousseff of Brazil
(who took office in January 2011), gained popular election to presidencies in
politically stable settings. How can we explain these cases? Did Fernández and
Bachelet help escalate the pace of women presidential candidates and offer
greater support for female leadership among the general public? While paths
to presidential power have become more varied in Latin America, this has not
occurred in South and Southeast Asia, where women still require family ties to
gain executive office. Attention to these questions necessitates in-depth regional
case studies.

The element of "family ties" may benefit from more thorough conceptu-
alization. What political position must a member of a woman's family attain
to count as a family link to power? What relationships can be considered
"familial"? If a woman possesses a family connection, to what extent does
she have to publicize this for it to be germane to her ascension to an executive post? Do family ties serve as catalysts to women seeking office (Hodson
1997)? Does the public view women with family ties differently than their
male counterparts, and do these perceptions interact with gender stereotypes and political institutions?

Candidate Strategies

The strategies employed by the diverse array of women candidates in their
quests for office constitute another fruitful area for future research. To what
extent do women candidates employ gendered tactics in their electoral pursuits, and which circumstances yield greatest success? While Murray's (2010a)
collection examines some recent female presidential bids, it presents only a
handful of cases, and the contributors fail to make consistent links between
campaign approaches and executive powers. Prime ministerial candidacies
remain somewhat mysterious. This is understandable, given that presidential

contests center more on individual candidates. However, more of the dynamics related to prime ministerial campaign tactics, paths, and powers should be examined.

Comparative Study of Gender Stereotypes and Discrimination

Much of the research concerning gender stereotypes of voters has been conducted in just a few Western countries (Dolan 2004; Herrnson, Lay, and Stokes 2003; Aalberg and Jenssen 2007; Huddy and Terkildsen 1993).[2] Applying the findings of these studies to many different regions and contexts appears problematic. More research relating stereotypes and executive office should be conducted in a greater variety of countries at both the elite and mass levels. The effects of the views of party elites on candidate recruitment are largely unknown outside the United States, Canada, and Western Europe (Niven 2010; Kittilson 1999, 2006; Cheng and Tavits 2011). Moreover, the studies that have been conducted have addressed the recruitment of candidates for legislative offices, not executive offices. With more data available, we will be able to make firmer connections between gendered constructs and women executives' paths and powers.

CONCLUSION

Women prime ministers and presidents have vastly increased in number since Sirimavo Bandaranaike assumed the Sri Lankan premiership in 1960. Five decades later, however, women executives remain seriously underrepresented as national leaders around the globe. Although this book has answered many key questions related to women's ascensions as well as the powers they exercise, more avenues require exploration. Future investigations should take diverse forms, including in-depth regional analyses, single case studies, and large-N statistical models. The resulting research agenda should center on the myriad ways women prime ministers and presidents link to women's representation.

Biographies of Women Leaders, 1960–2010

REGION: AFRICA

Sylvie Kinigi (1952–)
Prime Minister of Burundi (June 1993–February 1994)

Sylvie Kinigi was a student of economics at the University of Burundi before becoming a civil servant and adviser to the prime minister in 1991. As a member of the Hutu ethnic group who had married a Tutsi, she was in a unique position to help breach the rift between the two rival groups (Encyclopædia Britannica Online 2010a, 2010b; UNESCO 2011). Kinigi was elevated from bureaucrat to prime minister after the election of President Melchior Ndadaye in 1993. Four months following her appointment, President Ndadaye was assassinated in a coup, and Kinigi was asked to form a caretaker government. However, after the National Assembly elected a new president, Cyprien Ntaryamira, a new prime minister was appointed and Kinigi left government service. She became an outspoken proponent of reconciliation between Hutus and Tutsis and continues in that role today. Kinigi has held various positions in the United Nations, including special representative of the UN Secretary General to the Great Lakes region in Africa (Encyclopædia Britannica Online 2010a; UNESCO 2011; Reuters 1994).

Elisabeth Domitien (1925–April 26, 2005)
Prime Minister of Central African Republic (January 2, 1975–April 7, 1976)

Elisabeth Domitien was the first woman prime minister of Central African Republic and the first black woman ruler of an independent state (Zárate 2011). A businesswoman and politician, Domitien became involved in politics at an early age. She supported Jean-Bédel Bokassa, who assumed power in a 1965 coup (Encyclopædia Britannica Online 2010c). She became vice president of the Movement for the Social Evolution of Black Africa (MESAN), the country's only legal political party, in 1972. Three years later she was appointed prime minister by Bokassa, but she was dismissed in 1976 because of her opposition to Bokassa's institution of a monarchical state (Titley 1997). After Bokassa was ousted from office in 1979, Domitien was tried for covering up extortion within Bokassa's government (Encyclopædia Britannica Online 2010c). She served a brief prison term and was barred from participating in politics. Nevertheless, she remained influential in both business and politics until her death in 2005.

Rose Francine Rogombé (September 20, 1942–)
President of Gabon (June 10–October 16, 2009)

Born in Lambarene, Gabon, Rose Francine Rogombé studied in France but returned to Gabon to serve in the government. She worked as a magistrate before being named secretary of state for the advancement of women and human rights. She received a degree in theology in 2007 and was chosen as president of the Senate in February 2009 (Our Campaigns 2009; African Free Press 2009).

The death of President Omar Bongo in June 2009 propelled Rogombé into the presidency because the Gabonese constitution stipulates that the president of the Senate is the presidential successor (Radio Netherlands Worldwide 2009; Our Campaigns 2009). Although she served only on an interim basis (the first woman to hold that office), the political climate of Gabon was somewhat tenuous as concerns arose over a potential power vacuum (Koep 2009). Amid widespread criticism, however, Rogombé fulfilled her obligation as interim president and ordered a new election within the forty-five-day time frame designated by the constitution (Index Mundi 2012) After the election of a new president, Rogombé returned to her previous position as president of the Senate, in which she continues to serve.

Carmen Pereira (1937–)
President of Guinea-Bissau (May 14–May 16, 1984)

Carmen Pereira became involved in politics when Guinea-Bissau was fighting for its independence from Portugal. Women were likewise seeking liberation, but from the exploitative nature of the patriarchal system (Urdang 1975). Pereira, the daughter of a lawyer, was expected to hone her embroidery and other sewing skills and patiently wait for a husband (Coquery-Vidrovitch

1997). While she indeed found a husband, her career eventually extended far beyond household duties.

Pereira's membership in the African Party for the Independence of Guinea and Cape Verde (PAIGC) led her to assume several governmental posts. In 1973 she became the deputy president of the Assembléla Nacional Popular, a position she maintained until 1984 (Urdang 1975; Christensen 2011). From 1975 to 1980 Pereira served as president of the Parliament of Cape Verde. She also served as minister of health and social affairs, acting head of state for three days in 1984, a member of the Council of State, and minister of state for social affairs (Christensen 2011). She was deputy prime minister of Guinea-Bissau from 1990 until she was dismissed in 1992 by her successor, President João Bernardo Vieira.

Ellen Johnson Sirleaf (October 29, 1938–)
President of the Republic of Liberia (January 16, 2006–present)

Ellen Johnson Sirleaf was born in Liberia and came to the United States to attend the University of Colorado, where she studied economics. She then obtained a master of public administration degree from Harvard University. Johnson Sirleaf returned to Liberia following her education and immediately became embroiled in national politics, serving as finance minister. She narrowly escaped death in 1980 when all but four cabinet ministers were executed when Samuel Doe overthrew the government of President William Tolbert (CBC News Online 2006). After the coup, Johnson Sirleaf began protesting Doe's government. These activities eventually led her to flee Liberia. While working for Citibank during her exile in Kenya, she continued agitating for democratic transition in her home country. In 1985 she returned to Liberia to run for the Senate and was placed under house arrest for several months; when she was released she again went into exile in Kenya (CBC News Online 2006).

In addition to serving as a vice president for Citibank and HSCB, she worked for the United Nations Development Programme's Regional Bureau for Africa and for the World Bank and was president of the Liberia Bank for Development and Investment. She also served on the board of the International Monetary Fund. While initially supportive of Charles Taylor, who overthrew the Liberian government, she ultimately challenged him, leading Taylor to charge her with treason and exiling her again (BBC News 2005b; CBC News Online 2006).

When Taylor's government fell in 2005, Johnson Sirleaf successfully ran for the presidency. She restored necessary infrastructure, including electrical and water systems, in addition to providing general political stability. Although continually plagued by corruption, Johnson Sirleaf exposed criminal behavior within the government (BBC News 2005b; Cabellero 2006; CBC News Online 2006; Hough 2006; Independent Television Service 2008; PBS News Hour 2005; Whitaker 2010). In 2011, she was awarded the Nobel Peace Prize. She recently embarked on a second term as president of Liberia.

Luísa Dias Diogo (April 11, 1958–)
Prime Minister of Mozambique (February 17, 2004–January 16, 2010)

Luísa Dias Diogo obtained a bachelor's degree in economics from Eduardo Mondale University and began a lifelong career in Mozambique's finance ministry. She began as part of the technical staff of the program and worked her way up to head of the Department of Budget in the Ministry of Finance. She was appointed national director of the Budget Office in1992; in the same year, she completed her master's degree in financial economics (AfDevInfo 2008; Department of Public Information 2006). When she left the budget office, she went to work for the World Bank for one year before returning to the Ministry of Finance as the director of budget. She served five years as the deputy minister of finance and five years as the minister of finance before she was selected to be prime minister.

Diogo helped with public-sector financial reforms, restructuring foreign debt, reforming the tax system, and strengthening the financial position of Mozambique. She is currently working as cochair of the United Nations High-Level Panel on System-wide Coherence in the areas of development, humanitarian assistance, and environment (AfDevInfo 2008; Department of Public Information 2006). Diogo was ranked ninety-sixth in *Forbes* magazine's list of "the 100 Most Powerful Women of 2005." *Time* magazine also listed her as one of the "top 100 most influential and powerful people of 2004" (Encyclopedia of World Biography 2010; *Forbes* 2007).

Agathe Uwilingiyimana (May 23, 1953–April 6, 1994)
Prime Minister of Rwanda (July 18, 1993–April 7, 1994)

Agathe Uwilingiyimana was appointed prime minister of Rwanda during a time of continuing turmoil and tribulation in that nation. Prior to her appointment, Uwilingiyimana spent many years as a chemistry and math teacher (Yasinow 2006) before being elevated to minister of primary and secondary education, in which position she focused on making education available to all Rwandans. She served as prime minister for eight months, before the government fell apart. Rebels first destroyed the airplane in which President Juvenal Habyarimana and Burundi's new president, Cyprien Ntaryamira, were passengers. This same plane crash was responsible for elevating Sylvie Kinigi to Burundi's prime ministership (*New York Times* 1994). The next day, Uwilingiyimana's guards, provided by the United Nations, were killed and she was taken hostage. She was raped and, along with her husband, killed by her captors (*New York Times* 1994; Yasinow 2006). Ultimately, her attackers were convicted of genocide and murder (*New York Times* 1994; Simons 2007; Yasinow 2006).

Maria das Neves Ceita Batista de Sousa (1958–)
Prime Minister of São Tomé and Príncipe (October 3, 2002–September 18, 2004)

Maria das Neves was appointed prime minister of São Tomé and Príncipe after the dissolution of the previous government. Her appointment came during a long struggle between the office of the president and the Parliament. In order to strengthen their hands, the members of Parliament had attempted to rewrite the constitution. Das Neves was a consensus candidate among the three largest parties, and the president agreed to her appointment (*New York Times* 2003).

Das Neves was a civil servant in the Ministry of Finance, worked for the World Bank, and served as minister of economics and minister of commerce, industry, and tourism. The government survived a coup attempt, and Das Neves tendered her resignation after the government was restored. Her resignation was rebuffed; however, her government was dismissed on charges of corruption a year later (Africa Resource Center 2006). As prime minister, she focused on increasing tourism, promoting women's rights, and developing industry, specifically an oil industry (*New York Times* 2003; Afrol News 2002, 2003a, 2003b; Council of Women World Leaders 2011; Africa Resource Center 2006).

Maria do Carmo Silveira (1961–)
Prime Minister of São Tomé and Príncipe (June 8, 2005–April 21, 2006)

Less than a year after São Tomé and Príncipe witnessed the dismissal of its first female prime minister, President Fradique de Menezes selected another woman for that position. Maria do Carmo Silveira was governor of the National Bank from 2002 until 2005. She simultaneously served as prime minister and finance minister (Freedom House 2005). General elections were held the year following Silveira's appointment, and a coalition government assumed office (Encyclopedia.com 2007).

Mame Madior Boye (1940–)
Prime Minister of Senegal (March 3, 2001–November 4, 2002)

Mame Madior Boye was the councilor to the Supreme Court of Appeals and minister of justice and keeper of the seals before being selected as prime minister of Senegal in 2001 (Christensen 2011). Her position was to be temporary, and her primary responsibility was to oversee new elections (Jensen 2008). President Abdoulaye Wade was so impressed with her performance, however, that he appointed her to a full term following the elections. Controversy arose when a ferry disaster claimed the lives of almost one thousand people in October 2002, and Boye was dismissed as prime minister a month later (Jensen 2008).

Ivy Matsepe-Casaburri (September 18, 1937–April 6, 2009)
President of the Republic of South Africa (September 14–September 18, 2005; September 25, 2008)

Ivy Matsepe-Casaburri was born in Kroonstad in South Africa's Free State province. At the age of twenty-eight, she went into exile and would not return to South Africa for twenty-five years. During her time in exile, she enrolled in postgraduate studies in the United States and received a doctorate degree in sociology from Rutgers University (Ministry of Communications 2009; Who's Who Southern Africa 2009). Matsepe-Casaburri returned to South Africa in 1990 and became active in the areas of gender, education, economic development, and local government. In 1996 she became the first female premier of the Free State provincial government, a post she held until 1999.

Matsepe-Casaburri served as minister of communications from 1999 until her death in 2009. Twice during her tenure, she was named acting president of South Africa. In 2005 she served in that capacity for three days during the simultaneous absence of the president and the deputy president, and in 2008 she served for fourteen hours following the resignation of President Thabo Mbeki (Ministry of Communications 2009; Quintal 2008). During her long career, Matsepe-Casaburri taught at Rutgers University, was the senior lecturer and registrar at the United Nations Institute for Namibia, was the first woman and first black chairperson of the Board of Sentech, and was an activist on issues of education, gender, and research. She also received an honorary doctorate in law from Rutgers (Ministry of Communications 2009; Who's Who Southern Africa 2009).

REGION: ASIA

Sheikh Hasina (September 28, 1947–)
Prime Minister of Bangladesh (June 23, 1996–July 15, 2001;
January 6, 2009–present)

Sheikh Hasina's father, Sheikh Mujibur Rahman, led the independence movement that secured Bangladesh's freedom from Pakistan. However, he was assassinated in a coup that claimed not only his life but also the lives of his wife and three sons. Sheikh Hasina and her sister were in West Germany at the time of the coup (Bangladesh Awami League 2011), and Hasina remained outside of the country until she was elected leader of her party, the Awami League. Upon her return to Bangladesh, she assumed the role of opposition leader, and she was jailed a number of times in that role. She and Khaleda Zia (discussed in the next biography) struggled to free Bangladesh from military rule. When the military government was expelled, Khaleda Zia's party won parliamentary elections, but many of Zia's counterparts participated in the military government. As a result, Hasina continued to agitate for a caretaker government and new elections.

Eventually, her efforts led to elections and the Awami League won a parliamentary majority, leading to her installation as prime minister. She was eventually ousted by rival, Khaleda Zia, in 2001. She faced corruption and murder charges leveled by her enemies. Eventually both Hasina and Zia would be arrested following a military coup (Bangladesh Awami League 2011; Virtual Bangladesh 2006a; Green and Perry 2006; Banglapedia 2006). Once military rule ended, Hasina returned again as prime minister of Bangladesh in 2009. Despite threats of assassination, Hasina continues to pursue economic development and promote women's participation in various sectors of government (Bast 2010).

Khaleda Zia (August 15, 1945–)
Prime Minister of Bangladesh (March 20, 1991–March 30, 1996;
October 10, 2001–October 29, 2006)

Khaleda Zia's political life began when her husband, General Ziaur Rahman, was assassinated in a military coup (Banglapedia 2006). He had come to power as a result of a military takeover of the Bangladesh government. His death led to Zia's greater involvement in political party activities with the Bangladesh National Party (BNP), which set her at odds with Sheikh Hasina (discussed in the preceding biography). The military government eventually yielded to pressure brought to bear by Zia and Hasina as well as other parties. Like Hasina, Zia was imprisoned a number of times during their freedom fight.

In the election of 1991, Zia gained the prime ministership. She focused heavily on the role of women and on reducing poverty and improving education. She also concentrated a great deal on reducing the role of terrorists in Bangladesh. She served two terms before being defeated by Hasina. She retreated to the role of active opposition leadership until 2001, when she again defeated Hasina (Green and Perry 2006; Banglapedia 2006; Virtual Bangladesh 2006b). Upon the conclusion of Zia's second term, emergency rule in Bangladesh resumed for two years. Zia was arrested on corruption charges in 2007 but, like Hasina, gained release in 2008 (US Department of State 2010). Most recently, BNP activists have been protesting the disappearance of party members since Hasina's return to the premiership (Alam 2012).

Indira Gandhi (November 19, 1917–October 31, 1984)
Prime Minister of India (January 19, 1966–March 24, 1977; January 14, 1980–October 31, 1984)

Indira Gandhi was born into a politically active Indian family. Mahatma Gandhi (no relation) was a frequent guest in her family's home (IndiraGandhi.com 2008). She, along with family members, participated in India's independence movement. After India gained autonomy, her father, Jawaharlal Nehru, became the country's first prime minister. After her father's death, Gandhi was elected to Parliament in 1966 and was subsequently appointed prime minister when a death opened the position for contestation.

Gandhi led during a time of great turmoil for India, including a war between India and Pakistan and problems between East Pakistan (later Bangladesh) and West Pakistan. The war resulted in a military win for India and the granting of Bangladesh's independence from Pakistan (Kamat 2011). Gandhi was severely criticized for her heavy-handed approach to governance. She was accused of amassing too much power, ruling essentially as a dictator through issuing emergency rule. In 1977, she was voted out of power, but she returned to office in 1980, and her son Sanjay Gandhi was assumed to be her heir apparent. Upon his death in a plane crash, her other son, Rajiv Gandhi, began his political career. In October 1984, Indira Gandhi's bodyguards attacked and killed her. Rajiv Gandhi succeeded her (IndiraGhandi.com 2008; Kamat 2011), but Tamil militants murdered him in 1991.

Pratibha Patil (December 19, 1934–)
President of India (July 25, 2007–July 25, 2012)

Pratibha Patil has held numerous positions in local and national Indian government, including minister of tourism, social welfare, and housing; chief of her party; director of the National Federation of Urban Cooperative Banks and Credit Societies; and governor of Rajasthan. In all, Patil has held more than ten different positions in state and national government in India (President's Secretariat 2011).

A public supporter of Indira Gandhi, Patil spent ten days in jail for protesting Gandhi's arrest. In 2007, a male consensus candidate for the presidency was chosen by a group of left-wing politicians. However, on the day of the nomination, the coalition fell apart. The parties sought a more palatable candidate, leading to Patil's selection as the consensus choice (BBC News 2007b; President's Secretariat 2011). She easily won election at age seventy-two (BBC News 2007b; President's Secretariat 2011; NDTV Bureau 2007; Nilacharal Ltd. 2011).

Megawati Sukarnoputri (January 23, 1947–)
President of Indonesia (July 23, 2001–October 20, 2004)

Megawati Sukarnoputri's father, Sukarno, was considered the "Father of Indonesia"; he helped free the country from Dutch colonial rule after World War II. Sukarnoputri did not get involved in Indonesian politics until she was into her forties (BBC News 2004). During this time, General Suharto took over the Indonesian government and ruled as a dictator (CNN 2004; PBS News Hour 2001). His harsh governance propelled Sukarnoputri into action. She began protesting Suharto's government and resurrected her family's political party. Feeling threatened, Suharto refused to allow her to run for office. Eventually, Suharto was removed from power. In 1999, Sukarnoputri ran for president and reportedly gained the most votes (Sirry 2006, 477), but the Parliament instead appointed Abdurrahman Wahid, a Muslim cleric, to the presidency. Wahid successfully mobilized Muslim parties against a female presidential candidacy, though they were willing to elect Sukarnoputri vice president (Sirry 2006, 477). She succeeded Wahid after his impeachment in 2001.

Sukarnoputri brought stability to the government in the face of rising worldwide concerns about Indonesia's role in terrorism. A sluggish economy and continued terrorist incidents would ultimately cost her reelection in 2004 (BBC News 2004; PBS News Hour 2001; CNN 2004). The first direct presidential election in Indonesia was held in July 2004. Because the winner lacked a majority vote, Sukarnoputri, who ranked second, participated in a runoff election in September 2004, but she lost. Her third run in 2009 likewise proved unsuccessful (*Economist* 2009).

Nyam Osoryn Tuyaa (1958–)
Acting Prime Minister of Mongolia (July 22–July 30, 1999)

Nyam Osoryn Tuyaa assumed the duties of acting prime minister of Mongolia after the government fell in 1999. She served in that capacity for more than a week until the Mongolian Parliament selected a successor. Tuyaa remained in the new government as foreign minister (Jensen 2008; Christensen 2011).

Benazir Bhutto (June 21, 1953–December 27, 2007)
Prime Minister of Pakistan (December 2, 1988–August 6, 1990; October 19, 1993–November 5, 1996)

Raised a daughter of privilege in Pakistan, Bhutto was educated at Harvard University in the United States and at Oxford University in England before returning to Pakistan (Baker 2007). Her father, Zulfikar Ali Bhutto, served as prime minister and president, and he was hanged in 1979 for murdering a polit-ical rival (a charge he vehemently denied). Benazir, as her father's oldest child, took up the mantle of the Pakistan People's Party (PPP) and was eventually appointed prime minister (bhutto.org 2008). While she ran on promises of liber-ating Pakistan from some of its religious strictures, particularly as they related to women, her first administration was noted for its inactivity. She was ousted from government on charges of corruption in 1990. One of Bhutto's brothers was also killed while she was prime minister, and some of her family turned against her, accusing her and her husband, Asif Zardari, of being complicit in his murder.

However, Bhutto's departure from government proved brief. She gained reappointment as prime minister in 1993, after the government following her first term was also ousted. Her second stint was soon interrupted by charges of corruption, resulting in her husband's arrest and her family's departure from Pakistan. They remained exiled until 2007, when President Pervez Musharraf started clearing the way for her return to Pakistan and opened talks regard-ing a power-sharing agreement (Baker and Robinson 2007). Bhutto's trium-phant return proved short-lived. During a celebration of her homecoming in the Rawalpindi district, the same district where her father had been hanged, shots rang out and, shortly thereafter, a suicide bomb was detonated. The exact cause of Bhutto's death remains unclear (whether she was killed by a gunshot or by a blow to the head from the bomb concussions), but some suspect that the Taliban was involved in her assassination, likely because of her Western lean-ings (Baker 2007, 2008; Baker and Robinson 2007).

Corazon Aquino (January 25, 1933–August 1, 2009)
President of the Philippines (February 25, 1986–June 30, 1992)

Corazon "Cory" Aquino came from a wealthy and politically powerful family in the Philippines (Bacani 2010; Coronel 2006). At the end of World War II, her parents sent her and her siblings to the United States to finish their educations because of the residual effect of the war on the Philippines. Upon returning home, she abandoned her plans to become a lawyer in favor of marrying Benigno Aquino and starting a family (Bacani 2010; Coronel 2006). Her husband entered politics, first attaining a mayoral position. He became a vocal leader of the opposition to President Ferdinand Marcos, which eventually resulted in his arrest. He was held for a number of years, and upon his release the family moved to the United States so that he could seek medical treatment (Bacani 2010; Coronel 2006).

When the family returned to the Philippines to pressure the Marcos administration to hold free and fair elections (Benigno planned to run for the presidency), Benigno Aquino was assassinated (Bacani 2010; Coronel 2006). Following his death, Corazon Aquino was urged to run in her husband's place. She did so and won the election, but Marcos falsified the results, leading to the peaceful People's Revolution and Marcos's exile from the Philippines (Coronel 2006).

One of Corazon Aquino's first acts as president was to declare a revolution government (Coronel 2006). This allowed her to dismiss the legislature, rewrite the Constitution, pressure other leaders into leaving government, and begin a dialogue about land redistribution. Many of her critics noted, however, that she deferred the land redistribution plans to the legislature, which was composed primarily of landowners. Aquino survived numerous coup attempts and eventually oversaw the peaceful transfer of power (Bacani 2010; Coronel 2006). She died in 2009, and her son, Benigno Aquino III, now continues her presidential legacy.

Gloria Macapagal-Arroyo (April 5, 1947–)
President of the Philippines (January 20, 2001–June 30, 2010)

Gloria Macapagal-Arroyo was born into a politically active family in the Philippines. Her father, Diosdado Macapagal, was the ninth president of the nation, and many of her relatives, including siblings, nieces, and nephews, have been involved in governmental or nongovernmental service to the Philippines (KGMA 2011). Macapagal-Arroyo attended Catholic school in the Philippines before enrolling at Georgetown University in Washington, D.C. She finished her undergraduate education at Assumption College, and she later completed a doctorate in economics. Returning to the Philippines to enter government service, she held executive-level positions in the Department of Trade and Industry and the Department of Social Welfare and Development and served on the Garments and Textile Boards. She was elected senator and later vice president before she achieved the presidency in 2001.

Although many Filipinos initially welcomed Macapagal-Arroyo's presidency, her time in office was rocked by rumors of corruption, four impeachment attempts, and a number of coup efforts. She broke her promise not to seek a second term and was reelected amid allegations of vote fraud. In 2010, Filipinos elected Benigno Aquino III, the son of former President Corazon Aquino, as the new president of the Philippines. Macapagal-Arroyo was elected to Congress in the new government (Syjuco 2010).

Sang Chang (1939–)
Interim Prime Minister of South Korea (July 11–July 31, 2002)

Sang Chang became the designated prime minister of South Korea in July 2002, only to have her appointment vetoed by Parliament less than a month later. She holds a doctoral degree in theology from Princeton Theological College (Christensen 2011).

Myeong-Sook Han (March 24, 1944–)
Prime Minister of South Korea (April 19, 2006–March 7, 2007)

Myeong-Sook Han completed bachelor's and master's degrees in French literature from South Korea's prestigious Ewha Women's University. Shortly after she completed her studies, the government imprisoned her for two years because of her political philosophy. Upon her release, Han took a position as a lecturer in women's studies at Ewha Women's University (Kitchens 2006). Prior to being elevated to prime minister at age sixty-two, Han served as a member of the Unification, Foreign Affairs and Trade, and Environment and Labor Committees. She was also the minister of environment and the first minister of gender equality. Han resigned the prime ministership ten months after taking office to run (unsuccessfully) for the presidency. She advocated increased maternity leave, expansion of the U.S. Army base near Seoul, and greater German investment in South Korea (Kitchens 2006; Korea Society 2007). In 2010, Han was tried and acquitted of bribery charges and campaigned for the office of mayor of Seoul. She lost her mayoral bid to incumbent conservative Oh Se-hoon (Jackson 2010). She recently quit her post as opposition leader (United Press International 2012).

Sirimavo Bandaranaike (April 17, 1916–October 10, 2000)
Prime Minister of Sri Lanka (July 21, 1960–March 27, 1965; May 29, 1970–July 23, 1977; November 14, 1994–August 10, 2000)

Sirimavo Bandaranaike holds the distinction of being the world's first woman prime minister; she has served as Sri Lanka's prime minister three separate times. Bandaranaike's husband, Solomon Bandaranaike, was prime minister from 1956 until his assassination by a Buddhist monk in 1959. After his death, her political career began in earnest (BBC News 2000; Bandaranaike 2005). She was elected to the Senate and was appointed prime minister in 1960 at age forty-three. Her first term allowed her to show her skills in foreign policy. She successfully navigated relationships with India and China to help avoid an armed confrontation over a border dispute (BBC News 2000; Bandaranaike 2005; Government of Sri Lanka 2010).

After her first ouster as prime minister in 1965, she led the opposition. She regained the office in 1970, and during this term, she also served, simultaneously, as the minister of planning and economic affairs and the minister of defense and foreign affairs. Sri Lanka then implemented a dual executive, with a weak presidency, and Bandaranaike's second term was marked by a worldwide oil crisis, a food crisis, and an insurgency. She also initiated land reforms (BBC News 2000). In 1978, Sri Lanka established a presidential dominance system in an attempt to alleviate tensions between the government and Sinhalese Tamils. Opponents saw Bandaranaike as incapable of providing unity, and their alterations to the presidency deliberately sought to keep her from exercising dominant executive power. In 1980, her political rivals cast her from Parliament altogether, prohibiting her from running for president in 1983. When she again set her sights on the presidency in 1986, she lost the elections. She eventually won back her parliamentary seat in 1989. She returned to the prime ministership in 1994 when her daughter (President Chandrika Kumaratunga, discussed next) appointed her to the position (Liswood 1995, 8). She resigned in August 2000 and died in October of that year (Bandaranaike 2005; BBC News 2000; Government of Sri Lanka 2010).

Chandrika Kumaratunga (June 29, 1945–)
Prime Minister of Sri Lanka (August 19–November 14, 1994)
President of Sri Lanka (November 14, 1994–November 15, 2005)

Chandrika Kumaratunga comes from a politically active Sri Lankan family. Both her father and her husband lost their lives to political rivals. She was educated at St. Bridget's Convent and studied at the Aquinas University College in Colombo, Sri Lanka, receiving a baccalaureate in law. She completed a degree in political science at the University of Paris and was pursuing a Ph.D. in development economics when she was called home to serve her country (Gluckman 1996; Government of Sri Lanka 2008).

Kumaratunga's involvement in Sri Lankan politics began upon the appointment of her mother, Sirimavo Bandaranaike, as prime minister. The family

assumed that Bandaranaike's son, Anura, would succeed his mother, particularly given that Kumaratunga and her husband, Vijaya Kumaratunga, founded
an opposition party in the late 1970s. Vijaya Kumaratunga, a film idol turned
politician, was assassinated in 1988, and Chandrika and her children fled in fear
to Europe (Gluckman 1996). Kumaratunga returned to Sri Lanka in 1992 and
became her mother's heir apparent in the family party. She gained election as
chief minister of the Western Provincial Council in 1993 and in 1994, and was
appointed prime minister at the age of forty-nine. Three months later, she successfully gained the presidency. Upon her elevation to president, she appointed
her mother prime minister. She won a second presidential term in 1999 and
retired in 2005 due to term limits. Critics of Kumaratunga's presidency accused
her of being too ambitious, creative, and ineffective (Government of Sri Lanka
2008, 2010; Gluckman 1996).

REGION: CARIBBEAN

Eugenia Charles (May 15, 1919–September 6, 2005)
Prime Minister of Dominica (July 21, 1980–June 14, 1995)

Eugenia Charles studied law at the University of Toronto and then went on
to study at the London School of Economics. She eventually became a lawyer,
the first Dominican woman to do so, and specialized in property law (Pattullo
2005). In 1968 Charles helped form the Dominica Freedom Party and was subsequently elected to the House of Assembly and led the opposition. She was
later selected as Dominica's first female prime minister in 1980. Her tenure
in office was both revered and reviled. Supporters lauded her efforts to stabi-
lize Dominica and secure aid for the nation's devastated infrastructure after
the ravages of Hurricane David in 1979. Critics, on the other hand, accused
her of betrayal for supporting the invasion of Grenada by the United States in
1983 (Pattullo 2005). She survived several attempts to remove her from office.
Charles was made a Dame Commander of the Order of the British Empire in
1991, and she retired from politics in 1995.

Ertha Pascal-Trouillot (August 13, 1943–)
Acting President of Haiti (March 14, 1990–February 7, 1991)

Ertha Pascal-Trouillot was born to a blacksmith and a seamstress in Petion-Ville,
Haiti. She received her law degree from the Law School of Gonaives. In 1980,
she was appointed the first woman civil judge in Port-au-Prince, and she was

the first woman on the executive committee of the Haitian Bar Association (Haiti-Reference 2010). She was later the first woman selected to serve on Haiti's Court of Appeals. Her appointment as judge of the Court of Cassation paved the way for her succession to the presidency.

Pascal-Trouillot became provisional president of Haiti on March 14, 1990, after the removal of the military-dominated government following the ouster of dictator Jean-Claude Duvalier in 1986 (Jensen 2008). She gained this appointment after the head of the Supreme Court and other judges refused the position or were discounted (Jensen 2008). Political disagreements damaged Pascal-Trouillot's presidency, as charges of corruption and nepotism marred attempts to hold elections. She refused to resign. Following the election of Jean-Bertrand Aristide, Pascal-Trouillot was arrested and charged with complicity in an attempted coup. She gained release one month later.

Claudette Werleigh (1946–)
Prime Minister of Haiti (November 7, 1995–February 27, 1996)

Prior to being named prime minister by Jean-Bertrand Aristide, Claudette Werleigh served as minister for social affairs and foreign affairs in Ertha Pascal-Trouillot's administration (Diocese of Westminster 2010; Jensen 2008). She previously worked for numerous nongovernmental organizations, dealing primarily with adult literacy and humanitarian relief (Diocese of Westminster 2010). She received her education and training in the fields of medicine and law in the United States and Sweden, and then obtained a postgraduate specialization in adult nonformal education (Diocese of Westminster 2010; Pax Christi International 2006).

Portia Simpson-Miller (December 12, 1945–)
Prime Minister of Jamaica (March 30, 2006–September 11, 2007)

Portia Simpson-Miller came from a working-class family. She obtained a college degree at the University of Miami (Jensen 2008; Mascoll 2006). The resignation of Prime Minister Percival Patterson offered an opportunity for Simpson-Miller to succeed him. However, she first needed to gain the office of president of the ruling People's Party (Jensen 2008). Prior to being elected prime minister, Simpson-Miller was minister of local government, community development, and sport (Christensen 2011). She also served as the minister of tourism, entertainment, sports, and women's affairs, as well as minister of labor, social welfare, and sports. In 2006, she was named to *Forbes* magazine's list of the "100 Most

Powerful Women" (*Forbes* 2006). Her first term as prime minister ended in 2007, and she regained the position in January 2012.

Michèle Pierre-Louis (October 5, 1947–)
Prime Minister of Haiti (September 5, 2008–November 8, 2009)

Michele Duvivier Pierre-Louis was born in the southwestern city of Jeremie, Haiti. Following her primary education in Haiti, she enrolled at Queens College in New York, where she received a master's degree in economics. At the age of fifty-six she obtained a Ph.D. in humanities from St. Michael's College in Burlington, Vermont (Pierre-Louis and Ives 2008; Mahalo 2011). Prior to her prime ministership, she was the assistant director-general of the National Airport Authority, a national trainer for the Mission Alpha Catholic Church literacy program, a member of President Jean-Bertrand Aristide's cabinet, and executive director of Fondation Connaissance et Liberte (FOKAL), also known as the Knowledge and Freedom Foundation (Pierre-Louis and Ives 2008).

Pierre-Louis was a professor at Quisqueya University and FOKAL's director at the time of her prime ministerial nomination (Pierre-Louis and Ives 2008). Just fourteen months after her ascension, the Haitian Senate voted to remove Pierre-Louis from office (Guyler Delva 2009), alleging that she had done nothing to alleviate poverty in Haiti and was ineffective in rebuilding parts of the infrastructure following devastating storms in 2008. During her tenure, Pierre-Louis was instrumental in securing $1.2 billion in debt relief along with millions of dollars in funding from multiple donors (Mahalo 2011). She also continued her promotion of literacy and educational development. Since her removal from office, Pierre-Louis remains active in FOKAL and solicited aid for recovery efforts following the devastation caused by the earthquake that struck Haiti in early 2010 (Progressio 2010).

Kamla Persad-Bissessar (April 22, 1952–)
Prime Minister of Trinidad and Tobago (May 26, 2010–present)

Kamla Persad-Bissessar was born in Siparia, Trinidad, and received her primary education at Hindu and Presbyterian schools. She continued her education at Norwood Technical College and the University of the West Indies, where she obtained a bachelor of arts degree and a diploma in education (Parliament of the Republic of Trinidad and Tobago 2011; Sookraj 2010). She earned a law degree from the Hugh Wooding Law School in Trinidad and Tobago. In 2006, she received an executive master's degree in business administration from the

Arthur Lok Jack Graduate School of Business in Trinidad (Parliament of the Republic of Trinidad and Tobago 2011).

Persad-Bissessar entered politics in 1987 despite the hostile nature of the profession, especially toward women (Yearwood 2010). She was elected alderman for St. Patrick County Council in Siparia (Parliament of the Republic of Trinidad and Tobago 2011), a position she held from 1987 until 1991. In 1995 she was appointed the country's first attorney general and then minister of legal affairs in 1996 (Parliament of the Republic of Trinidad and Tobago 2011). She was the first female deputy political leader of the United National Congress (UNC) as well as the first woman leader of the opposition. She has been a member of Parliament for Siparia since 1995 (Parliament of the Republic of Trinidad and Tobago 2011). In the capacity of education minister, she succeeded in establishing universal secondary education as well as approximately thirty-two new secondary schools (Sookraj 2010). She was appointed Trinidad and Tobago's first female prime minister in May 2010 (Parliament of the Republic of Trinidad and Tobago 2011). Persad-Bissessar has promised to adopt policies that consider group dynamics and multiculturalism and has stated that she wishes to continue her advocacy in the advancement of education (Parliament of the Republic of Trinidad and Tobago 2011).

REGION: EUROPE

Reneta Indzhova (July 6, 1953–)
Interim Prime Minister of Bulgaria (October 16, 1994–January 25, 1995)

In 1994, when a deeply divided Bulgarian legislature failed to elect a prime minister, the president dissolved Parliament and appointed Reneta Indzhova interim prime minister (Jensen 2008; Perlez 1994). Prior to her appointment, Indzhova served as head of the privatization agency (Christensen 2010; Jensen 2008; Perlez 1994). It was Indzhova's duty to oversee new elections. Her brief stint as prime minister prompted her to pursue the office of president in 2001. She ran as an independent, and her candidacy was subsequently rejected by the Central Election Commission (Jensen 2008).

Jadranka Kosor (July 1, 1953–)
Prime Minister of Croatia (July 6, 2009–December 23, 2011)

Jadranka Kosor graduated from the Faculty of Law at the University of Zagreb in 1972. Following her education, she became a correspondent for the newspaper

Večernji list and Radio Zagreb (Government of the Republic of Croatia 2010). During the Croatian War of Independence, Kosor hosted a show for refugees at Croatian Radio (SETimes 2009). In 1995, she made the transition from journalist to politician and was elected to the House of Representatives. She was subsequently selected to serve as vice president of the Croatian Democratic Union (HDZ). From 1999 until 2002, she was president of the HDZ's Women's Association Katarina Zrinski (Government of the Republic of Croatia 2007; SETimes 2009). Kosor became the deputy president of the HDZ in 2002, followed by her appointment as deputy prime minister and minister of family and veterans' affairs in 2003.

Six days following the surprise resignation of Prime Minister Ivo Sanader, the ruling party elected Kosor Croatia's first female prime minister (BBC News 2009a; SETimes 2009). During her time in office, Kosor cracked down on widespread corruption in the government and was a proponent for Croatia's entry into the European Union. In October 2010, Kosor's government survived a no-confidence vote prompted by the opposition (Kuzmanovic 2010).

Tarja Halonen (December 24, 1943–)
President of the Republic of Finland (January 3, 2000–March 1, 2012)

Tarja Halonen has a law degree from the University of Helsinki (Halonen 2012). Beginning in 1970, she worked as a lawyer for the Finnish Trade Unions (Aimo-Koivisto 2006). She was appointed parliamentary secretary to the prime minister in 1974 and joined Parliament in 1979. She was also a member of the Helsinki City Council beginning in 1979. She was reelected to Parliament four times and the city council five times before leaving Parliament to become Finland's first female president in 2000 at age fifty-six. While a member of Parliament she worked on the Social Affairs Committee, the Legal Affairs Committee, and the Grand Committee. As a member of the cabinet, she served as minister of justice, minister of foreign affairs, and minister of social affairs and Health. She held the position of president of the European Union from July to December 1999 (Halonen 2012).

Anneli Tuulikki Jäätteenmäki (February 11, 1955–)
Prime Minister of Finland (April 17–June 24, 2003)

Born in Western Finland, Anneli Tuulikki Jäätteenmäki trained and worked as a lawyer before joining Parliament in 1987. While in Parliament she was a member of Finland's delegation to the Nordic Council, chairwoman of the Environment

Committee, minister for justice, and vice chairwoman of Finland's delegation to the Council of Europe. She also served as vice chairwoman and chairwoman of the Centre Party, the first woman leader of a Finnish party. In 2003, Jäätteenmäki led her party to victory and became prime minister (Jäätteenmäki 2008).

She served less than one year as prime minister before moving on to the European Parliament. Her resignation was forced after it was revealed that she had used classified documents in her campaign. She was tried for her role in the documents' release and was found not guilty (her codefendant, however, was convicted of leaking secrets). In the European Union she has worked on the Committee on Constitutional Affairs, the Women's Right and Gender Equality Committee, the Committee on Foreign Affairs, the Subcommittee on Security and Defense, and the Subcommittee on Climate Change (Jäätteenmäki 2008; Jensen 2008; Gibbs 2004).

Mari Kiviniemi (September 27, 1968–)
Prime Minister of Finland (June 22, 2010–June 22, 2011)

Mari Kiviniemi graduated from the University of Helsinki with a master's degree in social science. She has served as minister of public administration and local government, minister of foreign trade and development, and minister of the interior and as a member of Parliament since 1995 (Parliament of Finland 2012). She also was part of the Finnish Delegation to the Nordic Council. She has chaired or served as vice chair on various committees, including Parliamentary Commerce, Parliamentary Grand, and Foreign Affairs, and on the Supervisory Council of the Bank of Finland (Parliament of Finland 2012). Kiviniemi became the second female prime minister of Finland in June 2010 after her selection to the chairmanship of the Centre Party.

Edith Cresson (1934–)
Prime Minister of France (May 15, 1991–April 2, 1992)

Edith Cresson began her political career in the 1970s as a youth organizer. She caught the eye of President François Mitterrand and served in his cabinet as minister of agriculture, minister of foreign trade, minister of industry, and minister of European affairs before he nominated her for prime minister. She was previously the mayor of Châtellerault. As prime minister she was known for making colorful comments, which ultimately led to her removal (BBC News 1999; Sancton 1999). Upon her ouster, President Mitterrand sent her to the European Commission. She soon alienated European leadership by requesting to be made a vice president

Appendix

of the EC. Instead, she was given the task of overseeing research, education, and training programs. As the director for this group, she appointed her dentist to oversee AIDS research. Additionally, on her watch, a large sum of money for youth training programs was misappropriated (BBC News 1999; Sancton 1999).

Nino Burdzhanadze (July 16, 1964–)
President of Georgia (November 23, 2003–January 25, 2004)

Nino Burdzhanadze was educated at Tbilisi State University, where she received a degree in law. She earned a doctoral degree in international law from the Moscow Lomonosov State University. Following her education, she began teaching international law at Tbilisi State University and became involved in politics (Parliament of Georgia 2011). Burdzhanadze served as an expert consultant to the Committee on Foreign Relations as well the Ministry of Environment in the early 1990s. In 1995 she was elected to Parliament and chaired several committees, including the Foreign Relations Committee and the Constitutional and Legal Affairs Committee, as well as the Permanent Parliamentary Delegation to the United Kingdom. In 2003 Burdzhanadze was speaker of the Georgian Parliament when she and two of her fellow politicians led the movement to oust President Eduard Shevardnadze (Jensen 2008). Widespread street protests prompted Shevardnadze, who had headed a corrupt administration, to resign, clearing the way for Burdzhanadze to become interim president. She did not run in the subsequent election. She became acting president for a second time in 2007, when President Mikhail Saakashvili stepped down to campaign for reelection (Civil Georgia 2007).[1] Also in 2007, Burdzhanadze announced her intention to organize the Democratic Movement–United Georgia, an opposition party to President Saakashvili (Schepp 2008).

Burdzhanadze's experience in international relations earned her respect and recognition around the world. She openly questioned Saakashvili's handling of the war with Russia in 2008 (Schepp 2008). She has supported the European Union's involvement in the region, especially in regard to Georgia's conflict with Russia. She has also attempted to pursue better diplomatic relations with the Russian government, a move that has brought accusations of treason against her by members of the Georgian Parliament (RIA Novosti 2010a).

Sabine Bergmann-Pohl (April 20, 1946–)
President of East Germany (April 5–October 2, 1990)

Sabine Bergmann-Pohl holds the distinction of being the first and only female president of the German Democratic Republic as well as the last president of that country. By the time Bergmann-Pohl was elected president, the Berlin Wall had fallen and reunification with the Federal Republic of Germany was the predominant issue (Von Hellfeld 2010). The elections of 1990 were also the first free and fair elections held in East Germany.

Bergmann-Pohl, a physician with a specialization in lung diseases, joined the Christian Democratic Union of East Germany in 1981. She rose through the party ranks and became a member of the Volkskammer, or the People's Chamber (Von Hellfeld 2010; Marshall 1990). Reunification occurred just six months after Bergmann-Pohl took office. Following the reunification of Germany, she became the federal minister for special affairs for the new unified state. She was also named the parliamentary undersecretary of health and was a member of the German Parliament until 1998.

Angela Merkel (July 17, 1954–)
Chancellor of Germany (November 22, 2005–present)

Angela Merkel's father was a Protestant minister in Brandenburg, Germany. In the 1950s, he moved his family from Hamburg in West Germany to communist East Germany, where he ran a home for the mentally handicapped (Paterson 2010). Although living in a communist state, Merkel's family had access to Western newspapers brought in under church protection. Merkel was an industrious student and excelled in Russian. Following her primary education, she went on to the University of Leipzig to study chemistry, where she completed a Ph.D. in physics in 1986 (Christian Democratic Union 2011).

When the Berlin Wall fell in 1989, Merkel delved into the realm of politics and joined the democratic movement (Christian Democratic Union 2011). She worked for the press secretary for the final East German government, which was headed by Lothar de Maizière, and was named as the acting spokeswoman for that government. She then joined the German Parliament to focus on reunification issues. She served as minister for women and youth, party chairwoman, and minister for the environment, nature conservation, and nuclear safety. She was also elected leader of her party (Christian Democratic Union 2011; Paterson 2010; Government of Germany 2011).

In 2005, Merkel's party won a narrow victory, and Merkel had to rely on a "grand coalition" with the Social Democrats in order to claim the chancellorship (BBC News 2009b). Her job performance in office, however, won her the admiration of the German people. Prior to the world economic downturn of 2008, Merkel's economic policies had more than doubled the rate of German growth, and the German job market had improved. She also enjoyed high approval ratings (BBC 2005; Kulish 2007).

The elections of 2009 solidified Merkel's conservative government and allowed her to remain chancellor of Germany (Moulson and Eddy 2009). While her own party posted unimpressive results, the election effectively ended the "grand coalition" into which Merkel was forced four years prior. She was able to form a governing coalition with the promarket Free Democrats (Moulson and Eddy 2009; Paterson 2010). In 2010, Merkel's popularity seemed to dip because of a lack of government movement in regard to reforms (Paterson 2010). In addition, Merkel received sharp criticism from the European Central Bank and fellow European Union leaders for forcing a possible bailout of the debt-ridden Greek economy. She has also been accused of looking out for German interests rather than the interests of Europe (Paterson 2010).

Vigdís Finnbogadóttir (April 15, 1930–)
President of Iceland (August 1, 1980–August 1, 1996)

Vigdís Finnbogadóttir was born in the capital city of Reykjavík. Her mother was a nurse, and her father was a civil engineering professor. Finnbogadóttir studied French, literature, and drama at the University of Grenoble, the Sorbonne, and the University of Iceland (Women's International Center 2008; Club of Madrid 2003c). She worked with a number of theatrical organizations, including the Reykjavík Theatre Company, and served as a resource for information about the culture of Iceland. She began her political career as a member of the Advisory Committee on Cultural Affairs of the Nordic Council (Women's International Center 2008; Club of Madrid 2003c). She became chair of that committee in 1978 and was elected president of Iceland in 1980, the first woman to be democratically elected as the constitutional head of state. She was reelected in 1984, 1988, and 1992. She emphasized reforestation, land reclamation, education, language and cultural restoration, and the care of youth. Since her presidency, she has continued to focus on preserving not only the cultural traditions of Iceland but also the native traditions of all countries around the world. She has also been involved in a number of international organizations working in the areas of human rights and education (Women's International Center 2008; Club of Madrid 2003c; Vigdís Finnbogadóttir Institute of Foreign Languages 2008).

Jóhanna Sigurðardóttir (October 4, 1942–)
Prime Minister of Iceland (February 1, 2009–present)

Born in the capital of Reykjavík, Jóhanna Sigurðardóttir worked as a flight attendant and office clerk before becoming a member of Parliament in 1978

(BBC News 2009c; Prime Minister's Office 2010). As a parliamentarian, Sigurðardóttir served on a variety of committees, including Foreign Affairs, Industry, Constitutional Affairs, and Economy and Trade. She has been a member of the Icelandic delegation to the Inter-Parliamentary Union as well as the Icelandic delegation to the Organization for Security and Cooperation in Europe. Her diverse experience and popularity resulted in her selection as prime minister of Iceland in 2009. The selection of Sigurðardóttir, a lesbian, was considered a milestone for the gay rights movement (BBC News 2009c). A member of the National Movement Party—which she helped to form in 1995—she advocates for the mentally challenged and disabled, adult education, and the revision of social security (Prime Minister's Office 2010).

Mary McAleese (June 27, 1951–)
President of Ireland (November 11, 1997–November 10, 2011)

Mary McAleese, the oldest of nine children, was born in Belfast, Northern Ireland. She was the first woman to be pro-vice chancellor of Queen's University of Belfast. Prior to coming to presidential office she also served as the director of a television station, director of a public utility, and delegate to the White House Conference on Trade and Investment. McAleese followed Mary Robinson into office. She was reelected in 2004 as the only valid candidate for the presidency (*Irish Times* 2004). She was the first president of Ireland to come from Northern Ireland (Áras an Uachtaráin 2005a). She focused her work as president on "building bridges." Toward the end of her presidency, McAleese came under fire because of the cost to the Irish government of paying for her protection during her frequent trips to Northern Ireland (Murray 2009).

Mary Robinson (May 21, 1944–)
President of Ireland (December 3, 1990–September 12, 1997)

Mary Robinson holds both a master of arts and a law degree from Trinity College in Dublin and began her career as a professor of penal legislation, constitutional and criminal law, and the law of evidence (Áras an Uachtaráin 2005b). She additionally holds degrees from King's Inns Dublin and Harvard Law School. She joined Parliament in 1969 and worked on a number of committees there; in addition to serving on the Secondary Legislation Committee and the Joint Committee on Marital Breakdown, she chaired the Social Affairs Subcommittee and the Legal Affairs Committee. Simultaneously, from 1979 to 1983, she served on the Dublin City Council. Her legal practice focused on utilizing the law to strengthen human rights protections in Irish and European courts. In 1980, she was elected chancellor of Trinity College.

Robinson became the first female president of Ireland in 1990. As president, focused on international human rights issues. In 1997, she left office to become United Nations High Commissioner for Human Rights. In that position, she needled and prodded nations to do more to end human rights violations throughout the world. She served until 2002, when she left to take on a variety of human rights projects and concerns (Áras an Uachtaráin 2005b; Club of Madrid 2003b; Office of the High Commissioner for Human Rights 2011; Shipsey 2004; Elders Foundation 2011).

Vaira Vīķe-Freiberga (December 1, 1937–)
President of the Republic of Latvia (June 17, 1999–July 8, 2007)

Vaira Vīķe-Freiberga was born in Latvia and fled the country with her family in 1945 to escape Soviet occupation. She went to school in Germany, Morocco, and Canada. She earned bachelor's and master's degrees in psychology from the University of Toronto and a Ph.D. in experimental psychology from McGill University. At the University of Montreal, she taught courses in the psychology department and conducted research focusing on memory and language and the influence of drugs on cognitive processes. She also explored questions of Latvian identity and the political future of the Baltic states. She held a number of positions in the Canadian government. She returned to Latvia in 1998 and was named director of the Latvian Institute. At age sixty-one she was elected president of Latvia; she was reelected in 2003. She was active in helping Latvia to gain membership in the North Atlantic Treaty Organization (NATO) and the European Union (Chancery of the President of Latvia 2007).

Kazimira Danutė Prunskienė (February 26, 1943–)
Prime Minister of the Republic of Lithuania (March 17, 1990– January 10, 1991)

Kazimira Danutė Prunskienė was born in Vasiuliske in 1943, while Lithuania was a part of the Soviet Bloc. She attended Vilnius University, completed a doctorate in economics, and worked as an economics professor. In 1988 she became a part of the Sajudis Seimas (the Lithuanian parliament). A year later, she served as the deputy director of the Institute of Economics and deputy prime minister of Lithuania. At age forty-seven she became the first prime minister of the newly independent government of Lithuania.

At the end of her term as prime minister, she went to work at the Institute of Europe of Lithuania, a nonprofit science organization, and also became a part-time lecturer at the Vilnius Gediminas Technical University. She retained a number of governmental and quasi-governmental positions and relationships, including serving as a member of the International Committee of Economic Reforms and Cooperation and as a member of the Council of Women World Leaders. She continues to work on behalf of her political party (New Democratic Women's Party) and serves in the Seimas. In 1992 she was investigated for an alleged role in the Soviet KGB (Seimas of the Republic of Lithuania 2011b). She has run several times for the presidency, but always unsuccessfully.

Dalia Grybauskaitė (March 1, 1956–)
President of Lithuania (July 12, 2009–present)

Dalia Grybauskaitė was born in the capital city of Vilnius. She graduated from the Zhdanov University with a degree in political economic sciences (Baltic News Service 2009). Following her undergraduate education, Grybauskaitė worked as a lecturer in the Department of Political Economy at the Vilnius Higher Party School while she pursued a doctoral degree in economic sciences from the Moscow Academy of Social Studies. In 1991 she began working for the government of Lithuania as a director of programs (Baltic News Service 2009). She served as vice minister of finance and foreign affairs from 1999 to 2001 and headed the Finance Ministry from 2001 to 2004. In 2004, Grybauskaitė was appointed the European Union commissioner in charge of financial programming and budget. As a result of her work with the EU, she received endorsement from the EU commissioner to pursue the presidency of Lithuania. As president, she has vowed to provide tax breaks for small and medium-size businesses, to stimulate exports, and to demand transparency in her government (Reuters 2009).

Irena Degutienė (June 1, 1949–)
Acting Prime Minister of Lithuania (May 4–May 18, 1999; October 27–November 3, 1999)

Irena Degutienė was educated at Vilnius University and graduated with a degree in medicine (Seimas of the Republic of Lithuania 2011a). She worked for twenty years at the Vilnius Red Cross Hospital prior to being named deputy minister of health care in 1994. In 1996 she was elected to Parliament, and in 2000 she ran a successful reelection campaign. Twice in 1999 she was designated acting prime minister of Lithuania. In May, a bitter dispute between the president and Prime Minister Gediminas Vagnorius prompted the latter's resignation. The president appointed Degutienė to the position until a replacement could be selected. Later that year, Lithuania witnessed a second resignation by a prime minister, leading Degutienė, again, to fill the void (Jensen 2008).

Although Degutienė's role as a Lithuanian leader was brief, she has remained active in politics. She has been a member of Parliament and a delegate to the Baltic Assembly. She has served as the deputy chair of the Committee on Social Affairs and Labour (Seimas of the Republic of Lithuania 2011a). In 2009, Degutienė was the first woman to be installed as speaker of the Parliament (Seimas of the Republic of Lithuania 2011a).

Radmila Šekerinska (June 10, 1972–)
Interim Prime Minister of Macedonia (May 12–June 12, 2004; November 18–December 17, 2004)

Born in Skopje in the former Yugoslavia, Radmila Šekerinska attended the University of Skopje and received a degree in power engineering. She then obtained a master's degree from the Fletcher School of Law and Diplomacy at Tufts University (Academy for Cultural Diplomacy 2010). Between the periods when she was pursuing her educational degrees, Šekerinska worked in public relations at the Open Society Institute Macedonia and was elected to the Skopje City Council. In 1998 she was elected to the Macedonian Parliament and became a deputy coordinator of the Social-Democratic Union of Macedonia. After her reelection to Parliament she was appointed deputy prime minister, in which position she was responsible for facilitating Macedonia's entry into the European Union (Academy for Cultural Diplomacy 2010). Macedonia received candidate status in 2005. Šekerinska served briefly as prime minister in 2004 on two separate occasions. In 2006 she became party leader of the Social Democratic Alliance of Macedonia (SDSM), the first woman to lead the main opposition (SETimes 2006). She has authored numerous academic and scientific works, and the World Economic Forum has named her one of its Global Leaders of Tomorrow (Academy for Cultural Diplomacy 2010).

Agatha Barbara (March 11, 1923–February 4, 2002)
President of Malta (February 15, 1982–February 17, 1987)

Agatha Barbara began her career as a schoolteacher. She ran for election for the first time in 1947 and was the first woman elected to the Maltese House of

Representatives. She participated in every election from then until she gained the presidency in 1982, and won every electoral contest in which she participated. In addition to her role as a legislator, she was active in the fight for Malta's liberation from its colonial government. This advocacy netted her a prison sentence. As a legislator, she was selected to serve as minister of education, labor, culture, and welfare and as acting prime minister. She also served as minister of labor, social services, and culture. She was elected president of Malta in 1982 at age fifty-eight. As president, she focused on strengthening the Maltese position internationally. She was recognized by a number of countries, including Pakistan and China, for her work as a statesman (Department of Information—Malta 2005).

Zinaida Greceanîi (February 2, 1956–)
Prime Minister of Moldova (March 31, 2008–September 14, 2009)

Prior to being named prime minister of Moldova, Zinaida Greceanîi served as vice prime minister and coordinator of activity in charge of the financial sector (Christensen 2011). She also served as vice minister and first vice minister of finance, as well as minister of finance. The Communist Party lost its reelection bid in 2009 and Greceanîi, therefore, lost the premiership and returned to her position as a member of Parliament. Greceanîi made an unsuccessful attempt at the presidency that same year (Azeri-Press Agency 2009).

Gro Harlem Brundtland (April 20, 1939–)
Prime Minister of Norway (February 4–October 14, 1981; May 9, 1986–October 16, 1989; November 3, 1990–October 25, 1996)

Gro Harlem Brundtland completed her medical education at the University of Oslo and received a master of public health degree from Harvard University before returning to Oslo to work for the Board of Health, where she focused on children's health issues. She served as the minister of the environment, becoming head of her party, and then prime minister in 1981. In this capacity, she appointed eight women to her cabinet, a first for Norway. At age forty-one, she was the youngest prime minister in Norway's history. The Labour Party lost power in 1989, and Brundtland served as leader of the opposition party. When the Labour Party regained power in 1986, and again in 1990, she returned as prime minister. In 1996 Brundtland resigned as prime minister to pursue a career as the director general of the World Health Organization (Williams and CIMT Tech 1999a; World Health Organization 2011).

Hanna Suchocka (April 3, 1946–)
Prime Minister of Poland (July 11, 1992–October 26, 1993)

Hanna Suchocka has a master's degree in constitutional law and a Ph.D. in law
from the University of Adam Mickiewicz. She worked as a lecturer in law at
the University of Poznan and the Catholic University of Lublin. She entered
politics in 1980, becoming the legal adviser to the Solidarity trade union. She
also became a member of Parliament in 1980. In 1984 she was expelled from
her party and left Parliament but returned the same year. She served on the
Foreign Affairs Committee and the Constitutional Committee of the National
Assembly. She also served as minister of justice and attorney general for Poland.
She was prime minister for fifteen months, beginning in 1992. She focused on
shepherding Poland through the transition from communism to democracy.
After leaving the Polish government, Suchocka became Poland's ambassador to
the Holy See (Club of Madrid 2003a).

Maria de Lourdes Pintasilgo (January 18, 1930–July 10, 2004)
Prime Minister of Portugal (August 1, 1979–January 3, 1980)

Maria de Lourdes Pintasilgo grew up in the era of fascist dictator António de
Oliveira Salazar. Although a committed Catholic, she often defied the ultra-
conservative views of the church patriarchy and pursued her own progressive
ideas. She obtained an engineering degree in industrial chemistry in 1953. She
was a pioneer feminist, helping to establish Graal (the Grail) in Portugal, an
international Catholic women's association (O'Shaughnessy 2004; Women's
International Center 2004). After the Carnation Revolution in 1974, Pintasilgo
was appointed minister of social affairs; she later became Portugal's first envoy
to France (O'Shaughnessy 2004). In 1979, President António Ramalho Eanes
selected her to be prime minister, a position she held for five months. She ran
unsuccessfully for the presidency in 1986. Among the accomplishments of her
time in office were the establishment of universal social security, significant
health care improvements, and expanded education and labor legislation.

Nataša Mićić (November 2, 1965–)
Acting President of Serbia (December 29, 2002–February 4, 2004)

Nataša Mićić's rise to the presidency occurred as a result of a bitter political
conflict. She protested against the government of dictator Slobodan Milošević,
offering up her law office as the unofficial headquarters of Otpor, an anti-

Milošević resistance group. After Milošević was ousted from power, two years of Serbian instability failed to produce an acceptable replacement (Anastasijevic 2002). Subsequently, the office of the president of Serbia fell to Mićić because of her position as speaker of the Parliament. As acting president, she oversaw three presidential elections, but low voter turnout resulted in the voiding of each (Election Guide 2010). She eventually dissolved Parliament during this period. Throughout her political career, Mićić has focused on government transparency and investing in research and technology for Serbia.

Iveta Radičová (December 7, 1956–)
Prime Minister of Slovakia (July 8, 2010–April 4, 2012)

Iveta Radičová was born in Bratislava and was educated at the University of Bratislava, where she earned a degree in sociology as well as a doctoral degree in philosophy (*Slovak Spectator* 2010). She worked for a time as a lecturer at Comenius University and then as a staff member of the Slovak Academy of Sciences (SAV). In 2005 she became the director of the Institute of Sociology at SAV. She was Slovakia's first female professor of sociology. In 2006, Radičová was elected to Parliament and sat as the deputy chair of the Committee for Social Affairs and Housing. She campaigned for the presidency in 2009, competing well enough to enter the second round of voting. Although she was unsuccessful in the runoff election, her succession as party leader put her in the position to assume the office of prime minister (*Slovak Spectator* 2010). Economic woes, as well as diplomatic relations with Hungary, overshadowed the summer elections in Slovakia in 2010. The results of the election reflected the voters' choice for the country to go in a different direction: Radičová's center-right coalition was triumphant (BBC News 2010b). As leader of the best-polling party of the new coalition, Radičová was named Slovakia's prime minister, the first woman to hold that position (BBC News 2010b; *Slovak Spectator* 2010).

Ruth Dreifuss (January 9, 1940–)
President of Switzerland (January 1, 1999–January 1, 2000)

Ruth Dreifuss was born in St. Gall, Switzerland. Her family was forced to flee the country when she was a small child because of the impending Nazi occupation, but they eventually returned to Switzerland and settled in Geneva. Dreifuss began her career working as a journalist. She eventually completed a degree in mathematics and economics at Geneva University, where she joined the faculty for a time before leaving to work with trade unions. She then gained

employment in the Ministry of Foreign Affairs and sat on a number of its committees. She championed the causes of social insurance and labor laws, particularly as they relate to maternity leave. In 1981 she was elected to the general
secretariat of the Federation of Swiss Trade Unionists. In 1998 Dreifuss became
vice president of Switzerland, and in 1999 she earned the distinction of being
the first person of Jewish descent and the first woman to be president of the
Swiss Confederation (Williams and CIMT Tech 1999b).

Micheline Calmy-Rey (July 8, 1945–)
President of Switzerland (January 1, 2007–January 1, 2008)

Micheline Calmy-Rey completed a graduate degree in political science at the
Graduate Institute of International Studies in Geneva in 1968. She entered pol-
itics after operating a book distribution business for more than twenty years.
She was elected in 1981 to the Geneva Cantonal Parliament, ultimately serving
as the chair of the Finance Committee. She was elected to the Swiss Federal
Council in 2003 and served as the head of foreign affairs. In this capacity, she
worked on policies promoting peace, human rights, and poverty eradication.
She has also served on the Board of Directors of Swiss National Bank (Swiss
Federal Department of Foreign Affairs 2011). In 2008 she was elected president
of the Swiss Confederation. She regained the presidency in 2011.

Doris Leuthard (April 10, 1963–)
President of Switzerland (January 1, 2010–December 31, 2010)

Doris Leuthard was educated at the University of Zurich, where she studied
law. She practiced law in the firm of Fricker & Leuthard from 1991 until 2006,
during which time she held membership with the Aargau Cantonal Parliament,
the Expert Commission on Gender Equality, and the Justice Commission, as
well as the National Council (Swiss Confederation 2010). Leuthard was elected
to the Federal Council in 2006 and became head of the Federal Department of
Economic Affairs. In 2010 she was elected president of the Swiss Confederation
(Swiss Confederation 2010).

Tansu Çiller (May 24, 1946–)
Prime Minister of Turkey (June 25, 1993–March 7, 1996)

Tansu Çiller was born into a middle-class Turkish family. Her father had political ambitions that he was unable to fulfill, and this may have shaped Çiller's

own career in politics (Reinart 1999). She completed her master's and doctorate degrees in the United States. She and her family returned to Turkey in the
mid-1970s, and she began teaching economics at the university level. She was
elected to office in 1991 and became minister of the economy in a coalition government. She made a number of controversial declarations regarding Turkey's
finances and the role of the World Bank. While others intervened to prevent
her mistakes from damaging Turkey, they were unable to suppress the opposition forming against her. In 1993, however, she was appointed prime minister.
Allegations of wrongdoing followed her throughout her premiership, eventually forcing her into a coalition government. As a result, she lost the prime ministership (Reinart 1999).

Yuliya Tymoshenko (November 27, 1960–)
Prime Minister of Ukraine (February 4–September 8, 2005;
December 18, 2007–March 3, 2010)

Yuliya Tymoshenko attended Dneproptrovsk State University in 1979 to study
cybernetic engineering. When she finished her degree, she worked as an economy engineer at a machine-building plant, and in 1991 she began managing the Ukrainian Oil Corporation. She gained parliamentary office in 1996.
She became a deputy chief of her party and chair of the Strategic Budgeting
Committee. She was influential in shaping not only the tax codes of Ukraine
but also the fundamental financial principles under which the Ukrainian government operated. She also completed her Ph.D. in economics and became
vice premier minister under Viktor Yushchenko. She would be fired from this
position in January 2001 and arrested on corruption charges in February 2001.
However, she was released a month later because the allegations could not
be substantiated. In 2005, Yushchenko won election as president and subsequently nominated Tymoshenko as prime minister (Cutler 2010). She served
for seven months in 2005 and then returned to the office following elections
in 2007. During her second period in office, her relationship with President
Yushchenko seemed strained. She had not been his choice for prime minister; she came to power through election results favoring her coalition. She
confronted votes of no confidence in 2007 and again in 2008 (Cutler 2010).
In January 2010, Tymoshenko ran for the presidency against Yushchenko
and Viktor Yanukovych. While Yushchenko placed a distant third, the voting
results triggered a runoff election between Yanukovych, who came in first with
38 percent of the vote, and Tymoshenko, who placed second with 25 percent
(Levy 2010). She subsequently lost the February runoff election (Associated
Press 2010).

Margaret Thatcher (October 13, 1925–)
Prime Minister of the United Kingdom (May 4, 1979–November 28, 1990)

Margaret Thatcher was born in Grantham, England, the daughter of gro-cers. She attended school locally and went on to study chemistry at Oxford University. Raised in a religious family, she quickly become involved in conser-vative politics, as had her father before her (he held the position of mayor), and was president of the Conservative Student Association at Oxford. She twice ran unsuccessfully for a seat in Parliament.

In the 1950s she went back to school to become a tax attorney. She was even-tually elected to Parliament in 1959. As a member of the Conservative Party, she worked her way up to the position of education secretary and became party leader. In 1979 the Labour Party had lost favor in the country because of poor economic conditions and a number of labor union strikes, and when the Conservative Party gained a majority in Parliament, Thatcher became prime minister.

Thatcher's first term was plagued by bad economic news. The country entered into a recession, unemployment increased, and manufacturing plants closed down. During this period, the United Kingdom fought Argentina in the Falklands War, and Thatcher focused on changing her country's international military posture. By her second term, union reforms were reaffirmed and her relationship with President Ronald Reagan strengthened the United Kingdom's relationship with the United States. Hostilities also heated up between the British government and the Irish Republican Army, illustrated by a 1984 assas-sination attempt against Thatcher.

In her third and final term, with the economy fully recovered and the domes-tic and foreign policy of the country operating smoothly, she undertook a series of reforms to education, taxes, and the National Health Service. She oversaw the ending of the Cold War, the economic downturn of the late 1980s, and the first steps toward the European Union. She resigned the prime ministership on November 28, 1990, and then entered the House of Lords (Margaret Thatcher Foundation 2011; Satter 2009).

Milka Planinc (November 21, 1924–October 7, 2010)
Prime Minister of Yugoslavia (May 16, 1982–May 15, 1986)

Milka Planinc was born Milka Malada in Drniš, a small Croatian town for-merly part of Austria-Hungary. She fought in World War II in Josip Tito's par-tisan army, later earning the rank of lieutenant (Djokic 2010; Barlovac 2010). Planinc obtained power by rising through the Communist Party ranks over a period of thirty years. She was appointed head of an ideological propaganda committee in 1949. In 1965 she became education minister. After Tito's death in 1980, the Yugoslavian government restructured the executive branch. The National Assembly of the Federal Executive Council appointed Planinc, then president of the Central Committee of the League of Communists of Croatia, prime minister in 1982 (Opfell 1993, 118). Following the Yugoslav Wars of the 1990s, Planinc held nonpolitical positions.

REGION: LATIN AMERICA

Isabel Perón (February 4, 1931–)
President of Argentina (July 1, 1974–March 24, 1976)

Isabel Perón met her husband, Juan Perón, while he was in exile. He was an army colonel who had risen to the presidency originally through a military coup. They eventually returned to Argentina at a time when he was in poor health (BBC News 2008). At age seventy-eight, Juan Perón enjoyed renewed popularity and made one last presidential run. He selected his wife as his vice president. Some believed that when Juan Perón died, Isabel Perón would hold new elections rather than fill the presidency herself (BBC News 2008). Instead, she retained power and was elevated to the presidency upon her husband's death in 1974. Her leadership was marked by turmoil, including death squads that may have been responsible for as many as fifteen hundred deaths and "disappearances." Eventually, Isabel Perón was forced into European exile in Spain in 1981. In 2007, she returned to the public's attention when she was arrested and arraigned for her role in the activities of the Argentine death squads. Spanish courts subsequently rejected her extradition back to Argentina, ruling that the charges were not considered "crimes against humanity" and the statute of limitations had expired (BBC News 2008).

Cristina Fernández (February 19, 1953–)
President of Argentina (December 10, 2007–present)

Cristina Fernández is the second woman to serve as Argentina's president and the first to be popularly elected. She met her husband and predecessor, Néstor Kirchner, when they were both students protesting the Argentine government's undemocratic use of power (BBC News 2007a). They both then became active in government. Originally a psychology major, Fernández graduated from the University of La Plata in 1979 with a law degree. As a member of the Perónist

Justicialist Party (Partido Justicialista), she took part in the party's national convention in 1985 at age thirty-two and became a member of the Santa Cruz provincial legislature in 1989. Beginning in 1995, Fernández served in both the upper and lower houses of Argentina's Congress. Kirchner was elected president in 2003, and she was credited with helping him to victory. In 2007 Fernández was elected president of Argentina (Encyclopædia Britannica Online 2010d).

Fernández ran a campaign that promised more of the same, with emphasis on continuing the economic developments led by her husband and lowering the inflation rate in Argentina. She was so far in the lead that rather than actually campaign, she began meeting with world leaders to assist with the implementation of her economic and political plans for Argentina. Her first thirty days in office were marred by an allegation of illegal campaign contributions (BBC News 2007a; Carroll 2007).

In October 2010, Néstor Kirchner died of heart attack (*New York Times* 2010b). Many wondered how Kirchner's sudden death would affect his wife's reelection plans (Schweimler 2011), but she easily sailed to victory, attaining some of the highest vote totals in the country's history (Garlow 2011).

Lidia Gueiler Tejada (August 28, 1921–)
Acting President of Bolivia (November 17, 1979–July 18, 1980)

Lidia Gueiler Tejada came to power in Bolivia as part of a long history of governmental instability. An accountant by training, she served almost a decade in the Bolivian Congress before fleeing the country. When she returned from exile in 1979, she again ran for Congress. Upon her election, the presidency was in chaos, as no single candidate had received 50 percent of the votes. Her immediate predecessor held office for sixteen days before being overthrown in a military coup. Strikes in the country led to the military seeking a compromise, which resulted in Gueiler's being nominated for president by Congress at age fifty-eight (Encyclopædia Britannica Online 2010e).

Her leadership was never meant to be permanent. Rather, she was put in office to help create stability and work toward the return of an elected president. The military initially supported Gueiler's candidacy. However, a great deal of animosity developed between the United States and the military leaders of Bolivia, who felt that the U.S. government under President Jimmy Carter was attempting to manipulate the election's outcome. Specifically, they wanted to expel the U. S. ambassador from the country. The presidential elections resulted in no clear winner. Rather than see a leftist leader take control, the military overthrew the government. The coup was led by Luis García Meza Tejada, Gueiler's cousin. Coup leaders surrounded the place where Gueiler and her cabinet ministers had been taken hostage. Eventually, Gueiler made her way to the Vatican consulate and became an exile in Europe for almost two years. She later returned to Bolivia and assumed different diplomatic missions before retiring from public life in the early 1990s (Encyclopædia Britannica Online 2010e; Christensen 2011).

Michelle Bachelet (September 29, 1951–)
President of Chile (March 11, 2006–March 11, 2010)

On September 11, 1973, Augusto Pinochet launched a coup against the Chilean government. Michelle Bachelet's father, a general in the Chilean army, was imprisoned by Pinochet's government and died of cardiac failure during his detention. In 1975, Bachelet and her mother were forced to flee the country after months of detainment (Langman and Contreras 2005; *Newsweek* 2002). While in exile, Bachelet went to medical school to become a pediatrician, and after her return to Chile, she eventually gained appointment as the nation's first female health minister. Realizing the importance of understanding military strategy to executive leadership, she attended military academies in Santiago, Chile, and Washington, D.C., and was considered a standout student. Her military experience led to her being moved from the health ministry to a position as civilian head of the Chilean military (Langman and Contreras 2005; *Newsweek* 2002).

After assuming the presidency in 2006, Bachelet displayed a leadership style of active engagement and persuasion. Her primary platform was expansion of assistance to lower-class Chileans to close the income gap. However, critics questioned her ability, as a woman, to be an effective leader. While her initial cabinet was focused on gender parity, she quickly removed two women from the cabinet and replaced them with more experienced men (Langman and Contreras 2005; Clift 2007). Despite these problems, Bachelet took many positive steps toward advancing women's rights, and her presidency was largely deemed a success. She was selected to lead the newly created United Nations Entity for Gender Equality and the Empowerment of Women in 2010 (Lemmon 2011).

Laura Chinchilla (March 28, 1959–)
President of Costa Rica (May 8, 2010–present)

Born in the capital city of San José, Laura Chinchilla studied political science at the University of Costa Rica and then earned a master's degree in public policy from Georgetown University. She returned to Costa Rica following her education in the United States and worked as a consultant on security and judicial reform (Long and Miller Llana 2010; Inside Costa Rica 2010). Her first post in the Costa Rican government was vice minister of public security (Long and Miller Llana 2010). She was later named the first female minister of public security. In 2002 Chinchilla became a member of the legislative assembly and then in 2006 served as vice president and minister of justice in the administration of Óscar Arias Sánchez (Jaco Blog 2010; Long and Miller Llana 2010; Inside Costa Rica 2010). She resigned in October 2008 to run for president. Endorsed by Arias, she won the 2010 election with nearly 50 percent of the vote. She pledged to turn Costa Rica into the first developed country in Central America, campaigning on the issues of improved health care and citizen safety (Long and Miller Llana 2010). While she was not the wife or daughter of an executive or political opposition force, her father had been the comptroller general of Costa Rica for fifteen years (Jaco Blog 2010; Long and Miller Llana 2010; Inside Costa Rica 2010).

Rosalía Arteaga (December 5, 1956–)
Acting President of Ecuador (February 9–February 11, 1997)

Rosalía Arteaga held the presidency of Ecuador on an acting basis for only two days. She was elected to the vice presidency on a ticket that resulted in Abdalá Bucaram's ascending to the presidency. When Bucaram was impeached because of mental incompetence, Fabian Alcaron, the president of Congress, declared himself president, citing an unadopted constitutional amendment (Schemo 1997a; *New York Times* 1997). According to constitutional rules, however, as vice president Arteaga was the appropriate successor (Schemo 1997b). When President Bucaram refused to cede power, the military and Congress forced Alcaron to drop his claim to the presidency temporarily, resulting in Arteaga's interim appointment (Schemo 1997c). Two days after constitutional changes altered the line of succession to place the president of Congress first in line in the case of a presidential opening, Alcaron was sworn in as president (Schemo 1997d). Arteaga unsuccessfully ran for the presidency the next year. Following the resolution of the turmoil, Arteaga worked for the Amazon Cooperation Treaty Organization and served on the board of the Encyclopædia Britannica.

Janet Jagan (October 20, 1920–March 28, 2009)
President of Guyana (December 19, 1997–August 11, 1999)

Janet Jagan was born in Chicago, Illinois. A Marxist, she met her husband, Cheddi Jagan, at Northwestern University's dentistry school. Upon moving to Guyana, she immediately became involved in local politics. She worked to establish workers' unions and helped to lead the charge to end British oppression of the Guyanese people. Eventually, Cheddi Jagan was elected British Guyana's chief minister. Shortly thereafter, the British government disbanded the governing council and jailed both Jagans (Ko 2011; *Time* 1963).

Cheddi Jagan returned to office in 1957, and Guyana achieved independence in 1966. However, the country did not hold free elections until the early 1990s. When these elections were held, Cheddi Jagan was elected president of Guyana. Following his death in 1997, Janet Jagan first gained appointment as prime minister and then was elected president. After a heart attack, she resigned before her first term ended (Ko 2011). She continued working in the offices of the People's Progressive Party, which she cofounded with her husband (Ko 2011; Cheddi Jagan Research Center 1999).

Violeta Chamorro (October 18, 1929–)
President of Nicaragua (April 25, 1990–January 10, 1997)

Violeta Chamorro was born into a world of privilege in Nicaragua. Her family was wealthy, and Chamorro's education included private school in Texas. Her husband, Pedro Chamorro, was a journalist and a leading opponent of the Nicaraguan government who had family ties to the presidency. He was eventually gunned down in the streets of Managua, Nicaragua. His death led to the overthrow of the government by the Sandinistas and the establishment of a military junta. A falling out with the Sandinistas eventually led Violeta Chamorro to withdraw from the government and become one of its biggest critics (Hoge 1979; Flora 1988).When the Sandinistas were overthrown, Chamorro returned to public life and successfully ran for president as a restoration candidate, promising to undo the damage done to the government by the Sandinistas as well as their predecessors both at home and abroad. Comparisons were often made between Violeta Chamorro and Corazon Aquino, which Chamorro rejected (Managua 1990; Flora 1988; Purcell 1985; Robinson 1996; Uhlig 1990).

Chamorro's presidency was marked by strife as she tried to balance the demands of her country internally and externally. Nicaragua struggled financially because of its history of war and the fact that the Russians and Americans were conducting a proxy war there at the time. This turmoil included attempts by Sandinista rebels to take over the government. It also made other countries reluctant to invest in the country. Still, Chamorro's government was followed by a relatively smooth electoral transition (*New York Times* 1993; Rohter 1995).

Mireya Moscoso (July 1, 1946–)
President of Panama (September 1, 1999–September 1, 2004)

Mireya Moscoso came to prominence in Panama because of her husband, Arnulfo Arias, who was elected president of Panama three times (and deposed each time). He died in exile in Miami (Navarro 1999a). Moscoso, with a certificate in interior design from Miami Dade Community College, was dismissed by many people as undereducated and unable to lead. However, she returned to Panama and started a political party in her husband's honor before becoming president (Navarro 1999b; Gonzalez 1999). As president, she faced tough challenges. Panama was racked with poverty. She was the first presidential candidate to lead Panama without the pressure of the American military, but also without the benefit of American money and jobs in the Panama Canal (Navarro 1999c).

Beatriz Merino Lucero (November 15, 1947–)
Prime Minister of Peru (June 28, 2003–December 15, 2003)

Beatriz Merino Lucero served as a senator from 1990 until 1992 and then as a member of Peru's Congress from 1995 until 2000 (Christensen 2011). She was a vice presidential candidate in 2000 before becoming prime minister in 2003. President Alejandro Toledo dismissed her from that post only five months after she took power (Wildman 2004). He reportedly felt threatened by Merino's popularity and spread rumors about her sexuality (Wildman 2004).

REGION: MIDDLE EAST

Golda Meir (May 3, 1898–December 8, 1978)
Prime Minister of Israel (March 17, 1969–June 3, 1974)

Upon her death in 1978, *Time* magazine eulogized Golda Meir as an appropriate symbol of Israel because she was "above all tough." She was described as a pioneer in building the Jewish state and one of the world's most admired women leaders. Meir was born in the Ukraine, and the inequality of treatment faced by Russian Jews affected her profoundly. Her father emigrated to the United States in 1903 and settled in Milwaukee, sending for Meir, her mother, and her two sisters to join him three years later.

Meir joined Histadrut, a Jewish labor federation, in the 1940s and became head of its political department. Following the end of World War II, she acted as a fund-raiser for the Jewish government in the United States. She also served as an envoy to King Abdullah in Jordan to negotiate peace with the forming Israeli state. Once Israel became a state, Meir was named its first ambassador to Moscow. Additionally, she held the titles of minister of labor and foreign minister (Provizer 2003; Butt 1998).

Meir was the leader of Israel's Labor Party when the prime minister of Israel died. Upon his death, she was invited by her party to take over as prime minister to avoid a power struggle in the new nation. In office, she focused on establishing Israel as an enduring proposition in the Middle East and changed military policy from general response to swift and sure response on a grand scale. As prime minister, she oversaw the Six-Day War (Provizer 2003; Butt 1998). She was driven from office by the start of the October War in 1974 (*Time* 1978; Provizer 2003; Butt 1998).

Dalia Itzik (October 20, 1952–)
Acting President of Israel (January 25–July 15, 2007)

Dalia Itzik was first elected to the Knesset (the Israeli legislature) in 1992 (Israel Ministry of Foreign Affairs 2008). Previously, she had been a teacher and had served as deputy mayor of Jerusalem in charge of education. As a member of the Knesset, she worked on the Education and Culture Committee, the Committee for the Advancement of the Status of Women, the Science and Technology Committee, and the Internal Affairs and Environment Committee. She was named minister of the environment in 1999 and minister of industry and trade in 2001. In 2006, Itzik was selected speaker of the Knesset. She became acting president in 2007 when then President Moshe Katsav was granted a temporary suspension in order to address charges of rape and other offenses (Frenkel 2007).

REGION: NORTH AMERICA

Kim Campbell (March 10, 1947–)
Prime Minister of Canada (June 25–November 5, 1993)

A native of British Columbia, Kim Campbell received a degree in political science from the University of British Columbia, where she was active in the student government. Campbell earned a law degree in 1984 and practiced law in Vancouver until 1986. Her first public political work was as a trustee on the Vancouver School Board in 1983. She later served in the British Columbia

Legislative Assembly. In the federal government, she served in the cabinet as minister of Indian affairs and northern development, minister of justice, attorney general, and minister of defense. In 1993, Prime Minister Brian Mulroney announced that he would not be running for reelection. After much campaigning, Campbell won the party election to replace Mulroney. Upon her elevation to prime minister, she made cuts to the number of ministries and worked to reduce ministry expenses. Campbell's reelection possibilities were seriously handicapped by missteps in her campaign and a general Canadian fatigue with the Conservative Party following Mulroney's service. Campbell was defeated in the November 1993 election by the Liberal Party's Jean Chrétien (Bliss 2011; Farnsworth 1993a, 1993b).

REGION: OCEANIA

Julia Gillard (September 29, 1961–)
Prime Minister of Australia (June 24, 2010–present)

Julia Gillard was born in Barry, Wales, and emigrated to Australia in 1966 along with her parents and her older sister, Allison (Wills 2010). She grew up in Adelaide and attended Mitcham Demonstration School and Unley High School. Gillard enrolled at the University of Adelaide, then transferred to the University of Melbourne. She graduated from the University of Melbourne in 1990, receiving degrees in both law and arts. Following her education, she joined the law firm of Slater & Gordon and became one of the firm's first female partners.

Gillard served as chief of staff to the opposition leader of the state of Victoria from 1996 to 1998. She ran for and won the federal seat of Lalor for the Australian Labor Party in 1998 (Government of Australia 2012). As a proponent for social equity and education (Wills 2010), Gillard served on the House of Representatives Standing Committee on Employment, Education, and Workplace Relations from 1998 to 2001 (Government of Australia 2012). Following the Labor Party's victory in the 2007 federal election, she became deputy prime minister and minister for education, employment, and workplace relations and social inclusion. Gillard's rise in politics came under scrutiny in 2007 when it was revealed that as a student she was a "key figure in a socialist group that pushed radical policies and social agendas" (Wright 2007). The group advocated the cutting of Australia's ties to the United States, the introduction of death duties (inheritance taxes), and the redistribution of wealth.

Jenny Shipley (February 4, 1952–)
Prime Minister of New Zealand (December 8, 1997–December 10, 1999)

Jenny Shipley's political career began at the local level. Prior to becoming active in politics, she was a primary school teacher and farmer, having finished her degree from Christchurch Teachers College. She joined Parliament in 1987. While in Parliament, she served as minister of social welfare, minister of women's affairs, and minister of health. In 1997 she became prime minister of New Zealand. She focused on New Zealand's recovery from the Asian economic crisis, advanced a free trade agenda, and worked on a solution for East Timor. After her prime ministership ended in 1999, she spent four years as leader of the opposition before retiring from politics at age fifty. She then began a career as a consultant, speaker, and strategic adviser for the public and private sector. Since leaving office she has also sat on a number of boards of directors and consults as an adviser to some government agencies (Celebrity Speakers 2009; Official Website of the New Zealand Government 2009).

Helen Elizabeth Clark (February 26, 1950–)
Prime Minister of New Zealand (December 10, 1999–November 19, 2008)

Helen Elizabeth Clark gained prominence in the New Zealand Labour Party in 1978, working as an executive member of the Auckland Regional Council. She became a cabinet minister in 1987 and served over time as minister of housing, minister of conservation, minister of health, and deputy prime minister. In 1999, she became prime minister of New Zealand, leading the ruling coalition. As prime minister she worked to improve the welfare system and reduce unemployment (Serafin 2008; Associated Press 2008a) as part of an effort to shepherd New Zealand through the end of an economic bust. Ultimately, the economic crisis of 2008–2009 led to the ouster of Labour Party as the dominant force in New Zealand politics. In November 2008, Clark pledged to continue her work as a member of Parliament but resigned from the leadership of the Labour Party.

Table A-1. TENURES OF WOMEN LEADERS AND THEIR PREDECESSORS

Region	Country	WOMAN LEADER		PREDECESSOR	
		POSITION Name	Tenure (years, months)	POSITION Name	Tenure(years, months)
Africa	Burundi	PM Kinigi	7 m	PM Sibomana	**4 y, 8 m**
	Central African Republic	PM Domitien	1 y, 3 m	PM Bokassa*	**9 y**
	Liberia	PRES Johnson Sirleaf	**4 y, 6 m+**	PRES Blah	2 m
	Mozambique	PM Diogo	5 y, 11 m	PM Mocumbi	**9 y, 2 m**
	Rwanda	PM Uwilingiyimana	8 m	PM Nsengiy	**1 y, 3m**
	São Tomé and Príncipe	PM das Neves	**9 m**	PM Costa	6 m
		PM Silveira	**10 m**	PM d'Almeida	8 m
	Senegal	PM Boye	**1 y, 8 m**	PM Niasse	10 m
Asia	Bangladesh	PM Wajed	5 y	PM Zia	
		PM Zia	**10 y**	PM Ahmed	8 m
	India	PM Gandhi	**15 y, 11m**	PM Shastri	1 y, 7 m
		PRES Patil	3 y, 2 m+	PRES Kalam	5 y
	Indonesia	PRES Sukarnoputri	**3 y, 2 m**	PRES Wahid	1 y, 9 m
	Kyrgyzstan	PRES Otunbayeva	5 m+	PRES Bakiyev	5 y, 1 m
	Pakistan	PM Bhutto	1 y, 8 m	PM Junego	**4 y, 2 m**
		PM Bhutto	**3 y**	PM Sharif	2 y, 8 m
	Philippines	PRES Aquino	6 y, 4 m	PRES Marcos	**20 y**
		PRES Macapagal-Arroyo	**10y, 2 m**	PRES Estrada	2 y, 6 m
	South Korea	PM Han	10 m	PM Lee	**1 y, 8 m**
	Sri Lanka	PM Bandaranaike	**4 y, 8 m**	PM Senanayake	4 m
		PM Bandaranaike	**7 y, 1 m**	PM Senanayake	5 y, 2 m
		PM Bandaranaike	**5 y, 8 m**	PM Kumaratunga	1 y
		PRES Kumaratunga	**11 y**	PRES Wijetunga	1 y, 6 m

Caribbean	Dominica	PM Charles	**14 y, 10 m**	PM Seraphine	1 y, 1 m
	Jamaica	PM Simpson-Miller	1 y, 5 m	PM Patterson	**14 y**
	Haiti	PM Werleigh	3 m	PM Michel	**11 m**
		PM Pierre-Louis	1 y, 2 m	PM Alexis	**2 y, 2m**
	Trinidad and Tobago	PM Persad-Bissessar	6 m+	PM Manning	8 y, 5 m
Europe	Croatia	PM Kosor	1 y+	PM Sanader	6 y
	Finland	PRES Halonen	**10 y, 3 m+**	PRES Ahtisaari	6 y
		PM Jäättenmäki	2 m	PM Lipponen	**8 y**
		PM Kiviniemi	5 m+	PM Vanhanen	7 y
	France	PM Cresson	11 m	PM Rocard	**3 y**
	Germany	Chancellor Merkel	5 y+	Chancellor Schröder	7 y
	Iceland	PRES Finnbogadóttir	**16 y**	PM Eldjárn	12 y
		PM Jóhanna Sigurðardóttir	1 y, 10 m+	PM Haarde	3 y
	Ireland	PRES McAleese	12 y, 3 m+	PRES Robinson	6 y, 9 m
		PRES Robinson	6 y, 9 m	PRES Hillery	**14 y**
	Latvia	PRES Vīķe-Freiberga	**8 y**	PRES Ulmanis	6 y
	Lithuania	PM Prunskienė	9 m	No predecessor	
		PRES Grybauskaitė	1 y, 4 m+	PRES Adamkus	5 y
	Malta	PRES Barbara	5 y	PRES Buttigieg	5 y
	Moldova	PM Greceanîi	1 y, 5 m	PM Tarlev	**6 y, 11 m**
	Norway	PM Brundtland	8 m	PM Nordli	**5 y**
		PM Brundtland	3 y, 5 m	PM Willoch	**4 y, 6 m**
		PM Brundtland	**5 y, 11 m**	PM Syse	1 y
	Poland	PM Suchocka	**1 y, 3 m**	PM Pawlak	1 m

(continued)

Table A-1. CONTINUED

Region	Country	WOMAN LEADER		PREDECESSOR	
		POSITION Name	Tenure (years, months)	POSITION Name	Tenure(years, months)
	Slovakia	PM Radičová	4 m+	PM Fico	4 y
	Switzerland	PRES Dreifuss	1 y	PRES Cotti	1 y
		PRES Calmy-Rey	1 y	PRES Leuenberger	1 y
		PRES Leuthard	1 y	PRES Deiss	1 y
	Turkey	PM Çiller	**2 y, 8 m**	PM Demirel	1 y, 5 m
	Ukraine	PM Tymoshenko**	7 m	PM Yushchenko	**2 y, 1m**
		PM Tymoshenko	**2 y, 2 m**	PM Yanukovych	2 y, 1 m
	United Kingdom	PM Thatcher	**11 y, 6 m**	PM Callaghan	3 y, 1 m
Latin America	Yugoslavia	PM Planinc	4 y	PM Djuranović	**5 y, 2 m**
	Argentina	PRES I. Perón	**1 y, 8 m**	PRES J. Perón	1 y, 6 m (total 18 y)
		PRES C. Fernández	3 y+	PRES N. Kirchner	5 y, 7 m
	Chile	PRES Bachelet	6 y	PRES Escobar	6 y
	Costa Rica	PRES Chinchilla	10 m+	PRES Arias	4 y
	Guyana	PRES Jagan	**1 y, 7 m**	PRES Jagdeo	9 m
	Nicaragua	PRES Chamorro	**6 y, 8 m**	PRES Ortega	5 y, 3 m
	Panama	PRES Moscoso	5 y	PRES Balladares	5 y
	Peru	PM Merino	5 m	PM La Fuente	**11 m**
Middle East	Israel	PM Meir	**5 y, 2 m**	PM Eshkol	**5 y, 8 m**
North America	Canada	PM Campbell	4 m	PM Mulroney	**8 y, 9 m**

Oceania	New Zealand	PM Shipley	2 y	PM Bolger	**7 y, 1 m**
		PM Clark	**8 y, 11 m**	PM Shipley	2 y
	Australia	PM Gillard	6 m+	PM Rudd	2 y, 6 m

SOURCE: Author's analysis of data from the World Political Leaders (1945–2010) page of the Zárate's Political Collections Web site. Date durations for women leaders still in office were determined as of December 1, 2010.

NOTES: Women leaders are listed first, with their predecessors (not interim leaders) following. Bold numbers indicate longer durations. A plus sign indicates that the leader was still in office when the calculations were made (March 2010). Comparisons were not made when any of the following applied: (1) the successor was still in office when calculations made (March 2010) *and* the successor's tenure did not already exceed her predecessor's (Johnson Sirleaf and Blah, Liberia; Otunbayeva and Bakiyev, Kyrgyzstan; Persad-Bissessar and Manning, Trinidad and Tobago; Kiviniemi and Vanhanen, Finland; Merkel and Schröder, Germany; Grybauskaitė and Adamkus, Lithuania; Radičová and Fico, Slovakia; Gillard and Rudd, Australia); (2) a woman succeeded another woman (Wajed and Zia, Bangladesh; Bandaranaike and Kumaratunga, Sri Lanka; McAleese and Robinson, Ireland); (3) there was no predecessor (Prunskienė, Lithuania). Totals include nonconsecutive terms and multiple terms (Bhutto, Pakistan; Bandaranaike, Sri Lanka; Brundtland, Norway; Tymoshenko, Ukraine).

*Bokassa had already declared himself president prior as well. **The person who served immediately before Tymoshenko served only on an interim basis.

Table A-2. Male Leaders and Familial Ties

Country	Male Leader	Ties to
Antigua	Prime Minister Lester B. Bird	Father, Prime Minister Vere C. Bird
Armenia	Prime Minister Aram Sargsyan	Brother, Prime Minister Vazgen Sargsyan
Azerbaijan	President Ilham Aliev	Father, President Hedyar Aliev
Barbados	Prime Minister Tom Adams	Father, Prime Minister Grantley Adams
Belgium	Prime Minister Mark Eyskens	Father, Prime Minister Gaston Eyskens
Bolivia	President Adolfo Ballivián	Father, President José Ballivián
Botswana	President Ian Khama	Father, President Seretse Khama
Brazil	President H. R. da Fonseca	Uncle, President Deodoro Fonseca
Central African Republic	President Jean-Bédel Bokassa	Cousin, President David Dacko
Chile	President Jorge Alessandri Rodríguez	Father, President Arturo Rodríguez
	President Federico Errázuriz Echaurren	Father, Federico Marcos del Rosario Errázuriz Zañartu
	President Eduardo Frei Ruiz-Tagle	Father, President. Eduardo Frei Montalva
	President Pedro Elías Pablo Montt Montt	Father, President Manuel Montt Torres
	President Jorge Montt	Uncle, President Pedro Elías Pablo Montt Montt
	President Aníbal Pinto Garmendia	Father, President Francisco Antonio Pinto
Colombia	President Alfonso López Michelsen	Father, President Alfonso López Pumarejo
	President Andrés Pastrana Arango	Father, President Misael Pastrana Borrero
Comoros	President Ali Soilih	Brother, President Said Mohammed Djohar
Costa Rica	President Rafael Ángel Calderón Fournier	Father, President Rafael Ángel del Socorro Calderón Guardia
	President José María Figueres Olsen	Father, President José María Hipólito Figueres Ferrer
	President Ricardo Jiménez Oreamuno	Father, President Jesús María Ciriaco Jiménez Zamora
Democratic Republic of Congo	President Joseph Kabila Kabange	Father, President Laurent-Désiré Kabila
Djibouti	President Ismaïl Omar Guelleh	Uncle, President Hassan Gouled
Dominican Republic	President Hector Trujillo	Brother, President Rafael Trujillo
Ecuador	President Carlos Julio Arosemena Monroy	Father, President Carlos Julio Arosemena Tola
	President Galo Plaza Lasso	Father, President Leónidas Plaza Gutiérrez

Greece	Prime Minister Geórgios Papandréou	Father and Grandfather, Prime Ministers Andreas and Geórgios Papandréou
	Prime Minister Konstantinos Karamanlis	Uncle, Prime Minister Constantine
	Prime Minister Sophoklis Venizelos	Father, Prime Minister Eleftherios Venizelos
Haiti	President Jean-Claude Duvalier	Father, President François Duvalier
India	Prime Minister Rajiv Gandhi	Mother, Prime Minister Indira Gandhi; Grandfather, Prime Minister Jawaharlal Nehru
Israel	President Ezer Weizman	Father, President Chaim Azriel Weizman
Jamaica	Prime Minister Norman Manley	Father, Premier Norman Washington Manley; Cousin, Sir William Alexander Clarke Bustamante
Japan	Prime Minister Hugh Lawson	Cousin, Prime Minister Michael Manley
Jordan	Prime Minister Yasuo Fukuda	Father, Prime Minister Takeo Fukuda
Latvia	Prime Minister Adnan Badran	Brother, Prime Minister Mudar Seyyid Muhammad Badran
Lebanon	President Guntis Ulmanis	Father, Prime Minister and President Guntis Ulmanis
	Prime Minister Omar Abdul Hamid Karami	Father, Prime Minister Abdul Hamid Karami; Brother, Rashid Abdul Hamid Karami
Malaysia	Prime Minister Najib Tun Razak	Father, Prime Minister Abdul Razak
Marshall Islands	President Imata Kabua	Cousin, President Amata Kabua
Mauritius	Prime Minister Navinchandra Ramgoolam	Father, Prime Minister Seewoosagur Ramgoolam
Nepal	Prime Minister Girija Prasad Koirala	Brother, Prime Minister Bishweshwar Prasad Koirala; Brother, Prime Minister Matrika Prasad Koirala
Nicaragua	President Chamorro	Several generations of presidents
	President Juan Bautista Sacasa Sacasa	Father, Roberto Sacasa Sarria
	President Anastasio Somoza Debayle	Father, Anastasio Somoza García; Grandfather, Roberto Sacasa Sarria
Niger	President Ali Saibou	Cousin, President Seyni Kountché

(*continued*)

Table A-2. CONTINUED

Country	Male Leader	Ties to
Palau	President Thomas Remengesau	Father, President Thomas Remengesau Sr.
Pakistan	President Asif Zardari	Wife, Prime Minister Benazir Bhutto; Father-in-Law, Prime Minister and President Ali Bhutto
Panama	President Arnulfo Arias	Brother, President Harmodio Arias Madrid
	President Roberto Francisco Chiari Remón	Father, President Rodolfo Chiari Robles
Paraguay	President Francisco López Carrillo	Father, President Carlos Antonio López Ynsfrán
Peru	President Francisco Bermúdez Cerruti	Grandfather, President Remigio Morales Bermúdez
	President Manuel Prado y Ugarteche	Father, President Mariano Ignacio Prado Ochoa
Philippines	President Benigno Aquino III	Mother, President Corazon Aquino; Father, Benigno Aquino II
Singapore	Prime Minister Lee Hsien Loong	Father, Prime Minister Lee Kuan Yew
Sri Lanka	Prime Minister Dudley Shelton Senanayake	Father, Prime Minister Don Stephen Senanayake
Syria	President Bashar al-Assad	Father, President Hafez al-Assad
Sweden	Prime Minister Gerhard Louis De Geer	Father, Prime Minister Louis Gerhard De Geer
Togo	President Faure Essozimna Gnassingbé	Father, President Gnassingbé Eyadéma
United States	President George W. Bush	Father, President George H. W. Bush
	President Franklin D. Roosevelt	Cousin, President Theodore Roosevelt
	President John Quincy Adams	Father, President John Adams
Uruguay	President José Pablo Torcuato Batlle y Ordóñez	Father, President Lorenzo Cristóbal Manuel Batlle y Grau
	President Jorge Pacheco Areco	Great-Uncle, President Duncan Stewart
Vanuatu	Prime Minister Ham Lini Vanuaroroa	Brother, Prime Minister Walter Hadye Lini
	Prime Minister Barak Tame Sopé Mautamata	Uncle, President Ati George Sokomanu

Table A-3. Woman-versus-Woman Races

Country	Year	Name of Candidate	Percentage of Vote and Ranking (if available)
Argentina	1999	Mendez, L.	0.7%, 5th
		Walsh, P.	0.8%, 4th
	2003	Castro, A.	Unclear but less than 7%
		Carrió, E.	14%, 5th
	2007	Carrió, E.	23%, 2nd
		Ripoll, V.	1%, 8th
		C. Fernández	45%, 1st
Austria	1998	Schmidt, G.	11%, 3rd
		Knoll, G.	14%, 2nd
Benin	2006	Zannou, C.	0.32%, 17th
		Gbedo, M.	0.33%, 16th
Bosnia and Herzegovina	2006	Javor-Korjenić, I.	Less than 1%
		Avdalović, S.	Less than 1%
		Udovičić, S.	Less than 1%
Brazil	2006	Carvalho, H.	7%, 3rd
		Rangel, A.	Less than 1%, 5th
Chile	1999	Marín, G.	3%, 3rd
		Ruiz-Taige, S.	0.44%, 5th
Colombia	1974	Rojas, M.	Unclear
		Ramirez, M.	Unclear
	1994	Betancourt, R.	0.18%, 4th
		Gaitan, G.	0.3%, 9th
		de Castro, D.	0.1%, 18th
	2002	Sanin, N.	6%, 4th
		Pulecio, I.	0.5%, 5th
Costa Rica	2010	Chinchilla, L.	47%, 1st
		González León, M.	0.72, 6th
	1998	Brenes, N.	Less than 1%
		Ventura, Y.	Less than 1%
		Duarte, N.	Less than 1%
Croatia	2005	Adlešič, D.	2.68%, 4th
		Košta, D.	0.37%, 11th
		Kosor, J.	30%, 2nd
	2010	Škare-Ožbolt, V	1.89%, 11th
		Pusić, V.	7%, 5th
Democratic Republic of the Congo	2006	M'Poyo, J.	0.44%, 18th
		wa Mbombo, C.	0.38%, 20th
		N'landu Kavidi, W.	0.32%, 24th
		Mpolo, M.	0.21%, 30th
		Tosimiaka M'Fumfu, A.	Unclear

(continued)

Table A-3. CONTINUED

Country	Year	Name of Candidate	Percentage of Vote and Ranking (if available)
Ecuador	1998	Lima, M.	2%, 6th
		Serrano, R.	3%, 5th
	2009	Roldós Bucaram, M.	4%, 4th
		Jácome, M.	1.35%, 5th
Finland	1994	Kuuskaski, E.	Resigned
		Rehn, E.	30%, 2nd (Round 1)
	2000	Uosukainen, R.	12%, 3rd
		Halonen, T.	40%, 1st (Round 1)
		Hautala, H.	3%, 5th
	2006	Halonen, T.	52%, 1st (Round 1)
		Hautala, H.	3%, 5th
France	1981	Laguiller, A.	2%, 8th
		Bouchardeau, H.	1%, 10th
		Garaud, M.	1%, 11th
	2002	Boutin, C.	1.19%, 16th
		Taubira-Delannon, C.	2.32%, 13th
		Lepage-Jessua, C.	1.19%, 17th (but withdrew)
	2007	Royal, S.	26%, 2nd (Round 1)
		Buffet, M.	1.93%, 7th
Gabon	2009	Rekangalt, Y.	0.11%, 11th
		Duboze, V.	0.09%, 13th
		Assayi, A.	Withdrew
Germany	1999	Ranke-Heinemann, U.	Did not receive nomination
		Schipanski, B.	Did not receive nomination
Guatemala	1999	Reyes, C.	Less than 1%, 11th
		Castro, A.	Unclear
Iceland	1988	Finnbogadóttir, V.	95%, 1st
		Thorsteindóttir, S.	5%, 2nd
Ireland	1997	McAleese, M.	45%, 1st
		Banotti,M.	30%, 2nd
		Scallon, D.	13.8%, 3rd
		Roche, A.	7%, 4th
Italy	1992	Ferrari, M.	Unclear
		Lotti, N.	Unclear
		Anselmi, T.	Unclear
	1999	Jervelino, R.	Unclear
		Bonino, E.	Unclear
Kenya	1997	Wangari, M.	Withdrew
		Ngilu, C.	7.9%, 5th

Table A-3. CONTINUED

Country	Year	Name of Candidate	Percentage of Vote and Ranking (if available)
Latvia	1999*	Udre, I.	9%
		Paegle, V.	1st place, but did not attain necessary majority
Liberia	1997	Johnson Sirleaf	9.58%, 2nd (Round 1)
		Thompson, M.	0.9%, 12th (Round 1)
Lithuania	2004	Blinkeviciute, V.	1.6%, 4th
		Prunskienė, K.	21%, 2nd (Round 1)
	2009	Grybauskaitė, D.	69%, 1st
		Prunskienė, K.	3.91%, 5th
		Graužinienė-Šniokaitė, L.	3.61%, 6th
Macedonia	2009	Hoxha, M.	3.09%, 7th
		Taseva, S.	Unclear
Mexico	1994	Gonzales, C.	2.75%, 4th
		Toledano, M.	0.47%, 8th
Moldova	1996	Livitchi, M.	2.13%, 6th
		Gorea-Costin, U.	0.69%, 8th
		Abramcivc, V.	0.42%, 9th
Nicaragua	1990	Chamorro, V.	55%, 1st
		Echaverry, B.	0.36%, 8th
Nigeria	2003	Jubril, S.	0.4%, 6th
		Abayomi Jorge, A.	0.02%, 15th
		Adekunle-Obasanjo, M.	0.01%, 20th
Peru	2001	Nano, L.	23.8%, 3rd
		Ramos, M.	Unclear
		Negron, F.	Unclear
	2006	Cosso de Ocampo, M.	7.4%, 4th
		Villaran, S.	0.62%, 7th
Philippines	1992	Santiago, M.	19.7%, 2nd
		Marcos, I.	10.3%, 5th
	1998	Santiago, M.	2.96%, 7th
		Marcos, I.	Withdrew
		Faigao Sumagpang, M.	Unclear
		Delos Santos, E.	Unclear
		Arilla, M.	Unclear
		Sabeniano, M.	Unclear
		Penaranda	Unclear
Poland	1995	Gronkiewicz-Waltz, H.	2.4%, 6th
		Zytkiewicz, J.	Unclear
	2000	Górniak, K.	16%, 3rd
		Zytkiewicz, J.	Withdrew

(*continued*)

Table A-3. CONTINUED

Country	Year	Name of Candidate	Percentage of Vote and Ranking (if available)
Serbia	2004	Arandjelović, L.	38%, 11th
		Karadjordjević, E.	Withdrew
		Pop-Lazić, G.	Unclear
Slovakia	1999	Vasaryova, M.	6.6%, 3rd
		Schomegova, B.	Unclear
Slovenia	1992	Bebler, D.	Unclear
		Zangar-Slana, A.	Unclear
	2007	Pečarič, E.	0.89%, 6th
		Piberl, M.	0.48, 7th
Sri Lanka	1994	Kumaratunga, C.	64%, 1st
		Dissanayake, S.	34%, 1st
Ukraine	1999	Vitrenko, N.	4th, 11%
		Datsenko, V.	Unclear
	2010	Tymoshenko, Y.	25%, 1st (Round 1)
		Bohoslovska, I.	0.41%, 8th
		Pavlivna Suprun, L.	0.81%, 13th
United States	1972	Osteen Jenhess, L.	0.1%, 5th
		Chisholm, S.	Did not win nomination
		Mink, P.	Withdrew
		Abzug, B.	Withdrew
	1976	Wright, M.	0.06%, 15th
		McCormack, E.	Did not win nomination
	1980	McCormack, E.	0.04%, 7th
		Smith, M.	0.02%, 10th
		Griswold, D.	0.02%, 12th
		Johnson, S.	0.08%, 5th
	1988	Fulani, L.	0.24%, 5th
		Kenoyer, W.	0.2%, 17th
	1992	La Riva, G.	0%, 23rd
		Fulani, L.	0.6%, 6th
		Halyard, H.	0%, 16th
		Masters, I.	0%, 22nd
		Howard, M.	Did not win nomination
		Block, S.	Did not win nomination
	1996	Feinland, M.	0.03%, 7th
		Moorehead, M.	0.03%, 8th
		Hollis, M.	0%, 11th
		Templin, D.	0%, 13th
		Masters, I.	0%, 18th
		Doerschuck, G.	Did not win nomination
		Hoyd-Duffie, E.	Did not win nomination
		Jennings, A.	Did not win nomination

Table A-3. CONTINUED

Country	Year	Name of Candidate	Percentage of Vote and Ranking (if available)
		Harder, H.	Did not win nomination
		Howard, M.	Did not win nomination
		LeTulle, M.	Did not win nomination
		Duncan, S.	Did not win nomination
		Pharr, J.	Did not win nomination
	2000	Brown, C.	0%, 12th
		Moorehead, M	0%, 11th
		Rocker, A.	Did not win nomination
		Harder, H.	Did not win nomination
		Masters, I.	Did not win nomination
		Howard, M.	Did not win nomination
		Yaeger, D.	Did not win nomination
		Dole, E.	Withdrew
	2004	Moseley Braun, C.	Withdrew
		Howard, M.	Did not win nomination
	2008	Clinton, H.	Did not win nomination
		McKinney, C.	0.12%, 6th
		La Riva, G.	0%, 10th

SOURCES: Author's analysis of data from the Guide to the Female Presidential Candidates section of the Worldwide Guide to Women in Leadership Web site, the African Elections Web site, the Election Guide section of the International Foundation for Electoral Systems Web site, the Political Database of the Americas, the European Election Database, and the US Department of State Web site. For the United States, analysis includes additional data from Dave Leip's Atlas of U.S. Presidential Elections Web site.

*Vīķe-Freiberga, who eventually won, was introduced as a candidate after several rounds of voting had occurred.

CHAPTER 1

1. A total of 134 presidencies and 118 prime ministerships existed worldwide in 2015, resulting in a total of 252 executive posts. Of these, 233 positions were occupied by men, while only 19 were held by women. My calculations derive from analysis of data available on the World Political Leaders (1945–2015) page of the Zárate's Political Collections Web site, http://www.terra.es/personal2/monolith/00index. htm (accessed December 1, 2010).

2. Worldwide, 802 presidents held office from 1960 through 2010. I have excluded acting or interim leaders from this count and have considered each president as only one case even if he or she served previously, to avoid duplicate counts. My calculations derive from analysis of data available on the World Political Leaders (1945–2010) site, http://www.terra.es/personal2/monolith/00index.htm (accessed December 1, 2010).

3. Obviously, problems of endogeneity arise in the assessment of women leaders' impacts. Do women leaders arise in the first place because the public and political parties already accept them? I argue, based on the great diversity of cases of women executives worldwide, that the acceptance of women as leaders does not always exist as individual women ascend to their positions, particularly when so many come to office through alternate paths and during sudden openings. In these contexts as well as those more supportive of women as political players, women successfully rising to power can heighten the association of women with political leadership.

4. Eileen McDonagh (2009) connects the percentage of women in political institutions with a country's promotion of "maternalist" policies, including having hereditary monarchies open to women. However, my findings do not provide evidence for this link at the national executive level.

CHAPTER 2

1. New cases integrated in the revised edition include Angela Merkel (Germany), Gro Harlem Brundtland (Norway), and Sirimavo Bandaranaike (Sri Lanka). I have contributed a chapter on Ellen Johnson Sirleaf of Liberia (Jalalzai 2013).

2. The 1995 edition of Liswood's *Women World Leaders* contains interviews with fifteen women. The 2007 edition includes some presidents and prime ministers who more recently came to power.

3. I coauthored the North American chapter with Manon Tremblay (Jalalzai and Tremblay 2011).

4. *Reconciliation* was published posthumously.

5. Thompson and Lennartz (2006) draw a few comparisons between Merkel's background and path and those of Asian leaders.

6. The four women analyzed include Johnson Sirleaf of Liberia (Adams 2008), Michelle Bachelet of Chile (Tobar 2008), Tarja Halonen of Finland (Holli 2008), and Angela Merkel of Germany (Wiliarty 2008).

7. Merkel has since remarried.

8. This critical response section was initiated in response to my article, also published in *Politics & Gender*, "Women Rule: Shattering the Executive Glass Ceiling" (Jalalzai 2008).

9. Hodson concentrates on the South Asian cases of Bangladesh's Khaleda Zia, Sri Lanka's Chandrika Kumaratunga, and Pakistan's Benazir Bhutto.

10. While Inglehart and Norris (2003) identify clear divergences from their main theory—that cultural shifts shaped by modernization move populations toward greater support for gender equality—understanding these exceptions is not a main focus of their work.

11. Norris (1997) found that the women national leaders she studied received slightly less media coverage than their male counterparts (their immediate predecessors or successors in office), but she examined only ten paired cases. A major weakness of Cantrell and Bachman's (2008) article is that they analyze only three women: Ellen Johnson Sirleaf, Angela Merkel, and Michelle Bachelet. They also do not compare their coverage with men who held the same posts.

12. Cheng and Tavits's (2011) study focuses on Canada. See Tremblay and Pelletier (2001) for a contrary view.

13. My own recent fieldwork indicates that the same appears true for Laura Chinchilla of Costa Rica.

14. *German Politics* published a special issue in September 2011 devoted to analysis of Merkel's chancellorship; the contributors make critical links between gender and other aspects of her background.

15. In addition to Thatcher and Merkel, Beckwith (2010b) notes, this trajectory applies to Gro Harlem Brundtland in her rise to the Norwegian premiership.

16. It should be noted that not all parliamentary systems require the prime minister to be party head, as is the case in Germany.

17. Reynolds's (1999) study controls for more numerous factors than does Rule's (1985).

18. For example, Fish (2002) does not use rigorous statistical tests to bolster assertions about women's negative status. Further, Fish's model utilizes a limited time frame and measures Islam only crudely.

19. Quoted from Bhutto (1989, 44).

20. Beckwith (2000) excludes other social movements, such as women in national movements that lack gender content and where men dominate in leadership and decision making.

21. Baldez (2003) argues that where women participated in democratic struggles, they lacked a catalyst for the formation of a woman's movement. In contrast, if they faced exclusion, women might join together to demand a seat at the table.

22. Women's representation likely lags rather than follows a linear pattern (Salmond 2006).

23. Krook (2009) argues that this fit does not have to exist at the time of the initial adoption of the quota; it could evolve based on subsequent developments.

24. See the Inter-Parliamentary Union database, http://www.ipu.org/wmn-e/classif.htm (accessed June 25, 2008).

25. See the Inter-Parliamentary Union Database, http://www.ipu.org/wmn-e/classif.htm (accessed June 30, 2009).

26. As Murray (2010d) notes, more positive developments have occurred in France as of late.

27. One exception to this exists in Costa Rica, where, by law, at least one woman must appear on the presidential ballot, either as a presidential candidate or as one of the candidates vying for the two vice presidential slots (Quesada 2003).

28. The many prime ministers who are drawn from their countries' parliaments are subject to public vote when attaining their legislative seats.

29. For example, Germany's Angela Merkel inherited the particularly daunting task of serving in her first term as chancellor under the "grand coalition," which consisted of her party—the Christian Democratic Union (CDU)—and the Social Democratic Party (SPD). However, she navigated this coalition to many policy successes. The September 2009 elections resulted in a coalition of the CDU/Christian Social Union (CSU)–Frauen union, placing Merkel in an arguably more auspicious location within a more ideologically cohesive government. However, preliminary assessments indicate that internal disputes within her new coalition undercut Merkel's authority on the domestic front. Her having clear ideological divergences from the SPD required that she employ closer teamwork and conciliation, a style of governance that generally led to more favorable perceptions of Merkel's leadership style than she currently evokes (Jalalzai 2011).

30. This difference in the voting ages of women and men in the United Kingdom persisted until 1928.

CHAPTER 3

1. I exclude from this analysis women occupying positions not conforming to presidential or prime ministerial office. For example, the executive structure in San Marino is unique. Instead of a president or prime minister, two co-captain regents share power simultaneously for a six-month period. Unfortunately, this case selection excludes at least eight women leaders from San Marino. I also omit President Borjana Krišto because of the Federation of Bosnia's nontraditional and complex governmental structure. Bosnia's multiple executive entities includes a three-person presidency, with rotating chief executives. Krišto is not part of this collective, but is president of another executive system within Bosnia, making it difficult to compare her to others. Finally, while Switzerland's executive structure also appears unique, the Swiss president is elected from the seven-person Federal Council to serve a one-year term. Due to this seemingly unrivaled power of its president, I retain

Switzerland as a case. I also omit leaders of nonautonomous countries, given that
ultimate authority in such nations lies with other governments. As Siaroff (2003)
argues, these cases are "outside the spirit of debate" (288). I therefore eliminate the
following cases from analysis: the premier of the Åland Islands in Finland, two premiers from Bermuda, five prime ministers from Netherlands Antilles, and a prime
minister from the Faeroe Islands. Finally, a small number of women have served
in both prime ministerial and presidential capacities in the same country. Others
have led officially as interim leaders prior to securing more permanent appointments. Since the unit of analysis is the woman leader, I do not count each position
as a separate case. In each instance where the same woman held two different types
of executive positions, I generally analyze her in the position she held longer.

2. Scholars increasingly question critical mass theory, paying more attention to com-
   binations of key players (critical actors) and institutions than to percentages of
   women legislators (Childs and Krook 2006; Dahlerupe 2006).
3. One exception to this exists in Costa Rica, where, by law, at least one woman must
   appear on the presidential ballot, either as a presidential candidate or as one of
   candidates vying for the two vice presidential slots (Quesada 2003).
4. Exceptions include Argentina, which has been led by two different female presidents to date. A second woman (Rosario Fernández) recently gained appointment
   to the Peruvian premiership but served only from March 19 through July 28, 2011.
   Brazil's first female president, Dilma Rousseff, rose to power in January 2011.
   Because these women were elected or appointed after 2010, I exclude them from
   analysis here, but I will engage them in subsequent studies.
5. For example, women were granted suffrage in New Zealand in 1893, but women
   in Central African Republic did not receive the right to vote until 1986 (eleven
   years after a woman executive came to power). The percentages of women in other
   political institutions, including legislatures and cabinets, vary considerably, as do
   Gender-Related Development Index ratings. I dissect these numbers more thoroughly throughout this book.
6. The head of state could be either a president or a monarchical figure.
7. Still, there are exceptions to this rule. For example, Norway forbids the early disil-
   lusion of parliament (Strom and Swindle 2002). Also, some prime ministers require
   presidential consent (in dual-executive systems) to call early elections, though this
   may be more of a procedural requirement than a substantive obstacle.
8. An extensive literature exists emphasizing the socialization of women and girls
   toward cooperation rather than competition (Gilligan 1982) and the stereotypes
   held by the public that reinforce such gendered traits (Fox and Oxley 2003).
9. I deliberately say "less resistant" rather than "more open" here because I do not suggest that women are more apt than men to gain prime ministerships; all executive
   positions are heavily gendered, with men much more likely to hold any post.
10. I am excluding governors-general from this analysis.
11. Rather than dichotomous powers (one either has a power or does not), other schol-
    ars use a scaling approach to assess the degree to which executives hold powers
    (Shugart and Carey 1992; Taghiyev 2006). However, this procedure is quite com-
    plicated and offers no added benefit.

12. Another possible strategy for such cases is to divide the powers in half (Frye 1997).

13. An exception to this may be at transitional moments centered on unifying the country. For example, President Hamid Karzai of Afghanistan holds dominant executive power (Afghanistan is a unified presidential system) but lacks a party label.

14. See the World Political Leaders page of the Zárate's Political Collections Web site, http://www.terra.es/personal2/monolith/00index2.htm (accessed throughout the month of August 2009).

15. For inclusion, countries must meet the following criteria: they must be politically autonomous, must conform to a traditional executive structure, and must open executive office to contestation (even though politics may be less than democratic). I therefore exclude one-party communist states, absolute monarchies, and military dictatorships. Integration of these cases would only further illustrate men's dominance of executive positions.

16. I exclude temporary leaders. To avoid duplicate counts, I count presidents only once even if they served on multiple occasions during different periods of time. In any case, only men left office and later returned again as president. I tabulate counts from the World Political Leaders site, http://www.terra.es/personal2/monolith/00index2.htm (accessed throughout the month of August 2009).

17. While similar research designs also utilize successor comparisons (Norris 1997), since many women national leaders remain in office, I analyze only predecessors. To make paired cases more comparable, I evaluate only noninterim positions. Therefore, if a female leader was immediately preceded by an acting leader, I compare her to the last nonacting executive.

18. I examine one hundred leaders: fifty women and fifty men. Totals do not include the following:

    1. Pairs where the successor was still in office as these calculations were made: Johnson Sirleaf and Blah (Liberia), Otunbayeva and Bakiyev (Kyrgyzstan), Persad-Bissessar and Manning (Trinidad and Tobago), Kiviniemi and Vanhanen (Finland), Merkel and Schröder (Germany), Grybauskaitė and Adamkus (Lithuania), Radičová and Fico (Slovakia), Gillard and Rudd (Australia).
    2. Pairs where a woman succeeded another woman: Hasina and Zia (Bangladesh), Bandaranaike and Kumaratunga (Sri Lanka), McAleese and Robinson (Ireland).
    3. Cases where no predecessor exists: Prunskienė (Lithuania).

    The total includes women serving nonconsecutive terms multiple times: Bhutto (Pakistan), Bandaranaike (Sri Lanka), Brundtland (Norway), and Tymoshenko (Ukraine).

19. I focus only on women who already completed their terms, since tenures are unknown for the women currently serving.

20. Table A.1 in the appendix, "Tenures of Women Leaders and Their Predecessors," specifies the lengths of time those in each pair served.

21. See "What Is the G20?" (G20 2009).

22. Israel's status is not official, but it is highly likely that the nation has nuclear capabilities.

23. Women leaders who were in place before their countries possessed nuclear power include Bhutto, Gandhi, and Meir. Cresson and Patil were not in posts substantively influencing defense, and Bhutto's sway in defense matters has also been called into question because of the military's influential and independent role in Pakistan.

CHAPTER 4

1. While I retain Switzerland in my sample because only one person of the seven-member collective is appointed president, the president's sole power is chairing cabinet meetings. The Council or Federal Assembly exercises all other powers, leading me to classify the Swiss president as weak.
2. Only Sukarnoputri lacked a veto, because removal of veto power from the presidency was considered a necessary reform for the transition toward democracy in the post-Suharto era (Yudhini 2009). Sukarnoputri possessed limited emergency powers (Aglionby 2001).
3. Costa Rica abolished its standing army in 1949. International courts hear challenges to Costa Rican sovereignty and national defense. The president, however, commands law enforcement. In Panama, President Guillermo Endara officially eradicated the country's military forces in 1990, and the legislature ratified a constitutional amendment in 1994 allowing only special police forces to counter external attacks (Central Intelligence Agency 2011).
4. Sri Lanka's prime minister exercises more power in periods of cohabitation (when the president is in a party different from that of the majority of parliament). Kumaratunga actually appointed her mother, Sirimavo Bandaranaike, to her third and last prime ministerial term, which began in 1994 and ended in 2000 with her resignation due to health reasons. In 2001, Kumaratunga's party suffered a defeat in the parliamentary elections, leading to the selection of Ranil Wickramasinghe. By all accounts, though this cohabitation period was particularly conflictual, Kumaratunga still dominated. In fact, Kumaratunga stripped the United National Front (UNF) coalition of many of its powers, including several cabinet portfolios, such as defense, because she disagreed with the coalition's handling of peace negotiations with the Tamil Tigers (Sambandan 2003).
5. Macapagal-Arroyo later won popular election (though some disputed the election results), which increased her powers by one in her second term. Sukarnoputri waged an unsuccessful election bid after her first term expired. Perón was ousted in a military coup before her first term ended. Otunbayeva (Kyrgyzstan) was appointed as interim president and then retained by a public referendum.
6. Until 2004, no president of Iceland had ever refused to sign a bill. This changed under Finnbogadóttir's successor, President Ólafur Ragnar Grímsson.
7. Independent Irish presidents arise when parties select a consensus nominee prior to an election. In these cases, presidential elections are in essence unopposed contests that do not require a public vote. Mary Robinson, officially an independent, was affiliated with the Labour Party as a candidate. McAleese ran and ruled on the Fianna Fáil label her first term (van der Brug, van der Eijk, and Marsh 2000). Uncontested for her second term, she became an independent.
8. Indian constitution, http://indiacode.nic.in/coiweb/amend/amend42.htm (accessed August 1, 2009).

9. Holli (2008, 505) argues that the electoral reforms increased women's presidential prospects because they allowed women to engage in gender-based voting, challenging the "masculine" party hierarchies that had previously kept women from the position. However, women's support for female candidates has been undercut by men's tendency to vote for male candidates (Hellsten, Holli, and Wass 2007). Even when a country generally has more progressive views regarding gender and political roles, this does not assure uniform support for women presidential candidates. Further, women's success depends on institutional forms.

10. For discussion, see Halonen (2012).

11. The one exception is Jagan (Guyana).

12. This power is more overt in some cases than in others. Sheikh Hasina, for example, serves as both prime minister of Bangladesh and head of the armed forces ministry. See the Web site of the Prime Minister of Bangladesh, http://www.pmo.gov.bd/index.php?option=com_content&task=blogsection&id=37&Itemid=362 (accessed January 22, 2010).

13. See Germany's constitution at http://www.constitution.org/cons/germany.txt (accessed April 29, 2009).

14. German constitution, Article 63, http://www.constitution.org/cons/germany.txt (accessed April 27, 2009).

15. German constitution, Article 67, http://www.constitution.org/cons/germany.txt (accessed April 29, 2009).

16. See the Web site of the Office of the German Chancellor, http://www.bundeskanzlerin.de/Webs/BK/En/Angela-Merkel/angela-merkel.html;jsessionid=9BEDB0AF3386638537DCD7D8481F8D4F.s2t2.

17. Given Bhutto's vulnerability to dismissal, I deducted one point from her total powers, resulting in her score of 4 instead of 5.

18. See Pakistan's constitution, http://www.pakistani.org/pakistan/constitution/part12.ch2.html (accessed January 28, 2010).

19. Pakistan's constitution, http://www.pakistani.org/pakistan/constitution/musharraf_const_revival/lfo.html (accessed January 29, 2010).

20. At the time, Bhutto and Musharraf were negotiating the structure of executive power and the ending of prime ministerial term limits, as well as a plan to lift corruption charges that had been brought against Bhutto and her husband.

21. See Mozambique's constitution, Article 117, http://www.chr.up.ac.za/hr_docs/constitutions/docs/MozambiqueC(rev).doc (accessed January 29, 2010).

22. This concern is not unfounded. Presidents Kuchma and Viktor Yushchenko served first as prime ministers prior to their presidencies.

23. See Ukraine's constitution, Articles 106 and 107, http://www.rada.gov.ua/const/conengl.htm#r5 (accessed February 4, 2010).

24. Until confirmation, the nominee is technically "acting prime minister." In fact, Chang Sang's prime ministerial nomination faced parliamentary defeat.

25. See the South Korean constitution, http://www.servat.unibe.ch/icl/ks00000_.html (accessed February 4, 2010).

26. President Lee exercised this power in September 2009 (*New York Times* 2011a).

27. Han was disqualified from running and was charged with bribery, but was acquitted.

28. See Peru's constitution, http://web.parliament.go.th/parcy/sapa_db/cons_doc/constitutions/data/Peru/peru.pdf.

29. See the Web site "Worldwide Guide to Women in Leadership" (Christensen 2011).

30. In Merino's case, rumors that she was a lesbian sealed her demise (Wildman 2004).

31. Because the governmental structure changed three times during her three separate terms as prime minister, Bandaranaike is hard to classify in a position and system. Although she served as the sole executive of Sri Lanka during her first term, a weak presidency was created two years into her second term in 1972. In 1978, the presidential dominance system was established in an attempt to alleviate ethnic tensions between Sinhalese Tamils. As Reilly (1997) notes, "It was for this reason that the constitutional drafters were very conscious of the need to ensure that the new office of executive president would be filled by a national figure representative of all groups in society, and capable of encouraging consensual politics between those groups" (107). Opponents saw Bandaranaike as incapable of this; the creation of the presidency was a deliberate attempt to keep her from exercising dominant executive power. Bandaranaike set her sights on the presidency in 1986 but did not succeed. She eventually won back her parliamentary seat in 1989, and her daughter, Chandrika Kumaratunga, appointed her prime minister in 1994 (Liswood 1995, 8). She ruled in a dual-executive system more years than in a unified one (eleven and seventeen years, respectively); in the dual-executive structure, she held the weaker position longer (six versus five years). I therefore classify her as a weak prime minister in a presidential dominance system.

32. Senegal's Boye also lacked a party tie prior to her ascension, but she adopted the president's label.

CHAPTER 5

1. To determine each executive's age, I subtracted year of birth from year of entrance to executive office. Recognizing that some women served multiple terms, I assess only age at the first time the leader occupied the position.

2. Several countries specify the minimum age one must achieve to occupy executive office, and a few set a maximum.

3. I exclude the sixteen interim leaders from this part of the analysis. No one preceded Prunskienė as prime minister of Lithuania, and in Ireland, New Zealand, and Bangladesh, a woman succeeded another woman. This reduces the sample of paired cases of predecessors/successors from sixty-three to fifty-nine.

4. There are some exceptions. In Turkey, for example, an executive must have a college degree. See the Turkish constitution, Chapter II, Article 101, http://www.servat.unibe.ch/icl/tu00000_.html (accessed August 30, 2010).

5. I note cases where leaders pursued extensive study toward degrees but ultimately did not finish. Because such leaders did not complete their degrees, I include them within the degree category they last accomplished.

6. Information on Mame Madior Boye and Lidia Geuiler Tejada was obtained through e-mail correspondence with the Senegalese and Bolivian embassies, March 22, 2003, and March 24, 2003, respectively. Information on Elisabeth Domitien, Maria

das Neves, Maria do Carmo Silveira, and Milka Planinc derive from Jensen (2008). Other biographical sources utilized were the Council of Women World Leaders, http://www.cwwl.org/members.html; Worldwide Guide to Women in Leadership, http://www.guide2womenleaders.com; and Women's History, http://womenshistory.about.com.

7. See the biographies in the appendix for more information on the educational attainment of the individual women executives. Because the subsamples of the leaders and their professions and degree fields are so small, I do not perform tests of statistical significance.

8. Several women leaders who attended Catholic schools were from non-Catholic backgrounds, including Benazir Bhutto, a Muslim, and Sirimavo Bandaranaike, a Buddhist.

9. For details, see the biographies in the appendix.

10. These leaders are Juan Perón (Argentina), Moses Blah (Liberia), and Jean-Bédel Bokassa (Central African Republic). Information is unavailable for six male cases.

11. Data are unavailable for Dismas Nsengiyaremye (Rwanda), Manuel Pinto da Costa and Damião Vaz d'Almeida (São Tomé and Príncipe), Adrien Sibomana (Burundi), Jacques-Édouard Alexis (Haiti), and Veselin Djuranović (Yugoslavia). I placed information requests through various embassies but received no replies.

12. Michael Genovese, personal correspondence with the author, March 19, 2003.

13. Admittedly, women's access to governmental offices in parliamentary systems depends on whether or not their parties are in power. If their parties are in opposition, they might rise to the position of party leader without gaining governmental experience.

14. These women included Finnbogadóttir of Iceland, McAleese of Ireland, Aquino of the Philippines, and Bandaranaike of Sri Lanka. Aquino and Bandaranaike were political widows, and Finnbogadóttir and McAleese held largely ceremonial posts. Aquino and Bandaranaike are the only women in the sample who could be classified accurately as "housewives" or "homemakers."

15. Because there are so few cases within experience categories, I do not conduct chi-square tests regionally.

16. As before, since so few cases exist within experience categories, I do not conduct chi-square tests regionally.

17. Gender stereotypes related to perceived biological sex distinctions result in women and men being competent in different issue areas and possessing varying traits (Huddy and Terkildsen 1993; Fox and Oxley 2003; Sczesny et al. 2004). I understand, however, concerns that differentiating between "feminine" and "masculine" traits and issues reifies gender differences linked to biological sex, which is why I place quotes around these terms (see also Murray 2010b).

18. While the environment is typically considered "feminine," Escobar-Lemmon and Taylor-Robinson (2009) note that this entails energy policy, which in many Latin American contexts is a "masculine" domain. They consider such cases "unclassifiable" rather than gender-neutral.

19. Mari Kiviniemi (Finland) was also minister of foreign trade and development. She held this appointment only temporarily, while her colleague was on leave.

I therefore consider only her capacity as minister for public administration and local government.

20. Based on this small sample, I cannot conclude if this is a function of the ministry or of gender. Only one male predecessor served as defense minister.

21. Julia Gillard (Australia) was minister for education, employment, and workplace. Since this ministry combines both "feminine" and "masculine" issues, I count this as gender-neutral.

22. I analyze men preceding women's first terms in addition to men holding power just before women prime ministers returned to office. For example, Bhutto served at two different periods of time. I therefore compared her cabinet assignment during her first term to her first predecessor's and her second portfolio to her second predecessor's.

23. Of these, nine changed only once and four transferred at least three times. I identified the following patterns: three women stayed within "masculine," two went from gender-neutral to "masculine," two from "feminine" to gender-neutral, one stayed within gender-neutral, one moved from "masculine" to "feminine," one from "feminine" to "masculine," one from gender-neutral to "feminine," and one from "feminine" to "masculine" to gender-neutral.

24. Boye (Senegal) and Bachelet (Chile) each initially headed another department and Campbell (Canada) headed two. Upon gaining the prime ministership, Bhutto appointed herself head of the Defense Ministry. Only two women switched to foreign ministries. Werleigh (Haiti) initially entered the cabinet within the foreign ministry post, and Meir (Israel) gained this assignment after first serving in a different cabinet position.

25. This includes those staying in one department and the initial appointments of cabinet switchers.

26. The figure of "nearly one-quarter" is is derived from the fact that fifteen out of a total of sixty-three women leaders had experience heading masculine departments.

27. Exceptions are Néstor Kirchner (Argentina), Waldemar Pawlak (Poland), Óscar Arias (Costa Rica), Kurmanbek Bakiyev (Kyrgyzstan), and Lal Bahadur Shastri (India). Still, they accumulated official political experience prior to their presidencies or prime ministerships. Only Djuranović (Yugoslavia) ascended with only party activist experience.

28. Examples include Juan Perón (Argentina), Jean-Bédel Bokassa (Central African Republic), Daniel Ortega (Nicaragua), Ferdinand Marcos (the Philippines), and Moses Blah (Liberia).

29. The familial ties examined do not include relations to other family members holding positions of lower-level office, such as members of parliament, cabinets, or regional, local/city governments, although such ties may be important.

30. The only other Asian exception is former South Korean prime minister Han.

31. Chinchilla's father, however, served as national comptroller. Two women who ascended to executive posts in Peru and Brazil in 2011 lacked family ties. Bachelet's family connections are a source of debate.

32. Former Latvian president Guntis Ulmanis is the son of a former prime minister and president. General Bokassa, the former president and prime minister of Central African Republic, is the cousin of former president David Dacko.

33. The finding of *p* value less than .001 is calculated from an examination of fifteen of sixty-three women leaders and two of fifty-nine male leaders. The sample of male leaders is smaller because one woman succeeded no one and women preceded other women in three other cases.
34. Because this analysis focuses only on successful executive aspirants, no conclusions can be drawn about the qualifications of women who failed in their bids.

Chapter 6

1. As noted in Chapter 5, I define familial ties as relationships through blood or marriage to executives or to opposition leaders. Johnson Sirleaf's father, however, was a legislator, and Chinchilla's father served as comptroller. While we can explain Johnson Sirleaf's ascension in part by the highly unstable Liberian political environment, we cannot offer a similar explanation for Chinchilla's.
2. Isabel Perón was Juan Domingo Perón's third wife.
3. See Council of Women World Leaders, http://www.cwwl.org/council/bio-jagan-janet.html (accessed September 29, 2011).
4. Arias was elected to the presidency on three occasions, but each time he was ousted before he could complete his term.
5. The media refer to her in additional ways, including Cristina Kirchner and Cristina Fernández de Kirchner. I use Cristina Fernández, which is the appropriate shorthand used in Argentine culture (see Piscopo 2010, 206).
6. Presidents of Argentina can serve multiple consecutive terms. Legislators, however, cannot serve consecutively. This has led to congressmen alternating terms with their wives to save their seats (Rohter 2007a). Fernández and Kirchner's partnership is *not* equivalent to such placeholding, however.
7. Yingluck Shinawatra ascended to the Thai premiership in August 2011, after my cutoff point of 2010. Her brother, a former prime minister, is still alive.
8. For men the number is four; for women, two.
9. These observations derive from interviews with politicians, including President Chinchilla, conducted by the author in Costa Rica in 2011.
10. Burma's Aung San Suu Kyi won the 1991 parliamentary elections, but the military government refused to recognize these results, placing her under house arrest until November 2010. Though banned from running in the 2010 elections, she participated in the political transition (BBC News 2010a). She was finally sworn into parliament (for the first time) in May 2012, following the April elections. Her party, the National League for Democracy, made a very strong showing but gained only a small number of seats; the military is entitled to one-quarter of the seats (through a reservation mandate), and the military-backed ruling party holds a large majority (Harvey 2012). The prime ministership was abolished in 2011, and Burma's current president is former military leader Thein Sein (Harvey 2012). Since Suu Kyi never officially held the prime ministership, she is not included in the sample of women leaders examined here. Still, she is worth mentioning since she would have gained the premiership had the military not taken over. Moreover, this case illustrates that women may be restricted from holding power in various contexts; family ties are no guarantee of success.

11. Gandhi held this post initially for only one year and did not regain it until 1978. The Indian premier is not always party president.

12. Benigno Aquino also sought medical treatment for a heart condition in the United States (Komisar 1987).

13. Zia's regime took power in 1977 and arrested Zulfikar Ali Bhutto under unsubstantiated charges of conspiracy to murder. Bhutto was executed in 1979.

14. Benazir Bhutto's brothers were both studying overseas when their father was imprisoned and later murdered: Shah Nawaz Khan Bhutto reportedly by his wife in 1985 and Murtaza Bhutto by a police hit squad in 1986 (Burns 2007). Prior to his death, Murtaza had begun challenging his sister's claim as political heir, and his supporters accused Benazir Bhutto and her husband, Asif Zardari, of orchestrating his murder; these claims were never proven.

15. While Zardari went to prison for eight years, all corruption charges against him were eventually dropped, and a recent movement by Pakistan's Supreme Court to reopen charges failed (*New York Times* 2012). Benazir Bhutto did not go to prison for corruption, and the charges against her were dropped.

16. If Zardari remains in office, he could be the first civilian Pakistani president to serve a full term.

17. The government dropped the charges against her, including charges of extortion. The caretaker government was publicly embarrassed by media stories about how Hasina's deteriorating health had been exacerbated by her imprisonment (Herman 2008).

18. Ziaur Rahman was not related to Mujibur Rahman.

19. Following her husband's assassination, Khaleda Zia quickly mobilized politically, but she could not formally hold office until martial law was lifted.

20. The parliamentary system was fully restored before the 1991 elections.

21. The government did not drop charges against Zia or her son, but they were released on bail.

22. Diosdedo Macapagal died of natural causes in 1997.

23. In the Philippines, the vice president is elected at the same time as the president on a separate ballot. Macapagal-Arroyo wanted to run for president, but Estrada persuaded her to be his running mate.

24. PDI-P stands for Partai Demokrasi Indonesia Perjuangan, or Indonesian Democratic Party of Struggle (*Economist* 2009).

25. The People's Consultative Association elected the president and vice president in 1999.

26. Because Hasina lacked a male predecessor, the total number of pairs is reduced by one.

27. See Chapter 5 for a description of the coding for education and political experience.

28. Yingluck Shinawatra is an educated businesswoman. Because she entered office after 2010, I do not discuss her thoroughly, but her political ascension is worth noting.

29. As noted previously, Johnson Sirleaf's father was a legislator and Chinchilla's served as national comptroller.

30. The data on family links comes from numerous biographical databases and the World Political Leaders page of the Zárate's Political Collections Web site, http://www.terra.es/personal2/monolith/00index2.htm (accessed throughout 2010).

31. Family members need not hold duplicate positions; therefore, one could occupy the prime ministership and the other the presidency. In analyzing familial ties in this section, I use a narrower conception than advanced in earlier chapters. Whereas I previously included executives related to opposition leaders, that is not the case here.

32. I say "at least" because it is very likely that more of these relationships exist, particularly from much earlier points in history. I do not claim to present comprehensive information here.

33. The eleven countries are Central African Republic, Chile, Haiti, India, Israel, Latvia, Nicaragua, Pakistan, Panama, Peru, and Sri Lanka. Of these, women executives in Chile, Nicaragua, Pakistan, Panama, and Sri Lanka have had family ties.

34. These men had ties to Indira Gandhi, Benazir Bhutto, and Corazon Aquino, respectively. See Table A.2 in the appendix.

35. This is based on my analysis of data from the World Political Leaders site, http://www.terra.es/personal2/monolith/00index2.htm (accessed June 15, 2011).

36. This is based on an estimate of five thousand different male executives in power worldwide since 1960 and the seventy-three men with family ties previously derived.

37. One of the most striking stories in *My Truth* (Gandhi, 1980) involves Indira Gandhi's participation in the homespun movement. Since activists for Indian independence did not want Indians to rely on foreign imports, they wove khadi, a thick and very rough material. Gandhi tells a story of a woman visitor to her mother who complained of parents making children wear this material and gave Indira a beautiful foreign frock. Her mother ceded to Indira the power to decide whether or not to accept the gift, and, upon reflection, she refused it. The family friend pointed out that Indira's doll was also foreign made. In order to rectify this inconsistency, Indira later took the doll up to a terrace and set it on fire.

38. The denominator switches from sixty-three to seventy-nine when the entire sample of female leaders is analyzed.

39. See Burdzhanadze's biography in the appendix for more information.

40. Johnson Sirleaf was Tolbert's finance minister.

Chapter 7

1. While my 2008 *Politics & Gender* article "Women Rule" also presented a statistical model, that model had the following key differences from the current model. First, it examined 1996–2006, a period when fewer women held executive posts. The current data set also includes a greater quantity of countries. Furthermore, this revised model uses different measures of instability and political party systems. Finally, the new model includes five additional variables assessing whether each country has a history of people with family ties coming to power, has been ruled previously by a woman, features a multiparty system, enjoys membership in the G-20, and possesses nuclear capabilities.

2. When possible, however, I estimate values if regional data are available.

3. I use data from the International Institute for Democracy and Electoral Assistance (International IDEA) Web site, which outlines the institutional arrangements of countries worldwide. See International Foundation for Electoral Systems Election Guide, http://www.idea.int.

4. Data for both variables come from the United Nations Human Development Reports, http://hdrstats.undp.org/countries/data_sheets/cty_ds_USA.html.

5. Some evidence that women prime ministers and presidents appoint a greater proportion of females cabinet members exists. For example, Davis (1997) statistically confirms this in Western Europe. More recent qualitative case studies found that both Michelle Bachelet and Ellen Johnson Sirleaf, at least initially, appointed nearly equal proportions of men and women to their cabinets (Barnes and Jones 2011; Bauer 2011).

6. These areas are defined as follows. *Security:* Security effectiveness measures a country's general security and susceptibility to political violence and is based on three indicators (the number of wars a country engaged in, years between wars, and years since the end of the most recent war). Security legitimacy measures state repression on a five-point scale. Higher numbers indicate less effectiveness. Classifications stem from analysis of various human rights reports. *Politics:* Politics includes state durability, or the number of years a state exists without a major coup or other disruption such as assassination or resignation, and the current leader's tenure in office. Based on several indicators of state discrimination and polity fragmentation, political legitimacy specifies potential ethnic fractionalization of the population. *Economics:* Economic effectiveness incorporates the standardized gross domestic product per capita, and economic legitimacy illustrates the share of export trade in manufactured goods. Social effectiveness is based on the United Nations Human Development Index (HDI), which assesses life expectancy, educational attainment, and income of populations, rating countries on a scale of 0 and 1, with 1 indicating the highest level of development. *Social capacity:* Social legitimacy and effectiveness utilizes infant mortality rates (Marshall and Jaggers 2011).

7. Data on suffrage are from the Inter-Parliamentary Union, "Women's Suffrage: A World Chronology of the Recognition of Women's Rights to Vote and to Stand for Election," http://www.ipu.org/wmn-e/suffrage.htm.

8. Political activity is measured using an index that combines petition signing, boycotting, demonstrating, and engaging in political party work or belonging to a political group (Wolbrecht and Campbell 2007, 925).

9. Lawless and Fox's (2010) sample consisted of the "eligibility pool" made up of those who fit within the typical occupational backgrounds of politicians, including lawyers, business elite, activists, and educators.

10. Norris (1997) found that women national leaders receive slightly less media coverage than their male counterparts (their immediate predecessors or successors in office), but she examined only ten paired cases.

11. Still, the popularity of the first female leader likely mitigates the ascensions of future cases (Barnes and Jones 2011, 118). Assessing approval ratings appears problematic, however, given the absence of reliable comparative polling data.

12. Data on family links come from numerous biographical Web sites and the World Political Leaders page of the Zárate's Political Collections Web site, http://www.terra.es/personal2/monolith/00index2.htm (accessed March 2010–April 2010).

13. Scores are from the United Nations *Human Development Reports*, 2000–2008, http://hdr.undp.org.

14. While typically described as two-party, New Zealand has changed its party structure over the past decade and has become open to multiple competitive parties. For example, New Zealand's parliament comprised seven parties in 2008.
15. Pearson's $R = .49$.
16. I use different data exploring political instability in this book than in my 2008 article. Regardless of the data source, the variable fails to perform as expected.
17. While women in the United Kingdom gained suffrage in 1918, until 1928, they needed to be at least thirty years old to vote; men could vote at the age of twenty-one.
18. This is so if one uses the more liberal definition of familial ties discussed previously, including the case of Bachelet of Chile.
19. In previous work with Steven Jurek, I have defined family ties as having blood or marital connections to other politicians at any level. Investigating the backgrounds of all leaders in power in 2011, we found that African executives disproportionately possess these connections compared with executives in all other regions; these family links almost always benefit only men (Jurek and Jalalzai 2012).
20. As discussed in Chapter 6, however, women executives have a greater tendency to hail from politically unstable settings than do their male counterparts.

CHAPTER 8

1. Victoria Woodhull (1872, 1892) and Belva Lockwood (1884, 1888) were the first female presidential candidates. They both ran on the ticket of the Equal Rights Party, which was composed of proponents of equality for women and blacks.
2. During her first bid, Woodhull had not yet reached the minimum age to be president (Gutgold 2006).
3. In 1928 Angélica Mendoza ran for president in Argentina, and in 1930 Prudencia Ayala ran for president in El Salvador. Ayala, however, was legally restricted from running because she was female.
4. Again, Ayala was banned from running, thus I exclude her case from analysis. I retain Mendoza since she was not barred. The data analyzed come from the Guide to the Female Presidential Candidates section of the Worldwide Guide to Women in Leadership Web site, http://www.guide2womenleaders.com/index.html.
5. Crucially, this number did not include Perón, who succeeded her husband to the presidency.
6. I count distinct cases of women rather than the total number of female candidates decade by decade.
7. Women may be deemed ineligible to run for president in some countries for a variety of reasons; I excluded those deemed ineligible from my total list of presidential candidates.
8. This excludes Perón of Argentina (who was never a presidential candidate) and Sukarnoputri, who succeeded to the presidency in 2002 but was unable to win election subsequent to her succession to the presidency in 1999 (for the elections of 2004 and 2009). Indonesian presidential elections were indirect until 2004.
9. I collected election results for women presidential candidates from a variety of sources, including the African Elections Web site, http://africanelections.tripod.com; the Election Guide section of the International Foundation for Electoral

Systems Web site, http://www.electionguide.org; the Political Database of the Americas, http://pdba.georgetown.edu; the European Election Database, http://www.nsd.uib.no/european_election_database; and the US Department of State Web site, http://www.state.gov. For the United States, I also consulted Dave Leip's Atlas of U.S. Presidential Elections Web site, http://www.uselectionatlas.org, and the election results section of the Federal Election Commission's Web site, http://www.fec.gov/pubrec/electionresults.shtml.

10. I report the voting results only once for candidates who waged multiple unsuccessful bids (typically for their first race) unless they won office subsequently.

11. I excluded candidates from Bosnia-Herzegovina, which relies on a collectivist presidential structure; candidates from Taiwan, South Ossetia, Georgia, and Turkish-controlled Northern Cyprus because of ongoing disputes related to the countries' political recognition; and a candidate from Czechoslovakia in 1992 because a clear executive distribution of power did not exist.

12. Women presidents receiving votes in the 40 percent range include Chinchilla (Costa Rica, 47 percent), Fernández (Argentina, 45 percent), McAleese (Ireland, 45 percent), Moscoso (Panama, 45 percent), and Macapagal-Arroyo (Philippines, 40 percent). Only McAleese holds a weak presidency among these. Two received votes in the 30 percent range: Finnbogadóttir (Iceland, 34 percent) and Robinson (Ireland, 39 percent).

13. Those who achieved majorities are Grybauskaitė (Lithuania, 69 percent), Kumaratunga (Sri Lanka, 64 percent), Patil (India, 66 percent), Jagan (Guyana, 55 percent), and Chamorro (Nicaragua, 55 percent). Kumaratunga and Chamorro each effectively competed in a two-candidate election for the dominant presidency, and Grybauskaitė defeated six other candidates to secure her powerful post. Chamorro headed UNO, a coalition comprising fourteen parties. Patil faced one candidate but won through an electoral college vote (not tied to the public vote) for this weak position. Jagan's election to the dominant presidency hinged on her party's winning parliamentary elections and designating her president-elect upon victory. Roza Otunbayeva officially retained the presidency through a public referendum after a legislative appointment. She therefore faced no opposition candidates.

14. Bachelet of Chile garnered 46 percent initially and 54 percent subsequently; Johnson Sirleaf of Liberia won only 19.8 percent in the first round, positioning her second. She gained 60 percent of the vote, however, in the next round. Halonen of Finland first attained 40 percent prior to securing a bare majority in the following competition. Bachelet and Johnson Sirleaf were elected to dominant presidencies in unified systems, while Halonen gained a powerful presidency in a dual-executive system.

15. Finnbogadóttir faced no challengers in two of three subsequent elections. In her only contested election following her initial term, she won 95 percent of the vote, showing a marked improvement from her first performance. Halonen also improved in her second electoral contest to attain 52 percent of the vote in 2006.

16. South Korea's Han resigned the prime ministership to run for president in 2007 but voluntarily withdrew from the Democratic Party's primary to support another primary candidate, Hae-chan Lee; Lee did not win the presidential candidacy. Kosor of Croatia attempted to gain the presidency prior to her successful attainment of the premiership.

17. Examples include Zinaida Greceanîi (Moldova), Vaira Paegle (Latvia), and Ene Ergma (Estonia).

18. I exclude Jacqueline Lohouès-Oblé's 2010 candidacy in Côte d'Ivoire because the elections were repeatedly pushed back. African countries that have seen women presidential candidates include Algeria, Angola, Benin (two), Burkina Faso, Central African Republic, Congo-Brazzaville, Côte d'Ivoire, Democratic Republic of the Congo (five), Gabon (three), Guinea-Bissau (two), Kenya (two), Liberia (two including Johnson Sirleaf), Madagascar, Malawi, Mauritania, Nigeria (three), Rwanda, São Tomé and Príncipe, Senegal, Sierra Leone (two), Sudan, Tanzania, Togo, Uganda, and Zambia. Other women were also scheduled to run in presidential elections after I conducted this count. All women candidates running in Burundi and Rwanda, however, lost their bids, and presidential elections in Angola were postponed.

19. Positioned as vice president, Joyce Banda succeeded to the presidency of Malawi in April 2012 following the sudden death of the sitting president. As such, she did not gain the presidency through popular election (Tenthani 2012).

20. I excluded the 2009 candidacy of D. Sari of Indonesia, whose party was barred from competing in the elections.

21. Josefina Vázquez Mota competed in the 2012 Mexican presidential elections. She came in third place, securing 25 percent of the vote.

22. I did not include seven women write-in candidates and some who competed on one or a handful of ballots. The sample of thirty-seven female candidates from the United States therefore excludes Renderos, Chebib, Graham-Pendergast, Allen, Holmes, Lance-Council, Officewala, Miller, Duffy, Pueschel, and Ramsey-Rasmussen-Kennedy. I excluded Masters and Templin in 1984 and 2004, respectively.

23. A woman held interim presidential power in Israel.

24. While many countries in the Middle East have embarked on political transitions since 2011, so far these changes have not resulted in the ascensions of female prime ministers or presidents.

25. This sample stems from one used in Chapter 5 that analyzed 162 countries and examined the percentages of male and female leaders in office in 2009. In this chapter, however, I analyze only countries with presidents. I include politically autonomous countries conforming to a traditional executive structure, nonabsolute monarchies, and countries in which executive office is open to contestation (even though politics overall may be less than democratic). Some of the excluded cases, such as Iran, have never approved a female presidential candidate, so inclusion of those cases would further increase the percentage of countries lacking female candidates.

26. In Costa Rica (2010) and Finland (2000 and 2006) a woman won the presidency while her female opponent finished below second place.

CHAPTER 9

1. Human Rights Development Report Web site, http://hdr.undp.org/en/media/ HDR_20072008_GDI.pdf (accessed March 24, 2009).

2. National Center for Educational Statistics Web site, http://nces.ed.gov/pubs2005/ equity/Section12.asp (accessed March 24, 2009).

3. US Constitution, Article II, Section 1, http://www.usconstitution.net/const.html (accessed March 24, 2009).

4. Those who were not lawyers were John F. Kennedy, Lyndon B. Johnson, Jimmy Carter, Ronald Reagan, George H. W. Bush, and George W. Bush (Nelson 2009, 5).

5. Several female governors also have ascended to their offices not through popular election but through succession or appointment. Data are from the Center for American Women and Politics Web site, http://www.cawp.rutgers.edu.

6. Inter-Parliamentary Union Web site, http://www.ipu.org/wmn-e/classif.htm (accessed March 24, 2009).

7. This sample includes such women as Margaret Chase Smith, Patsy Mink, Shirley Chisholm, Bella Abzug, Patricia Schroeder, Hillary Clinton, Carol Moseley Braun, and Elizabeth Dole. Original analysis by the author.

8. World Values Survey Web site, online data analysis, http://www.wvsevsdb.com/wvs/WVSAnalizeQuestion.jsp (accessed May 24, 2010). I combine "strongly agree" and "agree" responses as well as "strongly disagree" and "disagree" responses.

9. To be considered "qualified," the candidate would have had to receive the nomination of the party with which the respondent was affiliated.

10. A major weakness of Heith's (2003) study is that she does not compare coverage of female candidates to the coverage of their male counterparts to see if men were subjected to similar reporting.

11. While some dictators hold on to power for lengthy periods, they usually operate in highly unstable contexts, making them vulnerable to ouster. Women may be looked upon as possible successors during democratization.

12. US Constitution, http://www.usconstitution.net/const.html (accessed March 24, 2009).

13. While Barack Obama is officially the forty-fourth president of the United States, this number includes President Grover Cleveland twice because he served two nonconsecutive terms.

14. Andrew Johnson and Bill Clinton were impeached but not convicted. Richard Nixon resigned when his impeachment and conviction seemed imminent.

15. In 2004, between the time he was nominated by the Republican Party and the general election, George W. Bush spent approximately $350 million; his opponent, John Kerry, spent $320 million. Both declined federal matching primary funds (Polsby and Wildavsky 2008). In the 2008 election, McCain, Clinton, and Obama all refused matching primary funds.

16. Obama's 2008 victory had a $600 million price tag (Luo 2008). In 2012, neither Obama nor his Republican challenger, Mitt Romney, accepted public financing for the primary and general elections (Blumenthal 2012). This is the first time that both major party candidates refused federal funding.

17. While Obama's 2008 election illustrates that a president can overcome these norms, his example still reinforces the unofficial presidential qualification of being male (Han 2007).

18. She was the only First Lady ever to have an office in the West Wing.

19. Among the many scandals involving the Clintons were Bill Clinton's affair with intern Monica Lewinsky and the Whitewater and "Travelgate" controversies.

20. Clinton was reportedly wrongly advised that delegates in some states would be allocated on a winner-take-all basis (Burden 2009, 36).

21. Obama did not place himself on the Michigan ballot because of the election date controversy and did not campaign in Florida, obviously altering electoral outcomes (CNN 2008).

22. The public viewed Kerry's prospects for handling the Iraq War slightly more positively than Bush's (Abramson, Aldrich, and Rohde 2010).

23. John Edwards also voted for the deployment, but he later apologized.

24. See a variety of 2008 poll results on PollingReport.com, http://www.pollingreport.com/wh08dem.htm.

25. This includes Bill Clinton's infamous comment diminishing Obama's primary win in South Carolina with comparisons to Jesse Jackson's victory in the state in 1984 and 1988. The remark was considered racially charged by some observers, given that both Obama and Jackson are African American (Burden 2009).

26. American female governors and members of Congress have historically benefited from family connections to politics (Jalalzai and Hankinson 2008).

27. Pastor Wright, an African American, had made several controversial claims during his sermons.

28. Even his supporters could not easily raise the issue of race. His eventual vice presidential nominee, Joe Biden, made waves when he referred to Obama as "the first mainstream African-American candidate who is articulate and bright and clean and a nice-looking guy" (Nelson 2009, 16).

29. African Americans seemed hesitant to support Obama initially because they did not view him as electable (Nelson 2009).

30. Some 96 percent of African Americans ultimately voted for Obama, increasing their Democratic support compared to the 2004 election (Abramson, Aldrich, and Rohde 2010).

31. In the general election, 56 percent of women voted for Obama, whereas 49 percent of men did (Center for American Women and Politics 2008).

32. Clinton's unpledged delegate count totaled 256 and Obama's 438; CNN Web site, http://www.cnn.com/ELECTION/2008/primaries/results/scorecard (accessed March 26, 2009). The number of delegates necessary to secure the nomination was 2,025.

33. I calculated the proportion of women in the French cabinet since 2000 to determine this number. Most recently, newly elected President François Hollande approved the prime minister's appointment of equal numbers of women and men to his cabinet. In 2012, therefore, women gained parity in the French cabinet for the first time in history (Associated Press 2012).

34. I examined the backgrounds of French presidents since the beginning of the Fifth Republic, consulting the biographical databases outlined in Chapter 5.

35. World Values Survey Web site, online data analysis, http://www.wvsevsdb.com/wvs/WVSAnalizeQuestion.jsp (accessed May 24, 2010). I combine "strongly agree" and "agree" responses as well as "strongly disagree" and "disagree" responses.

36. According to Sodaro (2008, 455), France had eleven types of regimes and fifteen constitutions.

37. Prior to reforms, the president served a seven-year term.

38. French constitution, Title II, Article 7, http://www.assemblee-nationale.fr/ english/8ab.asp (accessed May 24, 2010).

39. French constitution, Title II, Article 8, http://www.assemblee-nationale.fr/ english/8ab.asp (accessed May 24, 2010).

40. Parliamentary dismissal cannot occur multiple times within a one-year time frame. French constitution, Title II, Article 12, http://www.assemblee-nationale.fr/ english/8ab.asp (accessed May 25, 2010).

41. Presidential terms were reduced from seven years to five in part to prevent cohabitation. Parliamentary and presidential elections, still separate events, occur within the same year about one month apart.

42. Analysis of data available on the World Political Leaders page of the Zárate's Political Collections Web site, http://www.terra.es/personal2/monolith/00index2. htm (accessed May 27, 2010).

43. French constitution, Title II, Article 8, http://www.assemblee-nationale.fr/english/ 8ab.asp (accessed May 25, 2010).

44. French constitution, Title II, Article 9, http://www.assemblee-nationale.fr/english/ 8ab.asp (accessed May 25, 2010).

45. French constitution, Title II, Article 10, http://www.assemblee-nationale.fr/english/ 8ab.asp (accessed May 25, 2010).

46. French constitution, Title II, Article 11, http://www.assemblee-nationale.fr/english/ 8ab.asp (accessed May 27, 2010).

47. Based on its 2009 purchasing power parity, France has the world's ninth-largest economy (Central Intelligence Agency 2009).

48. The European Union is actually the highest-ranked world economy (Central Intelligence Agency 2009).

49. I analyzed each article written about Royal published in the *New York Times* through March 2009. I concentrated mostly on those about her rise to the Socialist Party nomination and the two rounds of the presidential race, although this time period also covers her subsequent loss in the Socialist Party leadership election in 2008. I understand that my lack of focus on French newspapers may be criticized, but I have also integrated secondary sources (particularly Murray 2010b) that present content analysis of French coverage.

50. Aubry, the daughter of Jacques Delors, has held various political posts, including several cabinet posts, first secretary of the party, and mayor of Lille.

51. Royal remains president of the Poitou-Charentes region.

CHAPTER 10

1. Based on my original analysis of the women in the *Glamour* article, twelve of the seventeen women featured hold dominant authority. Eight dominant women occupy prime ministerships, while only four women hold presidencies. Since dominant presidents are the most powerful executives, women's small numbers in this group are telling. Furthermore, we may question Roza Otunbayeva's powers, since the design of the presidency of Kyrgyzstan is in major flux, as noted in other parts of this book. Two women occupy powerful presidencies though weaker than the prime ministers, and three hold weak presidencies. Because of the Federation

of Bosnia's nontraditional and complex governmental structure, I omit President Borjana Krišto from analysis, although she is included in the *Glamour* article. See Table 10.1 for more information.

2. Most of this work has focused on the United States.

Appendix

1. According to the Georgian constitution, elections for the presidency must be held forty-five days following the vacancy of the office.

REFERENCES

Aalberg, Toril, and Anders Todal Jenssen. "Gender Stereotyping of Political Candidates." *Nordicom Review 28*, no. 1 (2007): 17–32.

Abramson, Paul R., John H. Aldrich, and David W. Rohde. *Change and Continuity in the 2008 Elections.* Washington, DC: CQ Press, 2010.

Academy for Cultural Diplomacy. "Radmila Šekerinska." http://www.culturaldiplomacy.org/academy/index.php?Radmila-Sekerinska.

Adams, Melinda. "Women's Executive Leadership in Africa: Ellen Johnson Sirleaf and Broader Patterns of Change." *Politics & Gender 4*, no. 3 (2008): 475–85.

Adams, Melinda. "Ma Ellen: Liberia's Iron Lady?" In *Cracking the Highest Glass Ceiling: A Global Comparison of Women's Campaigns for Executive Office*, edited by Rainbow Murray, 159–76. Santa Barbara, CA: Praeger, 2010.

Adams, William Lee. "Sheik Hasina Wajed, Prime Minister of Bangladesh." *Time*, August 5, 2011. http://www.time.com/time/specials/packages/article/0,28804,2005455_2005458_2005459,00.html.

Aday, Sean, and James Devitt. "Style over Substance: Newspaper Coverage of Elizabeth Dole's Presidential Bid." *Press/Politics 6*, no. 2 (2001): 52–73.

AfDevInfo. "AfDevInfo People Record Luisa Diogo." June 26, 2008. http://www.afdevinfo.com/htmlreports/peo/peo_1035.html.

Africa Resource Center. "African Women Presidents and Prime Ministers." *JENda Journal*, no. 9 (2006).

African Free Press. "Gabon: Mme Rogombé, une Magistrate Fidèle de Bongo aux Commondes." June 10, 2009. http://www.google.com/hostednews/afp/article/ALeqM5hcXpLY4gYYWQirLki9h5ZIS0OFow.

Afrol News. "São Tomé Gets Female Prime Minister." October 4, 2002. http://www.afrol.com/News2002/stp010_maria_neves.htm.

Afrol News. "Crisis Solved in São Tomé and Príncipe." January 25, 2003a. http://www.afrol.com/News2003/index_stp005.htm.

Afrol News. "São Toméan PM Steps Down After Coup." August 1, 2003b. http://www.afrol.com/articles/10333.

Aglionby, John. "Wahid Declares State of Emergency." *Guardian*, July 23, 2001. http://www.guardian.co.uk/world/2001/jul/23/indonesia.johnaglionby.

Ahmed, Leila. *Women and Gender in Islam*. New Haven, CT: Yale University Press, 1992.

Aimo-Koivisto, Antti. "Conan O'Brien Meets with Finnish Leader." *USA Today*, February 15, 2006. http://www.usatoday.com/life/people/2006-02-14-obrien-finland_x.htm.

Akhund, Iqbal. *Trial and Error: The Advent and Eclipse of Benazir Bhutto*. New York: Oxford University Press, 2000.

Alam, Shafiq. "Bangladesh Clashes over Missing Opposition Leader." *AFP*, April 23, 2012. http://www.google.com/hostednews/afp/article/ALeqM5iaTiU7D6WNS2grb 7dsd9aRkuiHxg?docId=CNG.a86eb6b2701ce148592ac01588b748be.9f1.

Alvarez, Sonia E. *Engendering Democracy in Brazil: Women's Movements in Transition Politics*. Princeton, NJ: Princeton University Press, 1990.

Anastasijevic, Dejan. " Madam President." *Time*, December 15, 2002. http://www.time.com/time/magazine/article/0,9171,399961,00.html.

Anderson, Nancy Fix. "Benazir Bhutto and Dynastic Politics: Her Father's Daughter, Her People's Sister." In *Women as National Leaders*, edited by Michael A. Genovese, 41–69. London: Sage, 1993.

Appel, Rebecca. "Women Earning More Doctoral Degrees than Men in U.S." *International Herald Tribune*, September 19, 2010. http://www.nytimes.com/2010/09/20/education/20iht-educBriefs20.html.

Áras an Uachtaráin. "Biographies: Mary McAleese." 2005a. http://www.president.ie/index.php?section=20&lang=eng.

Áras an Uachtaráin. "Biographies: Mary Robinson." 2005b. http://www.president.ie/index.php?section=31&lang=eng.

Associated Press. "Arnulfo Arias, 87, Panamanian Who Was President 3 Times." *New York Times*, August 11, 1988. http://www.nytimes.com/1988/08/11/obituaries/arnulf o-arias-87-panamanian-who-was-president-3-times.html.

Associated Press. "Conservative Ousts Prime Minister in New Zealand." *New York Times*, November 9, 2008a. http://www.nytimes.com/2008/11/09/world/asia/09iht-nz.1.17655275.html.

Associated Press. "Protesters Demand Arroyo's Ouster." *New York Times*, February 26, 2008b. http://query.nytimes.com/gst/fullpage.html?res=9A02EFDF103FF935A1575 1C0A96E9C8B63&scp=5&sq=Macapagal-Arroyo&st=nyt.

Associated Press. "Ukraine Premier Tymoshenko Concedes Election." National Public Radio, February 20, 2010. http://www.npr.org/templates/story/story.php?storyId=123924666.

Associated Press. "Women Play Big Role in France's New Cabinet." *U.S. News & World Report*, June 21, 2012.

Atkeson, Lonna Rae. "Not All Cues Are Created Equal: The Conditional Impact of Female Candidates on Political Engagement." *Journal of Politics 65*, no. 4 (2003): 1040–61.

Atkeson, Lonna Rae, and Nancy Carrillo. "More Is Better: The Influence of Collective Female Descriptive Representation on External Efficacy." *Politics & Gender 3*, no. 1 (2007): 79–101.

Azeri-Press Agency. "Moldovan Communist Party Names Prime Minister Zinaida Greceanii for Presidency." May 13, 2009. http://www.google.com/hostednews/afp/article/ALeqM5hL7k9wIMjcCg4QQwlSaPPg0288g?docId=CNG.a86eb6b2701ce14 8592ac01588b748be.8a1.

Bacani, Cesar R. "Essential Cory Aquino." Ninoy & Aquino Foundation. http://www.coryaquino.ph/index.php/essential.

Baker, Aryn. "Making a Martyr of Bhutto." *Time*, December 27, 2007. http://www.time.com/time/world/article/0,8599,1698472,00.html.

Baker, Aryn. "Bhutto's Incomplete Legacy." *Time*, February 17, 2008. http://www.time.com/time/world/article/0,8599,1714147,00.html.

Baker, Aryn, and Simon Robinson. "Missing Evidence from Bhutto's Murder." *Time*, December 31, 2007.

Baldez, Lisa. "Women's Movements and Democratic Transition in Chile, Brazil, East Germany, and Poland." *Comparative Politics 35*, no. 3 (2003): 253–72.

Baldez, Lisa. "The Gender Lacuna in Comparative Politics." *Perspectives on Politics 8*, no. 1 (2010): 199–205.

Baltic News Service. "Biography of Lithuania's President-Elect Gryauskaite." Lituanica, May 18, 2009. http://irzikevicius.wordpress.com/2009/05/18/biography-of-lithuania's-president-elect-grybauskaite.

Banaszak, Lee Ann. "Women's Movements and Women in the Movements." In *Political Women and American Democracy*, edited by Christina Wolbrecht, Karen Beckwith, and Lisa Baldez, 79–95. New York: Cambridge University Press, 2008.

Bandaranaike, Anura. "Sirimavo Bandaranaike: An Embodiment of Tolerance." Associated Newspapers of Ceylon, May 7, 2005. http://www.dailynews.lk/2005/05/07/fea01.htm.

Bangladesh Awami League. "Biography of Sheikh Hasina." http://www.albd.org/english/index.php?option=com_content&view=article&id=100%3Abiography-of-sheikh-hasina-01&catid=37&Itemid=98.

Banglapedia. "Zia, Begum Khaleda." 2006. http://www.banglapedia.org/httpdocs/HT/Z_0014.HTM.

Barlovac, Bojana. "Former Yugoslav PM Milka Planinc Dies." *Balkan Insight*, October 7, 2010. http://www.balkaninsight.com/en/article/former-yugoslav-pm-milka-planinc-dies.

Barnes, Tiffany D., and Mark P. Jones. "Latin America." In *Women in Executive Power*, edited by Gretchen Bauer and Manon Tremblay, 105–21. London: Routledge, 2011.

Barrioneuvo, Aleixi. "Argentine Ex-Leader Dies; Political Impact Is Murky." *New York Times*, October 27, 2010. http://www.nytimes.com/2010/10/28/world/americas/28argentina.html.

Bartholomeusz, Tessa. "Mothers of Buddhas, Mothers of Nations: Kumaratunga and Her Meteoric Rise to Power in Sri Lanka." *Feminist Studies 25*, no. 1 (1999): 211–25.

Bast, Andrew. "I Survived, Narrowly." *Newsweek*, October 10, 2010. http://www.newsweek.com/2010/10/10/q-a-with-bangladesh-p-m-sheikh-hasina-wajed.html.

Basu, Amrita, ed. *Women's Movements in the Global Era: The Power of Local Feminisms*. Boulder, CO: Westview Press, 2010.

Bauer, Gretchen. "Sub-Saharan Africa." In *Women in Executive Power*, edited by Gretchen Bauer and Manon Tremblay, 85–104. London: Routledge, 2011.

Bauer, Gretchen, and Manon Tremblay, eds. *Women in Executive Power*. London: Routledge, 2011.

Bauer, Jacqui. "Women and the 2005 Election in Liberia." *Journal of Modern African Studies 47*, no. 2 (2009):193–211.

BBC News. "World: Europe; Cresson: The 'Careless' Commissioner." March 16, 1999. http://news.bbc.co.uk/2/hi/europe/255053.stm.

BBC News. "Sirimavo Bandaranaike: First Woman Premier." October 10, 2000. http://news.bbc.co.uk/2/hi/south_asia/964914.stm.

BBC News. "Profile: Megawati Sukarnoputri." July 3, 2004. http://news.bbc.co.uk/1/hi/world/asia-pacific/1452246.stm.

BBC News. "Profile: Chandrika Kumaratunga." August 26, 2005a. http://news.bbc.co.uk/2/hi/south_asia/3239821.stm.

BBC News. "Profile: Liberia's 'Iron Lady.'" November 23, 2005b. http://news.bbc.co.uk/2/hi/africa/4395978.stm.

BBC News. "Profile: Cristina Fernandez de Kirchner." October 29, 2007a. http://www.bbc.co.uk/news/world-latin-america-12284208

BBC News. "Profile: Pratibha Patil July 21, 2007b. http://news.bbc.co.uk/2/hi/south_asia/6910097.stm.

BBC News. "Spain Rejects Peron Extradition." April 28, 2008. http://news.bbc.co.uk/2/hi/7372056.stm.

BBC News. "Croatia Closer to First Woman PM." July 4, 2009a. http://news.bbc.co.uk/2/hi/europe/8134577.stm.

BBC News. "Profile: Angela Merkel." September 27, 2009b. http://news.bbc.co.uk/1/hi/world/europe/4572387.stm.

BBC News. "Profile: Johanna Sigurdardottir." February 2, 2009c. http://news.bbc.co.uk/2/hi/7859258.stm.

BBC News. "Profile: Aung San Suu Kyi." November 15, 2010a. http://www.bbc.co.uk/news/world-asia-pacific-11685977.

BBC News. "First Slovak Female PM Iveta Radicova Takes Power." 2010b. http://www.bbc.co.uk/news/10567364.

BBC News. "Bangladesh Profile." Last updated March 4, 2011. http://www.bbc.co.uk/news/world-south-asia-12650944.

BBC World Service. "Women in Power Reveal What It Takes: Chandrika Kumaratunga." http://www.bbc.co.uk/worldservice/people/features/wiwp/dyncon/kum.shtml#.

Beckwith, Karen. "Beyond Compare? Women's Movements in Comparative Perspective." *European Journal of Political Research 37*, no. 4 (2000): 431–68.

Beckwith, Karen. "A Common Language of Gender?" *Politics & Gender 1*, no. 1 (2005): 128–37.

Beckwith, Karen. "Comparative Politics and the Logics of Comparative Gender." *Perspectives on Politics 8*, no. 1 (2010a): 159–68.

Beckwith, Karen. "Someday My Chance Will Come: Women Contesting for Executive Leadership in West Europe." Paper presented at the annual meeting of the American Political Science Association, Washington, DC, September 2010b.

Bennett, W. Lance. *News: The Politics of Illusion*. New York: Pearson Longman, 2009.

Bennhold, Katrin. "In French Race, 2 Rivals Feel Scorn of an Also-Ran." *New York Times*, April 26, 2007. http://www.nytimes.com/2007/04/26/world/europe/26france.html?ex=1335240000&en=0652289f54827619&ei=5088&partner=rssnyt&emc=rss.

Bennhold, Katrin. "Where Having It All Doesn't Mean Having Equality." *New York Times*, October 11, 2010. http://www.nytimes.com/2010/10/12/world/europe/12iht-fffrance.html?pagewanted=all.

Bhutto, Benazir. *Daughter of Destiny*. New York: Simon & Schuster, 1989.

Bhutto, Benazir. *Reconciliation: Islam, Democracy, and the West*. New York: HarperCollins, 2008.

Bhutto.org. "About Bhutto: 21 June 1953–27 December 2007." 2008. http://benazir. bhutto.org.

Birch, Sarah. "Ukraine: Presidential Power, Veto Strategies and Democratization." In *Semi-presidentialism in Central and Eastern Europe*, edited by Robert Elgie and Sophia Moestrup, 220–38. Manchester, England: Manchester University Press, 2008.

Black, Jerome H., and Lynda Erickson. "Women Candidates and Voter Bias: Do Women Politicians Need to Be Better?" *Electoral Studies 22*, no. 1 (2003): 81–100.

Bliss, Michael. "Kim Campbell." The Prime Ministers of Canada. Accessed 2011. http://www.prime-ministers.ca/campbell/intro.php.

Blondal, Karl. "Olafur Ragnar Grimsson, Iceland's New President." *Scandinavian Review 84*, no. 3 (1996): 4–11.

Blondel, Jean. "Introduction: Western European Cabinets in Comparative Perspective." In *Cabinets in Western Europe*, edited by Jean Blondel and Ferdinand Müller-Rommel, 1–17. London: Macmillan, 1988.

Blumenthal, Paul. "Presidential Election 2012 to Play Out on New Campaign Finance Field." *Huffington Post*, April 11, 2012. http://www.huffingtonpost.com/2012/04/11/presidential-election-campaign-finance-matching-funds-super-pacs_n_1417948.html.

Bond, Jon R., Cary Covington, and Richard Fleisher. "Explaining Challenger Quality in Congressional Elections." *Journal of Politics 47* (1985): 510–29.

Borrelli, MaryAnne. *The President's Cabinet: Gender, Power, and Representation*. Boulder, CO: Lynne Rienner, 2002.

Bouvard, Marguerite Guzman. *Revolutionizing Motherhood: The Mothers of the Plaza de Mayo*. Lanham, MD: Rowman & Littlefield, 2002.

Braden, Maria. *Women Politicians and the Media*. Lexington: University Press of Kentucky, 1996.

Brady, Jonann. "A Look Back at Hillary's Year in Pantsuits." *Good Morning America*, August 26, 2008. http://abcnews.go.com/GMA/Politics/story?id=5656295.

Bratton, Kathleen, and Leonard P. Ray. "Descriptive Representation, Policy Outcomes, and Municipal Day Care Coverage in Norway." *American Journal of Political Science 46* (2002): 428–37.

Bremner, Charles. "Bikini Shots Expose a Sea Change in Politics." *The Times*, August 9, 2006. http://www.timesonline.co.uk/tol/news/world/europe/article603568.ece.

Brundtland, Gro Harlem. *Madam Prime Minister: A Life in Power and Politics*. New York: Farrar, Straus and Giroux, 2002.

Burden, Barry. "The Nominations: Rules, Strategies, and Uncertainty." In *The Elections of 2008*, edited by Michael Nelson, 22–44. Washington, DC: CQ Press, 2009.

Burkett, Elinor. *Golda*. New York: Harper, 2008.

Burns, John F. "Benazir Bhutto, 54, Who Weathered Pakistan's Political Storm for 3 Decades, Dies." *New York Times*, December 28, 2007. http://www.nytimes.com/2007/12/28/world/asia/28bhutto.html.

Burns, Nancy, Kay Lehman Schlozman, and Sidney Verba. "The Political Worlds of Men and Women." In *The Private Roots of Public Action*, edited by Nancy Burns, Kay

Lehman Schlozman, and Sidney Verba, 99–136. Cambridge, MA: Harvard University Press, 2001.

Burrell, Barbara C. *A Woman's Place Is in the House: Campaigning for Congress in the Feminist Era*. Ann Arbor: University of Michigan Press, 1994.

Butt, Gerald. "Golda Meir." BBC News, April 21, 1998.

Bystrom, Dianne. "18 Million Cracks in the Glass Ceiling: The Rise and Fall of Hillary Rodham Clinton's Presidential Campaign." In *Cracking the Highest Glass Ceiling: A Global Comparison of Women's Campaigns for Executive Office*, edited by Rainbow Murray, 69–90. Santa Barbara, CA: Praeger, 2010.

Cabellero, Maria Cristina. "'Ma Ellen,' African Symbol of Hope, Returns to Harvard." *Harvard Gazette*, September 21, 2006. http://www.news.harvard.edu/gazette/2006/09.21/11-liberia.html.

Campbell, Robert. "Factbox—Costa Rica's President-Elect Laura Chinchilla." Reuters, February 7, 2010. http://www.reuters.com/article/idUSN0716657220100208.

Cantrell, Tania H., and Ingrid Bachman. "Who Is the Lady in the Window? A Comparison of International and National Press Coverage of First Female Government Heads." *Journalism Studies* 9, no. 3 (2008): 429–46.

Caraway, Teri L. "Inclusion and Democratization: Class, Gender, Race, and the Extension of Suffrage." *Comparative Politics* 36, no. 4 (2004): 443–60.

Caraway, Teri L. "Gendering Comparative Politics." *Perspectives on Politics* 8, no. 1 (2010): 169–75.

Carroll, Rory. "The Leading Contenders in Argentina's Election." *Guardian*, October 26, 2007. http://www.guardian.co.uk/world/2007/oct/26/argentina.rorycarroll.

Carroll, Susan J. "Reflections on Gender and Hillary Clinton's Presidential Campaign: The Good, the Bad, and the Misogynic." *Politics & Gender* 5, no. 1 (2009): 1–20.

CBC News Online. "Ellen Johnson-Sirleaf: Liberia's 'Iron Lady.'" March 28, 2006. http://www.cbc.ca/news/background/liberia/sirleaf.html.

Celebrity Speakers. "Right Honorable Jenny Shipley." 2009. http://www.csnz.co.nz/default,4296,rt_hon_jenny_shipley.sm;jsessionid=AD44C084C8287FC4A09FE7AA519C6786.

Center for American Women and Politics. "The Gender Gap: Voting Choices in Presidential Elections." 2008. http://www.cawp.rutgers.edu/fast_facts/voters/documents/GGPresVote.pdf.

Central Intelligence Agency. "The World Factbook 2009 Report." 2009. https://www.cia.gov/library/publications/the-world-factbook/rankorder/2001rank.html.

Central Intelligence Agency. "The World Factbook 2011 Report." August 23, 2011. https://www.cia.gov/library/publications/the-world-factbook/geos/pm.html.

Chamorro, Violeta. *Dreams of the Heart*. New York: Simon & Schuster, 1996.

Chancery of the President of Latvia. "Biography of Dr. Vaira Vike-Freiberga." April 17, 2007. http://www.president.lv/pk/preview/?module=print_content&module_name=content&cat_id=16&lng=en&p.

Chaney, Elsa M. *Supermadre: Women in Politics in Latin America*. Austin: University of Texas Press, 1979.

Cheddi Jagan Research Center. "Profile of Janet Jagan, O.E.—First Woman President of Guyana." 1999. http://www.jagan.org/janet_jagan3.htm#Profile%20of%20Janet%20

Jagan,%20O.E.%20%E2%80%93%20First%20Woman%20President%20of%20 Guyana.

Cheng, Christine, and Margit Tavits. "Informal Influences in Selecting Female Political Candidates." *Political Research Quarterly 64* (2011): 460–71.

Childs, Sarah. "Hitting the Target: Are Labour Women MPs 'Acting for' Women?" *Parliamentary Affairs 55* (2002): 143–53.

Childs, Sarah, and Mona Lena Krook. 2006. "Should Feminists Give Up on Critical Mass? A Contingent Yes." *Politics & Gender 2*, no. 4 (2006): 523–30.

Chodorow, Nancy J. *Femininities, Masculinities, Sexualities: Freud and Beyond.* Lexington: University Press of Kentucky, 1994.

Christensen, Martin K. I. "Worldwide Guide to Women in Leadership." June 9, 2011. http://www.guide2womenleaders.com/index.html.

Christian Democratic Union. "Dr. Angela Merkel." 2011. http://www.cdu.de/ en/3440_11274.htm.

Civil Georgia. "We Need a Landslide Election Victory—Saakashvili." November 24, 2007. http://www.civil.ge/eng/article.php?id=16421.

Clarke, Stephen. "No Sex, Please, We're French." *New York Times*, March 23, 2007. http:// www.nytimes.com/2007/03/23/opinion/23clarke.html.

Clemens, Clay. "From the Outside In: Angela Merkel as Opposition Leader, 2002–2005." *German Politics & Society 24*, no. 3 (2006): 41–81.

Clift, Ben. "The Ségolène Royal Phenomenon: Political Renewal in France?" *Political Quarterly 78*, no. 2 (2007): 282–91.

Clift, Eleanor. "Leadership Meets Machismo." *Newsweek,* May 10, 2007. http://www. newsweek.com/id/34804/page/1.

Club of Madrid. "Hanna Suchocka." 2003a. http://www.clubmadrid.org/en/miembro/ hanna_suchocka.

Club of Madrid. "Mary Robinson." 2003b. http://www.clubmadrid.org/en/miembro/ mary_robinson.

Club of Madrid. "Vigdís Finnbogadóttir." 2003c. http://www.clubmadrid.org/en/ miembro/Vigdís_Finnbogadóttir.

CNN. "Bangladesh's Zia Keen to Form Government." October 4, 2001. http://arti-cles.cnn.com/2001-10-04/world/bangla.elex_1_bangladesh-s-zia-hasina-s-awami-league-khaleda-zia?_s=PM:asiapcf.

CNN. "Ex-General Ahead in Indonesia." July 6, 2004. http://www.cnn.com/2004/ WORLD/asiapcf/07/05/indonesia.poll/index.html.

CNN. "Source: Obama Not Embracing Michigan Revote." March 19, 2008. http://www. cnn.com/2008/POLITICS/03/19/clinton.michigan/index.html.

Cohen, Mary, David Karol, Hans Noel, and John Zaller. "The Invisible Primary in Presidential Nominations, 1980–2004." In *The Making of the Presidential Candidates 2008*, edited William G. Mayer, 1–38. Lanham, MD: Rowman & Littlefield, 2008.

Col, Jeanne-Marie. "Managing Softly in Turbulent Times: Corazon C. Aquino, President of the Philippines." In *Women as National Leaders*, edited by Michael A. Genovese, 13–40. London: Sage, 1993.

Conde, Carlos H. "Arroyo Legacy Tour Troubles Her Critics." *New York Times*, May 7, 2010. http://www.nytimes.com/2010/05/07/world/asia/07iht-legacy.html?scp=1&sq= Arroyo%20Legacy%20Tour%20Troubles%20Her%20Critics&st=cse.

Connelly, Marjorie. "Sarkozy's Win, Group by Group." *New York Times*, May 8, 2007. http://query.nytimes.com/gst/fullpage.html?res=9F02E0D91631F93BA35756C0A96 19C8B63.

Coquery-Vidrovitch, Catherine. *African Women: A Modern History*. Translated by Beth Gillian Raps. Boulder, CO: Westview Press, 1997.

Coronel, Sheila. "Corazon Aquino." *Time*, November 13, 2006. http://www.time.com/time/magazine/article/0,9171,1554976,00.html.

Council of Women World Leaders. "Maria Das Neves: Prime Minister, São Tomé and Príncipe, 2002–2004." 2011. http://www.cwwl.org/council/bio-neves-maria.html.

Craske, Nikki. *Women and Politics in Latin America*. New Brunswick, NJ: Rutgers University Press, 1999.

Cutler, David. "Timeline: Ukrainian Politics Since the 2004 Orange Revolution." Reuters, January 14, 2010. http://www.reuters.com/article/idUSLDE60D2DQ20100114.

Dahl, Robert A. *How Democratic Is the Constitution?* New Haven, CT: Yale University Press, 2001.

Dahlburg, John-Thor. "Sri Lankan Premier Wins Presidency, Partial Results Show." *Los Angeles Times*, November 10, 1994. http://articles.latimes.com/1994-11-10/news/mn-61034_1_partial-results-show.

Dahlerupe, Drude. "The Story of the Theory of Critical Mass." *Politics & Gender 2*, no. 4 (2006): 511–22.

Darcy, R., Susan Welch, and Janet Clark. *Women, Elections, and Representation*. Lincoln: University of Nebraska Press, 1994.

Davidson-Schmich, Louise K. "Implementation of Political Party Gender Quotas: Evidence from the German Lander 1990–2000." *Party Politics 12*, no. 2 (2006): 211–32.

Davis, Rebecca Howard. *Women and Power in Parliamentary Democracies: Cabinet Appointments in Western Europe, 1968–1992*. Lincoln: University of Nebraska Press, 1997.

Department of Information—Malta. "Miss Agatha Barbara: President of Malta (1982–1987)." April 14, 2005. http://gov.mt/en/Government/Government%20of%20Malta/Presidents%20of%20Malta/Pages/Ms-Agatha-Barbara.aspx.

Department of Public Information. "Luísa Dias Diogo (Co-Chair), Prime Minister, Mozambique." United Nations. 2006. http://www.un.org/events/panel/html/diogo.html.

Deutsche Welle. "The Chancellor Vote Explained." November 10, 2005. http://www.dw-world.de/dw/article/0,,1737962,00.html.

de Vise, Daniel. "More Women than Men Got PhDs Last Year." *Washington Post*, September 14, 2010.

Diocese of Westminster. "Former Prime Minister of Haiti to Speak at Annual CAFOD Lecture." November 4, 2010. http://www.rcdow.org.uk/diocese/default.asp?library_ref=4&content_ref=3079.

Djokic, Dejan. "Milka Planinc Obituary." *Guardian*, October 10, 2010. http://www.guardian.co.uk/world/2010/oct/10/milka-planinc-obituary?INTCMP=SRCH.

Dodson, Debra L. *The Impact of Women in Congress*. New York: Oxford University Press, 2006.

Dolan, Julie. "Political Appointees in the United States: Does Gender Make a Difference?" *Political Science & Politics 34*, no. 2 (2001): 213–16.

Dolan, Kathleen. *Voting for Women: How the Public Evaluates Women Candidates.* Boulder, CO: Westview Press, 2004.

Dolan, Kathleen, and Lynne E. Ford. "Women in the State Legislatures: Feminist Identity and Legislative Behaviors." *American Politics Quarterly 23* (1995): 96–109.

Donno, Daniela, and Bruce M. Russett. "Islam, Authoritarianism, and Female Empowerment: What Are the Linkages?" *World Politics 56*, no. 4 (2004): 582–607.

Duerst-Lahti, Georgia. "Reconceiving Theories of Power: Consequences of Masculinism in the Executive Branch." In *The Other Elites*, edited by MaryAnne Borelli and Janet M. Martin, 11–32. Boulder, CO: Lynne Rienner, 1997.

Duerst-Lahti, Georgia. "Presidential Elections: Gendered Space and the Case of 2004." In *Gender and Elections: Shaping the Future of American Politics*, edited by Susan J. Carroll and Richard L. Fox, 12–42. New York: Cambridge University Press, 2006.

Duerst-Lahti, Georgia. "Masculinity on the Campaign Trail." In *Rethinking Madam President: Are We Ready for a Woman in the White House?*, edited by Lori Cox Han and Caroline Heldman, 87–112. Boulder, CO: Lynne Rienner, 2007.

Duerst-Lahti, Georgia, and Rita Mae Kelly, eds. *Gender Power, Leadership, and Governance.* Ann Arbor: University of Michigan Press, 1996.

Duverger, Maurice. "A New Political System Model: Semi-presidential Government." *European Journal of Political Research 8*, no. 2 (1980): 165–87.

Duverger, Maurice. *The Political Role of Women.* Paris: UNESCO, 1955. http://unesdoc. unesco.org/images/0005/000566/056649eo.pdf.

Economist. "More of the Same, Please: A Ringing Endorsement from the Voters." September 10, 2009. http://www.economist.com/node/14391430.

Edwards, George C., and Stephen J. Wayne. *Presidential Leadership: Politics and Policy Making,*7th ed. Boston: Wadsworth, 2005.

Elders Foundation. "Mary Robinson." 2011. http://theelders.org/mary-robinson? page=5.

Election Guide. "Country Profile: Serbia—News Archive." June 26, 2010. http://www. electionguide.org/country-news.php?ID=242.

Elgie, Robert. "The Classification of Democratic Regime Types: Conceptual Ambiguity and Contestable Assumptions." *European Journal of Political Research 33*, no. 2 (1998): 219–38.

Elgie, Robert, and Sophia Moestrup. "Semi-presidentialism: A Common Regime Type, but One That Should Be Avoided?" In *Semi-presidentialism in Central and Eastern Europe*, edited by Robert Elgie and Sophia Moestrup, 1–13. Manchester, England: Manchester University Press, 2008.

Encyclopædia Britannica Online. "Sylvie Kinigi." 2010a. http://www.britannica.com/ EBchecked/topic/1274402/Sylvie-Kinigi.

Encyclopædia Britannica Online. "Burundi." 2010b. http://www.britannica.com/ EBchecked/topic/85931/Burundi.

Encyclopædia Britannica Online. "Central African Republic." 2010c. http://www.britannica.com/EBchecked/topic/102152/Central-African-Republic/254022/Political-process.

Encyclopædia Britannica Online. "Cristina Fernandez de Kirchner." 2010d. http://www.britannica.com/EBchecked/topic/1100708/Cristina-Fernandez-de-Kirchner.

Encyclopædia Britannica Online. "Lidia Gueiler Tejada." 2010e. http://www.britannica.com/EBchecked/topic/248195/Lidia-Gueiler-Tejada.

Encyclopedia of World Biography. "Luisa Diogo Biography." 2010. http://www.notablebiographies.com/news/Ca-Ge/Diogo-Luisa.html.

Encyclopedia.com. "São Tomé and Príncipe." Worldmark Encyclopedia of the Nations. 2007. http://www.encyclopedia.com/doc/1G2-2586700119.html.

Erlanger, Steven, and Katrin Benhold. "French Socialists Face Division and Derision After Vote for Leader." New York Times, November 23, 2008. http://www.nytimes.com/2008/11/24/world/europe/24france.html?ref=segoleneroyal.

Escobar-Lemmon, Maria, and Michelle M. Taylor-Robinson. "Women Ministers in Latin American Government: When, Where, and Why." American Journal of Political Science 49, no. 4 (2005): 829–44.

Escobar-Lemmon, Maria, and Michelle M. Taylor-Robinson. "Getting to the Top: Career Paths of Women in Latin American Cabinets." Political Research Quarterly 62, no. 4 (2009): 685–99.

Everett, Jana. "Indira Gandhi and the Exercise of Power." In Women as National Leaders, edited by Michael A. Genovese, 103–34. London: Sage, 1993.

Falk, Erika. Women for President: Media Bias in Eight Campaigns. Chicago: University of Illinois Press, 2008.

Farnsworth, Clyde H. "Governing Tories in Canada Routed by Liberal Party." New York Times, October 26, 1993a. http://www.nytimes.com/1993/10/26/world/governing-tories-in-canada-routed-by-liberal-party.html?pagewanted=all&src=pm.

Farnsworth, Clyde H. "Kim Campbell Takes Oath as Canada's Prime Minister." New York Times, June 26, 1993b. http://www.nytimes.com/1993/06/26/world/kim-campbell-takes-oath-as-canada-s-prime-minister.html.

Farrar-Myers, Victoria. "A War Chest Full of Susan B. Anthony Dollars: Fund-Raising Issues for Female Presidential Candidates." In Anticipating Madam President, edited by Robert P. Watson and Ann Gordon, 81–93. Boulder, CO: Lynne Rienner, 2003.

Farrar-Myers, Victoria. "Money and the Art and Science of Candidate Viability." In Rethinking Madam President: Are We Ready for a Woman in the White House?, edited by Lori Cox Han and Caroline Heldman, 113–31. Boulder, CO: Lynne Rienner, 2007.

Ferree, Myra Marx. "Angela Merkel: What Does It Mean to Run as a Woman?" German Politics and Society 24, no. 1 (2006): 93–107.

Fish, Steven. "Islam and Authoritarianism." World Politics 55, no. 1 (2002): 4–37.

Flora, Lewis. "Violeta and Corazon." New York Times, February 12, 1988. http://www.nytimes.com/1988/02/12/opinion/foreign-affairs-violeta-and-corazon.html.

Forbes. "The 100 Most Powerful Women: #89 Portia Simpson Miller." August 31, 2006. http://www.forbes.com/lists/2006/11/06women_Portia-Simpson-Miller_MH76.html.

Forbes. "The 100 Most Powerful Women: #89 Luisa Diogo." August 30, 2007. http://www.forbes.com/lists/2007/11/biz-07women_Luisa-Diogo_ZTLN.html.

Forest, Maxime. "Central and Eastern Europe." In Women in Executive Power, edited by Gretchen Bauer and Manon Tremblay, 65–84. London: Routledge, 2011.

7

Fox, Richard L., and Zoe M. Oxley. "Gender Stereotyping in State Executive Elections: Candidate Selection and Success." *Journal of Politics* 65, no. 3 (2003): 833–50.

Franceschet, Susan, and Gwynn Thomas. "Michelle Bachelet's Rise to the Chilean Presidency." In *Cracking the Highest Glass Ceiling: A Global Comparison of Women's Campaigns for Executive Office*, edited by Rainbow Murray, 177–95. Santa Barbara, CA: Praeger, 2010.

Fraser, Antonia. *The Warrior Queens*. New York: Knopf, 1989.

Freedom House. "Freedom in the World: Sao Tome and Principe (2006)." December 19, 2005. http://www.unhcr.org/refworld/publisher,FREEHOU,,STP,473c558c49,0.html.

Frenkel, Sheera Claire. "Dalia Itzik Becomes Acting President." *Jerusalem Post*, January 25, 2007. http://www.jpost.com/Israel/Article.aspx?id=49225.

Friedman, Elisabeth Jay. "Seeking Rights from the Left: Gender and Sexuality in Latin America." In *Women's Movements in the Global Era: The Power of Local Feminisms*, edited by Amrita Basu, 285–314. Boulder, CO: Westview Press, 2010.

Frye, Timothy. "A Politics of Institutional Choice: Post-Communist Presidencies." *Comparative Politics Studies* 30, no. 5 (1997): 525–52.

Gandhi, Indira. *My Truth*. New York: Grove Press, 1980.

Garlow, Stephanie. "Cristina Fernandez de Kirchner Wins Re-election in Argentina." *GlobalPost*, October 23, 2011. http://www.globalpost.com/dispatches/globalpost-blogs/que-pasa/argentina-president-cristina-fernandez-kirchner-reelected.

Genovese, Michael A. "Women as National Leaders: What Do We Know?" In *Women as National Leaders*, edited by Michael A. Genovese, 211–17. London: Sage, 1993a.

Genovese, Michael A, ed. *Women as National Leaders*. London: Sage, 1993b.

Genovese, Michael A., and Janie S. Steckenrider eds. *Women as Political Leaders: Studies in Gender and Governing*. New York: Routledge, 2013 (forthcoming).

Geske, Mary, and Susan C. Bourque. "Grassroots Organizations and Women's Human Rights: Meeting the Challenge of the Global-Local Link." In *Women, Gender, and Human Rights: A Global Perspective*, edited by Marjorie Agosin, 246–62. New Brunswick, NJ: Rutgers University Press, 2001.

Gibbs, Walter. "World Briefing: Europe; Finland: Ex-Leader Acquitted on Secrets Charge." *New York Times*, March 20, 2004. http://www.nytimes.com/2004/03/20/world/world-briefing-europe-finland-ex-leader-acquitted-on-secrets-charge.html.

Gilligan, Nancy. *In a Different Voice: Psychological Theory and Women's Development*. Cambridge, MA: Harvard University Press, 1982.

Givhan, Robin. "Hillary Clinton's Tentative Dip into New Neckline Territory." *Washington Post*, July 20, 2007a. http://www.washingtonpost.com/wp-dyn/content/article/2007/07/19/AR2007071902668.html.

Givhan, Robin. "Wearing the Pants: Envisioning a Female Commander-in-Chief." *Washington Post*, December 9, 2007b. http://www.washingtonpost.com/wp-dyn/content/article/2007/12/08/AR2007120801502.html.

Gluckman, Ron. "Life under Siege." Gluckman.com. 1996. http://www.gluckman.com/ChandrikaKumaratunga.html.

Goldberg, Michelle. "Three A.M. Feminism." *New Republic*, June 25, 2008.

Gonzalez, David. "In Panama's New Dawn, Woman Takes Over." *New York Times*, September 2, 1999. http://www.nytimes.com/1999/09/02/world/in-panama-s-new-dawn-woman-takes-over.html?scp=1&sq=In%20Panama's%20New%20Dawn,%20Woman%20Takes%20Over&st=cse.

Government of Australia. "Your PM: Prime Minister Julia Gillard." 2012. http://www.pm.gov.au/your-pm.

Government of Germany. "Angela Merkel." The Federal Chancellor. 2011. http://www.bundeskanzlerin.de/Webs/BK/En/Angela-Merkel/angela-merkel.html.

Government of the Republic of Croatia. "Jadranka Kosor: Prime Minister." 2010. http://www.vlada.hr/en/naslovnica/o_vladi_rh/clanovi_vlade/jadranka_kosor_dipl_iur.

Government of Sri Lanka. "Hon Chandrika Bandaranaike Kumaratunga (1994–2005)." February 22, 2008. http://www.priu.gov.lk/execpres/cbk.html.

Government of Sri Lanka. "Former Prime Ministers Sri Lanka." April 23, 2010. http://www.priu.gov.lk/PrimeMinister/formerprimeministers.html#Hon.%20Sirimavo%20R.%20D.%20Bandaranaike%20(August%201994-August%202000.

Green, William, and Alex Perry. "We Have Arrested So Many." *Time,* April 10, 2006. http://www.time.com/time/world/article/0,8599,2053831,00.html.

Gresy, Brigitte, and Philip Dole. *The Equal Access of Women and Men in Work and Family Responsibilities in the Workplace.* Paris: General Inspectorate of Social Affairs, 2011. http://translate.google.com/translate?hl=en&sl=fr&u=http://www.igas.gouv.fr/spip.php%3Frubrique214&prev=/search%3Fq%3Dbrigitte%2Bgr%25C3%25A9sy%26hl%3Den%26biw%3D1440%26bih%3D782%26prmd%3Dimvns&sa=X&ei=7Rr3T6uaJYOI8QSxhqTjBg&sqi=2&ved=0CH8Q7gEwCw.

G20. "What Is the G20?" Accessed April 25, 2009. http://g20.org/index.php/en/g20.

Gutgold, Nichola D. *Paving the Way for Madam President.* Lanham, MD: Lexington Books, 2006.

Guyler Delva, Joseph. "Haiti Senate Ousts Prime Minister Pierre-Louis." Reuters, October 30, 2009. http://www.reuters.com/article/idUSTRE59T0OH20091030.

Haiti-Reference. "Profil d'Ertha Pascal-Trouillot." Last modified March 17, 2010. http://www.haiti-reference.com/histoire/notables/pascal-trouillot.html.

Halonen, Tarja. "President Tarja Kaarina Halonen." Accessed September 6, 2012. http://www.presidenthalonen.fi/en/tarja-halonen.

Han, Lori Cox. "Is the United States Really Ready for a Woman President?" In *Rethinking Madam President: Are We Ready for a Woman in the White House?,* edited by Lori Cox Han and Caroline Heldman, 1–15. Boulder, CO: Lynne Rienner, 2007.

Hardy, Molly O'Hagan. "Symbolic Power: Mary Robinson's Presidency and Eavan Boland's Poetry." *New Hibernia Review 12,* no. 3 (2008): 47–65.

Harris, David. "Liberia 2005: An Unusual African Post-conflict Election." *Journal of Modern African Studies 44,* no. 3 (2006): 375–95.

Harris, Lynn. "Female Heads of State: The Chosen Ones." *Glamour,* November 1, 2010. http://www.glamour.com/women-of-the-year/2010/female-heads-of-state.

Harvey, Rachel. "Burma's Aung San Suu Kyi Sworn in to Parliament." BBC News, May 2, 2012. http://www.bbc.co.uk/news/world-asia-17918414.

Haussman, Melissa. "Can Women Enter the 'Big Tents'? National Party Structures and Presidential Nominations." In *Anticipating Madam President,* edited by Robert P. Watson and Ann Gordon, 59–79. Boulder, CO: Lynne Rienner, 2003.

Healy, Patrick. "The Resume Factor: Those Two Terms as First Lady." *New York Times,* December 26, 2007a. http://www.nytimes.com/2007/12/26/us/politics/26clinton.html.

Healy, Patrick. "The Clinton Conundrum: What's behind the Laugh?" *New York Times*, December 12, 2007b. http://www.nytimes.com/2007/09/30/us/politics/30clinton.html?_r=2&oref=slogin&oref=slogin.

Healy, Patrick, and Michael Cooper. "Clinton Is Victor, Turning Back Obama; McCain Also Triumphs." *New York Times*, January 8, 2008. http://www.nytimes.com/2008/01/09/us/politics/09elect.html?_r=1&hp.

Heffernan, Richard. "The Prime Minister and the News Media: Political Communication as a Leadership Resource." *Parliamentary Affairs 59*, no. 4 (2006): 582–98.

Heith, Diane J. "The Lipstick Watch: Media Coverage, Gender, and Presidential Campaigns." In *Anticipating Madam President*, edited by Robert P. Watson and Ann Gordon, 123–30. Boulder, CO: Lynne Rienner, 2003.

Heldman, Caroline. "Cultural Barriers to a Female President in the United States." In *Rethinking Madam President: Are We Ready for a Woman in the White House?*, edited by Lori Cox Han and Caroline Heldman, 17–42. Boulder, CO: Lynne Rienner, 2007.

Heldman, Caroline, Susan J. Carroll, and Stephanie Olson. "'She Brought Only a Skirt': Print Media Coverage of Elizabeth Dole's Bid for the Republican Presidential Nomination." *Political Communication 22*, no. 3 (2005): 315–35.

Hellsten, Villiina, Anne Maria Holli, and Hanna Wass. 2007. "Sukupuolenmukainen äänestäminen vuoden 2006 presidentinvaaleissa." In *Presidentinvaalit 2006*, edited by Pekka Isotalus and Sami Borg. Helsinki: WSOY, 2007.

Helms, Ludger. "The Grand Coalition: Precedents and Prospects." *German Politics and Society 24*, no. 1 (2006): 47–66.

Henderson, Sarah L., and Alana S. Jeydel. *Participation and Protest: Women and Politics in a Global World*. New York: Oxford University Press, 2007.

Herman, Steve. "Bangladesh Caretaker Government Frees Former PM Hasina." Voice of America, June 11, 2008. http://www.voanews.com/english/news/a-13-2008-06-11-voa8-66752722.html.

Herrnson, Paul J., Celeste Lay, and Anita Stokes. "Women Running as Women: Candidate Gender, Campaign Issues, and Voter-Targeting Strategies." *Journal of Politics 65*, no. 1 (2003): 244–55.

Hill, Kevin. "Agatha Uwilingiyimana." In *Women in Law: A Bio-bibliographical Sourcebook*, edited by R. Salokar and Mary L. Volcansek, 323–28. Westport, CT: Greenwood Press, 1996a.

Hill, Kevin. "Sylvie Kinigi." *In Women in Law: A Bio-bibliographical Sourcebook*, edited by R. Salokar and Mary L. Volcansek, 118–22. Westport, CT: Greenwood Press, 1996b.

Hodson, Piper. "Routes to Power: An Examination of Political Change, Rulership, and Women's Access to Executive Office." In *The Other Elites*, edited by MaryAnne Borelli and Janet M. Martin, 33–47. Boulder, CO: Lynne Rienner, 1997.

Hoge, Warren. "Junta Allows 199 to Leave Nicaragua; 72 Denied Exit." *New York Times*, July 27, 1979.

Holli, Anne Maria. "Electoral Reform Opens Roads to Presidency for Finnish Women." *Politics & Gender 4*, no. 3 (2008): 496–509.

Hough, Lory. "Ellen!" *Kennedy School Bulletin*, Spring 2006. http://www.hks.harvard.edu/ksgpress/bulletin/spring2006/features/ellen.htm.

Htun, Mala N., and Mark P. Jones. "Engendering the Right to Participate in Decision-Making: Electoral Quotas and Women's Leadership in Latin America." In *Gender and the Politics of Rights and Democracy in Latin America*, edited by Nikki Craske and Maxine Molyneux, 32–54. New York: Palgrave, 2002.

Huddy, Leonie, and Tony E. Carey. "Group Politics Redux: Race and Gender in the 2008 Democratic Presidential Primaries." *Politics & Gender 5*, no. 1 (2009): 81–96.

Huddy, Leonie, and Nayda Terkildsen. "Gender Stereotypes and the Perception of Male and Female Candidates." *American Journal of Political Science 37*, no. 1 (1993): 119–47.

Hughes, Melanie M., and Pamela Paxton. "Familiar Theories from a New Perspective: The Implications of a Longitudinal Approach to Women in Politics Research." *Politics & Gender 3*, no. 3 (2007): 370–78.

Hughs, Libby. *Madam Prime Minister: A Biography of Margaret Thatcher*. New York: iUniverse.com, 2000.

Hunter, Alfred A., and Margaret A. Denton. "Do Female Candidates 'Lose Votes'? The Experience of Female Candidates in the 1979 and 1980 Canadian General Elections." *Canadian Review of Sociology and Anthropology 21*, no. 4 (1984): 395–406.

Independent Television Service. "Iron Ladies of Liberia, Her Life." *Independent Lens*, January 11, 2008. http://www.pbs.org/independentlens/ironladies/life.html.

Index Mundi. "Gabon Government Profile." 2012. http://www.indexmundi.com/gabon/government_profile.html.

IndiraGhandi.com. "About Indira Gandhi." 2008. http://www.indiragandhi.com/aboutindiragandhi.htm.

Inglehart, Ronald, and Pippa Norris. *The Rising Tide: Gender Equality and Cultural Change around the World*. New York: Cambridge University Press, 2003.

Inside Costa Rica. "Laura Chinchilla Miranda: Costa Rica's First Woman President." May 9, 2010. http://www.insidecostarica.com/dailynews/2010/may/09/costarica10050903.htm.

Inter-Parliamentary Union. "Women in National Parliaments." Accessed June 25, 2008. http://www.ipu.org/wmn-e/classif.htm.

Inter-Parliamentary Union. "Women's Suffrage: A World Chronology of the Recognition of Women's Rights to Vote and to Stand for Election." http://www.ipu.org/wmn-e/suffrage.htm.

Irish Times. "President Would Defeat Higgins, Poll Shows." February 2, 2004. http://www.irishtimes.com/newspaper/breaking/2004/0207/breaking4.html.

Israel Ministry of Foreign Affairs. "Dalia Itzik, MK." 2008. http://www.mfa.gov.il/MFA/MFAArchive/2000_2009/2002/11/Dalia+Itzik.htm.

Jäätteenmäki, Anneli. "My Story." Anneli Jaatteenmaki.net. 2008. http://www.anneli-jaatteenmaki.net/in-english/my-story.

Jackson, Andy. "Han Myeong-Sook Officially Starts Bid for Mayor of Seoul." Asian Correspondent.com, April 22, 2010. http://asiancorrespondent.com/31371/han-myeong-sook-officially-starts-bid-for-mayor-of-seoul.

Jackson-Laufer, Guida Myrl. *Women Rulers throughout the Ages: An Illustrated Guide*. Santa Barbara, CA: ABC-CLIO, 1999.

Jaco Blog. "Who Is Costa Rica's President Elect—Laura Chinchilla?" February 23, 2010. http://thejacoblog.com/who-is-costa-ricas-president-elect-laura-chinchilla.

Jalalzai, Farida. "Women Political Leaders: Past and Present." *Women & Politics 26*, nos. 3–4 (2004): 85–108.

Jalalzai, Farida. "Women Rule: Shattering the Executive Glass Ceiling." *Politics & Gender 4*, no. 2 (2008): 1–27.

Jalalzai, Farida. "The Snow Ball Effect of Women Leaders." Paper presented at the annual meeting of the Midwestern Political Science Association, Chicago, April 2010a.

Jalalzai, Farida. "Madam President: Gender, Power, and the Comparative Presidency." *Journal of Women, Politics & Policy 31* (2010b): 132–65.

Jalalzai, Farida. "A Critical Departure for Women Executives or More of the Same? The Powers of Chancellor Merkel." *German Politics 20*, no. 2 (2011): 428–48.

Jalalzai, Farida. "Ma Ellen—the Iron Lady of Liberia: Evaluating Ellen Johnson Sirleaf's Presidency." In *Women as Political Leaders: Studies in Gender and Governing*, edited by Michael A. Genovese and Janie S. Steckenrider. New York: Routledge, 2013 (forthcoming).

Jalalzai, Farida, and Chad A. Hankinson. "Political Widowhood in the United States: An Empirical Assessment of Underlying Assumptions of Representation." *Journal of Women, Politics & Policy 29*, no. 3 (2008): 395–426.

Jalalzai, Farida, and Mona Lena Krook. "Beyond Hillary and Benazir: Women's Leadership Worldwide." *International Political Science Review 31*, no. 1 (2010): 5–23.

Jalalzai, Farida, and Manon Tremblay. "Women in the Executive Branch in North America." In *Women in Executive Power*, edited by Gretchen Bauer and Manon Tremblay, 122–40. London: Routledge, 2011.

Jansen, Sharon. *The Monstrous Regiment of Women: Female Rulers in Early Modern Europe*. New York: Palgrave, 2002.

Jensen, Jane S. *Women Political Leaders: Breaking the Highest Glass Ceiling*. New York: Palgrave Macmillan, 2008.

Johnson Sirleaf, Ellen. *This Child Will Be Great: Memoir of a Remarkable Life by Africa's First Woman President*. New York: Harper, 2009.

Jones, Jeffrey M. "Some Americans Reluctant to Vote for Mormon, 72-Year-Old Presidential Candidates." Gallup, February 20, 2007. http://www.gallup.com/poll/26611/Some-Am ericans-Reluctant-Vote-Mormon-72YearOld-Presidential-Candidates.aspx.

Jones, Jeffrey M. "Perceived Honesty Gap for Clinton versus Obama, McCain." Gallup, March 18, 2008. http://www.gallup.com/poll/105097/Perceived-Honesty-Gap-Clinto n-Versus-Obama-McCain.aspx.

Jones, Mark P. "Gender Quotas, Electoral Laws, and the Election of Women: Lessons from the Argentine Provinces." *Comparative Political Studies 31*, no. 1 (1998): 3–21.

Jurek, Steven J., and Farida Jalalzai. "Representation at the Executive Level: Indistinguishable Elites, Multifarious Masses." *International Journal of Diversity in Organisations, Communities and Nations 11*, no. (2012): 71–84.

Kahn, Kim Fridkin. "The Distorted Mirror: Press Coverage of Women Candidates for Statewide Office." *Journal of Politics 56*, no. 1 (1994): 154–73.

Kamat, Vikas. "History of India—Indira Gandhi." Kamat's Potpourri, October 9, 2011. http://www.kamat.com/kalranga/itihas/indira_gandhi.htm.

Kathlene, Lynn. "Power and Influence of State Legislative Policymaking: The Interaction of Gender and Position in Committee Hearing Debates." *American Political Science Review 88*, no. 3 (1994): 560–76.

Kathlene, Lynn. "Alternative Views of Crime: Legislative Policymaking in Gendered Terms." *Journal of Politics 57*, no. 3 (1995): 696–723.

Katzenstein, Mary Fainsod. "Towards Equality? Cause and Consequences of the Political Prominence of Women in India." *Asian Survey 18*, no. 5 (1978): 473–86.

Kennedy, Carole. "Is the United States Ready for a Woman President? Is the Pope Protestant?" In *Anticipating Madam President*, edited by Robert P. Watson and Ann Gordon, 131–43. Boulder, CO: Lynne Rienner, 2003.

Kernell, Samuel. *Going Public: New Strategies of Presidential Leadership*. Washington, DC: CQ Press, 1997.

KGMA. "Gloria Macapagal Arroyo: Biography." 2011. http://www.macapagal.com/gma/biography/index.php.

King, Anthony. "The Outsider as Political Leader: The Case of Margaret Thatcher." *British Journal of Political Science 32*, no. 3 (2002): 435–54.

King, Gary, Robert Keohane, and Sidney Verba. *Designing Social Inquiry*. Princeton, NJ: Princeton University Press, 1994.

Kitchens, Susan. "The 100 Most Powerful Women: #68 Han Myung-sook." *Forbes*, August 31, 2006. http://www.forbes.com/lists/2006/11/06women_Han-Myung-sook_V02W.html.

Kittilson, Miki Caul. "Women's Representation in Parliament: The Role of Political Parties." *Party Politics 5*, no. 1 (1999): 79–98.

Kittilson, Miki Caul. *Challenging Parties, Changing Parliaments: Women and Elected Office in Contemporary Western Europe*. Columbus: Ohio State University Press, 2006.

Kittilson, Miki Caul, and Kim Fridkin. "Gender, Candidate Portrayals and Election Campaigns: A Comparative Perspective." *Politics & Gender 4*, no. 3 (2008): 371–92.

Ko, Lisa. "Independent Lens: Thunder in Guyana" Independent Television Service, 2011. http://www.pbs.org/independentlens/thunderinguyana/janet.html.

Koep, Hannah. "Instant View: Death of Gabon's President Bongo." Reuters, June 8, 2009. http://www.reuters.com/article/2009/06/08/us-gabon-bongo-future-instantview-idUSTRE5574RY20090608?pageNumber=1.

Kohli, Atul. *Democracy and Discontent*. Cambridge: Cambridge University Press, 1990.

Komisar, Lucy. *Corazon Aquino: The Story of a Revolution*. New York: George Braziller, 1987.

Korea Society. "Korea at a Turning Point." November 8, 2007. http://www.koreasociety.org/policy/policy/korea_at_a_turning_point.html.

Kosciejew, Marc. "Becoming Ellen Johnson-Sirleaf: The Controversial Political Career of Africa's 'Iron Lady.'" Conflict, Economy, Governance, Politics, Women's Rights, January 26, 2012. http://www.caaglop.com/robbenisland-blog/tag/ellen-johnson-sirleaf.

Krook, Mona Lena. *Quotas for Women in Politics: Gender and Candidate Selection Reform Worldwide*. New York: Oxford University Press, 2009.

Krupavicius, Algin. "Semi-presidentialism in Lithuania: Origins, Developments, and Challenges." In *Semi-presidentialism in Central and Eastern Europe*, edited by Robert Elgie and Sophia Moestrup, 65–84. Manchester, England: Manchester University Press, 2008.

Kuhn, R. "The French Presidential and Parliamentary Elections, 2007." *Representation 43*, no. 4 (2007): 323–36.

Kulish, Nicholas. "Two Years After Narrow Victory, Germany's Merkel Cruises on Her Popularity." *New York Times*, September 12, 2007. http://www.nytimes.com/2007/09/12/world/europe/12merkel.html.

Kuzmanovic, Jasmina. "Croatian Premier Kosor Survives No-Confidence Vote in Parliament." *Bloomberg Businessweek*, October 28, 2010. http://www.bloomberg.com/news/2010-10-28/croatian-premier-kosor-survives-no-confidence-vote-after-15-hour-debate.html.

Lambert, Caroline. "French Women in Politics: The Long Road to Parity." Brookings Institution, May 1, 2001. http://www.brookings.edu/articles/2001/05france_lambert.aspx.

Langman, Jimmy, and Joseph Contreras. "An Unlikely Pioneer." *Newsweek*, December 25, 2005. http://www.newsweek.com/id/51460.

Lawless, Jennifer L. "Women, War, and Winning Elections: Gender Stereotyping and the Post–September 11th Era." *Political Research Quarterly 57*, no. 3 (2004): 479–90.

Lawless, Jennifer L. "Sexism and Gender Bias in Election 2008: A More Complex Path for Women in Politics." *Politics & Gender 5*, no. 1 (2009): 70–80.

Lawless, Jennifer L., and Richard L. Fox. *It Still Takes a Candidate: Why Women Don't Run for Office*. New York: Cambridge University Press, 2010.

Lawrence, Regina G., and Melody Rose. *Hillary Clinton's Race for the White House: Gender Politics and the Media on the Campaign Trail*. Boulder, CO: Lynn Reiner, 2010.

Lemmon, Gayle Tzemach. "Michelle Bachelet Has a Mission." *Newsweek*, September 12, 2011. http://www.thedailybeast.com/newsweek/2011/09/11/michelle-bachelet-has-a-mission-to-help-the-world-s-women.html.

Levy, Clifford J. "Presidential Election in Ukraine Goes to a Runoff." *New York Times*, January 17, 2010. http://www.nytimes.com/2010/01/18/world/europe/18ukraine.html.

Library of Congress. "Bangladesh: Chronology of Important Events." September 1988. http://lcweb2.loc.gov/cgi-bin/query/r?frd/cstdy:@field(DOCID+bd0004).

Lijphart, Arend. *Patterns of Democracy: Government Forms and Performance in Thirty-Six Countries*. New Haven, CT: Yale University Press, 1999.

Liswood, Laura A. *Women World Leaders*. London: Pandora, 1995.

Liswood, Laura A. *Women World Leaders: Great Politicians Tell Their Stories*. Washington, DC: Council Press, 2007.

Long, Chrissie, and Sara Miller Llana. "Costa Rica Elects First Woman President, Inspiring the Region." *Christian Science Monitor*, February 8, 2010. http://www.csmonitor.com/World/Americas/2010/0208/Costa-Rica-elects-first-woman-president-inspiring-the-region.

Lorber, Judith. *The Paradoxes of Gender*. New Haven, CT: Yale University Press, 1994.

Lovenduski Joni. " Introduction: The Dynamics of Gender and Party." In *Gender and Party Politics*, edited by Joni Lovenduski and Pippa Norris, 1–15. London: Sage, 1993.

Lovenduski, Joni, and Pippa Norris, eds. *Gender and Party Politics*. London: Sage, 1993.

Luo, Michael. "Obama Recasts the Fundraising Landscape." *New York Times*, October 19, 2008. http://www.nytimes.com/2008/10/20/us/politics/20donate.html?_r=1&hp.

Lupia, Arthur, and Karen Strom. "Coalition Termination and the Strategic Timing of Parliamentary Elections." *American Political Science Review 89*, no. 3 (1995): 648–65.

Mahalo.com. "Michele Pierre-Louis." 2011. http://www.mahalo.com/michele-pierre-louis.

Managua, John Moody. "Chamorro: More than Just a Name?" *Time*, May 12, 1990. http://www.time.com/time/magazine/article/0,9171,969578-2,00.html.

Mansbridge, Jane. "Should Blacks Represent Blacks and Women Represent Women? A Contingent 'Yes.'" *Journal of Politics 61*, no. 3 (1999): 628–57.

Margaret Thatcher Foundation. "Essential Margaret Thatcher: Brief Biography." 2011. http://www.margaretthatcher.org/essential/biography.asp.

Marshall, Monty G ., Jack Goldstone, and Benjamin R. Cole. "State Fragility Index and Matrix 2008." In *Global Report 2009: Conflict, Governance, and State Fragility* edited by Monty G. Marshall and Benjamin R. Cole. Arlington, VA: Center for Systemic Peace, Center for Global Policy, 2009. http://www.systemicpeace.org/Global%20Report%202009.pdf.

Marshall, Monty G., and Keith Jaggers. "Polity IV Project: Political Regime Characteristics and Transitions, 1800–2010." Center for Systemic Peace. June 21, 2011. http://www.systemicpeace.org/polity/polity4.htm.

Marshall, Tyler. "New Parliament Picks a Leader for E. Germany." *Los Angeles Times*, April 6, 1990. http://articles.latimes.com/1990-04-06/news/mn-628_1_east-german.

Martin, Janet M. *The Presidency and Women: Promise, Performance, and Illusion.* College Station: Texas A&M University Press, 2003.

Mascoll, Philip. "Jamaica's First Female Prime Minister." Feminist eZine, February 26, 2006. http://www.feministezine.com/feminist/Jamaicas-First-Female-PM.html.

Matland, Richard E. "Institutional Variables Affecting Female Representation in National Legislatures: The Case of Norway." *Journal of Politics 55*, no. 3 (1993): 737–55.

Matland, Richard E. "Women's Representation in National Legislatures: Developed and Developing Countries." *Legislative Studies Quarterly 23*, no. 1 (1998a): 109–25.

Matland, Richard E. "Enhancing Women's Political Participation: Legislative Recruitment and Electoral Systems." In *Women in Parliament: Beyond Numbers*, edited by Azza Karam, 65–86. Stockholm: International IDEA, 1998b.

Matthews, Chris. "Hardball with Chris Matthews for Jan. 29." MSNBC, January 29, 2008. http://www.msnbc.msn.com/id/16886771.

McBride, Dorothy E., and Janine E. Parry. *Women's Rights in the USA: Policy Debates and Gender Roles.* New York: Routledge, 2010.

McDonagh, Eileen. *The Motherless State: Women's Political Leadership and American Democracy.* Chicago: University of Chicago Press, 2009.

McIntyre, Angus. *In Search of Megawati Sukarnoputri.* Clayton, Victoria, Australia: Monash University, 1997.

Miller, Melissa K., Jeffrey Peake, and Brittany Ann Boulton. "Testing the *Saturday Night Live* Hypothesis: Fairness and Bias in Newspaper Coverage of Hillary Clinton's Campaign." *Politics & Gender 6* (2010): 169–98.

Ministry of Communications. "Profile: Dr. Ivy Matsepe-Casaburri." Government of South Africa. 2009. http://www.gcis.gov.za/gcis/gcis_profile.jsp?id=1042.

Mohamad, Goenawan. "Mega, Mega." *Suara Independen (Independent Voice) 11*, no. 2 (1996): 2.

Moore, Gwen, and Gene Shackman. "Gender and Authority: A Cross-National Study." *Social Science Quarterly 77* (1996): 273–88.

Moran, Mary. *Liberia: The Voices of Democracy.* Philadelphia: University of Pennsylvania Press, 2008.

Moskin, Marietta D. *Margaret Thatcher of Great Britain.* Englewood Cliffs, NJ: Julian Messner, 1990.

Moulson, Geir, and Melissa Eddy. "Germany Election 2009: Angela Merkel Wins Second Term." *Huffington Post,* November 27, 2009. http://www.huffingtonpost.com/2009/09/27/germany-election-2009-ang_n_301202.html.

Müller, Wolfgang C., Torbjörn Bergman, and Kaare Strøm. "Parliamentary Democracy: Promises and Problems." In *Delegation and Accountability in Parliamentary Democracies,* edited by Kaare Strøm, Wolfgang C. Müller, and Torbjörn Bergman, 3–32. New York: Oxford University Press, 2003.

Murray, Alan. "McAleese Urged to Curb Costly 'Jaunts' to the North." *Independent,* February 8, 2009. http://www.independent.ie/national-news/mcaleese-urged-to-curb-costly-jaunts-to-the-north-1632514.html.

Murray, Rainbow, ed. *Cracking the Highest Glass Ceiling: A Global Comparison of Women's Campaigns for Executive Office.* Santa Barbara, CA: Praeger, 2010a.

Murray, Rainbow. "Introduction." In *Cracking the Highest Glass Ceiling: A Global Comparison of Women's Campaigns for Executive Office,* edited by Rainbow Murray, 3–27. Santa Barbara, CA: Praeger, 2010b.

Murray, Rainbow. "Madonna and Four Children: Ségolène Royal." In *Cracking the Highest Glass Ceiling: A Global Comparison of Women's Campaigns for Executive Office,* edited by Rainbow Murray, 49–68. Santa Barbara, CA: Praeger, 2010c.

Murray, Rainbow. "Second among Unequals? A Study of Whether France's 'Quota Women' Are Up to the Job." *Politics & Gender 6* (2010d): 93–118.

Murray, Rainbow, and Sheila Perry. "A Right Royal Mess: Why Did the French Say 'Non' to the Opportunity of Having a Woman President?" Paper presented at the annual meeting of the American Political Science Association, Boston, August 28–31, 2008.

Mushaben, Joyce. "Madam Chancellor: Angela Merkel and the Triangulation of German Foreign Policy." *Georgetown Journal of International Affairs 10,* no. 1 (2009): 27–35.

National Elections Commission. "2005 Voter Registration Statistics." Republic of Liberia. 2005. http://www.necliberia.org/Statistics_Maps/dstatistics10september2005.pdf.

Navarro, Mireya. "The Widow of Ex-Leader Wins Race in Panama." *New York Times,* May 3, 1999a. http://www.nytimes.com/1999/05/03/world/the-widow-of-ex-leader-wins-race-in-panama.html.

Navarro, Mireya. "Travel Advisory: Correspondent's Report; Panama Converting Canal Zone for Tourism." *New York Times,* August 29, 1999b. http://www.nytimes.com/1999/08/29/travel/travel-advisory-correspondent-s-report-panama-converting-canal-zone-for-tourism.html?scp=1&sq=Panama%20Converting%20Canal%20Zone%20for%20Tourism&st=cse.

Navarro, Mireya. "Woman in the News: Mireya Elisa Moscoso; Earnest Icon for Panama." *New York Times,* May 4, 1999c. http://www.nytimes.com/1999/05/04/world/woman-in-the-news-mireya-elisa-moscoso-earnest-icon-for-panama.html?.

NDTV Bureau. "Sonia Names Pratibha Patil for President." June 14, 2007. http://www.ndtv.com/convergence/ndtv/story.aspx?id=NEWEN20070015534.

Nelson, Michael. "The Setting." In *The Elections of 2008*, edited by Michael Nelson, 1–21. Washington, DC: CQ Press, 2009.

Neustadt, Richard. *Presidential Power and the Modern Presidency: The Politics of Leadership from Roosevelt to Reagan*. New York: Free Press, 1990.

New York Times. "Rebels in Nicaragua Take Officials Hostage." August 20, 1993. http://www.nytimes.com/1993/08/20/world/rebels-in-nicaragua-take-official s-hostage.html?scp=1&sq=Rebels%20in%20Nicaragua%20Take%20Officials%20 Hostage&st=cse.

New York Times. "Double Tragedy in Africa." April 10, 1994. http://www.nytimes.com/1994/04/10/opinion/double-tragedy-in-africa.html.

New York Times. "Political Madness in Ecuador." February 11, 1997. http://www.nytimes.com/1997/02/11/opinion/political-madness-in-ecuador.html.

New York Times. "Military Coup Ousts Government of São Tomé in West Africa." July 17, 2003. http://www.nytimes.com/2003/07/17/world/military-coup-ousts-government-of-sao-tome-in-west-africa.html?scp=1&sq=Military%20Coup%20 Ousts%20Government%20of%20S%C3%A3o%20Tom%C3%A9%20in%20West%20 Africa&st=cse.

New York Times. "Benazir Bhutto." April 16, 2010a. http://topics.nytimes.com/topics/ reference/timestopics/people/b/benazir_bhutto/index.html.

New York Times. "Times Topic: Nestor Kirchner." October 27, 2010b.

New York Times. "South Korea." August 25, 2011a. http://topics.nytimes.com/top/news/ international/countriesandterritories/southkorea/index.html.

New York Times. "Hillary Rodham Clinton." April 1, 2011b. http://topics.nytimes.com/ top/reference/timestopics/people/c/hillary_rodham_clinton/index.html.

New York Times. "Asif Ali Zardari." March 5, 2012. http://topics.nytimes.com/top/refer ence/timestopics/people/z/asif_ali_zardari/index.html.

Newsweek. "A General's Daughter: Michelle Bachelet, Latin America's First Female Defense Minister, Aims to Keep the Troops in Line." August 11, 2002. http://www.thedailybeast.com/newsweek/2002/08/11/a-general-s-daughter.html.

Nilacharal Ltd. "Pratibha Patil." 2011. http://www.nilacharal.com/enter/celeb/ PratibhaPatil.asp.

Niven, David. "Party Elites and Women Candidates: The Shape of Bias." In *Women, Gender, and Politics: A Reader*, edited by Mona Lena Krook and Sarah Childs, 151–58. New York: Oxford University Press, 2010.

Norris, Pippa. "Women Leaders Worldwide: A Splash of Color in the Photo Op." In *Women, Media, and Politics*, edited by Pippa Norris, 149–65. New York: Oxford University Press, 1997.

Norris, Pippa, and Joni Lovenduski. "Puzzles in Political Recruitment." In *Women, Gender, and Politics: A Reader*, edited by Mona Lena Krook and Sarah Childs, 135–40. New York: Oxford University Press, 2010.

Office of the High Commissioner for Human Rights. "Mary Robinson." United Nations. 2011. http://www.ohchr.org/EN/ABOUTUS/Pages/Robinson.aspx.

Official Website of the New Zealand Government. "Right Honorable Jenny Shipley." Last updated 2009. http://executive.govt.nz/96-99/minister/shipley/index.html.

Opfell, Olga S. *Women Prime Ministers and Presidents*. Jefferson, NC: McFarland, 1993.

Ortiz, Michelle Ray. "Moscoso Wins Panama Presidency." AP Online, May 2, 1999. http://www.highbeam.com/doc/1P1-23241605.html.

O'Shaughnessy, Hugh. "Obituary: Maria de Lourdes Pintasilgo, Europe's Second Female Prime Minister." *Independent*, July14, 2004. http://www.independent.co.uk/news/obituaries/maria-de-lourdes-pintasilgo-550094.html.

Our Campaigns. "Rose Francine Rogombé." Last modified 2009. http://www.ourcampaigns.com/CandidateDetail.html?CandidateID=216724.

Parkes, Stuart. *Understanding Contemporary Germany*. New York: Routledge, 1997.

Parliament of Finland. "Mari Kiviniemi/Finnish Centre Party." 2012. http://www.eduskunta.fi/triphome/bin/hex5000.sh?hnro=465&kieli=en.

Parliament of Georgia. "The Biography of the Chairperson of the Parliament of Georgia: Nino Burjanadze." 2011. http://www.Parliament.ge/index.php?lang_id=ENG&sec_id=28.

Parliamentof the Republic of Trinidad and Tobago. "The Honourable Kamla Persad-Bissessar, SC, MP." Parliament of the Republic of Trinidad and Tobago. 2011. http://www.ttParliament.org/members.php?mid=54&id=KPB01.

Paterson, Tony. "The Iron Frau: Angela Merkel." *Independent*, April 12, 2010. http://www.independent.co.uk/news/world/europe/the-iron-frau-angela-merkel-1941814.html.

Patterson, Thomas E. *We the People*. New York: McGraw-Hill, 2008.

Pattullo, Polly. "Dame Eugenia Charles: The Caribbean's First Woman PM, She Led Dominica for 15 Years." *Guardian*, September 8, 2005. http://www.guardian.co.uk/news/2005/sep/08/guardianobituaries.pollypattullo.

Pax Christi International. "Appointment of New Secretary General for Pax Christi International." November 18, 2006. http://www.paxchristi.org.uk/press_2005-2006.php.

Paxton, Pamela. "Women in National Legislatures: A Cross-National Analysis." *Social Science Research 26*, no. 4 (1997): 442–64.

Paxton, Pamela, and Melanie M. Hughes. *Women, Politics, and Power: A Global Perspective*. Los Angeles: Pine Forge Press, 2007.

PBS News Hour. "Changing Leaders." July 23, 2001. http://www.pbs.org/newshour/bb/asia/july-dec01/indonesia_7-23.html.

PBS News Hour. "President Ellen Johnson-Sirleaf." November 15, 2005. http://www.pbs.org/newshour/bb/africa/liberia/johnson-sirleaf-bio.html.

Perlez, Jane. "Ex-Communists in Bulgaria Are Poised for Return to Power." *New York Times*, December 18, 1994. http://query.nytimes.com/gst/fullpage.html?res=9C05E1DC1238F93BA25751C1A962958260.

Pierre-Louis, Yves, and Kim Ives. "Preval Nominates Michèle Pierre-Louis for Prime Minister." July 2, 2008. http://www.haitianalysis.com/2008/7/2/preval-nominates-michele-pierre-louis-for-prime-minister.

Piscopo, Jennifer. "Primera Donna or Prima Donna? Media Constructions of Cristina Fernandez de Kirchner in Argentina." In *Cracking the Highest Glass Ceiling: A Global Comparison of Women's Campaigns for Executive Office*, edited by Rainbow Murray, 197–219. Santa Barbara, CA: Praeger, 2010.

Pitkin, Hanna. *The Concept of Representation*. Berkeley: University of California Press, 1967.

Polity IV. "Polity IV Country Report 2008: Burundi." Center for Systemic Peace, 2008a. http://www.docstoc.com/docs/49075831/Polity-IV-Country-Report-2008-Bu.

Polity IV. "Polity IV Country Report 2008: Rwanda." Center for Systemic Peace, 2008b. http://www.docstoc.com/docs/48808143/Polity-IV-Country-Report-2008-Rw.

Polling Report. "White House 2008: Democratic Nomination." http://www.pollingreport.com/wh08dem.htm.

Polsby, Nelson W., and Aaron Wildavsky. *Presidential Elections: Strategies and Structures of American Politics*. Lanham, MD: Rowman & Littlefield, 2008.

President's Secretariat. "The President of India Pratibha Devisingh Patil." President of India.com. 2011. http://presidentofindia.nic.in/profile.html.

Prime Minister's Office. "Prime Minister of Iceland Jóhanna Sigurðardóttir." Government of Iceland. 2010. http://eng.forsaetisraduneyti.is/minister/cv.

Progressio. "Haiti: Michele Pierre-Louis Calls for Positive Change After the Earthquake." October 13, 2010. http://www.progressio.org.uk/blog/news/haiti-michele-pierre-loui s-calls-positive-change-after-earthquake.

Protsyk, Oleh, and Andrew Wilson. "Center Politics in Russia and Ukraine: Patronage, Power, and Virtuality." *Party Politics 9*, no. 6 (2003): 703–27.

Provizer, Norman. "Golda Meir: An Outline of a Unique Life—A Chronological Survey of Golda Meir's Life and Legacy." Metropolitan State University of Denver, Golda Meir Center for Political Leadership. 2003. http://www.mscd.edu/golda/goldameir/chronologyofgoldameir.

Przeworski, Adam, and Henry Teune. *The Logic of Comparative Social Inquiry*. New York: Wiley Interscience, 1970.

Purcell, Susan Kaufman. "Behind a Revolution." *New York Times*, July 20, 1985.

Quesada, Ana Isabel Garcia. "Putting the Mandate into Practice: Legal Reform in Costa Rica." Paper presented at the International IDEA workshop "The Implementation of Quotas—Latin American Experiences," Lima, Peru, February 23–24, 2003. http://www.quotaproject.org/CS/CS_Garcia_Costa_Rica.pdf.

Quintal, Angela. "No Wars, No Drama for Matsepe-Casaburri." IOL News, September 26, 2008. http://www.thepost.co.za/no-wars-no-drama-for-matsepe-casaburri-1.417900.

Radio Netherlands Worldwide. "Gabon Swears in Interim President." June 10, 2009. http://www.rnw.nl/english/article/gabon-swears-interim-president.

Randall, Colin. "What a Menage a Trois." *Daily Mail*, June 20, 2007.

Rasmussen, J. "Women's Role in Contemporary British Politics: Impediments to Parliamentary Candidates." *Parliamentary Affairs 36*, no. 1 (1983): 300–15.

Reilly, Ben. "Sri Lanka: Changes to Accommodate Diversity." In *The International Handbook of Electoral System Design*, edited by Andrew Reynolds and Ben Reilly, 107–28. Stockholm: International Institute for Democracy and Electoral Assistance, 1997. http://www.ifes.org/publication/799b329fa1126a43c9877959ca3d dbfa/esd_english.pdf.

Reinart, Ustun. "Ambition for All Seasons: Tansu Çiller." *Middle East Review of International Affairs 3*, no. 1 (1999). http://meria.idc.ac.il/journal/1999/issue1/jv3n1a6.html.

Reingold, Beth. *Representing Women: Sex, Gender, and Legislative Behavior in Arizona and California*. Chapel Hill: University of North Carolina Press, 2000.

Reuters. "Sylvie Kingi, Prime Minister of Burundi." December 23, 1994. http://www.hartford-hwp.com/archives/30/030.html.

Reuters. "Lithuanians Vote in Female President." Deutsche Welle, May 18, 2009. http://www.dw-world.de/dw/article/0,,4260641,00.html?maca=en-aa-top-861-rdf.

Reynolds, Andrew. "Women in the Legislatures and Executives of the World: Knocking at the Highest Glass Ceiling." *World Politics 51* (1999): 547–72.

RIA Novosti. "Georgian MPs Accuse Opposition Head of 'Treason' over Moscow Visit." April 3, 2010a. http://rianovosti.com/world/20100304/158093985.html.

RIA Novosti. "Otunbayeva Inaugurated as Kyrgyz President." July 3, 2010b. http://en.rian.ru/exsoviet/20100703/159673207.html.

Rich, Frank. "The Billary Road to Republican Victory." *New York Times*, January 27, 2008. http://www.nytimes.com/2008/01/27/opinion/27rich.html.

Richter, Linda K. "Explaining Theories of Female Leadership in South and South East Asia." *Pacific Affairs 63*, no. 1 (1991): 524–40.

Ritter, Gretchen. "Gender and Politics over Time." *Politics & Gender 3*, no. 3 (2007): 386–97.

Robinson, Linda. "Madam President." *New York Times*, September 15, 1996. http://www.nytimes.com/1996/09/15/books/madam-president.html?scp=1&sq=Madam%20President%20Robinson,%20Linda&st=cse.

Roces, Mina. "Negotiating Modernities: Filipino Women 1970–2000." In *Women in Asia: Tradition, Modernity, and Globalisation*, edited by Louise Edwards and Mina Roces, 112–38. Ann Arbor: University of Michigan Press, 2000.

Rohter, Larry. "President and Legislature Dueling in Nicaragua." *New York Times*, June 5, 1995. http://www.nytimes.com/1995/06/05/world/president-and-legislature-dueling-in-nicaragua.html?scp=1&sq=president%20and%20Legislature%20Dueling%20in%20Nicaragua&st=cse.

Rohter, Larry. "Argentina May See Shared Custody of Its Top Job." *New York Times*, March 3, 2007a. http://www.nytimes.com/2007/03/03/world/americas/03argentina.html.

Rohter, Larry. "Argentina's President Steps Aside to Support Wife as His Successor." *New York Times*, July 3, 2007b. http://www.nytimes.com/2007/07/03/world/americas/03argentina.html.

Rosenthal, Cindy Simon. *When Women Lead: Integrative Leadership in State Legislatures*. New York: Oxford University Press, 1998.

Rule, Wilma. "Twenty-Three Democracies and Women's Parliamentary Representation." Paper presented at the annual meeting of the International Political Science Association, Paris, 1985.

Rule, Wilma, and Joseph F. Zimmerman, eds. *Electoral Systems in Comparative Perspective: Their Impact on Women and Minorities*. Westport, CT: Greenwood Press, 1994.

Saint-Germain, Michelle A. "Women in Power in Nicaragua: Myth and Reality." In *Women as National Leaders*, edited by Michael A. Genovese, 70–102. London: Sage, 1993a.

Saint-Germain, Michelle A. "Paths to Power of Women Legislators in Costa Rica and Nicaragua." *Women's Studies International Forum 16*, no. 2 (1993b): 119–38.

Salmond, Rob. "Proportional Representation and Female Parliamentarians." *Legislative Studies Quarterly 31*, no. 2 (2006): 175–204.

Salo, Elaine. "South African Feminism: A Coming of Age?" In *Women's Movements in the Global Era: The Power of Local Feminisms*, edited by Amrita Basu, 29–55. Boulder, CO: Westview Press, 2010.

Sambandan, V. S., "A Crisis in Sri Lanka." *Frontline* 20, no. 24 (2003). http://www.hindu.com/thehindu/fline/fl2024/stories/20031205006900400.htm.

Sancton, Thomas. "Edith Cresson: How to Lose Friends and Alienate People." *Time*, March 29, 1999.

Sapiro, Virginia. "When Are Interests Interesting?" *American Political Science Review* 75, no. 3 (1981): 701–16.

Sardar, Ziauddin. "Kept in Power by Male Fantasy." *New Statesman*, August 7, 1998.

Sartori, Giovanni. *Comparative Constitutional Engineering*. London: Macmillan, 1997.

Satter, Raphael G. "Book Recounts Margaret Thatcher's Decline." CBS News, February 11, 2009. http://www.cbsnews.com/stories/2008/08/25/health/main4380977.shtml.

Schemo, Diana Jean. "3 Ecuadoreans Laying Claims to Presidency." *New York Times*, February 8, 1997a. http://www.nytimes.com/1997/02/08/world/3-ecuadoreans-lay-ing-claims-to-presidency.html?scp=1&sq=Three%20Ecuadoreans%20Laying%20Claims%20to%20Presidency&st=cse.

Schemo, Diana Jean. "Armed Forces in Ecuador Abandon Ousted Leader." *New York Times*, February 9, 1997b. http://www.nytimes.com/1997/02/09/world/armed-force s-in-ecuador-abandon-ousted-leader.html?scp=1&sq=Armed%20Forces%20in%20 Ecuador%20Abandon%20Ousted%20Leader.&st=cse.

Schemo, Diana Jean. "Ecuadorean Is Again Elected Interim President, Five Days Later." *New York Times*, February 12, 1997c. http://www.nytimes.com/1997/02/12/ world/ecuadorean-is-again-elected-interim-president-five-days-later.html?scp= 1&sq=Ecuadorean%20Is%20Again%20Elected%20Interim%20President,%20 Five%20Days%20Later&st=cse.

Schemo, Diana Jean. "Ecuadoreans Rally in Drive to Oust President." *New York Times*, February 6, 1997d. http://www.nytimes.com/1997/02/06/world/ecuadoreans-ral-ly-in-drive-to-oust-president.html?scp=1&sq=Ecuadoreans%20Rally%20in%20 Drive%20to%20Oust%20President&st=cse.

Schepp, Matthias. "I Can't Allow My Government to Lie to the World." Spiegel Online International, November 10, 2008. http://www.spiegel.de/international/ world/0,1518,589586,00.html.

Schmidt, Gregory D., and Kyle L. Saunders. "Effective Quotas, Relative Party Magnitude, and the Success of Female Candidates: Peruvian Municipal Elections in Comparative Perspective." *Comparative Political Studies 37*, no. 6 (2004): 704–34.

Schweimler, Daniel. "Argentine President Cristina Fernandez Eyes Second Term." BBC News, June 22, 2011. http://www.bbc.co.uk/news/world-latin-america-13872307.

Schwindt-Bayer, Leslie A. *Political Power and Women's Representation in Latin America*. New York: Oxford University Press, 2010.

Schwindt-Bayer, Leslie A. "Women Who Win: Social Backgrounds, Paths to Power and Political Ambition in Latin American Legislatures." *Politics & Gender 7*, no. 1 (2011): 1–33.

Schwindt-Bayer, Leslie A., and William Mishler. "An Integrated Model of Women's Representation." *Journal of Politics 67*, no. 2 (2005): 407–28.

Sciolino, Elaine. "Veteran French Socialist Steps Aside as Candidate for President." *New York Times*, September 29, 2006a. http://www.nytimes.com/2007/04/11/world/europe/11france.html.

Sciolino, Elaine. "Gender War à la Française Shakes Up Political Arena." *New York Times*, December 26, 2006b. http://www.nytimes.com/2006/12/26/world/europe/26france.html.

Sciolino, Elaine. "Socialists Back Woman in Race to Lead France." *New York Times*, November 17, 2006c. http://www.nytimes.com/2006/11/17/world/europe/17france.html.

Sciolino, Elaine. "France's Unfocused Candidates Vie for Undecided Voters." *New York Times*, April 11, 2007a. http://www.nytimes.com/2007/04/11/world/europe/11france.html.

Sciolino, Elaine. "Before French Vote, Candidate Asks Women to Pick Her." *New York Times*, April 19, 2007b. http://query.nytimes.com/gst/fullpage.html?res=9C03E4D91E3FF93AA25757C0A9619C8B63&sec=&spon=&pagewanted=2.

Sciolino, Elaine. "French Candidate Holds Curious Debate." *New York Times*, April 29, 2007c. http://www.nytimes.com/2007/04/29/world/europe/29france.html?_r=1&scp=2&sq=Sciolino%20April%2029,%202007&st=cse.

Sciolino, Elaine. "Candidates Spar Vigorously as French Vote Nears." *New York Times*, May 3, 2007d. http://www.nytimes.com/2007/05/03/world/europe/03iht-03france.5544182.html.

Sciolino, Elaine. "Sarkozy Wins in France and Vows Break with Past." *New York Times*, May 7, 2007e. http://www.nytimes.com/2007/05/07/world/europe/07france.html?scp=1&sq=Sciolino+May+7+2007&st=nyt.

Sczesny, Sabine, Janine Bosak, Daniel Neff, and Birgit Schyns. "Gender Stereotypes and the Attribution of Leadership Traits: A Cross-Cultural Comparison." *Sex Roles 41*, no. 11 (2004): 631–45.

Seimas of the Republic of Lithuania. "Irena Degutienė." 2011a. http://www3.lrs.lt/pls/inter/w5_show?p_a=5&p_asm_id=7207&p_r=786&p_k=2&p_b=3800.

Seimas of the Republic of Lithuania. "Kazimira Danutė Prunskienė." 2011b. http://www3.lrs.lt/docs3/kad5/w5_istorija.show5-p_r=786&p_k=2&p_a=5&p_asm_id=233.html.

Seltzer, Richard A., Jody Newman, and Melissa Vorhees Leighton. *Sex as a Political Variable: Women as Candidates and Voters in U.S. Elections*. Boulder, CO: Lynne Rienner, 1997.

Serafin, Tatiana. "The World's 100 Most Powerful Women: #56. Helen Clark: Prime Minister New Zealand." *Forbes*, August 27, 2008. http://www.forbes.com/lists/2008/11/biz_powerwomen08_Helen-Clark_EXX3.html.

SETimes. "Sekerinska Elected Leader of Macedonia's Main Opposition Party." November 6, 2006. http://www.setimes.com/cocoon/setimes/xhtml/en_GB/newsbriefs/setimes/newsbriefs/2006/11/06/nb-04.

SETimes. "Jadranka Kosor: Prime Minister of Croatia." July 9, 2009. http://www.setimes.com/cocoon/setimes/xhtml/en_GB/infoCountryPage/setimes/resource_centre/bios/kosor_jadranka?country=Croatia.

Shah, Aquil. "Democracy on Hold in Pakistan." *Journal of Democracy 13*, no. 1 (2002): 67–75.

Shipsey, Bill. "Mary Robinson Ambassador of Conscience 2004." Amnesty International. 2004. http://www.artforamnesty.org/aoc/biog_robinson.html (site discontinued).

Shugart, Mathew S., and John Carey. *Presidents and Assemblies.* Cambridge: Cambridge University Press, 1992.

Siamdoust, Nihad. "A Woman as President: Iran's Impossible Dream?" *Time*, May 20, 2009. http://www.time.com/time/world/article/0,8599,1899763,00.html.

Siaroff, Alan. "Comparative Presidencies: The Inadequacy of the Presidential, Semi-presidential and Parliamentary Distinction." *European Journal of Political Research 42*, no. 3 (2003): 287–312.

Sidner, Sara. "Yingluck Shinawatra Set to Be Thailand's First Female Premier." CNN, July 3, 2011. http://articles.cnn.com/2011-07-03/world/thailand.election_1_prime-minister-abhisit-vejjajiva-thai-government-thailand?_s=PM:WORLD.

Siggins, Lorna. *The Woman Who Took Power in the Park: Mary Robinson.* London: Trafalgar Square, 1997.

Simon, Roger. "Diamonds and Pearls for Hillary." Politico, December 12, 2007. http://www.politico.com/news/stories/1107/6926.html.

Simon, Roger. "Lost in Hillaryland." *Politico*, August 25, 2008. http://www.politico.com/news/stories/0808/12721.html.

Simons, Marlise. "World Briefing: Africa; Rwanda: Army Major Guilty in U.N. Killings." *New York Times*, July 5, 2007. http://query.nytimes.com/gst/fullpage.html?res=9C0CE2DE123EF936A35754C0A9619C8B63&scp=2&sq=World%20Briefing:%20Africa;%20Rwanda:%20Army%20Major%20Guility%20in%20U.%20N.%20Killings&st=cse.

Sirry, Mun'im A. "Political Islam in Indonesia." In *The Blackwell Companion to Contemporary Islamic Thought*, edited by Ibrahim M. Abu-Rabi, 466–82. Malden, MA: Blackwell, 2006.

Slovak Spectator. "Iveta Radičová." July 14, 2010. http://spectator.sme.sk/articles/view/39546/2/iveta_radicova.html.

Smith, Craig S. "French Contender Makes Her Presidential Case." *New York Times*, February 12, 2007. http://query.nytimes.com/gst/fullpage.html?res=980CE6DE1F3FF931A25751C0A9619C8B63&sec=&spon=&pagewanted=all.

Sodaro, Michael. *Comparative Politics.* New York: McGraw-Hill, 2008.

Sookraj, Radhica. "Kamla Came from Humble Beginnings." *Trinidad and Tobago Guardian*, May 26, 2010. http://test.guardian.co.tt/index.php?q=news/general/2010/05/26/kamla-came-humble-beginnings.

Streb, Matthew J., Barbara Burrell, Brian Frederick, and Michael A. Genovese. "Social Desirability Effects and Support for a Female American Woman President." *Public Opinion Quarterly 72*, no. 1 (2008): 76–89.

Strom, Karen, and Stephen M. Swindle. "Strategic Parliamentary Dissolution." *American Political Science Review 96*, no. 3 (2002): 575–91.

Studlar, Donley T., and Ian McAllister. "The Recruitment of Women to the Australian Legislature: Toward an Explanation of Women's Electoral Disadvantages." *Western Political Quarterly 44*, no. 3 (1991): 67–85.

Studlar, Donley T., and Ian McAllister. "Does a Critical Mass of Women Exist? A Comparative Analysis of Women's Legislative Representation Since 1950." *European Journal of Political Research 41*, no. 2 (2002): 233–53.

Sullivan, Amy. "Why Didn't More Women Vote for Hillary?" *Time*, June 5, 2008. http://www.time.com/time/magazine/article/0,9171,1812050,00.html.

Swers, Michele L. *The Differences Women Make: The Policy Impact of Women in Congress.* Chicago: University of Chicago Press, 2002.

Swiss Confederation. "Doris Leuthard, President of the Swiss Confederation." Federal Department of the Environment, Transport, Energy and Communications. November 3, 2010. http://www.uvek.admin.ch/org/vorsteher/01901/index.html?lang=en.

Swiss Federal Department of Foreign Affairs. "Micheline Calmy-Rey." January 19, 2011. http://www.eda.admin.ch/eda/en/home/dfa/head/portr.html.

Syjuco, Miguel. "And If This Leader Should Happen to Fall." *New York Times*, May 19, 2010. http://www.nytimes.com/2010/05/20/opinion/20iht-edsyjuco.html?scp=1&sq=And%20if%20This%20Leader%20Should%20Happen%20to%20Fall&st=cse.

Sykes, Patricia Lee. "Women as National Leaders: Patterns and Prospects." In *Women as National Leaders*, edited by Michael A. Genovese, 219–29. London: Sage, 1993.

Taagepera, Rein. "Beating the Law of Minority Attrition." In *Electoral Systems in Comparative Perspective: Their Impact on Women and Minorities*, edited by Wilma Rule and Joseph F. Zimmerman, 235–45. Westport, CT: Greenwood Press, 1994.

Taghiyev, Elgun A. "Measuring Presidential Power in Post Soviet Countries." *Central and Eastern European Political Science Journal 3* (2006): 11–21.

Taylor-Robinson, Michelle M., and Roseanna Michelle Heath. "Do Women Legislators Have Different Policy Priorities than Their Male Colleagues? A Critical Case Test." *Women & Politics 24*, no. 4 (2003): 77–101.

Telegraph. "Benazir Bhutto Obituary." December 27, 2007. http://www.telegraph.co.uk/news/obituaries/1573718/Obituary-Benazir-Bhutto.html.

Telegraph. "Ukraine: Yulia Tymoshenko Loses No-Confidence Vote." March 3, 2010. http://www.telegraph.co.uk/news/worldnews/europe/ukraine/7361459/Ukraine-Yulia-Tymoshenko-loses-no-confidence-vote.html.

Tenthani, Raphael. "Joyce Banda: Malawi's First Female President." BBC News, April 10, 2012. http://www.bbc.co.uk/news/world-africa-17662916.

Thatcher, Margaret. *The Downing Street Years.* New York: HarperCollins, 1995.

Thomas, Gwynn, and Melinda Adams. "Breaking the Final Glass Ceiling: The Influence of Gender in the Elections of Ellen Johnson Sirleaf and Michelle Bachelet." *Journal of Women, Politics & Policy 31*, no. 2 (2010): 105–31.

Thomas, Sue. *How Women Legislate.* New York: Oxford University Press, 1994.

Thompson, Mark R. "Female Leadership of Democratic Transitions in Asia." *Pacific Affairs 75*, no. 4 (2002–2003): 535–55.

Thompson, Mark R., and Ludmilla Lennartz. "The Making of Chancellor Merkel." *German Politics 15*, no. 1 (2006): 99–110.

Time. "Husband and Wife Team." May 3, 1963. http://www.time.com/time/printout/0,8816,828158,00.html.

Time. "Israel: A Tough, Maternal Legend." December 18, 1978. http://www.time.com/time/magazine/article/0,9171,916528,00.html.

Titley, Brian. *Dark Age: The Political Odyssey of Emperor Bokassa*. Montreal: McGill-Queen's University Press, 1997.

Tobar, Marcela Rios. "Seizing a Window of Opportunity: The Election of Michelle Bachelet in Chile." *Politics & Gender 4*, no. 3 (2008): 509–19.

Traub, James. "La Femme." *New York Times*, May 14, 2006. http://www.nytimes.com/2006/05/14/magazine/14royal.html.

Tremblay, Manon, and Réjean Pelletier. "More Women Constituency Party Presidents: A Strategy for Increasing the Number of Women Candidates in Canada?" *Party Politics 7*, no. 2 (2001): 157–90.

Tripp, Aili Mari. "The New Political Activism in Africa." *Journal of Democracy 12*, no. 3 (2001): 141–55.

Tripp, Aili Mari. "What Does the Rising Tide of Women in Executive Office Mean?" *Politics & Gender 4*, no. 3 (2008): 473–74.

Tripp, Aili Mari, Isabel Casimiro, Joy Kwesiga, and Alice Mungwa. *African Women's Movements: Transforming Political Landscapes*. New York: Cambridge University Press, 2009.

Tripp, Aili Mari, and Alice Kang. "The Global Impact of Quotas: On the Fast Track to Increased Female Legislative Representation." *Comparative Political Studies 41*, no. 3 (2008): 338–61.

Uhlig, Mart A. "Her Husband's Murder Sparked a Revolution That Brought the Sandinistas to Power. Now Violeta Chamorro Is Challenging Them in Nicaragua's Presidential Election." *New York Times*, February 11, 1990. http://www.nytimes.com/1990/02/11/magazine/opposing-ortega.html?ref=markauhlig.

United Nations Development Programme. "Gender-Related Development Index." *Human Development Report 2007/2008*. http://hdr.undp.org/en/media/HDR_20072008_GDI.pdf.

United Nations Educational, Scientific, and Cultural Organization (UNESCO). "Gender Mainstreaming." 2011. http://portal.unesco.org/en/ev.php-URL_ID=36816&URL_DO=DO_TOPIC&URL_SECTION=201.html.

United Press International. "Leader of S. Korean Opposition Party Quits." April 13, 2012. http://www.upi.com/Top_News/World-News/2012/04/13/Leader-of-S-Korean-opposition-party-quits/UPI-98071334341928.

Urdang, Stephanie. "Fighting Two Colonialisms: The Women's Struggle in Guinea-Bissau." *African Studies Review 18*, no. 3 (1975): 29–34.

US Department of State. "Background Note: Bangladesh." May 24, 2010. http://www.state.gov/r/pa/ei/bgn/3452.htm.

van der Brug, Wouter, Cees van der Eijk, and Michael Marsh. "Exploring Uncharted Territory: The Irish Presidential Elections 1997." *British Journal of Political Science 30* (2000): 631–50.

Vigdís Finnbogadóttir Institute of Foreign Languages. "Vigdís Finnbogadóttir." University of Iceland. 2008. http://www2.hi.is/page/svfe_toplink_Vigdís.

Virtual Bangladesh. "Sheikh Hasina." August 17, 2006a. http://www.virtualbangladesh.com/biography/hasina.html.

Virtual Bangladesh. "Khaleda Zia." August 17, 2006b. http://www.virtualbangladesh.com/biography/khaleda.html.

von Hellfeld, Matthias. "Twenty Years Ago: GDR's First Freely Elected Parliament Began Work." *Deutsche Welle*, April 4, 2010. http://www.dw-world.de/dw/article/0,,5424328,00.html.

Waldley, Susanne S. "Women and the Hindu Tradition." In *Women in India: Two Perspectives*, edited by D. Jacobson and S. Waldley, 119–39. Delhi: Manohar, 1977.

Waylen, Georgina. *Gender in Third World Politics*. Buckingham: Open University Press, 1996

Weir, Sara J. "Peronisma: Isabel Peron and the Politics of Argentina." In *Women as National Leaders*, edited by Michael A. Genovese, 161–75. London: Sage, 1993.

Whicker, Marcia Lynn, and Hedy Leonie Isaacs. "The Maleness of the American Presidency." In *Women in Politics: Outsiders or Insiders?*, edited by Lois Duke Whitaker, 221–32. Upper Saddle River, NJ: Prentice Hall, 1999.

Whitaker, Mark. "A Conversation with Ellen Johnson Sirleaf, President, Republic of Liberia." US Council on Foreign Relations. May 25, 2010. http://www.cfr.org/economics/conversation-ellen-johnson-sirleaf-president-republic-liberia/p22222.

Who's Who Southern Africa. "South Africa, Obituaries." April 6, 2009. http://www.whoswhosa.co.za/user/916.

Wildman, Sarah. "Prime Minister's Peril." *Advocate*, February 3, 2004, 15.

Wiliarty, Sarah. "Chancellor Angela Merkel: A Sign of Hope or the Exception That Proves the Rule?" *Politics & Gender 4*, no. 3 (2008): 485–96.

Wilkinson, Urrell. "Guyanese President Resigns for Health Reasons." Associated Press, August 9, 1999. http://www.lexisnexis.com/hottopics/lnacademic/?verb=sr&csi=7911.

Williams, Dessima, and CIMT Tech. "Gro Harlem Brundtland." Women Leaders and Transformation in Developing Countries. 1999a. http://www.unet.brandeis.edu/~dwilliam/profiles/brundtland.htm.

Williams, Dessima, and CIMT Tech. "Ruth Dreifuss (1940–)." Women Leaders and Transformation in Developing Countries. 1999b. http://people.brandeis.edu/~dwilliam/profiles/dreifuss.htm.

Wills, Daniel. "Julia Gillard's Parents 'Elated.'" *Daily Telegraph*, June 24, 2010. http://www.dailytelegraph.com.au/news/julia-gillards-parents-elated/story-e6freuy9-1225883750188.

Wolbrecht, Christina, and David E. Campbell. "Leading by Example: Female Members of Parliament as Political Role Models." *American Journal of Political Science 51*, no. 4 (2007): 921–39.

Women's International Center. "Maria da Lourdes Pintasilgo: Greatness through Power." 2004. http://www.wic.org/bio/pintasil.htm.

Women's International Center. "Vigdís Finnbogadóttir: President of Iceland." 2008. http://www.wic.org/bio/finnboga.htm.

World Health Organization. "Dr. Gro Harlem Brundtland, Director General." 2011. http://www.who.int/dg/brundtland/bruntland/en/index.html.

Wright, Lincoln. "Will Julia Gillard's Past Cause Red Faces?" *Herald Sun*, October 7, 2007. http://www.heraldsun.com.au/news/national/will-julias-past-cause-red-faces/story-e6frf7l6-1111114587478.

Wyatt, Caroline. "Profile: Segolene Royal." BBC News, November 17, 2006. http://news.bbc.co.uk/2/hi/europe/4625248.stm.

Yasinow, Melissa. "Win a Trip with Nick Kristof." *New York Times*, May 22, 2006. http://www.nytimes.com/2006/05/22/opinion/22yasinow_essay.html.

Yearwood, John. "Kamla Persad-Bissessar to Be Sworn in as Trinidad Prime Minister." *Miami Herald*, May 26, 2010. http://www.openlogger.com/u/14031/?kamla+persad-bissessar+to+be+sworn+in+as+trinidad+prime+minister+-+americas+-+miamiherald.com.

Yoon, Mi Yung. "Explaining Women's Legislative Representation in Sub-Saharan Africa." In *Women, Gender, and Politics: A Reader*, edited by Mona Lena Krook and Sarah Childs, 167–73. New York: Oxford University Press, 2010.

Young, Hugo. *The Iron Lady: A Biography of Margaret Thatcher.* New York: Noonday Press, 1990.

Yudhini, Etsi. "Indonesia's Presidentialism: Moderating Strong Presidents, Enhancing Representation." In *Making Presidentialism Work*, edited by the International Institute for Democracy and Electoral Assistance, 267–87. Mexico: Universidad Nacional Autónoma de México, 2009. http://www.idea.int/publications/making_presidentialism _work/index.cfm.

Zárate, Roberto Ortiz de. "Women World Leaders: 1945–2007." Zárate's Political Collections. Last modified April 23, 2011. http://www.terra.es/personal2/monolith/00women.htm.

WEB SITES

Data on Women in Various Levels of Politics

Center for American Women and Politics: http://www.cawp.rutgers.edu

Inter-Parliamentary Union (Women in National Parliaments): http://www.ipu.org/wmn-e/classif.htm

Women Watch (UN Information and Resources on Gender Equality and Empowerment of Women): http://www.un.org/womenwatch

Other Data on Women

Inter-Parliamentary Union (List of Dates of Women's Suffrage): http://www.ipu.org/wmn-e/suffrage.htm

National Center for Educational Statistics (Trends in Education Equity of Girls and Women): http://nces.ed.gov/pubs2005/equity.

United Nations Human Development Programme, GDI Indices: http://hdr.undp.org/en/statistics/indices/gdi_gem

Women's History: http://womenshistory.about.com

Biographical Details on Leaders

BBC News Profiles: http://www.bbc.co.uk

Council of Women World Leaders: http://www.cwwl.org/members.html
New York Times: http://www.nytimes.com
Women Presidential Candidates: http://www.guide2womenleaders.com/woman_presidential_candidates.htm
Worldwide Guide to Women in Leadership: http://www.guide2womenleaders.com
Zárate's Political Collections (Dates and Figures of the Worldwide Leadership Since 1945): http://www.terra.es/personal2/monolith

Government Structures, Rules, and Constitutions

Constitution Finder: http://confinder.richmond.edu
Constitution.org: http://www.constitution.org
Costa Rica Constitution: http://www.costaricalaw.com/legalnet/constitutional_law/engtit10.html
France Constitution: http://www.assemblee-nationale.fr/english/8ab.asp
Germany Constitution: http://www.constitution.org/cons/germany.txt
India Constitution: http://indiacode.nic.in/coiweb/amend/amend42.htm
Mozambique Constitution: http://www.chr.up.ac.za/hr_docs/constitutions/docs/MozambiqueC(rev).doc
Pakistan Constitution: http://www.pakistani.org/pakistan/constitution/part12.ch2.html
Peru Constitution: http://web.parliament.go.th/parcy/sapa_db/cons_doc/constitutions/data/Peru/peru.pdf
South Korea Constitution: http://www.servat.unibe.ch/icl/ks00000_.html
Turkey Constitution: http://www.servat.unibe.ch/icl/tu00000_.html
United States Constitution: http://www.usconstitution.net/const.html
Ukraine Constitution: http://www.rada.gov.ua/const/conengl.htm#
CIA World Factbook: http://www.cia.gov/library/publications/the-world-factbook/index.html
German Office of Chancellor: http://www.bundeskanzlerin.de/Webs/BK/En/Angela-Merkel/angela-merkel.html
Prime Minister of Bangladesh: http://www.pmo.gov.bd/index.php?option=com_content&task=blogsection&id=37&Itemid=362

Statistics on Candidates and Election Results

African Elections: http://africanelections.tripod.com/cf.html#1993_Presidential_Election
Dave Leip's Atlas of U.S. Presidential Elections: http://www.uselectionatlas.org
European Election Database: http://www.nsd.uib.no/european_election_database/about
Federal Election Commission: http://www.fec.gov
International Foundation for Electoral Systems: http://www.electionguide.org/results.php?ID=870
International Institute for Democracy and Electoral Assistance: http://www.idea.int

Political Database of the Americas: http://pdba.georgetown.edu
Polling Report: http://www.pollingreport.com
US Department of State: http://www.state.gov

DATABASES

National Center for Educational Statistics: http://nces.ed.gov/pubs2005/equity/
   Section12.asp
Polity IV Projects: http://www.systemicpeace.org/polity/polity4.htm
World Values Survey: http://www.wvsevsdb.com/wvs/WVSAnalizeQuestion.jsp

CPSIA information can be obtained at www.ICGtesting.com
Printed in the USA
BVOW08s0926050516

446836BV00002B/3/P